Anonymous

The Satires of Juvenal and Persius

Anonymous

The Satires of Juvenal and Persius

ISBN/EAN: 9783337371999

Printed in Europe, USA, Canada, Australia, Japan

Cover: Foto ©Thomas Meinert / pixelio.de

More available books at **www.hansebooks.com**

THE SATIRES

OF

JUVENAL AND PERSIUS.

WITH

ENGLISH NOTES,

CRITICAL AND EXPLANATORY,

FROM THE BEST COMMENTATORS.

BY

CHARLES ANTHON, LL.D.,

PROFESSOR OF THE GREEK AND LATIN LANGUAGES IN COLUMBIA COLLEGE,
NEW YORK, AND RECTOR OF THE GRAMMAR SCHOOL.

NEW YORK:

HARPER & BROTHERS, PUBLISHERS,

FRANKLIN SQUARE.

1863.

TO WM. HAWKESWORTH, ESQ.,

PROFESSOR OF ANCIENT LANGUAGES IN CHARLESTON COLLEGE, S.C.

MY DEAR PROFESSOR,

Allow me to dedicate this volume to you as a memorial not only of long-standing friendship, but also of sincere admiration for the noblest personal qualities, as well as for sound and unostentatious scholarship. You know very well that I would never have undertaken the work had it not been for your repeated solicitations; and if the result of my labours should now, in any way, disappoint your expectation, you will have only yourself to blame. I have endeavoured, as I promised you, to make a useful Variorum edition, and have, with that view, selected my materials from the best commentators, laying under contribution each and every one of them, whenever I found any thing that might tend to elucidate your favourite satirist. The only merit to which I can fairly lay claim, on my own account, is that of selection and arrangement, as well as an occasional balancing of authorities. In the text I have generally taken Jahn for my guide, and have also unsparingly removed whatever might tend to make Juvenal less readable in a lecture-room. On this point some may, perhaps, think that I have gone too far. But my own experience as an instructor is entirely in favour of the plan which I have adopted, and I am very sure that your opinion will coincide in this respect with my own.

Among the sources from which excellent materials have been obtained for the commentary, I may particularly mention the edition of Mayor, published in 1853, and also the German one of Heinrich. The English version by Evans has likewise been of great service, and even old Madan, though it is the fashion to decry him, has been found by me, on many occasions, a very useful companion, especially in his explanatory remarks. The American student has already been made acquainted with the notes of Madan by means of Leverett's Juvenal, to which edition they are appended in an abridged form. I have used them, however, much more sparingly than Leverett, and have never adopted any unless supported by other authorities.

With regard to Persius, you may remember that I intended to edit his Satires along with those of Juvenal until you dissuaded me from the attempt. I have therefore contented myself with merely giving the Latin text, unaccompanied by a single word of comment. This part of the volume, I am very sure, will meet with the undivided approbation of those critical friends of mine, who have uniformly condemned my commentaries as exuberant, if not useless, and over whose fairness and acumen you and I have had many a pleasant chat.

It only remains for me to subscribe myself, my dear Professor, your old and sincere friend,

C. A.

Col. College, *March 30th*, 1857.

LIFE OF JUVENAL.

(From Smith's Dictionary of Biography.)

DECIMUS JUNIUS JUVENALIS, according to his ancient biographers, was either the son or the "alumnus" of a rich freedman. These same authorities relate that he was born at the Volscian town of Aquinum; that he occupied himself, until he had nearly reached the term of middle age, in declaiming; that, having subsequently composed some clever lines upon Paris, the pantomime, he was induced to cultivate assiduously satirical composition; and that, in consequence of his attacks upon Paris becoming known to the court, the poet, although now an old man of eighty, was appointed to the command of a body of troops in a remote district of Egypt, where he died shortly afterward. It is supposed by some that the Paris who, according to these old biographers, was attacked by Juvenal, was the contemporary of Domitian, and that the poet was accordingly banished by this emperor. But this opinion is clearly untenable: 1. We know that Paris was killed in A.D. 83, upon suspicion of an intrigue with the Empress Domitia. 2. The Fourth Satire, as appears from the concluding lines, was written after the death of Domitian—that is, not earlier than A.D. 96. 3. The First Satire, as we learn from the forty-ninth line, was written after the condemnation of Marius Priscus—that is, not earlier than A.D. 100. These positions admit of no doubt, and hence

it is established that Juvenal was alive at least seven-
teen years after the death of Paris, and that some of
his Satires were composed after the death of Domitian.

The only facts with regard to Juvenal upon which
we can implicitly rely are, that he flourished toward
the close of the first century; that Aquinum, if not
the place of his nativity, was at least his chosen residence; and that he is, in all probability, the friend
whom Martial addresses in three epigrams. There is
perhaps another circumstance which we may admit.
We are told that he declaimed for many years of his
life, and every page in his writings bears evidence to
the accuracy of this assertion. Every piece is a finished rhetorical essay, energetic, glowing, and sono-
rous. He denounces vice in the most indignant terms;
but the obvious tone of exaggeration which pervades
all his invectives leaves us in doubt how far this sustained passion is real, and how far assumed for mere
show. The extant works of Juvenal consist of sixteen Satires, the last being a fragment of doubtful au-
thenticity, all composed in heroic hexameters.

SATIRARUM

LIBER PRIMUS.

SATIRA I.

SEMPER ego auditor tantum? nunquamne reponam,
Vexatus toties rauci Thescide Codri?
Impune ergo mihi cantaverit ille togatas,
Hic elegos? impune diem consumserit ingens
Telephus, aut, summi plena jam margine libri,
Scriptus et in tergo, nec dum finitus, Orestes?
   Nota magis nulli domus est sua, quam mihi lucus
Martis, et Æoliis vicinum rupibus antrum
Vulcani.   Quid agant venti, quas torqueat umbras
Æacus, unde alius furtivæ devehat aurum   10
Pelliculæ, quantas jaculetur Monychus ornos,
Frontonis platani convulsaque marmora clamant
Semper, et assiduo ruptæ lectore columnæ.
Exspectes eadem a summo minimoque poeta.
Et nos ergo manum ferulæ subduximus, et nos
Consilium dedimus Sullæ, privatus ut altum
Dormiret.   Stulta est clementia, quum tot ubique
Vatibus occurras, perituræ parcere chartæ.
   Cur tamen hoc potius libeat decurrere campo,
Per quem magnus equos Auruncæ flexit alumnus,   20
Si vacat et placidi rationem admittitis, edam.
Patricios omnes opibus quum provocet unus,
Quo tondente gravis juveni mihi barba sonabat;

A

Quum pars Niliacæ plebis, quum verna Canopi
Crispinus, Tyrias humero revocante lacernas,
Ventilet æstivum digitis sudantibus aurum,
Nec sufferre queat majoris pondera gemmæ:
Difficile est satiram non scribere.   Nam quis iniquæ
Tam patiens urbis, tam ferreus, ut teneat se,
Causidici nova quum veniat lectica Mathonis,   30
Plena ipso; post hunc magni delator amici,
Et cito rapturus de nobilitate comesa
Quod superest; quem Massa timet, quem munere palpat
Carus, et a trepido Thymele submissa Latino.
　　Quid referam, quanta siccum jecur ardeat ira,
Quum populum gregibus comitum premat hic spoliator
Pupilli prostantis?   Et hic damnatus inani
Judicio (quid enim salvis infamia nummis?)
Exsul ab octava Marius bibit, et fruitur Dis
Iratis; at tu victrix provincia ploras?   40
　　Hæc ego non credam Venusina digna lucerna?
Hæc ego non agitem?   Sed quid magis Heracleas
Aut Diomedeas aut mugitum Labyrinthi,
Et mare percussum puero fabrumque volantem;
Quum leno accipiat mœchi bona, si capiendi
Jus nullum uxori?
Quum fas esse putet curam sperare cohortis,
Qui bona donavit præsepibus et caret omni
Majorum censu, dum pervolat axe citato
Flaminiam, puer Automedon nam lora tenebat?   50
Nonne libet medio ceras implere capaces
Quadrivio: quum jam sexta cervice feratur
Hinc atque inde patens ac nuda pæne cathedra,
Et multum referens de Mæcenate supino,
Signator falso, qui se lautum atque beatum
Exiguis tabulis et gemma fecerat uda?
Occurrat matrona potens, quæ molle Calenum
Porrectura viro miscet sitiente rubetam,

Instituitque rudes melior Lucusta propinquas
Per famam et populum nigros efferre maritos?   60
    Aude aliquid brevibus Gyaris et carcere dignum,
Si vis esse aliquis! Probitas laudatur et—alget.
Criminibus debent hortos, prætoria, mensas,
Argentum vetus et stantem extra pocula caprum.
Si natura negat, facit indignatio versum,
Qualemcumque potest, quales ego vel Cluvienus.
    Ex quo Deucalion, nimbis tollentibus æquor,
Navigio montem ascendit sortesque poposcit,
Paulatimque anima caluerunt mollia saxa,
Quidquid agunt homines, votum, timor, ira, voluptas,   70
Gaudia, discursus, nostri est farrago libelli.
Et quando uberior vitiorum copia? quando
Major avaritiæ patuit sinus? alea quando
Hæc animos? Neque enim loculis comitantibus itur
Ad casum tabulæ, posita sed luditur arca.
Prœlia quanta illic dispensatore videbis
Armigero? Simplexne furor sestertia centum
Perdere, et horrenti tunicam non reddere servo?
Quis totidem erexit villas, quis fercula septem
Secreto cœnavit avus? Nunc sportula primo   80
Limine parva sedet, turbæ rapienda togatæ.
Ille tamen faciem prius inspicit et trepidat, ne
Suppositus venias ac falso nomine poscas.
Agnitus accipies; jubet a præcone vocari
Ipsos Trojugenas; nam vexant limen et ipsi
Nobiscum. "Da prætori, da deinde tribuno.
Sed libertinus prior est." "Prior," inquit, "ego adsum:
Cur timeam, dubitemve locum defendere, quamvis
Natus ad Euphraten, molles quod in aure fenestræ
Arguerint, licet ipse negem? sed quinque tabernæ   90
Quadringenta parant. Quid confert purpura major
Optandum, si Laurenti custodit in agro
Conductas Corvinus oves? ego possideo plus

Pallante et Licinis." Exspectent ergo tribuni ;
Vincant divitiæ, sacro nec cedat honori,
Nuper in hanc urbem pedibus qui venerat albis:
Quandoquidem inter nos sanctissima divitiarum
Majestas: etsi, funesta Pecunia, templo
Nondum habitas, nullas nummorum creximus aras,
Ut colitur Pax atque Fides, Victoria, Virtus,   100
Quæque salutato crepitat Concordia nido.
   Sed quum summus honor finito computet anno,
Sportula quid referat, quantum rationibus addat:
Quid facient comites, quibus hinc toga, calceus hinc est
Et panis fumusque domi? Densissima centum
Quadrantes lectica petit, sequiturque maritum
Languida vel prægnans et circumducitur uxor.
Hic petit absenti, nota jam callidus arte,
Ostendens vacuam et clausam pro conjuge sellam.
"Galla mea est," inquit. "Citius dimitte: moraris.   110
Profer, Galla, caput." "Noli vexare, quiescit."
   Ipse dies pulchro distinguitur ordine rerum:
Sportula, deinde forum, jurisque peritus Apollo,
Atque triumphales, inter quas ausus habere
Nescio quis titulos Ægyptius atque Alabarches.
Vestibulis abeunt veteres lassique clientes,
Votaque deponunt: quanquam longissima cœnæ
Spes homini: caulis miseris atque ignis emendus.
Optima silvarum interea pelagique vorabit
Rex horum, vacuisque toris tantum ipse jacebit.   120
Nam de tot pulchris et latis orbibus et tam
Antiquis una comedunt patrimonia mensa.
Nullus jam parasitus erit: sed quis feret istas
Luxuriæ sordes? Quanta est gula, quæ sibi totos
Ponit apros, animal propter convivia natum!
Pœna tamen præsens, quum tu deponis amictus
Turgidus, et crudum pavonem in balnea portas.
Hinc subitæ mortes atque intestata senectus.

It nova, nec tristis, per cunctas fabula cœnas,
Ducitur iratis plaudendum funus amicis. 130
   Nil erit ulterius, quod nostris moribus addat
Posteritas; eadem cupient facientque minores;
Omne in præcipiti vitium stetit.   Utere velis,
Totos pande sinus.   Dicas hic forsitan, "Unde
Ingenium par materiæ? unde illa priorum
Scribendi, quodcumque animo flagrante liberet,
Simplicitas, cujus non audeo dicere nomen?
Quid refert dictis ignoscat Mucius, an non?
Pone Tigellinum: tæda lucebis in illa,
Qua stantes ardent, qui fixo gutture fumant, 140
Et latum media sulcum diducis arena."
Qui dedit ergo tribus patruis aconita, vehatur
Pensilibus plumis, atque illinc despiciat nos?
"Quum veniet contra, digito compesce labellum:
Accusator erit, qui verbum dixerit, Hic est.
Securus licet Æneam Rutulumque ferocem
Committas; nulli gravis est percussus Achilles,
Aut multum quæsitus Hylas urnamque sequutus.
Ense velut stricto quoties Lucilius ardens
Infremuit, rubet auditor, cui frigida mens est 150
Criminibus; tacita sudant præcordia culpa.
Inde iræ et lacrimæ.   Tecum prius ergo voluta
Hæc animo ante tubas: galeatum sero duelli
Pœnitet."   Experiar, quid concedatur in illos,
Quorum Flaminia tegitur cinis atque Latina.

SATIRA III.

QUAMVIS digressu veteris confusus amici,
Laudo tamen, vacuis quod sedem figere Cumis
Destinet, atque unum civem donare Sibyllæ.
Janua Baiarum est et gratum litus amœni
Secessus.   Ego vel Prochytam præpono Suburæ.
Nam quid tam miserum, tam solum vidimus, ut non
Deterius credas horrere incendia, lapsus
Tectorum assiduos ac mille pericula sævæ
Urbis, et Augusto recitantes mense poetas?
Sed dum tota domus reda componitur una,   10
Substitit ad veteres arcus madidamque Capenam.
Hic, ubi nocturnæ Numa constituebat amicæ,
Nunc sacri fontis nemus et delubra locantur
Judæis; quorum cophinus fœnumque supellex;
Omnis enim populo mercedem pendere jussa est
Arbor, et ejectis mendicat silva Camenis.
In vallem Egeriæ descendimus et speluncas
Dissimiles veris.   Quanto præsentius esset
Numen aquæ, viridi si margine clauderet undas
Herba, nec ingenuum violarent marmora tophum!   20
Hic tunc Umbricius, " Quando artibus," inquit, " honestis
Nullus in urbe locus, nulla emolumenta laborum ;
Res hodie minor est, here quam fuit, atque eadem cras
Deteret exiguis aliquid : proponimus illuc
Ire, fatigatas ubi Dædalus exuit alas,
Dum nova canities, dum prima et recta senectus,
Dum superest Lachesi quod torqueat, et pedibus me
Porto meis, nullo dextram subeunte bacillo.
Cedamus patria : vivant Artorius istic
Et Catulus ; maneant qui nigrum in candida vertunt,   30
Quis facile est ædem conducere, flumina, portus,

Siccandam eluviem, portandum ad busta cadaver,
Et præbere caput domina venale sub hasta.
Quondam hi cornicines, et municipalis arenæ
Perpetui comites, notæque per oppida buccæ,
Munera nunc edunt et, verso pollice vulgi,
Quem libet, occidunt populariter : inde reversi
Conducunt foricas : et cur non omnia ? quum sint
Quales ex humili magna ad fastigia rerum
Extollit, quoties voluit Fortuna jocari.   40
Quid Romæ faciam ? Mentiri nescio ; librum,
Si malus est, nequeo laudare et poscere ; motus
Astrorum ignoro ; funus promittere patris
Nec volo, nec possum ; ranarum viscera nunquam
Inspexi. Ferre ad nuptam quæ mittit adulter,
Quæ mandat, norint alii : me nemo ministro
Fur erit, atque ideo nulli comes exeo, tanquam
Mancus, et exstinctæ corpus non utile dextræ.
Quis nunc diligitur, nisi conscius, et cui fervens
Æstuat occultis animus semperque tacendis ?   50
Nil tibi se debere putat, nil conferet unquam,
Participem qui te secreti fecit honesti :
Carus erit Verri, qui Verrem tempore, quo vult,
Accusare potest. Tanti tibi non sit opaci
Omnis arena Tagi, quodque in mare volvitur aurum,
Ut somno careas ponendaque præmia sumas
Tristis, et a magno semper timearis amico !
   Quæ nunc divitibus gens acceptissima nostris,
Et quos præcipue fugiam, properabo fateri ;
Nec pudor obstabit. Non possum ferre, Quirites,   60
Græcam urbem : quamvis quota portio fæcis Achæi ?
Jam pridem Syrus in Tiberim defluxit Orontes,
Et linguam, et mores, et cum tibicine chordas
Obliquas, nec non gentilia tympana secum
Vexit.
Rusticus ille tuus sumit trechedipna, Quirine,

Et ceromatico fert niceteria collo.
Hic alta Sicyone, ast hic Amydone relicta,
Hic Andro, ille Samo, hic Trallibus aut Alabandis,
Esquilias dictumque petunt a vimine collem,   70
Viscera magnarum domuum dominique futuri.
Ingenium velox, audacia perdita, sermo
Promtus et Isæo torrentior.   Ede, quid illum
Esse putes? quem vis hominem, secum attulit ad nos:
Grammaticus, rhetor, geometres, pictor, aliptes,
Augur, schœnobates, medicus, magus: omnia novit.
Græculus esuriens in cœlum, jusseris, ibit.
Ad summam, non Maurus erat neque Sarmata nec Thrax,
Qui sumsit pennas, mediis sed natus Athenis.
Horum ego non fugiam conchylia? me prior ille   80
Signabit? fultusque toro meliore recumbet,
Advectus Romam, quo pruna et cottana vento?
Usque adeo nihil est, quod nostra infantia cœlum
Hausit Aventini, bacca nutrita Sabina?
Quid, quod adulandi gens prudentissima laudat
Sermonem indocti, faciem deformis amici,
Et longum invalidi collum cervicibus æquat
Herculis, Antæum procul a tellure tenentis?
Hæc eadem licet et nobis laudare: sed illis
Creditur.   90
Nec tamen Antiochus, nec erit mirabilis illic
Aut Stratocles aut cum molli Demetrius Hæmo:
Natio comœda est.   Rides, meliore cachinno
Concutitur; flet, si lacrimas conspexit amici,
Nec dolet; igniculum brumæ si tempore poscas,
Accipit endromidem; si dixeris, "Æstuo," sudat.
Non sumus ergo pares: melior, qui semper et omni
Nocte dieque potest aliena sumere vultum
A facie, jactare manus, laudare paratus.
Scire volunt secreta domus atque inde timeri.   100
     Et quoniam cœpit Græcorum mentio, transi

Gymnasia atque audi facinus majoris abollæ.
Stoicus occidit Baream, delator amicum,
Discipulumque senex, ripa nutritus in illa,
Ad quam Gorgonei delapsa est pinna caballi.
Non est Romano cuiquam locus hic, ubi regnat
Protogenes aliquis vel Diphilus aut Hermarcus,
Qui gentis vitio nunquam partitur amicum,
Solus habet.   Nam quum facilem stillavit in aurem
Exiguum de naturæ patriæque veneno,   110
Limine summoveor; perierunt tempora longi
Servitii.   Nusquam minor est jactura clientis.
    Quod porro officium, ne nobis blandiar, aut quod
Pauperis hic meritum, si curet nocte togatus
Currere, quum Prætor lictorem impellat, et ire
Præcipitem jubeat, dudum vigilantibus orbis,
Ne prior Albinam et Modiam collega salutet?
Da testem Romæ tam sanctum, quam fuit hospes
Numinis Idæi; procedat vel Numa, vel qui
Servavit trepidam flagranti ex æde Minervam: 120
Protenus ad censum, de moribus ultima fiet
Quæstio: "quot pascit servos? quot possidet agri
Jugera? quam multa magnaque paropside cœnat?"
Quantum quisque sua nummorum servat in arca,
Tantum habet et fidei.   Jures licet et Samothracum
Et nostrorum aras, contemnere fulmina pauper
Creditur atque Deos, Dis ignoscentibus ipsis.
Quid, quod materiam præbet causasque jocorum
Omnibus hic idem, si fœda et scissa lacerna,
Si toga sordidula est et rupta calceus alter   130
Pelle patet; vel si, consuto vulnere, crassum
Atque recens linum ostendit non una cicatrix?
Nil habet infelix paupertas durius in se,
Quam quod ridiculos homines facit.   "Exeat," inquit,
"Si pudor est, et de pulvino surgat equestri,
Cujus res legi non sufficit, et sedeant hic

Lenonum pueri quocumque in fornice nati,
Hic plaudat nitidi praeconis filius inter
Pinnirapi cultos juvenes juvenesque lanistae.
Sic libitum vano, qui nos distinxit, Othoni.   140
Quis gener hic placuit censu minor atque puellae
Sarcinulis impar? quis pauper scribitur heres?
Quando in consilio est Aedilibus? Agmine facto
Debuerant olim tenues migrasse Quirites.
Haud facile emergunt, quorum virtutibus obstat
Res angusta domi: sed Romae durior illis
Conatus; magno hospitium miserabile, magno
Servorum ventres, et frugi coenula magno.
Fictilibus coenare pudet, quod turpe negavit
Translatus subito ad Marsos mensamque Sabellam,   150
Contentusque illic veneto duroque culullo.
    Pars magna Italiae est, si verum admittimus, in qua
Nemo togam sumit nisi mortuus.   Ipsa dierum
Festorum herboso colitur si quando theatro
Majestas, tandemque redit ad pulpita notum
Exodium, quum personae pallentis hiatum
In gremio matris formidat rusticus infans,
Aequales habitus illic similemque videbis
Orchestram et populum: clari velamen honoris,
Sufficiunt tunicae summis Aedilibus albae.   160
Hic ultra vires habitus nitor; hic aliquid plus
Quam satis est interdum aliena sumitur arca.
Commune id vitium est: hic vivimus ambitiosa
Paupertate omnes.   Quid te moror?   Omnia Romae
Cum pretio.   Quid das, ut Cossum aliquando salutes?
Ut te respiciat clauso Veiento labello?
Ille metit barbam, crinem hic deponit amati;
Plena domus libis venalibus!   Accipe, et istud
Fermentum tibi habe: praestare tributa clientes
Cogimur et cultis augere peculia servis.   170
    Quis timet aut timuit gelida Praeneste ruinam,

Aut positis nemorosa inter juga Volsiniis, aut
Simplicibus Gabiis, aut proni Tiburis arce?
Nos urbem colimus tenui tibicine fultam
Magna parte sui. Nam sic labentibus obstat
Villicus, et, veteris rimæ quum texit hiatum,
Securos pendente jubet dormire ruina.
Vivendum est illic, ubi nulla incendia, nulli
Nocte metus. Jam poscit aquam, jam frivola transfert
Ucalegon; tabulata tibi jam tertia fumant;   180
Tu nescis: nam si gradibus trepidatur ab imis,
Ultimus ardebit, quem tegula sola tuetur
A pluvia, molles ubi reddunt ova columbæ.
Lectus erat Codro Procula minor, urceoli sex,
Ornamentum abaci; nec non et parvulus infra ·
Cantharus, et recubans sub eodem marmore Chiron;
Jamque vetus Græcos servabat cista libellos,
Et divina opici rodebant carmina mures.
Nil habuit Codrus: quis enim negat? et tamen illud
Perdidit infelix totum nihil: ultimus autem   ʻ190
Ærumnæ cumulus, quod nudum et frustra rogantem
Nemo cibo, nemo hospitio tectoque juvabit.
Si magna Asturii cecidit domus, horrida mater,
Pullati proceres, differt vadimonia prætor;
Tunc geminus casus urbis, tunc odimus ignem.
Ardet adhuc, et jam accurrit qui marmora donet,
Conferat impensas: hic nuda et candida signa,
Hic aliquid præclarum Euphranoris et Polycleti,
Hic Asianorum vetera ornamenta deorum,
Hic libros dabit et forulos mediamque Minervam,   200
Hic modium argenti: meliora et plura reponit
Persicus, orborum lautissimus et merito jam
Suspectus, tanquam ipse suas incenderit ædes.
Si potes avelli Circensibus, optima Soræ
Aut Fabrateriæ domus aut Frusinone paratur,
Quanti nunc tenebras unum conducis in annum.

Hortulus hic puteusque brevis nec reste movendus
In tenues plantas facili diffunditur haustu.
Vive bidentis amans, et culti villicus horti,
Unde epulum possis centum dare Pythagoreis.   210
Est aliquid, quocumque loco, quocumque recessu,
Unius sese dominum fecisse lacertæ.

   Plurimus hic æger moritur vigilando : sed illum
Languorem peperit cibus imperfectus et hærens
Ardenti stomacho.   Nam quæ meritoria somnum
Admittunt?   Magnis opibus dormitur in Urbe :
Inde caput morbi.   Redarum transitus arcto
Vicorum in flexu, et stantis convicia mandræ,
Eripient somnum Druso vitulisque marinis.
Si vocat officium, turba cedente vehetur   220
Dives, et ingenti curret super ora Liburno,
Atque obiter leget aut scribet vel dormiet intus.
Namque facit somnum clausa lectica fenestra.
Ante tamen veniet ; nobis properantibus obstat
Unda prior, magno populus premit agmine lumbos
Qui sequitur ; ferit hic cubito, ferit assere duro
Alter ; at hic tignum capiti incutit, ille metretam.
Pinguia crura luto, planta mox undique magna
Calcor, et in digito clavus mihi militis hæret.

   Nonne vides quanto celebretur sportula fumo?   230
Centum convivæ ; sequitur sua quemque culina.
Corbulo vix ferret tot vasa ingentia, tot res
Impositas capiti, quot recto vertice portat
Servulus infelix et cursu ventilat ignem.
Scinduntur tunicæ sartæ : modo longa coruscat
Sarraco veniente abies, atque altera pinum
Plaustra vehunt ; nutant alte populoque minantur :
Nam si procubuit qui saxa Ligustica portat
Axis, et eversum fudit super agmina montem,
Quid superest de corporibus? quis membra, quis ossa 240
Invenit?   Obtritum vulgi perit omne cadaver

More animæ. ' Domus interea secura patellas
Jam lavat, et bucca foculum excitat, et sonat unctis
Striglibus, et pleno componit lintea gutto.
Hæc inter pueros varie properantur: at ille
Jam sedet in ripa, tetrumque novicius horret
Porthmea, nec sperat cœnosi gurgitis alnum,
Infelix, nec habet quem porrigat ore trientem.
Respice nunc alia ac diversa pericula noctis:
Quod spatium tectis sublimibus, unde cerebrum   250
Testa ferit, quoties rimosa et curta fenestris
Vasa cadunt; quanto percussum pondere signent
Et lædant silicem. Possis ignavus haberi
Et subiti casus improvidus, ad cœnam si
Intestatus eas. Adeo tot fata, quot illa
Nocte patent vigiles, te prætereunte, fenestræ.
Ergo optes, votumque feras miserabile tecum,
Ut sint contentæ patulas defundere pelves.
Ebrius ac petulans, qui nullum forte cecidit,
Dat pœnas, noctem patitur lugentis amicum   260
Pelidæ, cubat in faciem, mox deinde supinus.
Ergo non aliter poterit dormire? Quibusdam
Somnum rixa facit: sed, quamvis improbus annis,
Atque mero fervens, cavet hunc, quem coccina læna
Vitari jubet, et comitum longissimus ordo,
Multum præterea flammarum et aënea lampas:
Me, quem Luna solet deducere, vel breve lumen
Candelæ, cujus dispenso et tempero filum,
Contemnit. Miseræ cognosce procœmia rixæ,
Si rixa est, ubi tu pulsas, ego vapulo tantum.   270
Stat contra starique jubet; parere necesse est:
Nam quid agas, quum te furiosus cogat et idem
Fortior? Unde venis? exclamat: cujus aceto,
Cujus conche tumes? quis tecum sectile porrum
Sutor et elixi vervecis labra comedit?
Nil mihi respondes? Aut dic, aut accipe calcem.

Ede, ubi consistas, in qua te quæro proseucha.
Dicere si tentes aliquid, tacitusve recedas,
Tantundem est; feriunt pariter; vadimonia deinde
Irati faciunt.   Libertas pauperis hæc est: 280
Pulsatus rogat, et pugnis concisus adorat,
Ut liceat paucis cum dentibus inde reverti.
    Nec tamen hæc tantum metuas: nam qui spoliet te
Non deerit, clausis domibus, postquam omnis ubique
Fixa catenatæ siluit compago tabernæ.
Interdum et ferro subitus grassator agit rem,
Armato quoties tutæ custode tenentur
Et Pomtina palus et Gallinaria pinus.
Sic inde huc omnes tanquam ad vivaria currunt.
Qua fornace graves, qua non incude, catenæ?   290
Maximus in vinclis ferri modus, ut timeas, ne
Vomer deficiat, ne marræ et sarcula desint.
Felices proavorum atavos, felicia dicas
Secula, quæ quondam sub regibus atque tribunis
Viderunt uno contentam carcere Romam.
    His alias poteram et plures subnectere causas:
Sed jumenta vocant, et sol inclinat; eundum est.
Nam mihi commota jam dudum mulio virga
Innuit.   Ergo vale nostri memor, et quoties te
Roma tuo refici properantem reddet Aquino,   300
Me quoque ad Helvinam Cererem vestramque Dianam
Converte a Cumis.   Satirarum ego, ni pudet illas,
Adjutor gelidos veniam caligatus in agros."

[handwritten note, partly illegible] ... "nor will there be one wanting one to rob you (et "who may rob")"

SATIRA IV.

Ecce iterum Crispinus, et est mihi sæpe vocandus
Ad partes, monstrum nulla virtute redemtum
A vitiis, æger solaque libidine fortis.
Quid refert igitur, quantis jumenta fatiget
Porticibus, quanta nemorum vectetur in umbra,
Jugera quot vicina foro, quas emerit ædes?
Nemo malus felix, minime corruptor, et idem
Incestus, cum quo nuper vittata jacebat
Sanguine adhuc vivo terram subitura sacerdos.
Sed nunc de factis levioribus: et tamen alter   10
Si fecisset idem, caderet sub judice morum.
Nam quod turpe bonis, Titio Scioque, decebat
Crispinum.   Quid agas, quum dira et fœdior omni
Crimine persona est?   Mullum sex millibus emit,
Æquantem sane paribus sestertia libris,
Ut perhibent qui de magnis majora loquuntur.
Consilium laudo artificis, si munere tanto
Præcipuam in tabulis ceram senis abstulit orbi.
Est ratio ulterior, magnæ si misit amicæ,
Quæ vehitur clauso latis specularibus antro.   · 20
Nil tale exspectes: emit sibi.   Multa videmus,
Quæ miser et frugi non fecit Apicius.   Hoc tu,
Succinctus patria quondam, Crispine, papyro!
Hoc pretium squamæ!   Potuit fortasse minoris
Piscator, quam piscis, emi.   Provincia tanti
Vendit agros: sed majores Appulia vendit.
Quales tunc epulas ipsum glutisse putemus
Induperatorem, quum tot sestertia, partem
Exiguam et modicæ sumtam de margine cœnæ,
Purpureus magni ructarit scurra Palati,   30
Jam princeps equitum, magna qui voce solebat

Vendere municipes fracta de merce siluros!
Incipe, Calliope, licet et considere : non est
Cantandum, res vera agitur : narrate, puellæ
Pierides.

    Quum jam semianimum laceraret Flavius orbem
Ultimus, et calvo serviret Roma Neroni,
Incidit Adriaci spatium admirabile rhombi
Ante domum Veneris, quam Dorica sustinet Ancon,
Implevitque sinus : neque enim minor hæserat illis,   40
Quos operit glacies Mæotica, ruptaque tandem
Solibus effundit torpentis ad ostia Ponti,
Desidia tardos et longo frigore pingues.
Destinat hoc monstrum cymbæ linique magister
Pontifici summo.   Quis enim proponere talem,
Aut emere auderet, quum plena et litora multo
Delatore forent ?   Dispersi protinus algæ
Inquisitores agerent cum remige nudo,
Non dubitaturi fugitivum dicere piscem,
Depastumque diu vivaria Cæsaris ; inde   50
Elapsum veterem ad dominum debere reverti.
Si quid Palfurio, si credimus Armillato,
Quidquid conspicuum pulchrumque est æquore toto,
Res fisci est, ubicumque natat.   Donabitur ergo,
Ne pereat.   Jam letifero cedente pruinis
Autumno, jam quartanam sperantibus ægris,
Stridebat deformis hiems prædamque recentem
Servabat : tamen hic properat, velut urgeat Auster :
Utque lacus suberant, ubi, quanquam diruta, servat
Ignem Trojanum et Vestam colit Alba minorem,   60
Obstitit intranti miratrix turba parumper.
Ut cessit, facili patuerunt cardine valvæ ;
Exclusi spectant admissa opsonia Patres.
Itur ad Atriden.   Tum Picens, "Accipe," dixit,
"Privatis majora focis : genialis agatur
Iste dies : propera stomachum laxare saginis,

Et tua servatum consume in secula rhombum.
Ipse capi voluit." Quid apertius? et tamen illi
Surgebant cristæ. Nihil est, quod credere de se
Non possit, quum laudatur Dis æqua potestas.   70
Sed deerat pisci patinæ mensura. Vocantur
Ergo in consilium proceres, quos oderat ille;
In quorum facie miseræ magnæque sedebat
Pallor amicitiæ. Primus, clamante Liburno,
" Currite, jam sedit !" rapta properabat abolla
Pegasus, attonitæ positus modo villicus urbi.
Anne aliud tunc præfecti? quorum optimus atque
Interpres legum sanctissimus; omnia quanquam
Temporibus diris tractanda putabat inermi
Justitia. Venit et Crispi jucunda senectus,   80
Cujus erant mores, qualis facundia, mite
Ingenium. Maria ac terras populosque regenti
Quis comes utilior, si clade et peste sub illa
Sævitiam damnare et honestum afferre liceret
Consilium? Sed quid violentius aure tyranni,
Cum quo de pluviis aut æstibus aut nimboso
Vere loquuturi fatum pendebat amici?
Ille igitur nunquam direxit brachia contra
Torrentem, nec civis erat, qui libera posset
Verba animi proferre, et vitam impendere vero.   90
Sic multas hiemes atque octogesima vidit
Solstitia, his armis illa quoque tutus in aula.
Proximus ejusdem properabat Acilius ævi
Cum juvene, indigno, quem mors tam sæva maneret
Et domini gladiis tam festinata: sed olim
Prodigio par est in nobilitate senectus:
Unde fit, ut malim fraterculus esse Gigantis.
Profuit ergo nihil misero, quod cominus ursos
Figebat Numidas, Albana nudus arena
Venator. Quis enim jam non intelligat artes   100
Patricias? Quis priscum illud miratur acumen,

Brute, tuum?   Facile est barbato imponere regi.
Nec melior vultu, quamvis ignobilis, ibat
Rubrius, offensæ veteris reus atque tacendæ,
Et tamen improbior satiram scribente Nerone.
Montani quoque venter adest, abdomine tardus,
Et matutino sudans Crispinus amomo,
Quantum vix redolent duo funera; sævior illo
Pompeius tenui jugulos aperire susurro,
Et qui vulturibus servabat viscera Dacis   110
Fuscus, marmorea meditatus prœlia villa,
Et cum mortifero prudens Veiento Catullo,
Qui nunquam visæ flagrabat amore puellæ,
Grande et conspicuum nostro quoque tempore monstrum!
Cæcus adulator, dirusque a ponte satelles,
Dignus Aricinos qui mendicaret ad axes,
Blandaque devexæ jactaret basia redæ.
Nemo magis rhombum stupuit: nam plurima dixit
In lævum conversus: at illi dextra jacebat
Bellua.   Sic pugnas Cilicis laudabat et ictus,   120
Et pegma, et pueros inde ad velaria raptos.
Non cedit Veiento, sed ut fanaticus, œstro
Percussus, Bellona, tuo, divinat et, "Ingens
Omen habes," inquit, "magni clarique triumphi:
Regem aliquem capies, aut de temone Britanno
Excidet Arviragus: peregrina est bellua : cernis
Erectas in terga sudes?"   Hoc defuit unum
Fabricio, patriam ut rhombi memoraret et annos.
"Quidnam igitur censes? conciditur?" "Absit ab illo
Dedecus hoc," Montanus ait.   "Testa alta paretur,   130
Quæ tenui muro spatiosum colligat orbem.
Debetur magnus patinæ subitusque Prometheus.
Argillam atque rotam citius properate : sed ex hoc
Tempore jam, Cæsar, figuli tua castra sequantur."
Vicit digna viro sententia: noverat ille
Luxuriam imperii veterem noctesque Neronis

Jam medias aliamque famem, quum pulmo Falerno
Arderet   Nulli major fuit usus edendi
Tempestate mea.   Circeis nata forent, an
Lucrinum ad saxum Rutupinove edita fundo   140
Ostrea, callebat primo deprendere morsu;
Et semel aspecti littus dicebat echini.
Surgitur, et misso proceres exire jubentur
Concilio, quos Albanam dux magnus in arcem
Traxerat attonitos et festinare coactos,
Tanquam de Cattis aliquid torvisque Sicambris
Dicturus, tanquam diversis partibus orbis
Anxia præcipiti venisset epistola pinna.
    Atque utinam his potius nugis tota illa dedisset
Tempora sævitiæ, claras quibus abstulit urbi   150
Illustresque animas impune et vindice nullo!
Sed periit, postquam cerdonibus esse timendus
Cœperat: hoc nocuit Lamiarum cæde madenti.

SATIRA V.

Si te propositi nondum pudet, atque eadem est mens,
Ut bona summa putes aliena vivere quadra;
Si potes illa pati, quæ nec Sarmentus iniquas
Cæsaris ad mensas, nec vilis Galba tulisset:
Quamvis jurato metuam tibi credere testi.
Ventre nihil novi frugalius.   Hoc tamen ipsum
Defecisse puta, quod inani sufficit alvo:
Nulla crepido vacat? nusquam pons et tegetis pars
Dimidia brevior? tantine injuria cœnæ?
Tam jejuna fames, quum Pol sit honestius illic   10
Et tremere et sordes farris modere canini?
Primo fige loco, quod tu, discumbere jussus,
Mercedem solidam veterum capis officiorum.
Fructus amicitiæ magnæ cibus: imputat hunc rex,
Et, quamvis rarum, tamen imputat.   Ergo duos post
Si libuit menses neglectum adhibere clientem,
Tertia ne vacuo cessaret culcita lecto,
"Una simus," ait.   Votorum summa: quid ultra
Quæris?   Habet Trebius, propter quod rumpere somnum
Debeat et ligulas dimittere, sollicitus, ne   20
Tota salutatrix jam turba peregerit orbem,
Sideribus dubiis, aut illo tempore, quo se
Frigida circumagunt pigri sarraca Bootæ.
Qualis cœna tamen?   Vinum, quod sucida nolit
Lana pati: de conviva Corybanta videbis.
Jurgia proludunt: sed mox et pocula torques
Saucius, et rubra deterges vulnera mappa;
Inter vos quoties libertorumque cohortem
Pugna Saguntina fervet commissa lagena:
Ipse capillato diffusum Consule potat,   30
Calcatamque tenet bellis socialibus uvam,

Cardiaco nunquam cyathum missurus amico;
Cras bibet Albanis aliquid de montibus aut de
Setinis, cujus patriam titulumque senectus
Delevit multa veteris fuligine testæ:
Quale coronati Thrasea Helvidiusque bibebant
Brutorum et Cassî natalibus.   Ipse capaces
Heliadum crustas et inæquales beryllo
Virro tenet phialas: tibi non committitur aurum;
Vel, si quando datur, custos affixus ibidem,   40
Qui numeret gemmas, unguesque observet acutos.
Da veniam: præclara illic laudatur iaspis.
Nam Virro, ut multi, gemmas ad pocula transfert
A digitis, quas in vaginæ fronte solebat
Ponere zelotypo juvenis prælatus Iarbæ.
Tu Beneventani sutoris nomen habentem
Siccabis calicem, nasorum quatuor, ac jam
Quassatum, et rupto poscentem sulfura vitro.
Si stomachus domini fervet vinoque ciboque,
Frigidior Geticis petitur decocta pruinis: 50
     Non eadem vobis poni modo vina querebar:
Vos aliam potatis aquam.   Tibi pocula cursor
Gætulus dabit, aut nigri manus ossea Mauri,
Et cui per mediam nolis occurrere noctem,
Clivosæ veheris dum per monumenta Latinæ.
Flos Asiæ ante ipsum, pretio majore paratus,
Quam fuit et Tulli census pugnacis et Anci,
Et, ne te teneam, Romanorum omnia regum
Frivola.   Quod quum ita sit, tu Gætulum Ganymedem
Respice, quum sities.   Nescit tot millibus emtus   60
Pauperibus miscere puer: sed forma, sed ætas
Digna supercilio.   Quando ad te pervenit ille?
Quando vocatus adest calidæ gelidæque minister?
Quippe indignatur veteri parere clienti,
Quodque aliquid poscas et quod se stante recumbas.
Maxima quæque domus servis est plena superbis.

Ecce, alius quanto porrexit murmure panem
Vix fractum, solidæ jam mucida frusta farinæ,
Quæ genuinum agitent, non admittentia morsum !
Sed tener et niveus mollique siligine factus   70
Servatur domino.   Dextram cohibere memento.
Salva sit artoptæ reverentia : finge tamen te
Improbulum ; superest illic, qui ponere cogat.
" Vis tu consuetis, audax conviva, canistris
Impleri, panisque tui novisse colorem ?"
" Scilicet hoc fuerat, propter quod sæpe, relicta
Conjuge, per montem adversum gelidasque cucurri
Esquilias, fremeret sæva quum grandine vernus
Jupiter, et multo stillaret pænula nimbo !"
Aspice, quam longo distendat pectore lancem,   80
Quæ fertur domino, squilla, et quibus undique septa
Asparagis, qua despiciat convivia cauda,
Quum venit excelsi manibus sublata ministri.
Sed tibi dimidio constrictus cammarus ovo
Ponitur exigua, feralis cœna, patella.
Ipse Venafrano piscem perfundit : at hic, qui
Pallidus affertur misero tibi caulis, olebit
Laternam : illud enim vestris datur alveolis, quod
Canna Micipsarum prora subvexit acuta ;
Propter quod Romæ cum Bocchare nemo lavatur ;   90
Quod tutos etiam facit a serpentibus Afros.
Mullus erit domini, quem misit Corsica, vel quem
Tauromenitanæ rupes, quando omne peractum est
Et jam defecit nostrum mare, dum gula sævit,
Retibus assiduis penitus scrutante macello
Proxima, nec patimur Tyrrhenum crescere piscem.
Instruit ergo focum provincia : sumitur illinc
Quod captator emat Lænas, Aurelia vendat.
Virroni muræna datur, quæ maxima venit
Gurgite de Siculo : nam, dum se continet Auster,   100
Dum sedet et siccat madidas in carcere pennas,

Contemnunt mediam temeraria lina Charybdim.
Vos anguilla manet longæ cognata colubræ,
Aut glacie aspersus maculis Tiberinus, et ipse
Vernula riparum, pinguis torrente cloaca,
Et solitus mediæ cryptam penetrare Suburæ.
　　Ipsi pauca velim, facilem si præbeat aurem.
Nemo petit, modicis quæ mittebantur amicis
A Seneca, quæ Piso bonus, quæ Cotta solebat
Largiri : namque et titulis et fascibus olim　　　110
Major habebatur donandi gloria : solum
Poscimus, ut cœnes civiliter.　Hoc face et esto,
Esto, ut nunc multi, dives tibi, pauper amicis.
　　Anseris ante ipsum magni jecur, anseribus par
Altilis, et flavi dignus ferro Meleagri
Fumat aper : post hunc tradentur tubera, si ver
Tunc erit et facient optata tonitrua cœnas
Majores.　"Tibi habe frumentum," Allidius inquit,
"O Libye : disjunge boves, dum tubera mittas."
　　Structorem interea, ne qua indignatio desit,　　　120
Saltantem spectas et chironomunta volanti
Cultello, donec peragat dictata magistri
Omnia.　Nec minimo sane discrimine refert,
Quo gestu lepores et quo gallina secetur.
Duceris planta, velut ictus ab Hercule Cacus,
Et ponere foris, si quid tentaveris unquam
Hiscere, tanquam habeas tria nomina.　Quando propinat
Virro tibi sumitque tuis contacta labellis
Pocula? quis vestrum temerarius usque adeo, quis
Perditus, ut dicat regi, "bibe?"　Plurima sunt, quæ　130
Non audent homines pertusa dicere læna.
　　Quadringenta tibi si quis Deus aut similis Dis
Et melior fatis donaret ; homuncio, quantus
Ex nihilo fieres, quantus Virronis amicus?
"Da Trebio! pone ad Trebium!　Vis, frater, ab istis
Ilibus?"　O nummi, vobis hunc præstat honorem,
Vos estis fratres.　Dominus tamen et domini rex

Si vis tu fieri, nullus tibi parvulus aula
Luserit Æneas, nec filia dulcior illo :
Jucundum et carum sterilis facit uxor amicum.   140
Sed tua nunc Migale pariat licet, et pueros tres
In gremium patris fundat simul: ipse loquaci
Gaudebit nido ; viridem thoraca jubebit
Afferri, minimasque nuces, assemque rogatum,
Ad mensam quoties parasitus venerit infans.
Vilibus ancipites fungi ponentur amicis,
Boletus domino ; sed quales Claudius edit
Ante illum uxoris, post quem nil amplius edit.
    Virro sibi et reliquis Virronibus illa jubebit
Poma dari, quorum solo pascaris odore :   150
Qualia perpetuus Phæacum autumnus habebat,
Credere quæ possis surrepta sororibus Afris :
Tu scabie frueris mali, quod in aggere rodit,
Qui tegitur parma et galea, metuensque flagelli
Discit ab hirsuta jaculum torquere capella.
    Forsitan impensæ Virronem parcere credas.
Hoc agit, ut doleas : nam quæ comœdia, mimus
Quis melior plorante gula?   Ergo omnia fiunt,
Si nescis, ut per lacrimas effundere bilem
Cogaris, pressoque diu stridere molari.   160
Tu tibi liber homo et regis conviva videris :
Captum te nidore suæ putat ille culinæ :
Nec male conjectat.   Quis enim tam nudus, ut illum
Bis ferat, Etruscum puero si contigit aurum,
Vel nodus tantum et signum de paupere loro ?
Spes bene cœnandi vos decipit.   "Ecce, dabit jam
Semesum leporem atque aliquid de clunibus apri :
Ad nos jam veniet minor altilis."   Inde parato
Intactoque omnes et stricto pane tacetis.
Ille sapit, qui te sic utitur.   Omnia ferre   170
Si potes, et debes.   Pulsandum vertice raso
Præbebis quandoque caput, nec dura timebis
Flagra pati, his epulis et tali dignus amico.

S A T I R A R U M

LIBER TERTIUS.

SATIRA VII.

Et spes et ratio studiorum in Cæsare tantum:
Solus enim tristes hac tempestate Camenas
Respexit, quum jam celebres notique poetæ
Balneolum Gabiis, Romæ conducere furnos
Tentarent, nec fœdum alii, nec turpe putarent
Præcones fieri; quum, desertis Aganippes
Vallibus, esuriens migraret in atria Clio.
Nam si Pieria quadrans tibi nullus in umbra
Ostendatur, ames nomen victumque Machæræ,
Et vendas potius, commissa quod auctio vendit   10
Stantibus, œnophorum, tripodes, armaria, cistas,
Alcithoen Paccî, Thebas et Terea Fausti.
Hoc satius, quam si dicas sub judice, "Vidi,"
Quod non vidisti.   Faciant equites Asiani
Quanquam, et Cappadoces faciant equitesque Bithyni,
Altera quos nudo traducit Gallia talo.
Nemo tamen studiis indignum ferre laborem
Cogetur posthac, nectit quicunque canoris
Eloquium vocale modis, laurumque momordit.
Hoc agite, O juvenes: circumspicit et stimulat vos   20
Materiamque sibi Ducis indulgentia quærit.
Si qua aliunde putas rerum exspectanda tuarum
Præsidia, atque ideo croceæ membrana tabellæ
Impletur, lignorum aliquid posce ocius et, quæ

B

Componis, dona Veneris, Telesine, marito,
Aut clude et positos tinea pertunde libellos.
Frange miser calamos vigilataque prœlia dele,
Qui facis in parva sublimia carmina cella,
Ut dignus venias hederis et imagine macra.
Spes nulla ulterior : didicit jam dives avarus   30
Tantum admirari, tantum laudare disertos,
Ut pueri Junonis avem.   Sed defluit ætas
Et pelagi patiens et cassidis atque ligonis.
Tædia tunc subeunt animos, tunc seque suamque
Terpsichoren odit facunda et nuda senectus.

    Accipe nunc artes, ne quid tibi conferat iste,
Quem colis, et Musarum et Apollinis æde relicta.
Ipse facit versus atque uni cedit Homero
Propter mille annos : et, si dulcedine famæ
Succensus recites, maculosas commodat ædes ;   40
Hæc longe ferrata domus servire jubetur,
In qua sollicitas imitatur janua portas.
Scit dare libertos extrema in parte sedentes
Ordinis et magnas comitum disponere voces.
Nemo dabit regum, quanti subsellia constent,
Et quæ conducto pendent anabathra tigillo,
Quæque reportandis posita est orchestra cathedris.
Nos tamen hoc agimus tenuique in pulvere sulcos
Ducimus et litus sterili versamus aratro.
Nam si discedas, laqueo tenet ambitiosi   50
Consuetudo mali ; tenet insanabile multos
Scribendi cacoethes, et ægro in corde senescit.
Sed vatem egregium, cui non sit publica vena,
Qui nihil expositum soleat deducere, nec qui
Communi feriat carmen triviale moneta,
Hunc, qualem nequeo monstrare et sentio tantum,
Anxietate carens animus facit, omnis acerbi
Impatiens, cupidus silvarum aptusque bibendis
Fontibus Aonidum.   Neque enim cantare sub antro

Pierio thyrsumve potest contingere sana 60
Paupertas atque æris inops, quo nocte dieque
Corpus eget : satur est, quum dicit Horatius, Euœ !
Quis locus ingenio, nisi quum se carmine solo
Vexant, et dominis Cirrhæ Nysæque feruntur
Pectora nostra, duas non admittentia curas?
Magnæ mentis opus, nec de lodice paranda
Attonitæ, currus et equos faciesque Deorum
Aspicere, et qualis Rutulum confundat Erinnys.
Nam si Virgilio puer et tolerabile deesset
Hospitium, caderent omnes a crinibus hydri ; 70
Surda nihil gemeret`grave buccina. Poscimus, ut sit
Non minor antiquo Rubrenus Lappa cothurno,
Cujus et alveolos et lænam pignerat Atreus.
Non habet infelix Numitor, quod mittat amico :
Quintillæ quod donet, habet ; nec defuit illi,
Unde emeret multa pascendum carne leonem
Jam domitum : constat leviori bellua sumtu
Nimirum, et capiunt plus intestina poetæ.
Contentus fama jaceat Lucanus in hortis
Marmoreis : at Serrano tenuique Saleio 80
Gloria quantalibet quid erit, si gloria tantum est ?
Curritur ad vocem jucundam et carmen amicæ
Thebaidos, lætam fecit quum Statius Urbem
Promisitque diem. Tanta dulcedine captos
Afficit ille animos tantaque libidine vulgi
Auditur : sed, quum fregit subsellia versu,
Esurit, intactam Paridi nisi vendat Agaven.
Ille et militiæ multis largitur honorem,
Semestri vatum digitos circumligat auro.
Quod non dant proceres, dabit histrio : tu **Camerinos** 90
Et Bareas, tu nobilium magna atria curas?
Præfectos Pelopea facit, Philomela tribunos.
Haud tamen invideas vati, quem pulpita pascunt.
Quis tibi Mæcenas? quis nunc erit aut Proculeius

Aut Fabius? quis Cotta iterum? quis Lentulus alter?
Tunc par ingenio pretium; tunc utile multis
Pallere, et vinum toto nescire Decembri.
   Vester porro labor fecundior, historiarum
Scriptores? petit hic plus temporis atque olei plus:
Namque oblita modi millesima pagina surgit   100
Omnibus, et multa crescit damnosa papyro.
Sic ingens rerum numerus jubet atque operum lex.
Quae tamen inde seges? terrae quis fructus apertae?
Quis dabit historico, quantum daret acta legenti?
Sed genus ignavum, quod lecto gaudet et umbra!
   Dic igitur, quid causidicis civilia praestent
Officia, et magno comites in fasce libelli?
Ipsi magna sonant, sed tunc, quum creditor audit,
Praecipue, vel si tetigit latus acrior illo,
Qui venit ad dubium grandi cum codice nomen.   110
Tunc immensa cavi spirant mendacia folles,
Conspuiturque sinus.   Veram deprendere messem
Si libet, hinc centum patrimonia causidicorum,
Parte alia solum russati pone Lacernae.
Consedere Duces: surgis tu pallidus Ajax
Dicturus dubia pro libertate, bubulco
Judice.   Rumpe miser tensum jecur, ut tibi lasso
Figantur virides, scalarum gloria, palmae.
Quod vocis pretium? siccus petasunculus et vas
Pelamydum, aut veteres, Afrorum epimenia, bulbi,   120
Aut vinum Tiberi devectum, quinque lagenae,
Si quater egisti.   Si contigit aureus unus,
Inde cadunt partes, ex foedere, pragmaticorum.
"Aemilio dabitur, quantum licet, et melius nos
Egimus: hujus enim stat currus aeneus, alti
Quadrijuges in vestibulis, atque ipse feroci
Bellatore sedens curvatum hastile minatur
Eminus, et statua meditatur proelia lusca."
Sic Pedo conturbat, Matho deficit; exitus hic est

Tongilli, magno cum rhinocerote lavari   130
Qui solet, et vexat lutulenta balnea turba,
Perque forum juvenes longo premit assere **Medos,**
Emturus pueros, argentum, murrhina, villas :
Spondet enim Tyrio stlataria purpura filo.
Et tamen est illis hoc utile : purpura vendit
Causidicum, vendunt amethystina : convenit **illis**
Et strepitu et facie majoris vivere census.
Sed finem impensæ non servat prodiga **Roma.**
Fidimus eloquio?   Ciceroni nemo ducentos
Nunc dederit nummos, nisi fulserit annulus ingens.   140
Respicit hæc primum, qui litigat, an tibi servi
Octo, decem comites, an post te sella, togati
Ante pedes.   Ideo conducta Paullus agebat
Sardonyche, atque ideo pluris, quam Cossus agebat,
Quam Basilus.   Rara in tenui facundia panno.
Quando licet Basilo flentem producere matrem?
Quis bene dicentem Basilum ferat?   Accipiat te
Gallia, vel potius nutricula causidicorum
Africa, si placuit mercedem imponere linguæ.
    Declamare doces?   O ferrea pectora Vettî,   150
Quum perimit sævos classis numerosa tyrannos!
Nam quæcunque sedens modo legerat, hæc eadem stans
Proferet, atque eadem cantabit versibus isdem.
Occidit miseros crambe repetita magistros.
Quis color et quod sit causæ genus, atque ubi summa
Quæstio, quæ veniant diversa parte sagittæ,
Nosse velint omnes, mercedem solvere nemo.
"Mercedem appellas? quid enim scio?"   Culpa docentis
Scilicet arguitur, quod læva in parte mamillæ
Nil salit Arcadio juveni, cujus mihi sexta   160
Quaque die miserum dirus caput Hannibal implet ;
Quidquid id est, de quo deliberat, an petat Urbem
A Cannis, an post nimbos et fulmina cautus
Circumagat madidas a tempestate cohortes.

"Quantum vis stipulare, et protinus accipe quod do,
Ut toties illum pater audiat." Haec alii sex
Vel plures uno conclamant ore sophistae,
Et veras agitant lites, raptore relicto;
Fusa venena silent, malus ingratusque maritus,
Et quae jam veteres sanant mortaria caecos.   170
Ergo sibi dabit ipse rudem, si nostra movebunt
Consilia, et vitae diversum iter ingredietur,
Ad pugnam qui rhetorica descendit ab umbra,
Summula ne pereat, qua vilis tessera venit
Frumenti: quippe haec merces lautissima. Tenta,
Chrysogonus quanti doceat, vel Pollio quanti
Lautorum pueros, artem scindes Theodori.
Balnea sexcentis et pluris porticus, in qua
Gestetur dominus, quoties pluit. Anne serenum
Exspectet spargatque luto jumenta recenti?   180
Hic potius: namque hic mundae nitet ungula mulae.
Parte alia longis Numidarum fulta columnis
Surgat, et algentem rapiat coenatio solem.
Quanticunque domus, veniet qui fercula docte
Componat; veniet qui pulmentaria condat.
Hos inter sumtus sestertia Quintiliano,
Ut multum, duo sufficient: res nulla minoris
Constabit patri, quam filius. "Unde igitur tot
Quintilianus habet saltus?" Exempla novorum
Fatorum transi. Felix et pulcher et acer;   190
Felix et sapiens et nobilis et generosus,
Appositam nigrae lunam subtexit alutae:
Felix, orator quoque maximus et jaculator:
Et si perfrixit, cantat bene. Distat enim, quae
Sidera te excipiant modo primos incipientem
Edere vagitus et adhuc a matre rubentem.
Si Fortuna volet, fies de rhetore Consul:
Si volet haec eadem, fies de Consule rhetor.
Ventidius quid enim? quid Tullius? anne aliud, quam

Sidus et occulti miranda potentia fati?   200
Servis regna dabunt, captivis fata triumphos.
Felix ille tamen corvo quoque rarior albo.
Poenituit multos vanae sterilisque cathedrae,
Sicut Thrasymachi probat exitus atque Secundi
Carinatis: et hunc inopem vidistis, Athenae,
Nil praeter gelidas ausae conferre cicutas.
Di, majorum umbris tenuem et sine pondere terram
Spirantesque crocos et in urna perpetuum ver,
Qui praeceptorem sancti voluere parentis
Esse loco! Metuens virgae jam grandis Achilles   210
Cantabat patriis in montibus: et cui non tunc
Eliceret risum citharoedi cauda magistri?
Sed Rufum atque alios caedit sua quemque juventus,
Rufum, qui toties Ciceronem Allobroga dixit.
      Quis gremio Celadi doctique Palaemonis affert
Quantum grammaticus meruit labor? et tamen ex hoc
Quodcunque est (minus est autem, quam rhetoris aera)
Discipuli custos praemordet Acoenonetus,
Et, qui dispensat, frangit sibi.   Cede, Palaemon,
Et patere inde aliquid decrescere, non aliter, quam   220
Institor hibernae tegetis niveique cadurci;
Dummodo non pereat, mediae quod noctis ab hora
Sedisti, qua nemo faber, qua nemo sederet,
Qui docet obliquo lanam deducere ferro;
Dummodo non pereat totidem olfecisse lucernas,
Quot stabant pueri, quum totus decolor esset
Flaccus et haereret nigro fuligo Maroni.
Rara tamen merces, quae cognitione tribuni
Non egeat.   Sed vos saevas imponite leges,
Ut praeceptori verborum regula constet,   230
Ut legat historias, auctores noverit omnes,
Tanquam ungues digitosque suos: ut forte rogatus,
Dum petit aut thermas aut Phoebi balnea, dicat
Nutricem Anchisae, nomen patriamque novercae

Anchemoli ; dicat, quot Acestes vixerit annos,
Quot Siculus Phrygibus vini donaverit urnas.
Exigite, ut mores teneros ceu pollice ducat,
Ut si quis cera vultum facit ; exigite, ut sit
Et pater ipsius cœtus.
"Hæc," inquit, " cures et, quum se verterit annus,   240
Accipe, victori populus quod postulat, aurum."

SATIRA VIII.

STEMMATA quid faciunt? quid prodest, Pontice, longo
Sanguine censeri, pictosque ostendere vultus
Majorum, et stantes in curribus Æmilianos,
Et Curios jam dimidios, humerosque minorem
Corvinum, et Galbam auriculis nasoque carentem?
Quis fructus, generis tabula jactare capaci
[Corvinum, posthac multa contingere virga]
Fumosos equitum cum dictatore magistros,
Si coram Lepidis male vivitur? effigies quo
Tot bellatorum, si luditur alea pernox   10
Ante Numantinos; si dormire incipis ortu
Luciferi, quo signa duces et castra movebant?
Cur Allobrogicis et magna gaudeat ara
Natus in Herculeo Fabius Lare, si cupidus, si
Vanus, et Euganea quantumvis mollior agna;
Si tenerum attritus Catinensi pumice lumbum
Squalentes traducit avos emtorque veneni
Frangenda miseram funestat imagine gentem?
Tota licet veteres exornent undique ceræ
Atria, nobilitas sola est atque unica virtus.   20
Paullus vel Cossus vel Drusus moribus esto;
Hos ante effigies majorum pone tuorum;
Præcedant ipsas illi te Consule virgas.
Prima mihi debes animi bona: sanctus haberi
Justitiæque tenax factis dictisque mereris?
Agnosco procerem.   Salve, Gætulice, seu tu
Silanus, quocunque alio de sanguine, rarus
Civis et egregius patriæ contingis ovanti.
Exclamare libet, populus quod clamat, Osiri
Invento.   Quis enim generosum dixerit hunc, qui   30
Indignus genere et præclaro nomine tantum
B 2

Insignis? Nanum cujusdam Atlanta vocamus,
Æthiopem cygnum, pravam extortamque puellam
Europen; canibus pigris scabieque vetusta
Levibus, et siccæ lambentibus ora lucernæ,
Nomen erit pardus, tigris, leo, si quid adhuc est,
Quod fremat in terris violentius. Ergo cavebis
Et metues, ne tu sic Creticus aut Camerinus.
 His ego quem monui? tecum est mihi sermo, Rubelli
Plaute. Tumes alto Drusorum stemmate, tanquam 40
Feceris ipse aliquid, propter quod nobilis esses,
Et te conciperet quæ sanguine fulget Iuli,
Non quæ ventoso conducta sub aggere texit.
"Vos humiles," inquit, "vulgi pars ultima nostri,
Quorum nemo queat patriam monstrare parentis:
Ast ego Cecropides!" Vivas, et originis hujus
Gaudia longa feras: tamen ima plebe Quiritem
Facundum invenies; solet hic defendere causas
Nobilis indocti; veniet de plebe togata,
Qui juris nodos et legum ænigmata solvat. 50
Hic petit Euphraten juvenis domitique Batavi
Custodes aquilas, armis industrius: at tu
Nil nisi Cecropides, truncoque simillimus Hermæ,
Nullo quippe alio vincis discrimine, quam quod
Illi marmoreum caput est, tua vivit imago.
Dic mihi, Teucrorum proles, animalia muta
Quis generosa putet, nisi fortia? nempe volucrem
Sic laudamus equum, facili cui plurima palma
Fervet et exsultat rauco victoria Circo.
Nobilis hic, quocunque venit de gramine, cujus 60
Clara fuga ante alios et primus in æquore pulvis:
Sed venale pecus Coryphæi posteritas et
Hirpini, si rara jugo victoria sedit.
Nil ibi majorum respectus, gratia nulla
Umbrarum: dominos pretiis mutare jubentur
Exiguis, trito ducunt epiredia collo

Segnipedes, digniquc molam versare Nepotis.
Ergo ut miremur te, non tua, privum aliquid da,
Quod possim titulis incidere, præter honores,
Quos illis damus et dedimus, quibus omnia debes.   70
    Hæc satis ad juvenem, quem nobis fama superbum
Tradit et inflatum plenumque Nerone propinquo:
Rarus enim ferme sensus communis in illa
Fortuna.   Sed te censeri laude tuorum,
Pontice, noluerim sic, ut nihil ipse futuræ
Laudis agas.   Miserum est aliorum incumbere famæ,
Ne collapsa ruant subductis tecta columnis.
Stratus humi palmes viduas desiderat ulmos.
Esto bonus miles, tutor bonus, arbiter idem
Integer; ambiguæ si quando citabere testis   80
Incertæque rei, Phalaris licet imperet, ut sis
Falsus, et admoto dictet perjuria tauro:
Summum crede nefas animam præferre pudori
Et propter vitam vivendi perdere causas.
Dignus morte perit, cœnet licet ostrea centum
Gaurana, et Cosmi toto mergatur aheno.
Exspectata diu tandem provincia quum te
Rectorem accipiet, pone iræ fræna modumque,
Pone et avaritiæ: miserere inopum sociorum:
Ossa vides regum vacuis exsucta medullis.   90
Respice, quid moneant leges, quid curia mandet,
Præmia quanta bonos maneant, quam fulmine justo
Et Capito et Numitor ruerint, damnante Senatu,
Piratæ Cilicum.   Sed quid damnatio confert,
Quum Pansa eripiat, quidquid tibi Natta reliquit?
Præconem, Chærippe, tuis circumspice pannis,
Jamque tace: furor est post omnia perdere naulum.
Non idem gemitus olim, neque vulnus erat par
Damnorum, sociis florentibus et modo victis.
Plena domus tunc omnis, et ingens stabat acervus   100
Nummorum, Spartana chlamys, conchylia Coa,

Et cum Parrhasii tabulis signisque Myronis
Phidiacum vivebat ebur ; nec non Polycleti
Multus ubique labor ; raræ sine Mentore mensæ.
Inde Dolabella est atque hinc Antonius, inde
Sacrilegus Verres : referebant navibus altis
Occulta spolia et plures de pace triumphos.
Nunc sociis juga pauca boum, grex parvus equarum,
Et pater armenti capto eripietur agello ;
Ipsi deinde Lares, si quod spectabile signum,   110
Si quis in ædicula Deus unicus.   Hæc etenim sunt
Pro summis : nam sunt hæc maxima.' Despicias tu
Forsitan imbelles Rhodios unctamque Corinthum :
Despicias merito.   Quid resinata juventus,
Cruraque totius facient tibi levia gentis?
Horrida vitanda est Hispania, Gallicus axis
Illyricumque latus : parce et messoribus illis,
Qui saturant urbem, Circo scenæque vacantem.
Quanta autem inde feres tam diræ præmia culpæ,
Quum tenues nuper Marius discinxerit Afros?   120
Curandum imprimis, ne magna injuria fiat
Fortibus et miseris : tollas licet omne, quod usquam est
Auri atque argenti, scutum gladiumque relinques,
Et jacula et galeam : spoliatis arma supersunt.
    Quod modo proposui, non est sententia : verum
Credite me vobis folium recitare Sibyllæ.
Si tibi sancta cohors comitum, si nemo tribunal
Vendit Acersecomes, si nullum in conjuge crimen,
Nec per conventus et cuncta per oppida curvis
Unguibus ire parat nummos raptura Celæno :   130
Tunc licet a Pico numeres genus, altaque si te
Nomina delectant, omnem Titanida pugnam
Inter majores ipsumque Promethea ponas :
De quocunque voles proavum tibi sumito libro.
Quod si præcipitem rapit ambitio atque libido,
Si frangis virgas sociorum in sanguine, si te

Delectant hebetes lasso lictore secures:
Incipit ipsorum contra te stare parentum
Nobilitas, claramque facem præferre pudendis.
Omne animi vitium tanto conspectius in se   140
Crimen habet, quanto major qui peccat habetur.
Quo mihi, te solitum falsas signare tabellas
In templis, quæ fecit avus, statuamque parentis
Ante triumphalem? quo, si nocturnus adulter
Tempora Santonico velas adoperta cucullo?
Præter majorum cineres atque ossa volucri
Carpento rapitur pinguis Lateranus, et ipse,
Ipse rotam adstringit multo sufflamine Consul;
Nocte quidem: sed luna videt, sed sidera testes
Intendunt oculos.   Finitum tempus honoris   150
Quum fuerit, clara Lateranus luce fiagellum
Sumet, et occursum nunquam trepidabit amici
Jam senis, ac virga prior annuet, atque maniplos
Solvet, et infundet jumentis hordea lassis.
Interea dum lanatas robumque juvencum
More Numæ cædit Jovis ante altaria, jurat
Solam Eponam et facies olida ad præsepia pictas.
Sed quum pervigiles placet instaurare popinas,
Obvius assiduo Syrophœnix udus amomo
Currit, Idumææ Syrophœnix incola portæ.   160
Hospitis affectu dominum regemque salutat,
Et cum venali Cyane succincta lagena.
    Defensor culpæ dicet mihi, "fecimus et nos
Hæc juvenes."   Esto.   Desisti nempe, nec ultra
Fovisti errorem.   Breve sit, quod turpiter audes;
Quædam cum prima resecentur crimina barba;
Indulge veniam pueris: Damasippus ad illos
Thermarum calices inscriptaque lintea vadit,
Maturus bello, Armeniæ Syriæque tuendis
Amnibus, et Rheno atque Istro.   Præstare Neronem   170
Securum valet hæc ætas.   Mitte ostia, Cæsar,

Mitte: sed in magna legatum quære popina;
Invenies aliquo cum percussore jacentem,
Permixtum nautis et furibus ac fugitivis,
Inter carnifices et fabros sandapilarum,
Et resupinati cessantia tympana Galli.
Æqua ibi libertas, communia pocula, lectus
Non alius cuiquam, nec mensa remotior ulli.
Quid facias talem sortitus, Pontice, servum?
Nempe in Lucanos aut Tusca ergastula mittas.   180
At vos, Trojugenæ, vobis ignoscitis, et quæ
Turpia cerdoni, Volesos Brutumque decebunt.
Quid, si nunquam adeo fœdis adeoque pudendis
Utimur exemplis, ut non pejora supersint?
Consumtis opibus vocem, Damasippe, locasti
Sipario, clamosum ageres ut Phasma Catulli.
Laureolum velox etiam bene Lentulus egit,
Judice me dignus vera cruce. Nec tamen ipsi
Ignoscas populo: populi frons durior hujus,
Qui sedet et spectat triscurria patriciorum,   190
Planipedes audit Fabios, ridere potest qui
Mamercorum alapas. Quanti sua funera vendant,
Quid refert? Vendunt nullo cogente Nerone,
Nec dubitant celsi prætoris vendere ludis.
Finge tamen gladios inde, atque hinc pulpita pone:
Quid satius? Mortem sic quisquam exhorruit, ut sit
Zelotypus Thymeles, stupidi collega Corinthi?
Res haud mira tamen, citharœdo Principe, mimus
Nobilis. Hæc ultra quid erit, nisi ludus? Et illud
Dedecus urbis habes: nec mirmillonis in armis,   200
Nec clypeo Gracchum pugnantem aut falce supina.
(Damnat enim tales habitus; sed damnat et odit)
Nec galea faciem abscondit: movet ecce tridentem,
Postquam librata pendentia retia dextra
Nequidquam effudit; nudum ad spectacula vultum
Erigit et tota fugit agnoscendus arena.

Credamus tunicæ, de faucibus aurea quum se
Porrigat et longo jactetur spira galero.
Ergo ignominiam graviorem pertulit omni
Vulnere cum Graccho jussus pugnare sequutor. 210
    Libera si dentur populo suffragia, quis tam
Perditus, ut dubitet Senecam præferre Neroni;
Cujus supplicio non debuit una parari
Simia, nec serpens unus, nec culeus unus?
Par Agamemnonidæ crimen; sed causa facit rem
Dissimilem. Quippe ille Deis auctoribus ultor
Patris erat cæsi media inter pocula: sed nec
Electræ jugulo se polluit aut Spartani
Sanguine conjugii; nullis aconita propinquis
Miscuit, in scena nunquam cantavit Orestes, 220
Troica non scripsit. Quid enim Verginius armis
Debuit ulcisci magis, aut cum Vindice Galba,
Quod Nero tam sæva crudaque tyrannide fecit?
Hæc opera atque hæ sunt generosi Principis artes,
Gaudentis fœdo peregrina ad pulpita cantu
Prostitui, Graiæque apium meruisse coronæ.
Majorum effigies habeant insignia vocis:
Ante pedes Domiti longum tu pone Thyestæ
Syrma vel Antigones, seu personam Menalippes,
Et de marmoreo citharam suspende colosso. 230
Quid, Catilina, tuis natalibus atque Cethegi
Inveniet quisquam sublimius? Arma tamen vos
Nocturna et flammas domibus templisque parastis,
Ut Braccatorum pueri Senonumque minores;
Ausi, quod liceat tunica punire molesta.
Sed vigilat consul vexillaque vestra coercet.
Hic novus Arpinas, ignobilis et modo Romæ
Municipalis eques, galeatum ponit ubique
Præsidium attonitis, et in omni monte laborat.
Tantum igitur muros intra toga contulit illi 240
Nominis et tituli, quantum non Leucade, quantum

Thessaliæ campis Octavius abstulit udo
Cædibus assiduis gladio.   Sed Roma parentem,
Roma Patrem Patriæ Ciceronem libera dixit.
Arpinas alius Volscorum in monte solebat
Poscere mercedes, alieno lassus aratro;
Nodosam post hæc frangebat vertice vitem,
Si lentus pigra muniret castra dolabra :
Hic tamen et Cimbros et summa pericula rerum
Excipit, et solus trepidantem protegit urbem ;   250
Atque ideo, postquam ad Cimbros stragemque volabant
Qui nunquam attigerant majora cadavera corvi,
Nobilis ornatur lauro collega secunda.
Plebeiæ Deciorum animæ, plebeia fuerunt
Nomina : pro totis legionibus hi tamèn, et pro
Omnibus auxiliis, atque omni pube Latina,
Sufficiunt Dis infernis Terræque parenti :
Pluris enim Decii, quam quæ servantur ab illis.
Ancilla natus trabeam et diadema Quirini
Et fasces meruit, regum ultimus ille bonorum.   260
Prodita laxabant portarum claustra tyrannis
Exsulibus juvenes ipsius Consulis, et quos
Magnum aliquid dubia pro libertate deceret,
Quod miraretur cum Coclite Mucius, et quæ
Imperii fines, Tiberinum, virgo natavit.
Occulta ad Patres produxit crimina servus,
Matronis lugendus : at illos verbera justis
Afficiunt pœnis et legum prima securis.
  Malo pater tibi sit Thersites, dummodo tu sis
Æacidæ similis Vulcaniaque arma capessas,   270
Quam te Thersitæ similem producat Achilles.
Et tamen, ut longe repetas longeque revolvas
Nomen, ab infami gentem deducis asylo.
Majorum primus quisquis fuit ille tuorum,
Aut pastor fuit aut illud, quod dicere nolo.

SATIRARUM

LIBER QUARTUS.

SATIRA X.

OMNIBUS in terris, quæ sunt a Gadibus usque
Auroram et Gangen, pauci dignoscere possunt
Vera bona atque illis multum diversa, remota
Erroris nebula.   Quid enim ratione timemus
Aut cupimus? quid tam dextro pede concipis, **ut te**
Conatus non pœniteat votique peracti?
Evertere domos totas optantibus ipsis
Di faciles; nocitura toga, nocitura petuntur
Militia; torrens dicendi copia multis
Et sua mortifera est facundia; viribus ille   10
Confisus periit admirandisque lacertis.
Sed plures nimia congesta pecunia cura
Strangulat, et cuncta exsuperans patrimonia **census,**
Quanto delphinis balæna Britannica major.
    Temporibus diris igitur, jussuque Neronis,
Longinum et magnos Senecæ prædivitis hortos
Clausit, et egregias Lateranorum obsidet ædes
Tota cohors: rarus venit in cœnacula miles.
Pauca licet portes argenti vascula puri,
Nocte iter ingressus gladium contumque timebis,   20
Et motæ ad lunam trepidabis arundinis umbram:
Cantabit vacuus coram latrone viator.
Prima fere vota et cunctis notissima templis
Divitiæ, crescant ut opes, ut maxima toto

Nostra sit arca foro. Sed nulla aconita bibuntur
Fictilibus: tunc illa time, quum pocula sumes
Gemmata, et lato Setinum ardebit in auro.
Jamne igitur laudas, quod de sapientibus alter
Ridebat, quoties de limine moverat unum
Protuleratque pedem; flebat contrarius alter?   30
Sed facilis cuivis rigidi censura cachinni:
Mirandum est, unde ille oculis suffecerit humor.
Perpetuo risu pulmonem agitare solebat
Democritus, quanquam non esset urbibus illis
Prætexta et trabeæ, fasces, lectica, tribunal.
Quid, si vidisset prætorem curribus altis
Exstantem, et medio sublimem in pulvere Circi,
In tunica Jovis, et pictæ Sarrana ferentem
Ex humeris aulæa togæ, magnæque coronæ
Tantum orbem, quanto cervix non sufficit ulla?   40
Quippe tenet sudans hanc publicus, et, sibi Consul
Ne placeat, curru servus portatur eodem.
Da nunc et volucrem, sceptro quæ surgit eburno,
Illinc cornicines, hinc præcedentia longi
Agminis officia, et niveos ad fræna Quirites,
Defossa in loculis quos sportula fecit amicos.
Tum quoque materiam risus invenit ad omnes
Occursus hominum, cujus prudentia monstrat
Summos posse viros et magna exempla daturos
Vervecum in patria crassoque sub aere nasci.   50
Ridebat curas, nec non et gaudia vulgi,
Interdum et lacrimas, quum Fortunæ ipse minaci
Mandaret laqueum, mediumque ostenderet unguem.
     Ergo supervacua hæc aut perniciosa petuntur,
Propter quæ fas est genua incerare deorum.
Quosdam præcipitat subjecta potentia magnæ
Invidiæ; mergit longa atque insignis honorum
Pagina; descendunt statuæ restemque sequuntur.
Ipsas deinde rotas bigarum impacta securis

Cædit, et immeritis franguntur crura caballis. 60
Jam stridunt ignes, jam follibus atque caminis
Ardet adoratum populo caput, et crepat ingens
Sejanus: deinde ex facie toto orbe secunda
Fiunt urceoli, pelves, sartago, patellæ.
"Pone domi lauros, duc in Capitolia magnum
Cretatumque bovem: Sejanus ducitur unco
Spectandus! gaudent omnes. Quæ labra! quis illi
Vultus erat! nunquam, si quid mihi credis, amavi
Hunc hominem." "Sed quo cecidit sub crimine? quisnam
Delator? quibus indiciis, quo teste probavit?" 70
"Nil horum: verbosa et grandis epistola venit
A Capreis." "Bene habet; nil plus interrogo. Sed quid
Turba Remi?" "Sequitur fortunam, ut semper, et odit
Damnatos. Idem populus, si Nurtia Tusco
Favisset, si oppressa foret secura senectus
Principis, hac ipsa Sejanum diceret hora
Augustum. Jam pridem, ex quo suffragia nulli
Vendimus, effudit curas. Nam qui dabat olim
Imperium, fasces, legiones, omnia, nunc se
Continet, atque duas tantum res anxius optat, 80
Panem et Circenses." "Perituros audio multos."
"Nil dubium: magna est fornacula: pallidulus mî
Brutidius meus ad Martis fuit obvius aram.
Quam timeo, victus ne pœnas exigat Ajax,
Ut male defensus!" "Curramus præcipites et,
Dum jacet in ripa, calcemus Cæsaris hostem."
"Sed videant servi, ne quis neget et pavidum in jus
Cervice astricta dominum trahat." Hi sermones
Tunc de Sejano, secreta hæc murmura vulgi.
Visne salutari sicut Sejanus? habere 90
Tantundem, atque illi summas donare curules,
Illum exercitibus præponere? tutor haberi
Principis angusta Caprearum in rupe sedentis
Cum grege Chaldæo? Vis certe pila, cohortes,

Egregios equites et castra domestica.   Quidni
Hæc cupias? et qui nolunt occidere quenquam,
Posse volunt.   Sed quæ præclara et prospera tantum
Ut rebus lætis par sit mensura malorum?
Hujus, qui trahitur, prætextam sumere mavis,
An Fidenarum Gabiorumque esse potestas,   100
Et de mensura jus dicere, vasa minora
Frangere, pannosus vacuis Ædilis Ulubris?
Ergo quid optandum foret, ignorasse fateris
Sejanum: nam qui nimios optabat honores,
Et nimias poscebat opes, numerosa parabat
Excelsæ turris tabulata, unde altior esset
Casus, et impulsæ præceps immane ruinæ.
Quid Crassos, quid Pompeios evertit? et illum,
Ad sua qui domitos deduxit flagra Quirites?
Summus nempe locus nulla non arte petitus,   110
Magnaque numinibus vota exaudita malignis.
Ad generum Cereris sine cæde et vulnere pauci
Descendunt reges et sicca morte tyranni.

  Eloquium ac famam Demosthenis aut Ciceronis
Incipit optare, et totis Quinquatribus optat,
Quisquis adhuc uno partam colit asse Minervam,
Quem sequitur custos angustæ vernula capsæ.
Eloquio sed uterque periit orator; utrumque
Largus et exundans leto dedit ingenii fons.
Ingenio manus est et cervix cæsa; nec unquam   120
Sanguine causidici maduerunt rostra pusilli.
"O fortunatam natam me Consule Romam!"
Antonî gladios potuit contemnere, si sic
Omnia dixisset.   Ridenda poemata malo,
Quam te conspicuæ, divina Philippica, famæ,
Volveris a prima quæ proxima.   Sævus et illum
Exitus eripuit, quem mirabantur Athenæ
Torrentem et pleni moderantem fræna theatri.
Dîs ille adversis genitus fatoque sinistro,

Quem pater, ardentis massæ fuligine lippus, 130
A carbone et forcipibus gladiosque parante
Incude et luteo Vulcano ad rhetora misit.

Bellorum exuviæ, truncis affixa tropæis
Lorica, et fracta de casside buccula pendens,
Et curtum temone jugum, victæque triremis
Aplustre, et summo tristis captivus in arcu,
Humanis majora bonis creduntur: ad hoc se
Romanus Graiusque ac barbarus induperator
Erexit: causas discriminis atque laboris
Inde habuit. Tanto major famæ sitis est, quam 140
Virtutis. Quis enim virtutem amplectitur ipsam,
Præmia si tollas? Patriam tamen obruit olim
Gloria paucorum, et laudis titulique cupido
Hæsuri saxis cinerum custodibus, ad quæ
Discutienda valent sterilis mala robora ficus:
Quandoquidem data sunt ipsis quoque fata sepulcris.
Expende Hannibalem; quot libras in duce summo
Invenies? hic est quem non capit Africa Mauro
Percussa Oceano Niloque admota tepenti,
Rursus ad Æthiopum populos altosque elephantos. 150
Additur imperiis Hispania: Pyrenæum
Transilit. Opposuit natura Alpemque nivemque:
Diducit scopulos et montem rumpit aceto.
Jam tenet Italiam: tamen ultra pergere tendit:
"Actum," inquit, "nihil est, nisi Pœno milite portas
Frangimus et media vexillum pono Subura."
(O qualis facies et quali digna tabella,
Quum Gætula ducem portaret bellua luscum!)
Exitus ergo quis est? O gloria! vincitur idem
Nempe et in exsilium præceps fugit, atque ibi magnus 160
Mirandusque cliens sedet ad prætoria regis,
Donec Bithyno libeat vigilare tyranno.
Finem animæ, quæ res humanas miscuit olim,
Non gladii, non saxa dabunt, nec tela; sed ille

Cannarum vindex et tanti sanguinis ultor,
Annulus. I, demens, et sævas curre per Alpes,
Ut pueris placeas et declamatio fias!
Unus Pellæo juveni non sufficit orbis:
Æstuat infelix angusto limite mundi,
Ut Gyari clausus scopulis parvaque Seripho: 170
Quum tamen a figulis munitam intraverit urbem,
Sarcophago contentus erit. Mors sola fatetur,
Quantula sint hominum corpuscula. Creditur olim
Velificatus Athos, et quidquid Græcia mendax
Audet in historia: constratum classibus isdem
Suppositumque rotis solidum mare: credimus altos
Defecisse amnes, epotaque flumina Medo
Prandente, et madidis cantat quæ Sostratus alis.
Ille tamen qualis rediit Salamine relicta,
In Corum atque Eurum solitus sævire flagellis   180
Barbarus, Æolio nunquam hoc in carcere passos,
Ipsum compedibus qui vinxerat Ennosigæum?
Mitius id sane: quid? non et stigmate dignum
Credidit? Huic quisquam vellet servire Deorum?
Sed qualis rediit? nempe una nave, cruentis
Fluctibus, ac tarda per densa cadavera prora.
Has toties optata exegit gloria pœnas!
    "Da spatium vitæ, multos da, Jupiter, annos!"
Hoc recto vultu solum, hoc et pallidus optas.
Sed quam continuis et quantis longa senectus   190
Plena malis! Deformem et tetrum ante omnia vultum
Dissimilemque sui, deformem pro cute pellem,
Pendentesque genas, et tales aspice rugas,
Quales, umbriferos ubi pandit Tabraca saltus,
In vetula scalpit jam mater simia bucca.
Plurima sunt juvenum discrimina: pulcrior ille
Hoc, atque ille alio; multum hic robustior illo:
Una senum facies, cum voce trementia membra,
Et jam leve caput madidique infantia nasi.

Frangendus misero gingiva panis inermi :   200
Usque adeo gravis uxori natisque sibique,
Ut captatori moveat fastidia Cosso.
Non eadem vini atque cibi, torpente palato,
Gaudia.
        Nam quæ cantante voluptas,
Sit licet eximius, citharœdo, sitve Seleucus,
Et quibus aurata mos est fulgere lacerna?
Quid refert, magni sedeat qua parte theatri,
Qui vix cornicines exaudiet atque tubarum
Concentus? clamore opus est, ut sentiat auris,   210
Quem dicat venisse puer, quot nunciet horas.
Præterea minimus gelido jam in corpore sanguis
Febre calet sola; circumsilit agmine facto
Morborum omne genus : quorum si nomina quæras,
Promtius expediam,
Quot Themison ægros autumno occiderit uno,
Quot Basilus socios, quot circumscripserit Hirrus
Pupillos ;
Percurram citius, quot villas possideat nunc,
Quo tondente gravis juveni mihi barba sonabat.   220
Ille humero, hic lumbis, hic coxa debilis ; ambos
Perdidit ille oculos et luscis invidet ; hujus
Pallida labra cibum accipiunt digitis alienis.
Ipse ad conspectum cœnæ diducere rictum
Suetus, hiat tantum, ceu pullus hirundinis, ad quem
Ore volat pleno mater jejuna.   Sed omni
Membrorum damno major dementia, quæ nec
Nomina servorum, nec vultum agnoscit amici,
Cum quo præterita cœnavit nocte, nec illos,
Quos genuit, quos eduxit.   Nam codice sævo   230
Heredes vetat esse suos ; bona tota feruntur
Ad Phialen : tantum artificis valet halitus oris.
Ut vigeant sensus animi, ducenda tamen sunt
Funera natorum, rogus aspiciendus amatæ

Conjugis et fratris, plenæque sororibus urnæ.
Hæc data pœna diu viventibus, ut, renovata
Semper clade domus, multis in luctibus inque
Perpetuo mœrore et nigra veste senescant.
Rex Pylius, magno si quidquam credis Homero,
Exemplum vitæ fuit a cornice secundæ.   240
"Felix nimirum, qui tot per secula mortem
Distulit, atque suos jam dextra computat annos,
Quique novum toties mustum bibit."   Oro, parumper
Attendas, quantum de legibus ipse queratur
Fatorum, et nimio de stamine, quum videt acris
Antilochi barbam ardentem; quum quærit ab omni,
Quisquis adest socius, cur hæc in tempora duret,
Quod facinus dignum tam longo admiserit ævo?
Hæc eadem Peleus, raptum quum luget Achillem,
Atque alius, cui fas Ithacum lugere natantem.   250
Incolumi Troja Priamus venisset ad umbras
Assaraci, magnis solemnibus, Hectore funus
Portante, ac reliquis fratrum cervicibus, inter
Iliadum lacrimas, ut primos edere planctus
Cassandra inciperet scissaque Polyxena palla,
Si foret exstinctus diverso tempore, quo non
Cœperat audaces Paris ædificare carinas.
Longa dies igitur quid contulit? omnia vidit
Eversa et flammis Asiam ferroque cadentem.
Tunc miles tremulus posita tulit arma tiara,   260
Et ruit ante aram summi Jovis, ut vetulus bos,
Qui domini cultris tenue et miserabile collum
Præbet, ab ingrato jam fastiditus aratro.
Exitus ille utcunque hominis: sed torva canino
Latravit rictu, quæ post hunc vixerat, uxor.
Festino ad nostros, et regem transeo Ponti,
Et Crœsum, quem vox justi facunda Solonis
Respicere ad longæ jussit spatia ultima vitæ.
Exsilium et carcer, Minturnarumque paludes,
Et mendicatus victa Carthagine panis   270

Hinc causas habuere. Quid illo cive tulisset
Natura in terris, quid Roma beatius unquam,
Si, circumducto captivorum agmine et omni
Bellorum pompa, animam exhalasset opimam,
Quum de Teutonico vellet descendere curru?
Provida Pompeio dederat Campania febres
Optandas: sed multae urbes et publica vota
Vicerunt. Igitur Fortuna ipsius et urbis
Servatum victo caput abstulit. Hoc cruciatu   280
Lentulus, hac poena caruit ceciditque Cethegus
Integer, et jacuit Catilina cadavere toto.

    Formam optat modico pueris, majore puellis
Murmure, quum Veneris fanum videt anxia mater,
Usque ad delicias votorum. "Cur tamen," inquit,
"Corripias? Pulcra gaudet Latona Diana."
Sed vetat optari faciem Lucretia, qualem
Ipsa habuit: cuperet Rutilae Virginia gibbum
Accipere atque suam Rutilae dare. Filius autem
Corporis egregii miseros trepidosque parentes
Semper habet. Rara est adeo concordia formae   290
Atque pudicitiae. Sanctos licet horrida mores
Tradiderit domus, ac veteres imitata Sabinos;
Praeterea castum ingenium vultumque modesto
Sanguine ferventem tribuat natura benigna
Larga manu: (quid enim puero conferre potest plus
Custode et cura natura potentior omni?)
Non licet esse viros: nam prodiga corruptoris
Improbitas ipsos audet tentare parentes.
"Sed casto quid forma nocet?" Quid profuit immo
Hippolyto grave propositum? quid Bellerophonti?   300
Erubuit nempe haec, ceu fastidita, repulsa;
Nec Sthenoboea minus, quam Cressa, excanduit, et se
Concussere ambae. Mulier saevissima tunc est,
Quum stimulos odio pudor admovet. Elige, quidnam
Suadendum esse putes, cui nubere Caesaris uxor

C

Destinat.   Optimus hic et formosissimus idem
Gentis patriciæ rapitur miser exstinguendus
Messalinæ oculis: dudum sedet illa parato
Flammeolo, Tyriusque palam genialis in hortis
Sternitur, et ritu decies centena dabuntur   310
Antiquo: veniet cum signatoribus auspex.
Hæc tu secreta et paucis commissa putabas?
Non nisi legitime vult nubere.   Quid placeat, dic:
Ni parere velis, pereundum erit ante lucernas:
Si scelus admittas, dabitur mora parvula, dum res
Nota urbi et populo contingat principis aures.
Dedecus ille domus sciet ultimus: interea tu
Obsequere imperio: sit tanti vita dierum
Paucorum.   Quidquid melius leviusque putaris,
Præbenda est gladio pulcra hæc et candida cervix.   320
      "Nil ergo optabunt homines?"   Si consilium vis,
Permittes ipsis expendere numinibus, quid
Conveniat nobis, rebusque sit utile nostris.
Nam pro jucundis aptissima quæque dabunt Di.
Carior est illis homo, quam sibi.   Nos, animorum
Impulsu et cæca magnaque cupidine ducti,
Conjugium petimus partumque uxoris: at illis
Notum, qui pueri qualisque futura sit uxor.
Ut tamen et poscas aliquid, voveasque sacellis
Exta, et candiduli divina tomacula porci: 33(
Orandum est, ut sit mens sana in corpore sano.
Fortem posce animum, mortis terrore carentem,
Qui spatium vitæ extremum inter munera ponat
Naturæ, qui ferre queat quoscunque labores,
Nesciat irasci, cupiat nihil, et potiores
Herculis ærumnas credat sævosque labores
Et Venere et coenis et pluma Sardanapali.
Monstro quod ipse tibi possis dare: semita certe
Tranquillæ per virtutem patet unica vitæ.
Nullum numen habes, si sit prudentia: nos te,   340
Nos facimus, Fortuna, Deam coeloque locamus.

SATIRA XI.

Atticus eximie si coenat, lautus habetur:
Si Rutilus, demens.   Quid enim majore cachinno
Excipitur vulgi, quam pauper Apicius?   Omnis
Convictus, thermæ, stationes, omne theatrum
De Rutilo.   Nam dum valida ac juvenalia membra
Sufficiunt galeæ, dumque ardens sanguine, fertur
(Non cogente quidem, sed nec prohibente tribuno),
Scripturus leges et regia verba lanistæ.
Multos porro vides, quos sæpe elusus ad ipsum
Creditor introitum solet exspectare macelli,   10
Et quibus in solo vivendi causa palato est.
Egregius coenat meliusque miserrimus horum,
Et cito casurus jam perlucente ruina.
Interea gustus elementa per omnia quærunt,
Nunquam animo pretiis obstantibus: interius si
Attendas, magis illa juvant, quæ pluris emuntur.
Ergo haud difficile est perituram arcessere summam,
Lancibus oppositis vel matris imagine fracta,
Et quadringentis nummis condire gulosum
Fictile.   Sic veniunt ad miscellanea ludi.   20
Refert ergo, quis hæc eadem paret: in Rutilo nam
Luxuria est, in Ventidio laudabile nomen
Sumit et a censu famam trahit.   Illum ego jure
Despiciam, qui scit, quanto sublimior Atlas
Omnibus in Libya sit montibus, hic tamen idem
Ignoret, quantum ferrata distet ab arca
Sacculus.   E coelo descendit γνῶθι σεαυτόν,
Figendum et memori tractandum pectore, sive
Conjugium quæras, vel sacri in parte Senatus
Esse velis (nec enim loricam poscit Achillis   30
Thersites, in qua se traducebat Ulixes

Ancipitem), seu tu magno discrimine causam
Protegere affectas; te consule, dic tibi, quis sis,
Orator vehemens, an Curtius et Matho buccæ.
Noscenda est mensura sui spectandaque rebus
In summis minimisque; etiam quum piscis emetur,
Ne mullum cupias, quum sit tibi gobio tantum
In loculis.   Quis enim te, deficiente crumena,
Et crescente gula, manet exitus, ære paterno
Ac rebus mersis in ventrem, fenoris atque   40
Argenti gravis et pecorum agrorumque capacem?
Talibus a dominis post cuncta novissimus exit
Annulus, et digito mendicat Pollio nudo.
Non præmaturi cineres, nec funus acerbum
Luxuriæ, sed morte magis metuenda senectus.
Hi plerumque gradus: conducta pecunia Romæ
Et coram dominis consumitur: inde ubi paullum
Nescio quid superest et pallet fenoris auctor,
Qui vertere solum, Baias et ostrea currunt.
Cedere namque foro jam non est deterius, quam   50
Esquilias a ferventi migrare Subura.
Ille dolor solus patriam fugientibus, illa
Mœstitia est caruisse anno Circensibus uno.
Sanguinis in facie non hæret gutta: morantur
Pauci ridiculum fugientem ex urbe Pudorem.
   Experiere hodie, numquid pulcherrima dictu,
Persice, non præstem vita vel moribus et re;
Sed laudem siliquas occultus ganeo; pultes
Coram aliis dictem puero, sed in aure placentas.
Nam quum sis conviva mihi promissus, habebis   60
Evandrum, venies Tirynthius, aut minor illo
Hospes, et ipse tamen contingens sanguine cœlum:
Alter aquis, alter flammis ad sidera missus.
Fercula nunc audi nullis ornata macellis.
De Tiburtino veniet pinguissimus agro
Hædulus et toto grege mollior, inscius herbæ,

Necdum ausus virgas humilis mordere salicti,
Qui plus lactis habet, quam sanguinis; et montani
Asparagi, posito quos legit villica fuso.
Grandia praeterea tortoque calentia foeno   70
Ova adsunt ipsis cum matribus, et servatae
Parte anni, quales fuerant in vitibus, uvae:
Signinum Syriumque pirum, de corbibus isdem
Aemula Picenis et odoris mala recentis,
Nec metuenda tibi, siccatum frigore postquam
Autumnum et crudi posuere pericula succi.
Haec olim nostri jam luxuriosa Senatus
Coena fuit.   Curius, parvo quae legerat horto,
Ipse focis brevibus ponebat oluscula, quae nunc
Squalidus in magna fastidit compede fossor.   80
Sicci terga suis, rara pendentia crate,
Moris erat quondam festis servare diebus,
Et natalicium cognatis ponere lardum,
Accedente nova, si quam dabat hostia, carne.
Cognatorum aliquis, titulo ter consulis, atque
Castrorum imperiis et dictatoris honore
Functus, ad has epulas solito maturius ibat,
Erectum domito referens a monte ligonem.
Quum tremerent autem Fabios durumque Catonem
Et Scauros et Fabricios, postremo severos   90
Censoris mores etiam collega timeret;
Nemo inter curas et seria duxit habendum,
Qualis in Oceani fluctu testudo nataret,
Clarum Trojugenis factura ac nobile fulcrum:
Sed nudo latere et parvis frons aerea lectis
Vile coronati caput ostendebat aselli,
Ad quod lascivi ludebant ruris alumni.
Tales ergo cibi, qualis domus atque supellex.
Tunc rudis, et Graias mirari nescius artes,
Urbibus eversis, praedarum in parte reperta   100
Magnorum artificum frangebat pocula miles,

Ut phaleris gauderet equus, cælataque cassis
Romuleæ simulacra feræ mansuescere jussæ
Imperii fato, geminos sub rupe Quirinos,
Ac nudam effigiem clypeo venientis et hasta
Pendentisque Dei, perituro ostenderet hosti.
Argenti quod erat, solis fulgebat in armis.
Ponebant igitur Tusco farrata catino ;
Omnia tunc, quibus invideas, si lividulus sis.
Templorum quoque majestas præsentior, et vox   110
Nocte fere media, mediamque audita per urbem,
Litore ab Oceani Gallis venientibus et Dis
Officium vatis peragentibus, his monuit nos.
Hanc rebus Latiis curam præstare solebat
Fictilis et nullo violatus Jupiter auro.
Illa domi natas nostraque ex arbore mensas
Tempora viderunt: hos lignum stabat in usus,
Annosam si forte nucem dejecerat Eurus.
At nunc divitibus cœnandi nulla voluptas,
Nil rhombus, nil dama sapit, putere videntur   120
Unguenta atque rosæ, latos nisi sustinet orbes
Grande ebur, et magno sublimis pardus hiatu,
Dentibus ex illis, quos mittit porta Syenes
Et Mauri celeres et Mauro obscurior Indus,
Et quos deposuit Nabathæo bellua saltu,
Jam nimios capitique graves.   Hinc surgit orexis,
Hinc stomacho bilis : nam pes argenteus illis,
Annulus in digito quod ferreus.   Ergo superbum
Convivam caveo, qui me sibi comparat, et res
Despicit exiguas.   Adeo nulla uncia nobis   130
Est eboris, nec tessellæ, nec calculus ex hac
Materia : quin ipsa manubria cultellorum
Ossea : non tamen his ulla unquam opsonia fiunt
Rancidula, aut ideo pejor gallina secatur.
Sed nec structor erit, cui cedere debeat omnis
Pergula, discipulus Trypheri doctoris, apud quem

Sumine cum magno lepus, atque aper, et pygargus,
Et Scythicæ volucres, et phœnicopterus ingens,
Et Gætulus oryx hebeti lautissima ferro
Cæditur, et tota sonat ulmea cœna Subura.   140
Nec frustum capreæ subducere, nec latus Afræ
Novit avis noster tirunculus, ac rudis omni
Tempore, et exiguæ furtis imbutus ofellæ.
Plebeios calices et paucis assibus emtos
Porriget incultus puer atque a frigore tutus;
Non Phryx aut Lycius, non a mangone petitus
Quisquam erit; in magno quum posces, posce Latine.
Idem habitus cunctis, tonsi rectique capilli,
Atque hodie tantum propter convivia pexi.
Pastoris duri est hic filius, ille bubulci: 150
Suspirat longo non visam tempore matrem,
Et casulam, et notos tristis desiderat hædos,
Ingenui vultus puer ingenuique pudoris,
Quales esse decet, quos ardens purpura vestit.
Hic tibi vina dabit, diffusa in montibus illis,
A quibus ipse venit, quorum sub vertice lusit:
Namque una atque eadem est vini patria atque ministri.
Nostra dabunt multos hodie convivia ludos:
Conditor Iliados cantabitur, atque Maronis
Altisoni dubiam facientia carmina palmam.   160
Quid refert, tales versus qua voce legantur?
    Sed nunc dilatis averte negotia curis,
Et gratam requiem dona tibi, quando licebit
Per totam cessare diem: non fenoris ulla
Mentio.
Protinus ante meum, quidquid dolet, exue limen:
Pone domum et servos et quidquid frangitur illis
Aut perit: ingratos ante omnia pone sodales.
    Interea Megalesiacæ spectacula mappæ,
Idæum sollemne, colunt, similisque triumpho   170
Præda caballorum prætor sedet ac, mihi pace

Immensæ nimiæque licet si dicere plebis,
Totam hodie Romam Circus capit et fragor aurem
Percutit, eventum viridis quo colligo panni.
Nam si deficeret, mœstam attonitamque videres
Hanc urbem, veluti Cannarum in pulvere victis
Consulibus.   Spectent juvenes, quos clamor et audax
Sponsio, quos cultæ decet assedisse puellæ:
Nostra bibat vernum contracta cuticula solem,
Effugiatque togam.   Jam nunc in balnea, salva   180
Fronte, licet vadas, quanquam solida hora supersit
Ad sextam.   Facere hoc non possis quinque diebus
Continuis, quia sunt talis quoque tædia vitæ
Magna.   Voluptates commendat rarior usus.

SATIRA XII.

Natali, Corvine, die mihi dulcior hæc lux,
Qua festus promissa Deis animalia cespes
Exspectat; niveam Reginæ ducimus agnam,
Par vellus dabitur pugnanti Gorgone Maura.
Sed procul extensum petulans quatit hostia funem,
Tarpeio servata Jovi, frontemque coruscat:
Quippe ferox vitulus, templis maturus et aræ,
Spargendusque mero, quem jam pudet ubera matris
Ducere, qui vexat nascenti robora cornu.
Si res ampla domi similisque affectibus esset,   10
Pinguior Hispulla traheretur taurus, et ipsa
Mole piger, nec finitima nutritus in herba,
Læta sed ostendens Clitumni pascua sanguis
Iret, et a grandi cervix ferienda ministro,
Ob reditum trepidantis adhuc horrendaque passi
Nuper et incolumem sese mirantis amici.
Nam præter pelagi casus et fulminis ictus
Evasit.   Densæ cœlum abscondere tenebræ
Nube una, subitusque antennas impulit ignis,
Quum se quisque illo percussum crederet, et mox   20
Attonitus nullum conferri posse putaret
Naufragium velis ardentibus.   Omnia fiunt
Talia, tam graviter, si quando poetica surgit
Tempestas.   Genus ecce aliud discriminis: audi
Et miserere iterum: quanquam sint cetera sortis
Ejusdem: pars dira quidem, sed cognita multis,
Et quam votiva testantur fana tabella
Plurima.   Pictores quis nescit ab Iside pasci?
Accidit et nostro similis fortuna Catullo.
Quum plenus fluctu medius foret alveus, et jam,   30
Alternum puppis latus evertentibus undis,
C 2

Arbori incertæ, nullam prudentia cani
Rectoris quum ferret opem : decidere jactu
Cœpit cum ventis.
" Fundite, quæ mea sunt," dicebat, " cuncta," Catullus,
Præcipitare volens etiam pulcherrima, vestem
Purpuream, teneris quoque Mæcenatibus aptam,
Atque alias, quarum generosi graminis ipsum
Infecit natura pecus, sed et egregius fons
Viribus occultis et Bæticus adjuvat aer.   40
Ille nec argentum dubitabat mittere, lances
Parthenio factas, urnæ cratera capacem,
Et dignum sitiente Pholo vel conjuge Fusci ;
Adde et bascaudas et mille escalia, multum
Cælati, biberat quo callidus emtor Olynthi.
Sed quis nunc alius, qua mundi parte, quis audet
Argento præferre caput rebusque salutem ?
    Non propter vitam faciunt patrimonia quidam,
Sed vitio cæci propter patrimonia vivunt.
Jactatur rerum utilium pars maxima : sed nec   50
Damna levant.   Tunc, adversis urgentibus, illuc
Decidit, ut malum ferro submitteret ; ac se
Explicat angustum ; discriminis ultima, quando
Præsidia afferimus navem factura minorem.
I nunc et ventis animam committe, dolato
Confisus ligno, digitis a morte remotus
Quatuor, aut septem si sit latissima tæda!
Mox cum reticulis et pane et ventre lagenæ
Aspice sumendas in tempestate secures.
Sed postquam jacuit planum mare, tempora postquam   60
Prospera vectoris fatumque valentius Euro
Et pelago ; postquam Parcæ meliora benigna
Pensa manu ducunt hilares, et staminis albi
Lanificæ, modica nec multum fortior aura
Ventus adest : inopi miserabilis arte cucurrit
Vestibus extentis et, quod superaverat unum,

Velo prora suo. Jam deficientibus Austris,
Spes vitæ cum sole redit: tum gratus Iulo,
Atque novercali sedes prælata Lavino,
Conspicitur sublimis apex, cui candida nomen   70
Scrofa dedit, lætis Phrygibus mirabile sumen,
Et nunquam visis triginta clara mamillis.
Tandem intrat positas inclusa per æquora moles
Tyrrhenamque Pharon porrectaque brachia rursum,
Quæ pelago occurrunt medio longeque relinquunt
Italiam.   Non sic igitur mirabere portus,
Quos natura dedit: sed trunca puppe magister
Interiora petit, Baianæ pervia cymbæ,
Tuti stagna sinus, gaudent ubi vertice raso
Garrula securi narrare pericula nautæ.   80
Ite igitur, pueri, linguis animisque faventes,
Sertaque delubris et farra imponite cultris,
Ac molles ornate focos glebamque virentem!
Jam sequar et, sacro quod præstat rite peracto,
Inde domum repetam, graciles ubi parva coronas
Accipiunt fragili simulacra nitentia cera.
Hic nostrum placabo Jovem, Laribusque paternis
Thura dabo, atque omnes violæ jactabo colores.
Cuncta nitent; longos erexit janua ramos,
Et matutinis operatur festa lucernis.   90
    Nec suspecta tibi sint hæc, Corvine: Catullus,
Pro cujus reditu tot pono altaria, parvos
Tres habet heredes.   Libet exspectare, quis ægram
Et claudentem oculos gallinam impendat amico
Tam sterili.   Verum hæc nimia est impensa: coturnix
Nulla unquam pro patre cadet.   Sentire calorem
Si cœpit locuples Gallita et Paccius orbi,
Legitime fixis vestitur tota tabellis
Porticus; exsistunt qui promittant hecatomben,
Quatenus hic non sunt nec venales elephanti,   100
Nec Latio, aut usquam sub nostro sidere talis

Bellua concipitur: sed furva gente petita
Arboribus Rutulis et Turni pascitur agro,
Cæsaris armentum, nulli servire paratum
Privato: siquidem Tyrio parere solebant
Hannibali, et nostris ducibus, regique Molosso,
Horum majores, ac dorso ferre cohortes,
Partem aliquam belli, et euntem in prœlia turrim.
Nulla igitur mora per Novium, mora nulla per Istrum
Pacuvium, quin illud ebur ducatur ad aras,   110
Et cadat ante Lares Gallitæ victima, sola
Tantis digna Deis et captatoribus horum.
Alter enim, si concedas mactare, vovebit
De grege servorum magna et pulcherrima quæque
Corpora; vel pueris et frontibus ancillarum
Imponet vittas, et, si qua est nubilis illi
Iphigenia domi, dabit hanc altaribus, etsi
Non sperat tragicæ furtiva piacula cervæ.
Laudo meum civem, nec comparo testamento
Mille rates: nam si Libitinam evaserit æger,   120
Delebit tabulas, inclusus carcere nassæ,
Post meritum sane mirandum, atque omnia soli
Forsan Pacuvio breviter dabit.   Ille superbus
Incedet victis rivalibus.   Ergo vides, quam
Grande operæ pretium faciat jugulata Mycenis.
    Vivat Pacuvius, quæso, vel Nestora totum;
Possideat, quantum rapuit Nero; montibus aurum
Exæquet; nec amet quenquam, nec ametur ab ullo!

SATIRARUM

LIBER QUINTUS.

SATIRA XIII.

EXEMPLO quodcunque malo committitur, ipsi
Displicet auctori.   Prima est hæc ultio, quod se
Judice nemo nocens absolvitur, improba quamvis
Gratia fallaci Prætoris vicerit urna.
Quid sentire putas omnes, Calvine, recenti
De scelere et fidei violatæ crimine?   Sed nec
Tam tenuis census tibi contigit, ut mediocris
Jacturæ te mergat onus; nec rara videmus,
Quæ pateris.   Casus multis hic cognitus, ac jam
Tritus, et e medio fortunæ ductus acervo.   10
Ponamus nimios gemitus: flagrantior æquo
Non debet dolor esse viri, nec vulnere major.
Tu quamvis levium minimam exiguamque malorum
Particulam vix ferre potes, spumantibus ardens
Visceribus, sacrum tibi quod non reddat amicus
Depositum? stupet hæc, qui jam post terga reliquit
Sexaginta annos, Fonteio Consule natus?
An nihil in melius tot rerum proficis usu?
Magna quidem, sacris quæ dat præcepta libellis,
Victrix fortunæ sapientia: ducimus autem   20
Hos quoque felices, qui ferre incommoda vitæ,
Nec jactare jugum, vita didicere magistra.
Quæ tam festa dies, ut cesset prodere furem,
Perfidiam, fraudes atque omni ex crimine lucrum

Quæsitum, et partos gladio vel pyxide nummos?
Rari quippe boni: numerus vix est totidem, quot
Thebarum portæ vel divitis ostia Nili.
Nona ætas agitur pejoraque secula ferri
Temporibus, quorum sceleri non invenit ipsa
Nomen et a nullo posuit natura metallo.   30
Nos hominum Divumque fidem clamore ciemus,
Quanto Fæsidium laudat vocalis agentem
Sportula.   Dic, senior bulla dignissime, nescis
Quas habeat Veneres aliena pecunia? nescis
Quem tua simplicitas risum vulgo moveat, quum
Exigis a quoquam, ne pejeret et putet ullis
Esse aliquod numen templis aræque rubenti?
Quondam hoc indigenæ vivebant more, priusquam
Sumeret agrestem posito diademate falcem
Saturnus fugiens, tunc, quum virguncula Juno,   40
Et privatus adhuc Idæis Jupiter antris.
Nulla super nubes convivia cœlicolarum,
Nec puer Iliacus, formosa nec Herculis uxor
Ad cyathos, et jam siccato nectare tergens
Brachia Vulcanus Liparæa nigra taberna.
Prandebat sibi quisque Deus, nec turba Deorum
Talis, ut est hodie, contentaque sidera paucis
Numinibus miserum urgebant Atlanta minori
Pondere.   Nondum aliquis sortitus triste profundi
Imperium, aut Sicula torvus cum conjuge Pluton;   50
Nec rota, nec Furiæ, nec saxum aut vulturis atri
Pœna; sed infernis hilares sine regibus umbræ.
Improbitas illo fuit admirabilis ævo,
Credebant quo grande nefas et morte piandum,
Si juvenis vetulo non assurrexerat et si
Barbato cuicumque puer, licet ipse videret
Plura domi fraga et majores glandis acervos.
Tam venerabile erat præcedere quatuor annis,
Primaque par adeo sacræ lanugo senectæ!

Nunc, si depositum non infitietur amicus,   60
Si reddat veterem cum tota ærugine follem,
Prodigiosa fides et Tuscis digna libellis,
Quæque coronata lustrari debeat agna.
Egregium sanctumque virum si cerno, bimembri
Hoc monstrum puero aut miranti sub aratro
Piscibus inventis et fetæ comparo mulæ,
Sollicitus, tanquam lapides effuderit imber,
Examenque apium longa consederit uva
Culmine delubri, tanquam in mare fluxerit amnis
Gurgitibus miris et lactis vortice torrens.   70
    Intercepta decem quereris sestertia fraude
Sacrilega?   Quid si bis centum perdidit alter
Hoc arcana modo? majorem tertius illa
Summam, quam patulæ vix ceperat angulus arcæ?
Tam facile et pronum est superos contemnere testes,
Si mortalis idem nemo sciat!   Aspice, quanta
Voce neget; quæ sit ficti constantia vultus.
Per solis radios Tarpeiaque fulmina jurat,
Et Martis frameam et Cirrhæi spicula vatis,
Per calamos venatricis pharetramque puellæ,   80
Perque tuum, pater Ægæi Neptune, tridentem:
Addit et Herculeos arcus hastamque Minervæ,
Quidquid habent telorum armamentaria cœli.
Si vero et pater est, "Comedam," inquit, "flebile nati
Sinciput elixi Pharioque madentis aceto."
    Sunt in Fortunæ qui casibus omnia ponunt,
Et nullo credunt mundum rectore moveri,
Natura volvente vices et lucis et anni,
Atque ideo intrepidi quæcunque altaria tangunt.
Est alius metuens, ne crimen pœna sequatur: 90
Hic putat esse Deos et pejerat, atque ita secum:
"Decernat, quodcumque volet, de corpore nostro
Isis, et irato feriat mea lumina sistro,
Dummodo vel cæcus teneam, quos abnego, nummos.

Et Phthisis et vomicæ putres et dimidium crus
Sunt tanti?   Pauper locupletem optare podagram
Nec dubitet Ladas, si non eget Anticyra nec
Archigene.   Quid enim velocis gloria plantæ
Præstat, et esuriens Pisææ ramus olivæ?
Ut sit magna, tamen certe lenta ira Deorum est.   100
Si curant igitur cunctos punire nocentes,
Quando ad me venient? sed et exorabile numen
Fortasse experiar: solet his ignoscere.   Multi
Committunt eadem diverso crimina fato:
Ille crucem sceleris pretium tulit, hic diadema."
Sic animum diræ trepidum formidine culpæ
Confirmant.   Tunc te sacra ad delubra vocantem
Præcedit, trahere immo ultro ac vexare paratus.
Nam quum magna malæ superest audacia causæ,
Creditur a multis fiducia.   Mimum agit ille,   110
Urbani qualem fugitivus scurra Catulli:
Tu miser exclamas, ut Stentora vincere possis,
Vel potius, quantum Gradivus Homericus: "Audis,
Jupiter, hæc, nec labra moves, quum mittere vocem
Debueras vel marmoreus vel aheneus? aut cur
In carbone tuo charta pia thura soluta
Ponimus, et sectum vituli jecur albaque porci
Omenta?   Ut video, nullum discrimen habendum est
Effigies inter vestras statuamque Vagelli."
    Accipe quæ contra valeat solatia ferre,   120
Et qui nec Cynicos, nec Stoica dogmata legit
A Cynicis tunica distantia, non Epicurum
Suspicit exigui lætum plantaribus horti.
Curentur dubii medicis majoribus ægri:
Tu venam vel discipulo committe Philippi.
Si nullum in terris tam detestabile factum
Ostendis, taceo; nec pugnis cædere pectus
Te veto, nec plana faciem contundere palma,
Quandoquidem accepto claudenda est janua damno.

Et majore domus gemitu, majore tumultu 130
Planguntur nummi, quam funera. Nemo dolorem
Fingit in hoc casu, vestem diducere summam
Contentus, vexare oculos humore coacto.
Ploratur lacrimis amissa pecunia veris.
Sed si cuncta vides simili fora plena querela,
Si, decies lectis diversa parte tabellis,
Vana supervacui dicunt chirographa ligni,
Arguit ipsorum quos litera gemmaque princeps
Sardonychum, loculis quæ custoditur eburnis:
Ten', O delicias! extra communia censes 140
Ponendum? Qui tu gallinæ filius albæ,
Nos viles pulli nati infelicibus ovis?
Rem pateris modicam et mediocri bile ferendam,
Si flectas oculos majora ad crimina. Confer
Conductum latronem, incendia sulfure cœpta
Atque dolo, primos quum janua colligit ignes:
Confer et hos, veteris qui tollunt grandia templi
Pocula adorandæ robiginis, et populorum
Dona, vel antiquo positas a rege coronas.
Hæc ibi si non sunt, minor exstat sacrilegus, qui 150
Radat inaurati femur Herculis et faciem ipsam
Neptuni; qui bracteolam de Castore ducat.
An dubitet, solitus totum conflare Tonantem?
Confer et artifices mercatoremque veneni,
Et deducendum corio bovis in mare, cum quo
Clauditur adversis innoxia simia fatis.
Hæc quota pars scelerum, quæ custos Gallicus urbis
Usque a Lucifero, donec lux occidat, audit?
Humani generis mores tibi nosse volenti
Sufficit una domus. Paucos consume dies, et 160
Dicere te miserum, postquam illinc veneris, aude.
Quis tumidum guttur miratur in Alpibus? aut quis
In Meroe crasso majorem infante mamillam?
Cærula quis stupuit Germani lumina, flavam

Cæsariem et madido torquentem cornua cirro?
Nempe quod hæc illis natura est omnibus una.
Ad subitas Thracum volucres nubemque sonoram
Pygmæus parvis currit bellator in armis:
Mox impar hosti raptusque per aera curvis
Unguibus a sæva fertur grue. Si videas hoc   170
Gentibus in nostris, risu quatiare: sed illic,
Quanquam eadem assidue spectentur proelia, ridet
Nemo, ubi tota cohors pede non est altior uno.
  "Nullane perjuri capitis fraudisque nefandæ
Poena erit?"   Abreptum crede hunc graviore catena
Protinus, et nostro (quid plus velit ira?) necari
Arbitrio: manet illa tamen jactura, nec unquam
Depositum tibi sospes erit: sed corpore trunco
Invidiosa dabit minimus solatia sanguis:
At vindicta bonum vita jucundius ipsa.   180
Nempe hoc indocti, quorum præcordia nullis
Interdum aut levibus videas flagrantia causis.
Quantulacunque adeo est occasio, sufficit iræ:
Chrysippus non dicet idem, nec mite Thaletis
Ingenium, dulcique senex vicinus Hymetto,
Qui partem acceptæ sæva inter vincla cicutæ
Accusatori nollet dare.   Plurima felix
Paullatim vitia atque errores exuit omnes,
Prima docet rectum Sapientia: quippe minuti
Semper et infirmi est animi exiguique voluptas   190
Ultio.   Continuo sic collige, quod vindicta
Nemo magis gaudet, quam femina.   Cur tamen hos tu
Evasisse putes, quos diri conscia facti
Mens habet attonitos et surdo verbere cædit
Occultum quatiente animo tortore flagellum?
Poena autem vehemens ac multo sævior illis,
Quas et Cædicius gravis invenit aut Rhadamanthus,
Nocte dieque suum gestare in pectore testem.
Spartano cuidam respondit Pythia vates:

Haud impunitum quondam fore, quod dubitaret   200
Depositum retinere et fraudem jure tueri
Jurando: quærebat enim, quæ numinis esset
Mens, et an hoc illi facinus suaderet Apollo?
Reddidit ergo, metu, non moribus; et tamen omnem
Vocem adyti dignam templo veramque probavit,
Exstinctus tota pariter cum prole domoque
Et, quamvis longa deductis gente, propinquis.
Has patitur pœnas peccandi sola voluntas.
Nam scelus intra se tacitum qui cogitat ullum,
Facti crimen habet. "Cedo, si conata peregit?"   210
Perpetua anxietas nec mensæ tempore cessat,
Faucibus, ut morbo, siccis interque molares
Difficili crescente cibo: Setina misellus
Exspuit; Albani veteris pretiosa senectus
Displicet; ostendas melius, densissima ruga
Cogitur in frontem, velut acri ducta Falerno.
Nocte brevem si forte indulsit cura soporem,
Et toto versata toro jam membra quiescunt,
Continuo templum et violati numinis aras
Et, quod præcipuis mentem sudoribus urget,   220
Te videt in somnis; tua sacra et major imago
Humana turbat pavidum cogitque fateri.
Hi sunt, qui trepidant et ad omnia fulgura pallent,
Quum tonat, exanimes primo quoque murmure cœli;
Non quasi fortuitus, nec ventorum rabie, sed
Iratus cadat in terras et judicet ignis.
Illa nihil nocuit, cura graviore timetur
Proxima tempestas, velut hoc dilata sereno.
Præterea, lateris vigili cum febre dolorem
Si cœpere pati, missum ad sua corpora morbum   230
Infesto credunt a numine; saxa Deorum
Hæc et tela putant. Pecudem spondere sacello
Balantem et Laribus cristam promittere galli
Non audent: quid enim sperare nocentibus ægris

Concessum? vel quæ non dignior hostia vita?
Mobilis et varia est ferme natura malorum.
Quum scelus admittunt, superest constantia: quid fas
Atque nefas, tandem incipiunt sentire peractis
Criminibus.   Tamen ad mores natura recurrit
Damnatos, fixa et mutari nescia.   Nam quis   240
Peccandi finem posuit sibi? quando recepit
Ejectum semel attrita de fronte ruborem?
Quisnam hominum est, quem tu contentum videris uno
Flagitio?   Dabit in laqueum vestigia noster
Perfidus et nigri patietur carceris uncum,
Aut maris Ægæi rupem scopulosque frequentes
Exsulibus magnis.   Poena gaudebis amara
Nominis invisi tandemque fatebere lætus,
Nec surdum, nec Tiresiam quenquam esse Deorum.

SATIRA XIV.

Plurima sunt, Fuscine, et fama digna sinistra
Et nitidis maculam hæsuram figentia rebus,
Quæ monstrant ipsi pueris traduntque parentes.
Si damnosa senem juvat alea, ludit et heres
Bullatus, parvoque eadem movet arma fritillo.
Nec melius de se cuiquam sperare propinquo
Concedet juvenis, qui radere tubera terræ,
Boletum condire et eodem jure natantes
Mergere ficedulas didicit, nebulone parente
Et cana monstrante gula.   Quum septimus annus   10
Transierit puero, nondum omni dente renato,
Barbatos licet admoveas mille inde magistros,
Hinc totidem, cupiet lauto cœnare paratu
Semper, et a magna non degenerare culina.
Mitem animum et mores modicis erroribus æquos
Præcipit, atque animas servorum et corpora nostra
Materia constare putat paribusque elementis?
An sævire docet Rutilus, qui gaudet acerbo
Plagarum strepitu et nullam Sirena flagellis
Comparat, Antiphates trepidi Laris ac Polyphemus,   20
Tum felix, quoties aliquis tortore vocato
Uritur ardenti duo propter lintea ferro?
Quid suadet juveni lætus stridore catenæ,
Quem mire afficiunt inscripta ergastula, carcer
Rusticus?   o
Sic natura jubet: velocius et citius nos
Corrumpunt vitiorum exempla domestica, magnis
Quum subeunt animos auctoribus.   Unus et alter
Forsitan hæc spernant juvenes, quibus arte benigna
Et meliore luto finxit præcordia Titan: 30
Sed reliquos fugienda patrum vestigia ducunt,

Et monstrata diu veteris trahit orbita culpæ.
Abstineas igitur damnandis: hujus enim vel
Una potens ratio est, ne crimina nostra sequantur
Ex nobis geniti: quoniam dociles imitandis
Turpibus ac pravis omnes sumus, et Catilinam
Quocunque in populo videas, quocunque sub axe:
Sed nec Brutus erit, Bruti nec avunculus usquam. *anywhere*
Nil dictu fœdum visuque hæc limina tangat,
Intra quæ puer est.   40
Maxima debetur puero reverentia.   Si quid
Turpe paras, ne tu pueri contemseris annos,
Sed peccaturo obstet tibi filius infans.   *hinder*
Nam si quid dignum Censoris fecerit ira
Quandoque, et similem tibi se non corpore tantum
Nec vultu dederit, morum quoque filius, et qui
Omnia deterius tua per vestigia peccet:
Corripies nimirum et castigabis acerbo
Clamore ac post hæc tabulas mutare parabis!
Unde tibi frontem libertatemque parentis,   50
Quum facias pejora senex vacuumque cerebro
Jam pridem caput hoc ventosa cucurbita quærat?
   Hospite venturo, cessabit nemo tuorum.
"Verre pavimentum, nitidas ostende columnas,
Arida cum totâ descendat araneâ telâ;   *spider*   *net*
Hic leve argentum, vasa aspera tergeat alter:"
Vox domini furit instantis virgamque tenentis.
Ergo miser trepidas, ne stercore fœda canino
Atria displiceant oculis venientis amici,
Ne perfusa luto sit porticus (et tamen uno   60
Semodio scobis hæc emendat servulus unus):
Illud non agitas, ut sanctam filius omni
Aspiciat sine labe domum vitioque carentem?
Gratum est, quod patriæ civem populoque dedisti,
Si facis, ut patriæ sit idoneus, utilis agris,
Utilis et bellorum et pacis rebus agendis.

Plurimum enim intererit, quibus artibus et quibus hunc tu
Moribus instituas. Serpente ciconia pullos
Nutrit et inventa per devia rura lacerta:
Illi eadem sumtis quærunt animalia pinnis.　　　　　　　70
Vultur, jumento et canibus crucibusque relictis,
Ad fetus properat, partemque cadaveris affert.
Hic est ergo cibus magni quoque vulturis et se
Pascentis, propria quum jam facit arbore nidos.
Sed leporem aut capream famulæ Jovis et generosæ
In saltu venantur aves: hinc præda cubili
Ponitur: inde autem, quum se matura levarit
Progenies stimulante fame, festinat ad illam,
Quam primum prædam rupto gustaverat ovo.

　　Ædificator erat Cetronius et modo curvo　　　　　　80
Litore Caietæ, summa nunc Tiburis arce,
Nunc Prænestinis in montibus alta parabat
Culmina villarum, Græcis longeque petitis
Marmoribus, vincens Fortunæ atque Herculis ædem:
Ut spado vincebat Capitolia nostra Posides.
Dum sic ergo habitat Cetronius, imminuit rem,
Fregit opes, nec parva tamen mensura relictæ
Partis erat: totam hanc turbavit filius amens,
Dum meliore novas attollit marmore villas.

　　Quidam sortiti metuentem sabbata patrem,　　　　　90
Nil præter nubes et cœli numen adorant,
Nec distare putant humana carne suillam,
Qua pater abstinuit;
Romanas autem soliti contemnere leges,
Judaicum ediscunt et servant ac metuunt jus,
Tradidit arcano quodcunque volumine Moses.
Sed pater in causa, cui septima quæque fuit lux
Ignava, et partem vitæ non attigit ullam.

　　Sponte tamen juvenes imitantur cetera; solam
Inviti quoque avaritiam exercere jubentur.　　　　　100
Fallit enim vitium specie virtutis et umbra,

Quum sit triste habitu vultuque et veste severum.
Nec dubie tanquam frugi laudatur avarus,
Tanquam parcus homo, et rerum tutela suarum
Certa magis, quam si fortunas servet easdem
Hesperidum serpens aut Ponticus.   Adde quod hunc, de
Quo loquor, egregium populus putat acquirendi
Artificem : quippe his crescunt patrimonia fabris!
Sed crescunt quocunque modo majoraque fiunt
Incude assidua semperque ardente camino.   110
Et pater ergo animi felices credit avaros,
Qui miratur opes, qui nulla exempla beati
Pauperis esse putat : juvenes hortatur, ut illam
Ire viam pergant, et eidem incumbere sectæ.
Sunt quædam vitiorum elementa : his protinus illos
Imbuit et cogit minimas ediscere sordes.
Mox acquirendi docet insatiabile votum.
Servorum ventres modio castigat iniquo,
Ipse quoque esuriens : neque enim omnia sustinet unquam
Mucida cærulei panis consumere frusta,   120
Hesternum solitus medio servare minutal
Septembri, nec non differre in tempora cœnæ
Alterius conchem æstivi cum parte lacerti
Signatam, vel dimidio putrique siluro,
Filaque sectivi numerata includere porri.
Invitatus ad hæc aliquis de ponte negabit.
Sed quo divitias hæc per tormenta coactas,
Quum furor haud dubius, quum sit manifesta phrenesis,
Ut locuples moriaris, egentis vivere fato ?
Interea pleno quum turget sacculus ore,   130
Crescit amor nummi, quantum ipsa pecunia crevit ;
Et minus hanc optat qui non habet.   Ergo paratur
Altera villa tibi, quum rus non sufficit unum,
Et proferre libet fines, majorque videtur
Et melior vicina seges : mercaris et hanc et
Arbusta et densa montem qui canet oliva.

Quorum si pretio dominus non vincitur ullo,
Nocte boves macri lassoque famelica collo
Jumenta ad virides hujus mittuntur aristas;
Nec prius inde domum, quam tota novalia sævos   140
In ventres abeant, ut credas falcibus actum.
Dicere vix possis, quam multi talia plorent,
Et quot venales injuria fecerit agros.
Sed qui sermones! quam fœdæ buccina famæ!
"Quid nocet hæc?" inquit. "Tunicam mihi lato lupini,
Quam si me toto laudet vicinia pago,
Exigui ruris paucissima farra secantem."
Scilicet et morbis et debilitate carebis,
Et luctum et curam effugies, et tempora vitæ
Longa tibi post hæc fato meliore dabuntur,   150
Si tantum culti solus possederis agri,
Quantum sub Tatio populus Romanus arabat.
Mox etiam fractis ætate ac Punica passis
Prœlia, vel Pyrrhum immanem, gladiosque Molossos,
Tandem pro multis vix jugera bina dabantur
Vulneribus. Merces hæc sanguinis atque laboris
Nullis visa unquam meritis minor, aut ingratæ
Curta fides patriæ. Saturabat glebula talis
Patrem ipsum turbamque casæ, qua feta jacebat
Uxor, et infantes ludebant quatuor, unus   160
Vernula, tres domini: sed magnis fratribus horum,
A scrobe vel sulco redeuntibus, altera cœna
Amplior et grandes fumabant pultibus ollæ.
Nunc modus hic agri nostro non sufficit horto.
Inde fere scelerum causæ; nec plura venena
Miscuit, aut ferro grassatur sæpius ullum
Humanæ mentis vitium, quam sæva cupido
Immodici census: nam dives qui fieri vult,
Et cito vult fieri. Sed quæ reverentia legum,
Quis metus aut pudor est unquam properantis avari?   170
"Vivite contenti casulis et collibus istis,

D

O pueri!" Marsus dicebat et Hernicus olim
Vestinusque senex; "panem quæramus aratro,
Qui satis est mensis: laudant hoc numina ruris,
Quorum ope et auxilio gratæ post munus aristæ
Contingunt homini veteris fastidia quercus.
Nil vetitum fecisse volet, quem non pudet alto
Per glaciem perone tegi, qui summovet Euros
Pellibus inversis. Peregrina ignotaque nobis
Ad scelus atque nefas, quæcunque est, purpura ducit." 180
     Hæc illi veteres præcepta minoribus: at nunc
Post finem autumni media de nocte supinum
Clamosus juvenem pater excitat: "Accipe ceras,
Scribe, puer, vigila, causas age, perlege rubras
Majorum leges, aut vitem posce libello.
Sed caput intactum buxo naresque pilosas
Annotet, et grandes miretur Lælius alas.
Dirue Maurorum attegias, castella Brigantum,
Ut locupletem aquilam tibi sexagesimus annus
Afferat: aut, longos castrorum ferre labores   190
Si piget, et trepidum solvunt tibi cornua ventrem
Cum lituis audita, pares, quod vendere possis
Pluris dimidio, nec te fastidia mercis
Ullius subeant ablegandæ Tiberim ultra,
Neu credas ponendum aliquid discriminis inter
Unguenta et corium. Lucri bonus est odor ex re
Qualibet. Illa tuo sententia semper in ore
Versetur, Dis atque ipso Jove digna, poetæ:
Unde habeas, quærit nemo: sed oportet habere."
Hoc monstrant vetulæ pueris repentibus assæ,   200
Hoc discunt omnes ante alpha et beta puellæ.
Talibus instantem monitis quemcunque parentem
Sic possem affari: "Dic, o vanissime, quis te
Festinare jubet? meliorem præsto magistro
Discipulum. ° Securus abi: vinceris, ut Ajax
Præteriit Telamonem, ut Pelea vicit Achilles.

Parcendum est teneris; nondum implevere medullas
Maturæ mala nequitiæ.   Quum pectere barbam
Cœperit, et longi mucronem admittere cultri,
Falsus erit testis, vendet perjuria summa   210
Exigua, Cereris tangens aramque pedemque.
Elatam jam crede nurum, si limina vestra
Mortifera cum dote subit.   Quibus illa premetur
Per somnum digitis! nam quæ terraque marique
Acquirenda putas, brevior via conferet illi.
Nullus enim magni sceleris labor."   " Hæc ego nunquam
Mandavi," dices olim, " nec talia suasi."
Mentis causa malæ tamen est et origo penes te.
Nam quisquis magni census præcepit amorem
Et lævo monitu pueros producit avaros,   220
[Et qui per fraudes patrimonia conduplicare]
Dat libertatem, et totas effundit habenas
Curriculo: quem si revoces, subsistere nescit,
Et te contemto rapitur metisque relictis.
Nemo satis credit tantum delinquere, quantum
Permittas: adeo indulgent sibi latius ipsi.
Quum dicis juveni, stultum, qui donet amico,
Qui paupertatem levet attollatque propinqui;
Et spoliare doces et circumscribere et omni
Crimine divitias acquirere, quarum amor in te,   230
Quantus erat patriæ Deciorum in pectore, quantum
Dilexit Thebas, si Græcia vera, Menœceus:
In quorum sulcis legiones dentibus anguis
Cum clypeis nascuntur, et horrida bella capessunt
Continuo, tanquam et tubicen surrexerit una.
Ergo ignem, cujus scintillas ipse dedisti,
Flagrantem late et rapientem cuncta videbis.
Nec tibi parcetur misero, trepidumque magistrum
In cavea magno fremitu leo tollet alumnus.
    Nota mathematicis genesis tua: sed grave tardas   240
Exspectare colus.   Morieris stamine nondum

Abrupto.   Jam nunc obstas et vota moraris,
Jam torquet juvenem longa et cervina senectus.
Ocius Archigenen quære, atque eme quod Mithridates
Composuit, si vis aliam decerpere ficum
Atque alias tractare rosas.   Medicamen habendum est,
Sorbere ante cibum quod debeat et pater et rex.

     Monstro voluptatem egregiam, cui nulla theatra,
Nulla æquare queas prætoris pulpita lauti,
Si spectes, quanto capitis discrimine constent   250
Incrementa domus, ærata multus in arca
Fiscus, et ad vigilem ponendi Castora nummi,
Ex quo Mars Ultor galeam quoque perdidit, et res
Non potuit servare suas.   Ergo omnia Floræ
Et Cereris licet et Cybeles aulæa relinquas :
Tanto majores humana negotia ludi.

     An magis oblectant animum jactata petauro
Corpora, quique solet rectum descendere funem,
Quam tu, Corycia semper qui puppe moraris
Atque habitas, Coro semper tollendus et Austro,   260
Perditus ac vilis sacci mercator olentis ;
Qui gaudes pingue antiquæ de litore Cretæ
Passum, et municipes Jovis advexisse lagenas?
Hic tamen ancipiti figens vestigia planta
Victum illa mercede parat, brumamque famemque
Illa reste cavet : tu propter mille talenta
Et centum villas temerarius.   Aspice portus
Et plenum magnis trabibus mare ; plus hominum est jam
In pelago ; veniet classis, quocunque vocarit
Spes lucri, nec Carpathium Gætulaque tantum   270
Æquora transiliet, sed longe Calpe relicta,
Audiet Herculeo stridentem gurgite solem.
Grande operæ pretium est, ut tenso folle reverti
Inde domum possis, tumidaque superbus aluta,
Oceani monstra et juvenes vidisse marinos.
Non unus mentes agitat furor.   Ille sororis

In manibus vultu Eumenidum terretur et igni,
Hic bove percusso mugire Agamemnona credit
Aut Ithacum.   Parcat tunicis licet atque lacernis,
Curatoris eget qui navem mercibus implet   280
Ad summum latus, et tabula distinguitur unda,
Quum sit causa mali tanti et discriminis hujus
Concisum argentum in titulos faciesque minutas.
Occurrunt nubes et fulgura: "solvite funem,"
Frumenti dominus clamat piperisque coemti;
"Nil color hic cœli, nil fascia nigra minatur;
Æstivum tonat."   Infelix hac forsitan ipsa
Nocte cadet fractis trabibus, fluctuque premetur
Obrutus, et zonam læva morsuque tenebit.
Sed cujus votis modo non suffecerat aurum,   290
Quod Tagus et rutila volvit Pactolus arena,
Frigida sufficient velantes inguina panni
Exiguusque cibus, mersa rate naufragus assem
Dum rogat, et picta se tempestate tuetur.
    Tantis parta malis cura majore metuque
Servantur.   Misera est magni custodia census.
Dispositis prædives hamis vigilare cohortem
Servorum noctu Licinus jubet, attonitus pro
Electro signisque suis Phrygiaque columna,
Atque ebore et lata testudine.   Dolia nudi   300
Non ardent Cynici; si fregeris, altera fiet
Cras domus, aut eadem plumbo commissa manebit.
Sensit Alexander, testa quum vidit in illa
Magnum habitatorem, quanto felicior hic, qui
Nil cuperet, quam qui totum sibi posceret orbem,
Passurus gestis æquanda pericula rebus.
Nullum numen habes, si sit prudentia: nos te,
Nos facimus, Fortuna, Deam.   Mensura tamen quæ
Sufficiat census, si quis me consulat, edam:
In quantum sitis atque fames et frigora poscunt,   310
    Quantum, Epicure, tibi parvis suffecit in hortis,

Quantum Socratici ceperunt ante penates.
Nunquam aliud natura, aliud sapientia dicit.
   Acribus exemplis videor te claudere. Misce
Ergo aliquid nostris de moribus: effice summam,
Bis septem ordinibus quam lex dignatur Othonis.   *lesus m?*
Hæc quoque si rugam trahit extenditque labellum,
Sume duos Equites, fac tertia quadringenta.
Si nondum implevi gremium, si panditur ultra,
Nec Crœsi fortuna unquam, nec Persica regna   320
Sufficient animo, nec divitiæ Narcissi,
Indulsit Cæsar cui Claudius omnia, cujus
Paruit imperiis, uxorem occidere jussus.

SATIRA XV.

QUIS nescit, Volusi Bithynice, qualia demens
Ægyptus portenta colat?   Crocodilon adorat
Pars hæc, illa pavet saturam serpentibus ibin.
Effigies sacri nitet aurea cercopitheci,
Dimidio magicæ resonant ubi Memnone chordæ,
Atque vetus Thebe centum jacet obruta portis.
Illic aeluros, hic piscem fluminis, illic
Oppida tota canem venerantur, nemo Dianam.
Porrum et cæpe nefas violare et frangere morsu.
O sanctas gentes, quibus hæc nascuntur in hortis   10
Numina!   Lanatis animalibus abstinet omnis
Mensa; nefas illic fetum jugulare capellæ:
Carnibus humanis vesci licet.   Attonito quum
Tale super cœnam facinus narraret Ulixes
Alcinoo, bilem aut risum fortasse quibusdam
Moverat, ut mendax aretalogus.   " In mare nemo
Hunc abicit, sæva dignum veraque Charybdi,
Fingentem immanes Læstrygonas atque Cyclopas?
Nam citius Scyllam vel concurrentia saxa
Cyanea, plenos et tempestatibus utres   20
Crediderim, aut tenui percussum verbere Circes
Et cum remigibus grunnisse Elpenora porcis.
Tam vacui capitis populum Phæaca putavit?"
Sic aliquis merito nondum ebrius, et minimum qui
De Corcyræa temetum duxerat urna:
Solus enim hæc Ithacus nullo sub teste canebat.
Nos miranda quidem, sed nuper consule Junio
Gesta super calidæ referemus mœnia Copti,
Nos vulgi scelus et cunctis graviora cothurnis.
Nam scelus, a Pyrrha quamquam omnia syrmata volvas, 30
Nullus apud tragicos populus facit.   Accipe, nostro
Dira quod exemplum feritas produxerit ævo.

Inter finitimos vetus atque antiqua simultas,
Immortale odium et nunquam sanabile vulnus
Ardet adhuc, Ombos et Tentyra. Summus utrinque
Inde furor vulgo, quod numina vicinorum
Odit uterque locus, quum solos credat habendos
Esse Deos, quos ipse colit. Sed tempore festo
Alterius populi rapienda occasio cunctis
Visa inimicorum primoribus ac ducibus, ne   40
Lætum hilaremque diem, ne magnæ gaudia cœnæ
Sentirent, positis ad templa et compita mensis
Pervigilique toro, quem nocte ac luce jacentem
Septimus interdum sol invenit. Horrida sane
Ægyptus; sed luxuria, quantum ipse notavi,
Barbara famoso non cedit turba Canopo.
Adde, quod et facilis victoria de madidis et
Blæsis atque mero titubantibus. Inde virorum
Saltatus nigro tibicine, qualiacunque
Unguenta et flores multæque in .ronte coronæ: 50
Hinc jejunum odium. Sed jurgia prima sonare
Incipiunt animis ardentibus: hæc tuba rixæ.
Dein clamore pari concurritur, et vice teli
Sævit nuda manus: paucæ sine vulnere malæ;
Vix cuiquam aut nulli toto certamine nasus
Integer. Aspiceres jam cuncta per agmina vultus
Dimidios, alias facies et hiantia ruptis
Ossa genis, plenos oculorum sanguine pugnos.
Ludere se credunt ipsi tamen et pueriles
Exercere acies, quod nulla cadavera calcent: 60
Et sane quo tot rixantis millia turbæ,
Si vivunt omnes? Ergo acrior impetus, et jam
Saxa inclinatis per humum quæsita lacertis
Incipiunt torquere, domestica seditioni
Tela; nec hunc lapidem, quales et Turnus et Ajax,
Vel quo Tydides percussit pondere coxam
Æneæ; sed quem valeant emittere dextræ

Illis dissimiles et nostro tempore natæ.
Nam genus hoc vivo jam decrescebat Homero.
Terra malos homines nunc educat atque pusillos :   70
Ergo Deus, quicunque aspexit, ridet et odit.
    A diverticulo repetatur fabula.   Postquam
Subsidiis aucti, pars altera promere ferrum
Audet, et infestis pugnam instaurare sagittis :
Terga fuga celeri præstantibus omnibus, instant
Qui vicina colunt umbrosæ Tentyra palmæ.
Labitur hinc quidam, nimia formidine cursum
Præcipitans, capiturque : ast illum in plurima sectum
Frusta et particulas, ut multis mortuus unus
Sufficeret, totum corrosis ossibus edit   80
Victrix turba : nec ardenti decoxit aeno
Aut verubus : longum usque adeo tardumque putavit
Exspectare focos, contenta cadavere crudo.
Hic gaudere libet, quod non violaverit ignem,
Quem summa cœli raptum de parte Prometheus
Donavit terris.   Elemento gratulor, et te
Exsultare reor.   Sed qui mordere cadaver
Sustinuit, nil unquam hac carne libentius edit.
Nam scelere in tanto ne quæras et dubites, an
Prima voluptatem gula senserit.   Ultimus autem,   90
Qui stetit absumto jam toto corpore, ductis
Per terram digitis, aliquid de sanguine gustat.
Vascones, hæc fama est, alimentis talibus olim
Produxere animas : sed res diversa, sed illic
Fortunæ invidia est bellorumque ultima, casus
Extremi, longæ dira obsidionis egestas.
Hujus enim, quod nunc agitur, miserabile debet
Exemplum esse cibi : sicut modo dicta mihi gens
Post omnes herbas, post cuncta animalia, quidquid
Cogebat vacui ventris furor, hostibus ipsis   100
Pallorem ac maciem et tenues miserantibus artus,
Membra aliena fame lacerabant, esse parati
         D 2

Et sua. Quisnam hominum veniam dare, quisve Deorum
Viribus abnuerit dira atque immania passis,
Et quibus illorum poterant ignoscere manes,
Quorum corporibus vescebantur?   Melius nos
Zenonis praecepta monent: nec enim omnia, quaedam
Pro vita facienda putat.   Sed Cantaber unde
Stoicus, antiqui praesertim aetate Metelli?
Nunc totus Graias nostrasque habet orbis Athenas.   110
Gallia causidicos docuit facunda Britannos:
De conducendo loquitur jam rhetore Thule.
Nobilis ille tamen populus, quem diximus, et par
Virtute atque fide, sed major clade, Saguntus
Tale quid excusat.   Maeotide saevior ara
Ægyptus: quippe illa nefandi Taurica sacri
Inventrix homines (ut jam, quae carmina tradunt,
Digna fide credas) tantum immolat, ulterius nil
Aut gravius cultro timet hostia.   Quis modo casus
Impulit hos? quae tanta fames infestaque vallo   120
Arma coegerunt tam detestabile monstrum
Audere?   Anne aliam, terra Memphitide sicca,
Invidiam facerent nolenti surgere Nilo?
Qua nec terribiles Cimbri, nec Britones unquam,
Sauromataeque truces aut immanes Agathyrsi,
Hac saevit rabie imbelle et inutile vulgus,
Parvula fictilibus solitum dare vela phaselis,
Et brevibus pictae remis incumbere testae.
Nec poenam sceleri invenies, nec digna parabis
Supplicia his populis, in quorum mente pares sunt   130
Et similes ira atque fames.   Mollissima corda
Humano generi dare se natura fatetur,
Quae lacrimas dedit: haec nostri pars optima sensus.
Plorare ergo jubet casum lugentis amici
Squaloremque rei, pupillum ad jura vocantem
Circumscriptorem, cujus manantia fletu
Ora puellares faciunt incerta capilli.
Naturae imperio gemimus, quum funus adultae

Virginis occurrit, vel terra clauditur infans,
Et minor igne rogi. Quis enim bonus et face dignus   140
Arcana, qualem Cereris vult esse sacerdos,
Ulla aliena sibi credat mala? Separat hoc nos
A grege mutorum, atque ideo venerabile soli
Sortiti ingenium, divinorumque capaces,
Atque exercendis capiendisque artibus apti,
Sensum a coelesti demissum traximus arce,
Cujus egent prona et terram spectantia. Mundi
Principio indulsit communis conditor illis
Tantum animas, nobis animum quoque, mutuus ut nos
Affectus petere auxilium et praestare juberet,   150
Dispersos trahere in populum, migrare vetusto
De nemore et proavis habitatas linquere silvas;
Ædificare domos, Laribus conjungere nostris
Tectum aliud, tutos vicino limine somnos
Ut collata daret fiducia; protegere armis
Lapsum, aut ingenti nutantem vulnere civem,
Communi dare signa tuba, defendier isdem
Turribus, atque una portarum clave teneri.
Sed jam serpentum major concordia: parcit
Cognatis maculis similis fera. Quando leoni   160
Fortior eripuit vitam leo? quo nemore unquam
Exspiravit aper majoris dentibus apri?
Indica tigris agit rabida cum tigride pacem
Perpetuam: saevis inter se convenit ursis.
Ast homini ferrum letale incude nefanda
Produxisse parum est; quum rastra et sarcula tantum
Assueti coquere, et marris ac vomere lassi
Nescierint primi gladios extendere fabri.
Aspicimus populos, quorum non sufficit irae
Occidisse aliquem; sed pectora, brachia, vultum   170
Crediderint genus esse cibi. Quid diceret ergo,
Vel quo non fugeret, si nunc haec monstra videret
Pythagoras, cunctis animalibus abstinuit qui
Tanquam homine et ventri indulsit non omne legumen?

SATIRA XVI.

Quis numerare queat felicis præmia, Galle,
Militiæ? Nam si subeuntur prospera castra,
Me pavidum excipiat tironem porta secundo
Sidere. Plus etenim fati valet hora benigni,
Quam si nos Veneris commendet epistola Marti
Et Samia genitrix quæ delectatur arena.

   Commoda tractemus primum communia: quorum
Haud minimum illud erit, ne te pulsare togatus
Audeat; immo etsi pulsetur, dissimulet, nec
Audeat excussos prætori ostendere dentes,   **10**
Et nigram in facie tumidis livoribus offam,
Atque oculum, medico nil promittente, relictum.
Bardaicus judex datur hæc punire volenti,
Calceus et grandes magna ad subsellia suræ,
Legibus antiquis castrorum et more Camilli
Servato, miles ne vallum litiget extra
Et procul a signis. Justissima Centurionum
Cognitio est igitur de milite; nec mihi deerit
Ultio, si justæ defertur causa querelæ.
Tota cohors tamen est inimica, omnesque manipli   **20**
Consensu magno efficiunt, curabilis ut sit
Vindicta et gravior quam injuria. Dignum erit ergo
Declamatoris mulino corde Vagelli,
Quum duo crura habeas, offendere tot caligas, tot
Millia clavorum. Quis tam procul absit ab urbe
Præterea? quis tam Pylades, molem aggeris ultra
Ut veniat? Lacrimæ siccentur protinus, et se
Excusaturos non sollicitemus amicos.
Da testem, judex quum dixerit; audeat ille,
Nescio quis, pugnos qui vidit, dicere, Vidi?   **30**
Et credam dignum barba, dignumque capillis

Majorum.   Citius falsum producere testem
Contra paganum possis, quam vera loquentem
Contra fortunam armati contraque pudorem.
    Præmia nunc alia atque alia emolumenta notemus
Sacramentorum.   Convallem ruris aviti
Improbus aut campum mihi si vicinus ademit
Et sacrum effodit medio de limite saxum,
Quod mea cum patulo coluit puls annua libo;
Debitor aut sumtos pergit non reddere nummos,   40
Vana supervacui dicens chirographa ligni:
Exspectandus erit, qui lites inchoet, annus
Totius populi: sed tunc quoque mille ferenda
Tædia, mille moræ; toties subsellia tantum
Sternuntur; tum facundo ponente lacernas
Cædicio, et Fusco jam micturiente, parati
Digredimur: lentaque fori pugnamus arena.
Ast illis, quos arma tegunt et balteus ambit,
Quod placitum est ipsis, præstatur tempus agendi,
Nec res atteritur longo sufflamine litis.   50
    Solis præterea testandi militibus jus
Vivo patre datur: nam, quæ sunt parta labore
Militiæ, placuit non esse in corpore census,
Omne tenet cujus regimen pater.   Ergo Coranum
Signorum comitem, castrorumque æra merentem,
Quamvis jam tremulus, captat pater.   Hunc favor æquus
Provehit, et pulcro reddit sua dona labori.
Ipsius certe ducis hoc referre videtur,
Ut, qui fortis erit, sit felicissimus idem,
Ut læti phaleris omnes et torquibus omnes.   60

A. PERSII FLACCI

SATIRÆ.

A. PERSII FLACCI

S A T I R Æ.

PROLOGUS.

Nec fonte labra prolui caballino,
Nec in bicipiti somniasse Parnasso
Memini, ut repente sic poeta prodirem:
Heliconidasque pallidamque Pirenen
Illis remitto, quorum imagines lambunt
Hederæ sequaces: ipse semipaganus
Ad sacra vatum carmen affero nostrum.
Quis expedivit psittaco suum χαῖρε,
Picasque docuit verba nostra conari?
Magister artis ingenique largitor   10
Venter, negatas artifex sequi voces.
Quod si dolosi spes refulserit nummi,
Corvos poetas et poetridas picas
Cantare credas Pegaseïum nectar.

SATIRA I.

O curas hominum! o quantum est in rebus inane!
"Quis leget hæc?" Min' tu istud ais? "Nemo hercule!"
   Nemo?
"Vel duo, vel nemo; turpe et miserabile!" Quare?
Ne mihi Polydamas et Troïades Labeonem
Prætulerint? Nugæ. Non, si quid turbida Roma
Elevet, accedas, examenve improbum in illa
Castiges trutina; nec te quæsiveris extra!
Nam Romæ quis non . . .? ah, si fas dicere . . .! Sed fas
Tunc, quum ad canitiem et nostrum istud vivere triste   10
Aspexi, ac nucibus facimus quæcunque relictis,
Quum sapimus patruos; tunc, tunc ignoscite. Nolo:
(Quid faciam)? sed sum petulanti splene cachinno.
  Scribimus, inclusus numeros ille, hic pede liber,
Grande aliquid, quod pulmo animæ prælargus anhelet.
Scilicet hæc populo, pexusque togaque recenti
Et natalitia tandem cum sardonyche albus,
Sede leget celsa, liquido quum plasmate guttur
Mobile colluerit, patranti fractus ocello.
Hic neque more probo videas nec voce serena   20
Ingentes trepidare Titos, quum carmina lumbum
Intrant, et tremulo scalpuntur ubi intima versu.
Tun', vetule, auriculis alienis colligis escas?
Auriculis, quibus et dicas cute perditus, ohe!
Quo didicisse, nisi hoc fermentum et quæ semel intus
Innata est, rupto jecore, exierit caprificus?
En pallor, seniumque! O mores! usque adeone
Scire tuum nihil est, nisi te scire hoc sciat alter?
"At pulchrum est digito monstrari et dicier, hic est!
Ten' cirratorum centum dictata fuisse   30
Pro nihilo pendas?" Ecce inter pocula quærunt

Romulidæ saturi, quid dia poemata narrent.
Hic aliquis, cui circum humeros hyacinthina læna est
Rancidulum quiddam balba de nare loquutus,
Phyllidas, Hypsipylas, vatum et plorabile si quid,
Eliquat, ac tenero supplantat verba palato.
Assensere viri. Nunc non cinis'ille poetæ
Felix? non levior cippus nunc imprimit ossa?
Laudant convivæ: nunc non e manibus illis,
Nunc non e tumulo fortunataque favilla   40
Nascentur violæ? "Rides," ait, "et nimis uncis
Naribus indulges, an erit qui velle recuset
Os populi meruisse, et cedro digna loquutus,
Linquere nec scombros metuentia carmina, nec thus?"
  Quisquis es, O, modo quem ex adverso dicere feci,
Non ego, quum scribo, si forte quid aptius exit,
Quamquam hæc rara avis est, si quid tamen aptius exit,
Laudari metuam: neque enim mihi cornea fibra est:
Sed recti finemque extremumque esse recuso
Euge tuum et *belle*. Nam belle hoc excute totum: 50
Quid non intus habet? Non hic est Ilias Accî
Ebria veratro? non, si qua elegidia crudi
Dictarunt proceres? non, quicquid denique lectis
Scribitur in citreis? Calidum scis ponere sumen,
Scis comitem horridulum trita donare lacerna,
Et, Verum, inquis, amo; verum mihi dicite de me.
Qui pote? Vis dicam? nugaris, quum tibi, calve,
Pinguis aqualiculus protenso sesquipede extet.
O Jane, a tergo quem nulla ciconia pinsit,
Nec manus auriculas imitari mobilis albas,   60
Nec linguæ, quantum sitiat canis Appula, tantum!
Vos, o patricius sanguis, quos vivere fas est
Occipiti cæco, posticæ occurrite sannæ!
  Quis populi sermo est? quis enim, nisi carmina molli
Nunc demum numero fluere, ut per leve severos
Effundat junctura ungues? scit tendere versum

Non secus ac si oculo rubricam dirigat uno.
Sive opus in mores, in luxum et prandia regum
Dicere, res grandes nostro dat Musa poetæ.
  Ecce modo heroas sensus afferre docemus   70
Nugari solitos Græce, nec ponere lucum
Artifices, nec rus saturum laudare, ubi corbes
Et focus et porci et fumosa Palilia fœno;
(Unde Remus, sulcoque terens dentalia, Quinti,
Quum trepida ante boves dictatorem induit uxor,
Et tua aratra domum lictor tulit). Euge, poeta!
  Est nunc Briseïs quem venosus liber Accî,
Sunt quos Pacuviusque et verrucosa moretur
Antiopa, *"ærumnis cor luctificabile fulta."*
Hos pueris monitus patres infundere lippos   80
Quum videas, quærisne, unde hæc sartago loquendi
Venerit in linguas; unde istud dedecus, in quo
Trossulus exsultat tibi per subsellia levis?
Nilne pudet capiti non posse pericula cano
Pellere, quin tepidum hoc optes audire, *decenter?*
  Fur es, ait Pedio. Pedius quid? crimina rasis
Librat in antithetis, doctus posuisse figuras.
Laudatur: bellum hoc! hoc bellum?
Men' moveat? quippe et, cantet si naufragus, assem
Protulerim? cantas, quum fracta te in trabe pictum   90
Ex humero portas? Verum, nec nocte paratum,
Plorabit qui me volet incurvasse querela.
  "Sed numeris decor est et junctura addita crudis.
Claudere sic versum didicit Berecyntius Atys,
Et qui cæruleum dirimebat Nerea delphin;
Sic costam longo subduximus Apennino.
Arma virum, nonne hoc spumosum et cortice pingui,
Ut ramale vetus, prægrandi subere coctum?"
Quidnam igitur tenerum, et laxa cervice legendum?
Torva Mimalloneis implerunt cornua bombis,   100
Et raptum vitulo caput ablatura superbo

Bassaris, et lyncem Mænas flexura corymbis
Euion ingeminat : reparabilis assonat Echo.
Hæc fierent, si testiculi vena ulla paterni
Viveret in nobis? summa delumbe saliva
Hoc natat; in labris et in udo est Mænas et **Atys**;
Nec pluteum cædit, nec demorsos sapit unguis.
  "Sed quid opus teneras mordaci radere vero
Auriculas? vide sis, ne majorum tibi forte
Limina frigescant : sonat hic de nare canina   110
Littera." Per me quidem sint omnia protinus alba;
Nil moror.   Euge! omnes, omnes bene miræ eritis res!
Hoc juvat?   Hic, inquis, veto quisquam faxit oletum.
Pinge duos angues : pueri, sacer est locus.
Discedo.   Secuit Lucilius urbem,
Te, Lupe, te, Muci, et genuinum fregit in illis:
Omne vafer vitium ridenti Flaccus amico
Tangit, et admissus circum præcordia ludit,
Callidus excusso populum suspendere naso :
Men' mutire nefas? nec clam, nec cum scrobe, nusquam.
Hic tamen infodiam.   Vidi, vidi ipse, libelle :   120
Auriculas asini Mida rex habet.   Hoc ego opertum,
Hoc ridere meum, tam nil, nulla tibi vendo
Iliade.   Audaci quicunque afflate Cratino,
Iratum Eupolidem prægrandi cum sene palles,
Aspice et hæc, si forte aliquid decoctius audis.
Inde vaporata lector mihi ferveat aure,
Non hic, qui in crepidas Graiorum ludere gestit,
Sordidus, et lusco qui possit dicere, Lusce,
Sese aliquem credens, Italo quod honore supinus   130
Fregerit heminas Arreti ædilis iniquas;
Nec qui abaco numeros, et secto in pulvere **metas**
Scit risisse vafer, multum gaudere paratus,
Si cynico barbam petulans nonaria vellat.
His mane edictum, post prandia Callirhoen do.

SATIRA II.

Hunc, Macrine, diem numera meliore lapillo,
Qui tibi labentes apponit candidus annos;
Funde merum Genio.   Non tu prece poscis emaci,
Quæ nisi seductis nequeas committere Divis.
At bona pars procerum tacita libabit acerra.
Haud cuivis promtum est murmurque humilesque susurros
Tollere de templis, et aperto vivere voto?
Mens bona, fama, fides, hæc clare et ut audiat hospes:
Illa sibi introrsum et sub lingua immurmurat: "O si
Ebulliat patrui præclarum funus! et, O si   10
Sub rastro crepet argenti mihi 'seria, dextro
Hercule! pupillumve utinam, quem proximus heres
Impello, expungam! namque et scabiosus, et acri
Bile tumet.   Nerio jam tertia ducitur uxor!"
Hæc sancte ut poscas, Tiberino in gurgite mergis
Mane caput bis terque, et noctem flumine purgas.
    Heus age, responde; minimum est quod scire laboro:
De Jove quid sentis? estne ut præponere cures
Hunc cuiquam?   "Cuinam? vis Staio? an scilicet hæres,
Quis potior judex, puerisve quis aptior orbis?   20
Hoc igitur, quo tu Jovis aurem impellere tentas,
Dic agedum Staio: proh Jupiter! o bone, clamet,
Jupiter! at sese non clamet Jupiter ipse?
Ignovisse putas, quia, quum tonat, ocius ilex
Sulfure discutitur sacro, quam tuque domusque.
An quia non fibris ovium Ergennaque jubente
Triste jaces lucis evitandumque bidental,
Idcirco stolidam præbet tibi vellere barbam
Jupiter? aut quidnam est, qua tu mercede Deorum
Emeris auriculas? pulmone et lactibus unctis?   30
    Ecce avia, aut metuens Divum matertera, cunis

Exemit puerum, frontemque atque uda labella
Infami digito et lustralibus ante salivis
Expiat, urentes oculos inhibere perita.
Tunc manibus quatit, et spem macram supplice voto
Nunc Licini in campos, nunc Crassi mittit in ædes.
Hunc optent generum rex et regina; puellæ
Hunc rapiant; quicquid calcaverit hic, rosa fiat!
Ast ego nutrici non mando vota; negato,
Jupiter, hæc illi, quamvis te albata rogarit.   40
    Poscis opem nervis corpusque fidele senectæ.
Esto age: sed grandes patinæ tuccetaque crassa
Annuere his superos vetuere Jovemque morantur.
    Rem struere exoptas cæso bove, Mercuriumque
Arcessis fibra: da fortunare Penates,
Da pecus et gregibus fetum!   Quo, pessime, pacto,
Tot tibi quum in flammas junicum omenta liquescant?
Et tamen hic extis et opimo vincere ferto
Intendit: "Jam crescit ager, jam crescit ovile,
Jam dabitur, jam, jam!" donec deceptus et exspes   50
Nequicquam fundo suspiret nummus in imo.
    Si tibi crateras argenti incusaque pingui
Auro dona feram, sudes et pectore lævo
Excutiat guttas lætari prætrepidum cor.
Hinc illud subiit, auro sacras quod ovato
Perducis facies: nam fratres inter ahenos
Somnia pituita qui purgatissima mittunt
Præcipui sunto, sitque illis aurea barba.
    Aurum vasa Numæ Saturniaque impulit æra,   60
Vestalesque urnas et Tuscum fictile mutat.
O curvæ in terras animæ et cœlestium inanes?
Quid juvat hoc, templis nostros immittere mores,
Et bona Dis ex hac scelerata ducere pulpa?
Hæc sibi corrupto casiam dissolvit olivo,
Hæc Calabrum coxit vitiato murice vellus,
Hæc baccam conchæ rasisse, et stringere venas

Ferventis massæ crudo de pulvere jussit.
Peccat et hæc, peccat: vitio tamen utitur.   At vos
Dicite, pontifices, in sacro quid facit aurum?
Nempe hoc quod Veneri donatæ a virgine puppæ.   70
Quin damus id Superis, de magna quod dare lance
Non possit magni Messalæ lippa propago:
Compositum jus fasque animo, sanctosque recessus
Mentis, et incoctum generoso pectus honesto?
Hæc cedo, ut admoveam templis, et farre litabo.

SATIRA III.

NEMPE hoc assidue: jam clarum mane fenestras
Intrat et angustas extendit lumine rimas,
Stertimus, indomitum quod despumare Falernum
Sufficiat, quinta dum linea tangitur umbra.
"En quid agis? siccas insana Canicula messes
Jamdudum coquit, et patula pecus omne sub ulmo est."
Unus ait comitum. "Verumne? itane? ocius adsit
Huc aliquis! nemon'?" Turgescit vitrea bilis,
Finditur, Arcadiæ pecuaria rudere dicas.
    Jam liber et bicolor positis membrana capillis,   10
Inque manus chartæ nodosaque venit arundo.
Tunc queritur, crassus calamo quod pendeat humor,
Nigra quod infusa vanescat sepia lympha;
Dilutas queritur geminet quod fistula guttas.
    O miser! inque dies ultra miser, huccine rerum
Venimus? at cur non potius, teneroque columbo
Et similis regum pueris, pappare minutum
Poscis, et iratus mammæ lallare recusas?
"An tali studeam calamo?" Cui verba? quid istas
Succinis ambages? tibi luditur; effluis amens.   20
Contemnere: sonat vitium percussa, maligne
Respondet viridi non cocta fidelia limo.
Udum et molle lutum es, nunc, nunc properandus et acri
Fingendus sine fine rota. Sed rure paterno
Est tibi far modicum, purum et sine labe salinum;
(Quid metuas?) cultrixque foci secura patella est;
Hoc satis? an deceat pulmonem rumpere ventis,
Stemmate quod Tusco ramum millesime ducis,
Censoremque tuum vel quod trabeate salutas?
Ad populum phaleras: ego te intus et in cute novi.   30
Non pudet ad morem discincti vivere Nattæ?

E

Sed stupet hic vitio, et fibris increvit opimum
Pingue; caret culpa, nescit, quid perdat, et alto
Demersus summa rursus non bullit in unda.
    Magne pater Divum, sævos punire tyrannos
Haud alia ratione velis, quum dira libido
Moverit ingenium ferventi tincta veneno:
Virtutem videant intabescantque relicta.
Anne magis Siculi gemuerunt æra juvenci,
Aut magis auratis pendens laquearibus ensis   40
Purpureas subter cervices terruit, Imus,
Imus præcipites, quam si sibi dicat, et intus
Palleat infelix quod proxima nesciat uxor?
    Sæpe oculos, memini, tangebam parvus olivo,
Grandia si nollem morituri verba Catonis
Discere, non sano multum laudanda magistro,
Quæ pater adductis sudans audiret amicis.
Jure etenim id summum, quid dexter senio ferret
Scire, erat in voto; damnosa canicula quantum
Raderet; angustæ collo non fallier orcæ;   50
Neu quis callidior buxum torquere flagello.
    Haud tibi inexpertum curvos deprendere mores,
Quæque docet sapiens braccatis illita Medis
Porticus; insomnis quibus et detonsa juventus
Invigilat, siliquis et grandi pasta polenta;
Et tibi, quæ Samios diduxit litera ramos,
Surgentem dextro monstravit limite callem:
Stertis adhuc, laxumque caput, compage soluta,
Oscitat hesternum, dissutis undique malis.
Est aliquid quo tendis, et in quod dirigis arcum?   60
An passim sequeris corvos testaque lutoque
Securus quo pes ferat, atque ex tempore vivis?
    Helleborum frustra, cum jam cutis ægra tumebit,
Poscentes videas: venienti occurrite morbo!
Et quid opus Cratero magnos promittere montes?
Discite, O miseri, et causas cognoscite rerum,

Quid sumus, aut quidnam victuri gignimur; ordo
Quis datus, et metæ qua mollis flexus et unde;
Quis modus argento, quid fas optare, quid asper
Utile nummus habet; patriæ carisque propinquis   70
Quantum elargiri deceat; quem te Deus esse
Jussit, et humana qua parte locatus es in re.
Disce, neque invideas, quod multa fidelia putet
In locuplete penu, defensis pinguibus Umbris,
Et piper et pernæ, Marsi monumenta clientis;
Mænaque quod prima nondum defecerit orca.
    Hic aliquis de gente hircosa Centurionum
Dicat: "Quod sapio, satis est mihi; non ego curo
Esse quod Arcesilas ærumnosique Solones,
Obstipo capite et figentes lumine terram,   80
Murmura quum secum et rabiosa silentia rodunt,
Atque exporrecto trutinantur verba labello,
Ægroti veteris meditantes somnia, gigni
De nihilo nihil, in nihilum nil posse reverti.
Hoc est, quod palles? cur quis non prandeat, hoc est?"
His populus ridet, multumque torosa juventus
Ingeminat tremulos naso crispante cachinnos.
    Inspice; nescio quid trepidat mihi pectus, et ægris
Faucibus exsuperat gravis halitus; inspice, sodes!
Qui dicit medico, jussus requiescere, postquam   90
Tertia compositas vidit nox currere venas,
De majore domo, modicum sitiente lagena,
Lenia loturo sibi Surrentina rogavit.
Heus, bone, tu palles! "Nihil est." Videas tamen istud,
Quicquid id est: surgit tacite tibi lutea pellis.
"At tu deterius palles; ne sis mihi tutor;
Jam pridem hunc sepeli; tu restas." Perge, tacebo.
Turgidus hic epulis atque albo ventre lavatur,
Gutture sulfureas lentum exhalante mephites.
Sed tremor inter vina subit, calidumque trientem   100
Excutit e manibus, dentes crepuere retecti,

Uncta cadunt laxis tunc pulmentaria labris.
Hinc tuba, candelæ, tandemque beatulus alto
Compositus lecto, crassisque lutatus amomis,
In portam rigidos calces extendit: at illum
Hesterni capite induto subiere Quirites.

  Tange, miser, venas et pone in pectore dextram,
"Nil calet hic;" summosque pedes attinge manusque,
"Non frigent." Visa est si forte pecunia, sive
Candida vicini subrisit molle puella,   110
Cor tibi rite salit? Positum est algente catino
Durum olus, et populi cribro decussa farina,
Tentemus fauces: tenero latet ulcus in ore
Putre, quod haud deceat plebeia radere beta.
Alges, quum excussit membris timor albus aristas;
Nunc face supposita fervescit sanguis, et ira
Scintillant oculi, dicisque facisque, quod ipse
Non sani esse hominis non sanus juret Orestes.

SATIRA IV.

REM populi tractas? (barbatum hæc crede **magistrum**
Dicere, sorbitio tollit quem dira cicutæ),
Quo fretus, dic, o magni pupille Pericli.
Scilicet ingenium et rerum prudentia velox
Ante pilos venit; dicenda tacendaque calles!
Ergo ubi commota fervet plebecula bile,
Fert animus calidæ fecisse silentia turbæ
Majestate manus: quid deinde loquere?   Quirites,
Hoc, puto, non justum est; illud male, rectius illud.
Scis etenim justum gemina suspendere lance   10
Ancipitis libræ; rectum discernis, ubi inter
Curva subit, vel quum fallit pede regula varo,
Et potis es nigrûm vitio præfigere theta.
Quin tu igitur, summa nequicquam pelle decorus,
Ante diem blando caudam jactare popello
Desinis, Anticyras melior sorbere meracas?
Quæ tibi summa boni est?   Uncta vixisse patella
Semper, et assiduo curata cuticula sole.
Exspecta, haud aliud respondeat hæc anus.   I nunc:
"Dinomaches ego sum," suffla; "sum candidus." Esto, 20
Dum ne deterius sapiat pannucea Baucis,
Quum bene discincto cantaverit ocima vernæ.
    Ut nemo in sese tentat descendere, nemo,
Sed præcedentis spectatur mantica tergo!
Quæsieris, Nostin' Vectidî prædia?   "Cujus?"
Dives arat Curibus quantum non milvus oberret.
"Hunc ais, hunc Dis iratis, Genioque sinistro!
Qui, quandoque jugum pertusa ad compita figit,
Seriolæ veterem metuens deradere limum
Ingemit, Hoc bene sit! tunicatum cum sale mordens   30

Cæpe et, farrata pueris plaudentibus olla,
Pannosam fæcem morientis sorbet aceti?"
   At si unctus cesses et figas in cute solem,
Est, prope te ignotus cubito qui tangat, et acre
Despuat in mores.
"Quinque palæstritæ licet hæc plantaria vellant,
Non tamen ista filix ullo mansuescit aratro."
   Cædimus, inque vicem præbemus crura sagittis.
Vivitur hoc pacto; sic novimus!   Ilia subter
Cæcum vulnus habes: sed lato balteus auro   40
Prætegit.   Ut mavis, da verba et decipe nervos,
Si potes.   "Egregium quum me vicinia dicat,
Non credam?"   Viso si palles improbe nummo,
Si Puteal multa cautus vibice flagellas:
Nequicquam populo bibulas donaveris aures.
Respue, quod non es; tollat sua munera cerdo;
Tecum habita; noris, quam sit tibi curta supellex.

SATIRA V.

VATIBUS hic mos est, centum sibi poscere voces,
Centum ora et linguas optare in carmina centum,
Fabula seu mœsto ponatur hianda tragœdo,
Vulnera seu Parthi ducentis ab inguine ferrum.
"Quorsum hæc? aut quantas robusti carminis offas
Ingeris, ut par sit centeno gutture niti?
Grande loquuturi nebulas Helicone legunto,
Si quibus aut Prognes, aut si quibus olla Thyestæ
Fervebit, sæpe insulso cœnanda Glyconi.
Tu neque anhelanti, coquitur dum massa camino,   10
Folle premis ventos, nec clauso murmure raucus
Nescio quid tecum grave cornicaris inepte,
Nec stloppo tumidas intendis rumpere buccas:
Verba togæ sequeris junctura callidus acri,
Ore teres modico, pallentes radere mores
Doctus et ingenuo culpam defigere ludo.
Hinc trahe quæ dicas, mensasque relinque Mycenis
Cum capite et pedibus, plebeiaque prandia noris."
    Non equidem hoc studeo, bullatis ut mihi nugis
Pagina turgescat dare pondus idonea fumo.   20
Secreti loquimur: tibi nunc, hortante Camena,
Excutienda damus præcordia, quantaque nostræ
Pars tua sit, Cornute, animæ, tibi, dulcis amice,
Ostendisse juvat. Pulsa, dignoscere cautus
Quid solidum crepet, et pictæ tectoria linguæ.
His ego centenas ausim deposcere voces
Ut, quantum mihi te sinuoso in pectore fixi,
Voce traham pura, totumque hoc verba resignent,
Quod latet arcana non enarrabile fibra.
    Quum primum pavido custos mihi purpura cessit,   30
Bullaque succinctis laribus donata pependit;

Quum blandi comites totaque impune Subura
Permisit sparsisse oculos jam candibus umbo;
Quumque iter ambiguum est, et vitæ nescius error
Diducit trepidas ramosa in compita mentes,
Me tibi supposui: teneros tu suscipis annos
Socratico, Cornute, sinu; tunc fallere sollers
Apposita intortos extendit regula mores,
Et premitur ratione animus vincique laborat,
Artificemque tuo ducit sub pollice vultum.   40
Tecum etenim longos memini consumere soles,
Et tecum primas epulis decerpere noctes.
Unum opus et requiem pariter disponimus ambo,
Atque verecunda laxamus seria mensa.
Non equidem hoc dubites, amborum fœdere certo
Consentire dies et ab uno sidere duci:
Nostra vel æquali suspendit tempora libra
Parca tenax veri, seu nata fidelibus hora
Dividit in geminos concordia fata duorum,
Saturnumve gravem nostro Jove frangimus una: 50
Nescio quod, certe est, quod me tibi temperat, astrum.
     Mille hominum species et rerum discolor usus;
Velle suum cuique est, nec voto vivitur uno.
Mercibus hic Italis mutat sub sole recenti
Rugosum piper et pallentis grana cumini;
Hic satur irriguo mavult turgescere somno;
Hic Campo indulget; hunc alea decoquit:
Sed quum lapidosa chiragra
Fregerit articulos veteris ramalia fagi,
Tunc crassos transisse dies lucemque palustrem,   60
Et sibi jam miseri vitam ingemuere relictam.
     At te nocturnis juvat impallescere chartis:
Cultor enim juvenum purgatas inseris aures
Fruge Cleanthea, petite hinc juvenesque senesque
Finem animo certum serisque viatica canis!
"Cras hoc fiet." Idem cras fiet. "Quid? quasi magnum

Nempe, diem donas!" Sed quum lux altera venit,
Jam cras hesternum heu! consumsimus: ecce aliud cras
Egerit hos annos, et semper paulum erit ultra.
Nam quamvis prope te, quamvis temone sub uno   70
Vertentem sese frustra sectabere canthum,
Quum rota posterior curras et in axe secundo.
   Libertate opus est: non hac, qua, quisque Velina
Publius emeruit, scabiosum tesserula far
Possidet. Heu steriles veri, quibus una Quiritem
Vertigo facit! hic Dama est non tressis agaso,
Vappa et lippus, et in tenui farragine mendax.
Verterit hunc dominus, momento turbinis exit
Marcus Dama. Papæ! Marco spondente recusas
Credere tu nummos? Marco sub judice palles?   80
Marcus dixit, ita est: assigna, Marce, tabellas.
"Hæc mera libertas! hoc nobis pilea donant!
An quisquam est alius liber, nisi ducere vitam
Cui licet, ut voluit? licet ut volo vivere: non sum
Liberior Bruto?" Mendose colligis, inquit
Stoicus hic aurem mordaci lotus aceto;
Hoc, reliqua accipio, *licet ut volo vivere*, tolle.
"Vindicta postquam meus a prætore recessi,
Cur mihi non liceat jussit quodcunque voluntas,
Excepto si quid Masuri rubrica vetavit?"   90
   Disce, sed ira cadat naso rugosaque sanna,
Dum veteres avias tibi de pulmone revello.
Non prætoris erat stultis dare tenuia rerum
Officia, atque usum rapidæ permittere vitæ.
Sambucam citius caloni aptaveris alto.
Stat contra ratio et secretam gannit in aurem,
Ne liceat facere id, quod quis vitiabit agendo.
Publica lex hominum naturaque continet hoc fas,
Ut teneat vetitos inscitia debilis actus.
Diluis helleborum, certo compescere puncto   100
Nescius examen: vetat hoc natura medendi.

Navem si poscat sibi peronatus arator
Luciferi rudis, exclamet Melicerta periisse
Frontem de rebus: tibi recto vivere talo
Ars dedit? et veri speciem dignoscere calles,
Ne qua subærato mendosum tinniat auro?
Quæque sequenda forent, quæque evitanda vicissim,
Illa prius creta, mox hæc carbone notasti?
Es modicus voti, presso lare, dulcis amicis?
Jam nunc astringas, jam nunc granaria laxes: 110
Inque luto fixum possis transcendere nummum,
Nec glutto sorbere salivam Mercurialem?
    "Hæc mea sunt, teneo," quum vere dixeris, esto
Liberque ac sapiens prætoribus et Jove dextro:
Sin tu, quum fueris nostræ paulo ante farinæ,
Pelliculam veterem retines, et fronte politus
Astutam vapido servas sub pectore vulpem:
Quæ dederam supra, repeto, funemque reduco:
Ni tibi concessit ratio, digitum exsere, peccas:
Et quid tam parvum?   Sed nullo thure litabis,   120
Hæreat in stultis brevis ut semuncia recti.
Hæc miscere nefas; nec, quum sis cetera fossor,
Tres tantum ad numeros satyrum moveare Bathylli.
"Liber ego."   Unde datum hoc sumis, tot subdite rebus?
An dominum ignoras, nisi quem vindicta relaxat?
I puer, et strigiles Crispini ad balnea defer,
Si increpuit, cessas nugator? servitium acre
Te nihil impellit, nec quicquam extrinsecus intrat,
Quod nervos agitet: sed si intus et in jecore ægro
Nascuntur domini, qui tu impunitior exis   130
Atque hic, quem ad strigiles scutica et metus egit herilis?
    Mane piger stertis.   Surge, inquit Avaritia; heia
Surge.   Negas, instat, Surge, inquit.   "Non queo."   Surge.
"Et quid agam?"   Rogitas? saperdas advehe Ponto,
Castoreum, stuppas, ebenum, thus, lubrica Coa;
Tolle recens primus piper e sitiente camelo.

Verte aliquid; jura.   "Sed Jupiter audiet."   Eheu!
Varo, regustatum digito terebrare salinum
Contentus perages, si vivere cum Jove tendis.
Jam puer it pellem succinctus et œnophorum aptus.   140
Ocius ad navem!   Nihil obstat, quin trabe vasta
Ægœum rapias, nisi sollers luxuria ante
Seductum moneat: Quo deinde, insane, ruis? quo?
Quid tibi vis? calido sub pectore mascula bilis
Intumuit, quam non extinxerit urna cicutæ.
Tun' mare transilias? tibi, torta cannabe fulto,
Cœna sit in transtro, Veientanumque rubellum
Exhalet vapida læsum pice sessilis obba?
Quid petis? ut nummi, quos hic quincunce modesto
Nutrieras, peragant avidos sudare deunces?   150
Indulge Genio, carpamus dulcia; nostrum est,
Quod vivis: cinis et Manes et fabula fies;
[Vive memor leti, fugit hora, hoc quod loquor inde est.]
    En quid agis? duplici in diversum scinderis hamo;
Hunccine, an hunc sequeris?   Subeas alternus oportet
Ancipiti obsequio dominos, alternus oberres:
Nec tu, quum obstiteris semel, instantique negaris
Parere imperio, Rupi jam vincula, dicas.
Nam et luctata canis nodum abripit: attamen illi,
Quum fugit, a collo trahitur pars longa catenæ.   160
    Dave, cito, hoc credas jubeo, finire dolores
Præteritos meditor (crudum Chærestratus unguem
Abrodens ait hæc).   An siccis dedecus obstem
Cognatis?   An rem patriam rumore sinistro
Limen ad obscenum frangam, dum Chrysidis udas
Ebrius ante fores extincta cum face canto?
Euge, puer, sapias, Dîs depellentibus agnam
Percute.   Sed, censen', plorabit, Dave, relicta?
Nugaris: solea, puer, objurgabere rubra.
Ne trepidare velis atque arctos rodere casses.   170
Nunc ferus et violens: at si vocet, haud mora, dicas,

Quidnam igitur faciam? ne nunc, quum arcessat et ultro
Supplicet, accedam? Si totus et integer illinc
Exieras, ne nunc. Hic, hic quem quærimus, hic est,
Non in festuca, lictor quam jactat ineptus.
Jus habet ille sui palpo, quem ducit hiantem
Cretata ambitio? Vigila et cicer ingere large
Rixanti populo, nostra ut Floralia possint
Aprici meminisse senes. Quid pulcrius? At quum
Herodis venere dies, unctaque fenestra   180
Dispositæ pinguem nebulam vomuere lucernæ
Portantes violas, rubrumque amplexa catinum
Cauda natat thunni, tumet alba fidelia vino:
Labra moves tacitus, recutitaque sabbata palles.
Tunc nigri lemures ovoque pericula rupto,
Tunc grandes Galli et cum sistro lusca sacerdos
Incussere Deos inflantes corpora, si non
Prædictum ter mane caput gustaveris alli.
    Dixeris hæc inter varicosos Centuriones,
Continuo crassum ridet Vulfenius ingens,   190
Et centum Græcos curto centusse licetur.

SATIRA VI.

ADMOVIT jam bruma foco te, Basse, Sabino?
Jamne lyra et tetrico vivunt tibi pectine chordae?
Mire opifex, numeris veterum, primordia rerum
Atque marem strepitum fidis intendisse Latinae,
Mox juvenes agitare jocis et pollice honesto
Egregius lusisse senes.   Mihi nunc Ligus ora
Intepet, hibernatque meum mare, qua latus ingens
Dant scopuli, et multa litus se valle receptat.
Lunai portum est operae cognoscere, cives!
Cor jubet hoc Enni, postquam desertuit esse   10
Maeonides Quintus, pavone ex Pythagoreo.
Hic ego securus vulgi et quid praeparet Auster
Infelix pecori, securus et angulus ille
Vicini nostro quia pinguior; etsi adeo omnes
Ditescant orti pejoribus, usque recusem
Curvus ob id minui senio, aut coenare sine uncto,
Et signum in vapida naso tetigisse lagena.
Discrepet hinc alius.   Geminos, horoscope, varo
Producis Genio: solis natalibus est qui
Tingat olus siccum muria vafer in calice empta,   20
Ipse sacrum irrorans patinae piper; hic bona dente
Grandia magnanimus peragit puer.   Utar ego, utar,
Nec rhombos ideo libertis ponere lautus,
Nec tenuem sollers turdarum nosse salivam.
Messe tenus propria vive, et granaria, fas est,
Emole: quid metuas? occa, et seges altera in herba est.
Ast vocat officium; trabe rupta, Bruttia saxa
Prendit amicus inops, remque omnem surdaque vota
Condidit Ionio: jacet ipse in litore et una
Ingentes de puppe Dei, jamque obvia mergis   30
Costa ratis lacerae.   Nunc et de cespite vivo

Frange aliquid, largire inopi, ne pictus oberret
Cærulea in tabula. Sed cœnam funeris heres
Negliget iratus, quod rem curtaveris; urnæ
Ossa inodora dabit, seu spirent cinnama surdum,
Seu ceraso peccent casiæ, nescire paratus.
Tunc bona incolumis minuas? Et Bestius urget
Doctores Graios: "Ita fit, postquam sapere urbi
Cum pipere et palmis venit nostrum hoc maris expers,
Fœniseeæ crassó vitiarunt unguine pultes."   40
Hæc cinere ulterior metuas! At tu, meus heres,
Quisquis eris, paulum a turba seductior audi.
O bone, num ignoras? missa est a Cæsare laurus
Insignem ob cladem Germanæ pubis, et aris
Frigidus excutitur cinis; ac jam postibus arma,
Jam chlamydes regum, jam lutea gausapa captis
Essedaque, ingentesque locat Cæsonia Rhenos.
Dîs igitur Genioque ducis centum paria ob res
Egregie gestas induco; quis vetat? aude;
Væ, nisi connives! Oleum artocreasque popello   50
Largior; an prohibes? dic clare! "Non adeo," inquis:
"Exossatus ager juxta est." Age, si mihi nulla
Jam reliqua ex amitis, patruelis nulla, proneptis
Nulla manet patrui, sterilis matertera vixit,
Deque avia nihilum superest, accedo Bovillas
Clivumque ad Virbî, præsto est mihi Manius heres.
"Progenies terræ?" Quære ex me, quis mihi quartus
Sit pater: haud prompte, dicam tamen; adde etiam unum,
Unum etiam; Terræ est jam filius: et mihi ritu
Manius hic generis prope major avunculus exit.   60
Qui prior es, cur me in decursu lampada poscis?
Sum tibi Mercurius; venio Deus huc ego, ut ille
Pingitur: an renuis? vin' tu gaudere relictis?
Deest aliquid summæ; minui mihi: sed tibi totum est,
Quicquid id est. Ubi sit, fuge quærere, quod mihi quon-
          dam

Legarat Tadius, neu dicta repone paterna:
"Fænoris accedat merces; hinc exime sumtus!"
"Quid reliquum est?" Reliquum? nunc, nunc impensius
    unge,
Unge, puer, caules. Mihi festa luce coquatur
Urtica et fissa fumosum sinciput aure,   '   70
Ut tuus iste nepos fiat satur anseris extis?
Mihi trama figuræ
Sit reliqua: ast illi tremat omento popa venter?
   Vende animam lucro: mercare atque excute solers
Omne latus mundi, ne sit præstantior alter
Cappadocas rigida pingues plausisse catasta.
Rem duplica. Feci: jam triplex, jam mihi quarto,
Jam decies redit in rugam. Depunge, ubi sistam.
Inventus, Chrysippe, tui finitor acervi.   80

NOTES.

NOTES.

SATIRE I.

ARGUMENT.

THIS satire seems, from several incidental circumstances, to have been produced subsequently to most of them, and was probably drawn up after the author had determined to collect and publish his works, as a kind of introduction. It must have been made public, at all events, after A.D. 100, the third year of Trajan, for in that year Marius Priscus (see v. 39, *seq.*) was condemned.

He abruptly breaks silence with an impassioned complaint of the importunity of bad writers in reciting their productions, and with a resolution of retaliating upon them; and, after ridiculing their frivolous taste in the choice of their subjects, he declares his own intention of devoting himself to satire. After exposing the corruption of men, the profligacy of women, the luxury of courtiers, the baseness of informers and fortune-hunters, the treachery of guardians, and the peculation of officers of state, he censures the general passion for gambling, the avarice and gluttony of the rich, and the miserable poverty and subjection of their dependents; and after some bitter reflections on the danger of satirizing living villainy, he concludes with a resolution to attack it under the mask of departed names. (*Evans.*)

1-2. *Semper ego auditor tantum?* Supply *ero.* "Shall I ever be a hearer only?" *i. e.*, a listener merely to others while reciting their productions. An abrupt commencement, in true satiric tone. *Ego* being expressed is meant to be emphatic.—*Nunquamne reponam.* "Shall I never pay back?" *i. e.*, in kind, by reading my own productions. A metaphor taken from the repaying of a debt.—*Rauci Theseide Codri.* "With the Theseis of the hoarse-bawling Codrus;" *i. e.*, of Codrus rendered actually hoarse by the frequent and loud reading of his wretched poem on the exploits of Theseus. It was too

long to be finished in one or two recitations. Hence *toties*. As regards the form *Theseis*, compare that of the *Æneis* of Virgil.—
Codri. We have retained here the ordinary reading. Jahn and
others, however, give *Cordi*, which is certainly the usual Latin form ;
but the MSS. are against it. Perhaps the same individual is meant
who is alluded to in *Sat.* iii., 184.

3–6. *Togatas.* "His comedies." Supply *fabulas.* In the *fabu-
læ togatæ* the plot and characters were Roman, the name being derived from the *toga*, or main article of Roman attire. In the *palliatæ*,
so called from the Greek *pallium*, the plot and characters were Grecian. The *prætextatæ* were not so much tragedies as historical
plays.—*Elegos.* "His love-sick ditties." Literally, "his elegies."
The *elegi* were small poems on mournful or tender subjects, in alter-
nate hexameters and pentameters.—*Ingens Telephus.* "Bulky Telephus." Some prolix and stupid play, having for its subject the
well-known legend of Telephus, king of Mysia, who was wounded by
the spear of Achilles and cured by its rust.—*Aut summi plena*, &c.
"Or Orestes, the margin of the manuscript already full to the very
edge, written also on the back," &c. Another almost interminable
play on the legend of Orestes, son of Agamemnon and Clytæmnestra, who slew his guilty mother, and was driven mad, in consequence, by the Furies.—*Margine libri*, &c. The ancients usually
wrote on only one side of the paper or parchment, leaving a margin
more or less broad. When they wrote also on the back, as in the
present instance, the works were called *Opisthographi*, and were said
to be written " *aversa charta.*"

7–8. *Quam mihi.* Because these themes have been so incessantly
dinned into his ears.—*Lucus Martis.* We have our choice here of
three localities : either the grove sacred to Mars, near Alba, where
Rhea Silvia brought forth Romulus and Remus ; or a grove of Mars
on the Appian Way, where, according to the old scholiast, poets were
accustomed to recite; or the grove of this same deity in Colchis,
from an oak in which the golden fleece was suspended. Heinrich
declares in favor of the last ; but the first is most probable, as being
a strictly national theme, connected with the legend of the origin of
Rome.—*Æoliis vicinum rupibus antrum*, &c. By the "Æolian rocks"
are meant the Lipari Islands, in one of which Æolus reigned. The
" cave of Vulcan" is the adjacent Ætna, not, as some think, the isl-
and of Hiera (now *Volcano*), one of the Lipari group.

9–11. *Quid agant venti.* "What the winds may be doing." Alluding to some tedious didactic poem on the power and agency of
the winds by land and sea. Some think the reference is to a poem

on the legend of Boreas carrying off Orithyia.—*Quas torqueat Æacus umbras.* "What shades Æacus may be torturing," *i. e.*, torturing into a confession of their guilt. Æacus, in the world below, sat in judgment on the shades from Europe. The allusion is to some poem on the scenes and punishments of the other world.—*Alius.* Observe the irony. The matter is so trite and hackneyed that there is no need even of mentioning the well-known name of Jason; he is merely called "another."—*Furtivæ aurum pelliculæ.* "The gold of the stolen skin," *i. e.*, the golden fleece. *Pelliculæ*, contemptuously for *velleris.*—*Quantas jaculetur*, &c. Alluding to the conflict between the Centaurs and Lapithæ. Monychus, one of the former, greatly distinguished himself by hurling whole trees at the foe.—*Mŭnychus.* A very appropriate name for a Centaur, being derived from μῶνος (Doric for μόνος), "single," and ὄνυξ, "a hoof;" or else formed by syncope from μονώνυχος, and meaning "of solid (or uncloven) hoof," as an epithet of the horse.

12-14. *Frontonis platani.* Julius Fronto was a munificent, though not, perhaps, a very discriminating patron of literature. He was thrice consul, and once a colleague of Trajan, A.D. 97. His mansion is here indicated as the scene of recitation, surrounded by plane-trees, for the sake of coolness and shade.—*Convulsaque marmora clamant.* "And the (inlaid) marbles, actually shaken by the din, loudly re-echo," *i. e.*, they echo forth these hackneyed themes in long and loud reverberations.—*Marmora.* The walls were inlaid or incrusted with marble. Compare the *secta marmora* of Lucan (10, 114). Some erroneously think that tessellated pavements are meant.—*Ruptæ.* "Split." Poetic exaggeration, like *convulsa* in the previous line.—*Exspectes eadem*, &c. The *cacoëthes scribendi* has become a regular epidemic. Compare Horace, *Epist.* ii., 1, 117: "*Scribimus indocti doctique poemata passim.*"

15-18. *Et nos ergo manum*, &c. "We too, therefore, have withdrawn our hand from beneath the ferule," *i. e.*, we too have been at school. The train of ideas is as follows: Since therefore all, whether good or bad, write poems, I too, who have been at school, to learn the arts of poetry and declamation, and who am thus one of the educated, will do the same thing.—*Et nos consilium dedimus*, &c. Boys were taught rhetoric and declamation at the Roman schools by having a thesis proposed, on which they were to take opposite sides. The subject which Juvenal had to handle was of the deliberative kind, namely, whether Sulla ought to have laid down the dictatorship, and retired to private life, or to have continued at the head of the Roman state. It may be supposed to have been couched in the following form : *Deliberat Sulla, an dictaturam depo-nat.* Juvenal espoused the affirmative. Sulla did resign his dicta-torship, and died the following year.—*Periturœ.* " Destined in some way or other to be wasted," *i. e.,* in being written on by some one or other.

19-21. *Hoc campo.* The field of satire is meant. The meta-phor is taken from the chariot races at the Circensian games.—*Magnus Auruncœ alumnus.* Lucilius is meant, who first gave a regu-lar and artistic form to Roman satire. He was a native of Suessa Aurunca, in Latium.—*Et placidi rationem admittitis.* " And with kindly feelings are prepared to listen to reason."

22-23. *Patricios omnes,* &c. " When a single individual vies in wealth with the whole body of patricians." Some individual is here meant who had risen from a low line of life to the possession of im-mense riches, by turning informer, as well as by other detestable arts. The commentators take pains to ascertain the individual, but without much success. According to some, Juvenal has in view a certain Licinius, a barber and freed man of Augustus, while others think that he means Cinnamus, on whom we have an epigram in Martial (vii., 64).—*Provocet.* The verb *provocare* properly means " to challenge to a conflict," as here, a conflict of riches.—*Quo ton-dente, gravis,* &c. " Who clipping it, my beard, grown exuberant unto me while in early manhood, was accustomed to resound," *i. e.,* who used to trim my beard when I was a young man. Some, less correctly, give *gravis* here the meaning of " troublesome."

24-26. *Pars Niliacœ plebis.* " One of the very rabble of the Nile," *i. e.,* a fellow from the very dregs of the populace of Egypt. —*Verna Canopi.* " A born slave of Canopus." Not only a slave, but a slave born of a slave. And, what is still worse, a native of Canopus, one of the most dissolute places in all Egypt. Canopus was a short distance to the east of Alexandrea.—*Crispinus.* This man rose under Nero from the condition of a slave to riches and honours. His connection with that monster recommended him sub-sequently to Domitian, with whom also he seems to have been in high favour.—*Tyrias humero revocante lacernas.* " His shoulder every moment hitching up his scarlet cloak." The cloak was a costly one of Tyrian purple, and an ample one, as indicated by the plural. The parvenu allows it every moment, however, to slip off his shoulder, and drag on the ground, as if to show his careless in-difference for riches.—*Ventilet.* " Airs." He waves his hand slow-ly to and fro, in order to cool, as it were, his summer ring, and manages, at the same time, to display the gem to public view. The

Romans had become so effeminate as to wear a lighter ring in summer. Even this summer ring, however, Crispinus finds oppressively
hot.

28-34. *Iniquæ urbis.* "Of this iniquitous city." Heinrich takes
iniquæ here in the sense of *non ferendæ* or *intolerabilis.* Some render it "unfair," *i. e.*, unjust in its opinion of men and things. But
this wants force.—*Tam ferreus.* "So steeled in bosom."—*Nova
lectica.* "The bran-new litter." Matho had been starving as a
lawyer, but had now, on a sudden, become very wealthy as an informer. Hence the double hit in *causidicus* and *nova.* The *lectica,*
or litter, resembled somewhat an Oriental palanquin. It was fitted
up with a bed or mattress, and also with a pillow to support the
head, so that a person could read or write in it with ease. It was
carried by means of poles, supported on the shoulders of slaves.—
Plena ipso. "Full of his important self." An allusion, not to cor-
pulence, as some think, but to the haughty airs of an upstart.—*Delator.* No one in particular is meant. The blow is aimed at the
class of informers generally.—*De nobilitate comesa.* The nobility
were impoverished, not only by the exactions of the prince, but also
by the large sums which they were compelled to pay to the dreaded
informers.—*Massa.* The allusion is to Bæbius Massa, who was a
notorious informer in the reign of Domitian. He and Metius Carus, another informer, mentioned immediately after, are compelled
to propitiate an informer still more powerful than themselves.—
Palpat. "Coaxes." A metaphor taken from patting and coaxing
a horse.—*Et a trepido,* &c. "And Thymele sent secretly by the
trembling Latinus." Latinus, a celebrated mime-player in the time
of Domitian, and a favourite of that emperor, is also compelled to
propitiate the powerful informer, and secretly sends to him, with
rich presents, his wife Thymele, also celebrated as a female per-
former of mimes.

35-40. *Jecur.* The ancients considered the liver as the seat of
the passions.—*Spoliator pupilli prostantis.* "The plunderer of his
ward reduced (in consequence) to a life of infamy." The guardian
defrauds and plunders his ward, and the latter, impoverished in
means and corrupted in principles, is driven for support to an infamous course of life.—*Inani judicio.* "By an unavailing sentence."
Literally, an "empty" one, *i. e.*, one that leaves him still in possession of a large portion of his ill-gotten gains. The allusion is to
Marius Priscus, proconsul of Africa, who was tried in the third
year of Trajan for extortion in his province, and condemned to dis-
gorge into the public treasury 700,000 sesterces (about $27,000),

and also banished from Italy. The penalty was a mere trifle compared with the vast sums which he had accumulated, and, what was still worse, the province got no portion of the penalty.—*Infamia*. Part of the punishment for extortion was the kind of *infamia* called *intestabilitas.*—*Ab octava bibit*. "Begins to carouse from the eighth hour." Two o'clock, according to our mode of computing. The ninth hour (three o'clock) was the earliest time at which the temperate dined. Marius, however, begins an hour earlier.—*Et fruitur Dis iratis*. "And derives enjoyment from the angry gods, *i. e.*, laughs at them.—*Victrix*. "Though victorious in thy suit." *Victrix* is a forensic term, applied to the province as having succeeded against Marius. — *Ploras*. The province, after being put to the trouble and expense of a prosecution, obtains no real remuneration, but is left to deplore her losses.

41–44. *Venusina digna lucerna*. "Worthy of the Venusinian lamp," *i. e.*, of the satiric pen, and the caustic lucubrations of a Horace. Venusium, or Venusia, in Apulia, was Horace's native place. As regards the employment of the term *lucerna*, compare the language of Horace himself: "*Et, prius orto sole, vigil, calamum, et chartas, et scrinia posco.* (*Epist.* ii., 1, 112.)—*Sed quid magis Heracleas*, &c. "But why rather narrate the fabulous legends of a Hercules or a Diomede?" Supply *dicam* or *canam* from the preceding *agitem*, and after *Heracleas* and *Diomedeas* understand *fabulas*. Juvenal here anticipates the supposed objections of those who might, perhaps, advise him to employ his pen on some fabulous and safer subject. But why, replies the poet, should I prefer these hackneyed fables to the bold and unblushing realities of actual life.—*Diomedeas*. Alluding to the Thracian king, who fed his horses on human flesh.—*Mugitum Labyrinthi*. The legend of the Minotaur.—*Puero*. Icarus. The dative instead of *ab* with the ablative. (*Zumpt*, § 419.)—*Fabrum*. "Artificer." Dædalus.

45–50. *Quum leno accipiat*, &c. "When the pander-husband can take the property of the adulterer, since the wife herself has no right to receive it." The reference is to the *Lex Voconia* (B.C. 174). This law forbade a woman to be made *hæres ex asse*, that is, sole heiress. The subsequent *Lex Julia Papia Poppæa* gave women this privilege, however, if they had a certain number of children. A man who was the father of one child could take as universal heir. Accordingly, the satirist says that, if the wife is under a legal incapacity to take an inheritance, the husband may be able to take it; and therefore he winks at the dishonour of his wife, to win the favour of the adulterer and be made his heir. (*Long, ad loc.*)—*Quum fas esse putet*, &c. The allusion here is probably to the *Præfectura cohortis sociorum*, for which some ruined spendthrift is asking, the son, in all likelihood, of a senator, who, as a proof of his shamelessness, expects to be excused from one of the requirements of the service, namely, the having been previously a centurion. (*Madvig, ad loc.*) Some commentators, however, rejecting this general view, make the poet refer to Cornelius Fuscus, a youth of illustrious origin, who had officiated as charioteer to Nero, and had ruined himself by his extravagance in horses and stables. At a subsequent period he was made captain of the body-guard by Domitian, and fell in the Dacian war. Compare *Sat.* iv., 111.—*Præsepibus*. "On stables."—*Dum pervolat*, &c. Observe the peculiar employment of *dum* with the present, in the dependent clause, after a past tense in the principal one. He lost all his hereditary estate whilst he drove, and by driving, &c. — *Flaminiam*. Supply *viam*. The Flaminian Way was the Great North Road, and led from Rome to Ariminum. The portion here meant is that which skirted the whole length of the Campus Martius, and consequently formed the most conspicuous thoroughfare in Rome. It is now the *Corso*.— *Puer Automedon*, &c. "For, while yet a boy, he held the reins like Automedon of old." Automedon was the youthful charioteer of Achilles. The Achilles of Homer and the Roman Nero are here brought into amusing juxtaposition.

51-56. *Nonne libet.* "Does not one feel inclined?"—*Medio quadrivio.* "In the very middle of the crossways," *i. e.*, in the open and crowded streets; such is the effrontery of the times. *Quadrivium* is a place where four ways meet, and where there would always be more or less of a crowd.—*Ceras.* Used here for *ceratas tabellas*, "tablets." These tablets were thin pieces of wood, covered over on the inner side with wax, on which the ancients wrote with a sharp instrument called *stylus*. They were fastened together at the back by means of wires, which answered the purpose of hinges, so that they opened and shut like our books. To prevent the wax of one tablet rubbing against that of the other, there was a raised margin around each.—*Sexta cervice.* "On a sixth neck," *i. e.*, on the shoulders of six slaves. The litter-pole rested on the shoulder of the slave, leaning somewhat against the neck. The rich and fashionable had six litter-carriers, sometimes even eight. When six were employed, they were called *hexaphŏri* (ἑξάφοροι, from ἕξ, "six," and φέρω, "to carry"); when eight, *octophŏri* (ὀκτόφοροι).— *Patens.* "Conspicuous to the view." The litter was commonly shut in by curtains. On the present occasion, however, the curtains

F

are drawn aside, and the unblushing occupant within is fully exposed to the view.—*Ac nuda pœne cathedra.* "And almost in an uncurtained female chair." The *cathedra* here meant was a kind of easy-chair in which women were accustomed to be carried abroad instead of the *lectica.* In the present case, therefore, the open litter of the individual alluded to may almost, according to the satirist, be compared to an uncurtained female seat. So that we have here a union of impudence and effeminacy.

Et multum referens, &c. "And aping much (that is told us) of the effeminate Mæcenas." Literally, "bringing back to mind," or "recalling." Heinrich and others are wrong in making *de* with the ablative here a mere circumlocution for the genitive. The reference is rather to a matter of tradition respecting by-gone times. Mæcenas, though an able statesman, was remarkable for his luxurious and effeminate mode of life.—*Signator falso.* "Some forger of wills." Literally, "some sealer with a false seal," *signo* being understood after *falso,* as is implied by *signator.* A valid will would require, of course, the seals of witnesses to be appended. In the present case, however, a false will is substituted with false seals. Compare *Cic. pro Cluent.,* c. 14 : "*Testamentum, in alias tabulas transscriptum, signis adulterinis obsignavit.*" Ruperti and others prefer placing a comma after *signator,* and connecting *falso* (which will then mean "by forgery") with what follows, but this makes an awkward juxtaposition with *exiguis tabulis.*—*Lautum atque beatum.* "A man of splendour and wealth." *Beatum* poetically for *divitem.*— *Exiguis tabulis.* "By means of brief tablets," *i. e.,* by means of a few brief words. It would be enough to say, "*Titius hæres meus esto.*" Compare *Gaius,* ii., § 117.—*Gemma uda.* The signet was moistened before sealing, to prevent the wax from adhering to it.

57–58. *Occurrat matrona potens.* "When some powerful matron meets the view." Supply *cum* from the preceding clause. The subjunctive is the true reading here, and the interrogation with which the passage began (*nonne libet,* &c.) is continued on to *maritos.* The common text has *occurrit,* changing the construction, and places a full stop after *maritos.* The meaning will then be, "Next some powerful matron meets the view," &c. This, however, is much less spirited.—*Calenum.* Supply *vinum.* The wine of Cales, in Campania, was very celebrated. The territory which produced it was adjacent to the Falernian district.—*Viro sitiente.* "Her husband thirsting." Ablative absolute. Some, less correctly, make *sitiente* an old form of the dative for *sitienti.* The poet means that the husband is too thirsty to examine the contents of the cup.—*Rubetam.*

"The venom of the toad." *Rubeta* is the animal itself put for the venom which it was supposed to produce. There is great doubt, however, whether the toad is actually meant here. Some suppose the reference to be made to the *rana rubeta*, a species of frog found in brushwood (*rubus*), much used in magic and in poisons. Its blood, according to Ælian (*N. A.*, xvii., 12), when mixed with wine, often produced instant death. Others, however, make the *rubeta* to be the same with the *Bufo cornutus*, a horned frog. The Greek term is φρῦνος. (*Adams, s. v.*)

59–60. *Melior Lucusta.* "A more skilful Lucusta (even than she of former days)." Lucusta was a female in the time of Nero, famed for her skill in concocting poisons. Through her means, Agrippina poisoned off the Emperor Claudius, and Nero dispatched Britannicus. The true form of the name is *Lūcusta*, with the antepenult long. The common reading, *Locusta*, ought to have the antepenult short, from the analogy of *lŏcusta*, "the locust."—*Rudes.* Hitherto "inexperienced" in the art of poisoning.—*Per famam et populum,* &c. "To carry forth for interment their livid husbands amid busy rumours and the crowding populace." The people would crowd around to observe the discoloration occasioned by the poison. Observe that *efferre* is here in reality equivalent to *efferendos curare.* Heinrich makes *per famam et populum* a hendiadys for *per famam populi,* but this is less spirited.

61–66. *Aude aliquid,* &c. The leading idea is this: If you wish to come into notice at Rome, commit some act of great rascality, which ought to consign you to banishment or a prison, but which at Rome will prove the most effectual means of making you wealthy and powerful. The poet has principally in view the profligate favourites of bad emperors, who were wont to enrich and advance themselves by acts which ought to have subjected them to the severest punishment.—*Brevibus Gyaris dignum.* "Worthy of narrow Gyarus," *i. e.*, that ought to send you thither into exile. Gyarus was a small island, forming one of the group of the Cyclades, and to the southwest of Andros. It was inhabited by a few poor fishermen, and was little better than a barren rock. Hence it was one of the most dreaded places of exile in the whole Roman empire. There are two forms of the name, *Gyarus* (-*i*) and *Gyara* (-*orum*).—*Si vis esse aliquis.* "If you wish to be somebody." Compare the Greek εἰναί τις —*Alget.* "Starves." There should be a dash before this in the editions, the sense being suspended for a moment, in order that the closing word may come in with more emphasis, and, as it were, unexpectedly.

Prœtoria. "Their palaces." *Prœtorium,* when denoting an abode, properly means the official residence of the governor of a province, and then any splendid structure in general.—*Mensas.* For the dwellings of the opulent, tables were made of the most beautiful and costly kinds of wood.—*Argentum vetus.* "Their old plate," *i. e.,* silver vessels, the work of early and celebrated artificers.—*Et stantem extra pocula caprum.* "And the goat standing forth in relief from the cup," *i. e.,* a drinking-cup adorned with rich work in high relief. The goat, as peculiarly destructive of the vine, was sacrificed to Bacchus, and hence formed an appropriate device on drinking-cups.—*Si natura negat.* "If nature denies the vein," *i. e.,* the poetic vein requisite for the proper handling of such themes.—*Cluvienus.* A fictitious name for some stupid contemporary of the satirist's. Juvenal names him here along with himself, in order to satirize him the more by the very comparison.

67–71. *Ex quo,* &c. Juvenal means by this that his satire will take for its field of operations the whole range of human life, with all the varied feelings and motives that have been accustomed to sway it from the earliest ages.—*Tollentibus.* Supply *in altum.*—*Montem.* Parnassus, in Phocis.—*Sortesque poposcit.* "And asked for an oracle." According to the legend, Deucalion consulted the sanctuary of Themis, on Mount Parnassus, for the purpose of ascertaining in what way the race of man might be restored. *Sortes* is here used in its general sense of an oracular response. The primitive import of the term, however, refers to the practice, so frequent in the Italian nations, of endeavouring to ascertain the future by the drawing of lots, a practice that prevailed even in many of the ancient Italian temples.—*Paulatimque anima,* &c. "And the softening stones grew gradually warm with life." The stones were "the bones of their mother," which the oracle directed Deucalion and Pyrrha to throw behind them.—*Votum.* "Their every wish."—*Discursus.* "Their every pursuit." Literally, "their running to and fro."—*Nostri est farrago libelli.* "From the motley subject of my little work." *Farrago* literally means "mixed fodder" for cattle. Here, however, it is figuratively employed to indicate "a medley," "an olio."

72–75. *Quando major avaritiæ,* &c. "When did a deeper gulf of avarice open on the view?" Literally, "a more ample bosom." A metaphor borrowed from the Roman dress. The *sinus* was a part of the toga, hanging down in front, over the bosom, like a sling, and thus forming a kind of receptacle in which various things could be carried. It answered, therefore, the same purpose as a modern pocket. Some commentators, however, make *sinus* mean here the bosom of a sail, and consider the idea to be, "when were the sails of avarice more widely spread?" The explanation which we have adopted appears the more natural and forcible.—*Alea quando hæc animos.* "When did gambling like this of ours sway the minds of men?" We have given *hæc*, the ingenious conjecture of Heinecke. The common reading is *hos*, "When had gambling its present spirits?" or, making *hos* equivalent to *tot*, "When did gambling influence so many minds?" With *animos*, whether we read *hæc* or *hos*, supply *cepit.*—*Loculis comitantibus.* "Caskets accompanying them." They do not go to the gaming-table, as we would say, with purses, but the steward brings a whole money-chest, which is staked and played for at once. *Loculus* means a small casket, divided into compartments, and made of ivory or wood.—*Luditur.* Taken impersonally.

76–81. *Dispensatore armigero.* "The steward being the armour-bearer." The steward supplies the gold, the weapons of gambling warfare.—*Simplex.* "Common" or "ordinary."—*Sestertia centum.* "A hundred thousand sesterces." About $3900.—*Reddere.* "To give (what is merely his due)." *Reddo* here carries with it the idea of bestowing something that is due for services performed.—*Quis totidem*, &c. With *quis* supply *avus* from the succeeding clause.—*Secreto.* "By himself," *i. e.*, without his clients.—*Sportula parva*, &c. "A little basket has its seat," *i. e.*, is placed. *Parva*, incorrectly rendered here by some "diminished," is purposely employed to mark the contrast between the size of the basket and the rich patron's supper of seven *fercula.* The Romans, in the days of freedom, entertained their clients, after the latter had attended them in public, at a supper, which was called *cœna recta.* But, after the extinction of liberty, when the clients had lost all political influence, instead of being regularly entertained, they merely received a portion of food in a small basket called *sportula*, which they carried to their own homes. For the sake of convenience, it soon became customary to give an equivalent in money, the sum established by general usage being 100 *quadrantes* (about 24 cents). The donation in money, however, did not entirely supersede the *sportula* in kind, as may be seen from Juvenal himself (*Sat.* iii., 230, *seqq.*).—*Primo limine.* The *sportulæ* were placed in the vestibule of the mansion. —*Turbæ togatæ.* Said contemptuously of the Romans thronging to receive the *sportula.* The toga was always worn by clients when attending on their patrons.

82–85. *Ille.* The steward, or dispenser of the dole; not, as some

maintain, the master. — *Suppositus.* "A fraudulent substitute."
More literally, "put in the place of another." In order to guard
against imposition and fraud on the part of the applicants, a regular
roll was kept at each mansion of the persons entitled to receive the
sportula. The individuals, moreover, were required to appear in
person.—*Ipsos Trojugenas.* "The very descendants of the Trojans,"
i. e., men of some of the oldest families in Rome, but now so reduced ·
in means as not to be ashamed to come forward as applicants for the
dole.—*Nobiscum.* "With us poor folk."

86–93. *Da prætori,* &c. The language of the steward to one of
his assistants.—*Sed libertinus prior est.* "But there is a freedman
here before them." The reply of the assistant to the steward.—*Inquit.* "Exclaims the freedman." Supply *libertinus.* The freedman
says this on overhearing the remark of the assistant.—*Natus ad
Euphraten.* "Though born on the banks of the Euphrates," *i. e.,*
even though originally a slave from the East. Immense numbers of
slaves came from Armenia, Cappadocia, Mesopotamia, and other
countries watered by the Euphrates.—*Molles fenestræ.* "The soft
windows," *i. e.,* the openings or holes bored in the soft part of the
ear to receive ear-rings. Among most of the Oriental nations, men
wore ear-rings as well as women. Heinrich and others less correctly connect with *molles* the idea of effeminacy.—*Arguerint.* "Will
clearly prove, I think." Impudent irony. Observe the force of the
subjunctive. — *Sed quinque tabernæ,* &c. "But then my five shops
bring me in a rent of four hundred thousand sestertii," *i. e.,* but then,
even if I am of servile origin, my shops in the forum bring me in a
revenue equal to an equestrian fortune. The sum here mentioned
would be in our currency equal to $15,600.—*Quadringenta.* Supply
sestertia. — *Purpura major.* "The greater purple," *i. e.,* the lati-
clave. By this is meant the rank of senator. The allusion is to the
broad band or stripe of purple adorning the tunic of the senatorian
order, called *latus clavus,* and thus distinguished from the *angustus
clavus,* or narrow stripe (*purpura minor*) of the equestrian order.—
Optandum. "To be wished for in preference." — *Laurenti.* Lau-
rentum was one of the most ancient towns of Latium, lying between
Ostia and Ardea, not far from the sea.—*Corvinus.* "A Corvinus,"
i. e., a descendant of the old and illustrious house of the Valerii.—
Custodit conductus oves. "Undertakes, for a sum of money, to keep
another's flocks." Equivalent to *conducit custodiendas oves.*

94–101. *Pallante et Licinis.* "Than Pallas and the Licini," *i. e.,*
than Pallas and many a Licinus. Pallas, the freedman of the Emperor Claudius, was enormously rich; so, also, was Licinus, a freed-

man of Julius Cæsar, and subsequently a favourite of Augustus. The plural form *Licinis* is meant to indicate Licinus and others like him. (*Madvig, L. G.*, § 50, *Obs.* 4.) Some, less correctly, make *Licinis* here to be a contraction for *Liciniis*, and refer the term to M. Licinius Crassus, famed for his riches, as well as to other wealthy members of the Licinian time.—*Sacro nec cedat honori*. "Nor let him yield even to the sacred office (of tribune)." The persons of the tribunes were sacred and inviolable.—*Nuper*. So sudden is the advancement of these upstarts.—*Pedibus albis*. "With whitened feet." The feet of imported or foreign slaves were whitened with chalk.—*Nummorum*. We would expect here the dative *nummis*. The genitive, however, is in imitation of the Greek, ἱστάναι βωμόν τινος.—*Quæque salutato*, &c. "And Concord, whose temple resounds with chatterings when the nest is greeted (by the parent stork on its return)." Literally, "which chatters when the nest is greeted." Referring either to the chattering of the young storks when the parent bird, which has been in quest of food, returns to its nest in the temple, or to the noise made by the parent bird's striking its beak, in order to announce its return. In either event, we must suppose the temple to be now deserted by men, and to serve, in its ruined state, as a habitation for the stork. Hence the general idea is, "and Concord, whose temple is now deserted and in ruins."

102-111. *Summus honor*. "Magistrates of the highest rank." Compare line 86.—*Referat*. "Brings them in."—*Rationibus*. "To their yearly income."—*Comites*. "The poor clients." So called from their accompanying the patron in public.—*Hinc*. From the 100 *quadrantes*.—*Fumusque domi*. "And the smoky fuel of home," *i. e.*, and the green fuel that fills with smoke their homes. Literally, "the smoke of home."—*Densissima lectica*. "A very dense array of litters." The upper classes crowd out the poor.—*Sequiturque maritum*. Every claimant for the *sportula* had to appear in person, the wife as well as the husband.—*Languida vel prægnans*. "Sick or near her time."—*Absenti*. Supply *uxori*.—*Nota jam callidus arte*. "Showing his cunning by a trick now well known." The trick consisted in pretending that his absent wife was lying unwell, and asleep in the litter.—*Sellam*. Used here loosely for *lecticam*. Strictly speaking, however, the *sella* was the same as the *cathedra*. Consult note on line 53.—*Moraris*. Better without the mark of interrogation: "You are keeping us back." With the question, as given in most editions, it will be, "Do you hesitate?"—*Profer, Galla, caput*. The language of the steward, who wishes to be convinced, by his own eyes, of the presence of the wife.—*Noli vexare, quiescit.* "Ah! don't disturb her; she has just fallen asleep." Observe the force of the inceptive.

112–115. *Ipse dies,* &c. The poet, having exposed the meanness and avarice of the upper classes, now proceeds to ridicule their idle mode of spending the day.—*Pulchro ordine rerum.* "By a fine routine of employments." Ironical.—*Sportula.* "First the sportula." —*Forum.* The forum of Augustus is meant, in which the *judicia publica* were held. Here stood a statue of Apollo; and as the god was, as it were, a daily ear-witness of legal pleadings, he is called by the poet *juris peritus,* "learned in the law."—*Triumphales.* "The triumphal statues." 'Supply *statuas.* These were the statues of some of the most distinguished men of the republic, with which Augustus had adorned his forum.—*Nescio quis Ægyptius,* &c. "Some Egyptian and chief tax-gatherer or other." *Alabarches* is meant to be explanatory of *Ægyptius.* The Alabarches appears to have been the chief magistrate of the Jews at Alexandria; but whose duties, as far as the government was concerned, consisted in raising and paying the taxes. The term is derived from ἀλάβη, "ink," and ἄρχω. The common text has *Arabarches,* "Arabian prefect," a title sometimes given to the governor of the district of Thebais, in the time of the empire. The true reading, however, is *Alabarches.* The person alluded to is unknown, and various conjectures have been fruitlessly started.

116–124. *Vestibulis abeunt,* &c. "At length the old and wearied clients depart from the vestibules." The poor clients, after attending their lordly patron during the whole day, have now escorted him to his home, and have ranged themselves in the vestibule, in eager expectation of being invited to supper. But no such invitation comes, and they depart at length to their respective homes, with the paltry boon of a hundred *quadrantes.*—*Vota.* "Their eager wishes," *i. e.,* for the *cœna recta.*—*Quanquam longissima,* &c. "Although each poor fellow has been entertaining a very long-protracted hope of a supper."—*Caules atque ignis.* "Greens and green fuel."—*Emendus.* With the hundred *quadrantes.*—*Rex horum.* "The lordly patron of these."—*Vacuisque toris,* &c. "And he himself only will recline on empty couches," *i. e.,* all alone by himself, in solitary state. The usual number of couches in a triclinium, or banqueting-room, was three, and three persons usually occupied one couch, so that the regular number for a supper-party would be nine. —*Orbibus.* "Dishes." Some, less correctly, suppose round tables to be meant, which would be changed with every course.—*Antiquis.*

Old family plate, which ought to remind them of old-fashioned hospitality.—*Comedunt.* The plural, as indicating the whole class of
such persons.—*Una mensa.* "At a single course." Less correctly,
"at a single meal." The tables, as already remarked, were changed
at each course.—*Nullus jam parasitus erit.* "'Tis true, there will
now no longer be any parasite." The idea contained in this and
the succeeding clause is : One consolation, 'tis true, will be that the
breed of parasites will become extinct. And yet it may be question-
ed whether even a parasite could sit still and see such a disgusting
exhibition of selfish gluttony.—*Luxuriæ sordes.* "Filthiness of luxury," *i. e.,* foul gluttony.

125-130. *Animal propter convivia natum.* Intended to be served
up to a company of friends, and not to a μονοφά)ος. Juvenal quotes
here a common saying of the day. Compare Varro : "*Suillum pecus
donatum ab natura dicunt ad epulandum.* (*R. R.,* ii., 4, 10.) Boar's
flesh was held in high repute by the Romans. When the animal
was served up whole, it formed the *caput cœnæ,* or chief dish.—*Præsens.* "Close at hand." The idea is borrowed from the ἐπιφάνεια,
or *præsentia deorum.—Crudum pavonem.* "The undigested peacock."
The peacock was regarded as a very great delicacy by the Romans,
but as being very indigestible. It is said to have been first introduced by Hortensius the orator, at an inaugural supper.—*Hinc.*
From gluttony thus indulged in.—*Intestata senectus.* The good
friends of the deceased had been forming hopes of rich legacies.
His sudden death, however, arising from the injudicious use of the
bath after a gluttonous meal, has anticipated the making of a will,
and given all their expectations to the winds. When there was no
will, the property went to the nearest agnati, and there were no
legacies. (*Gaius,* iii., 18.)—*It nova, nec tristis,* &c. "A fresh piece
of news, and one calling forth no sorrow, goes the round of every
supper-party," *i. e.,* the news of the old glutton's death is spread
abroad, and no one is sorry, because he never cared sufficiently for
his friends to make a will in proper season for their advantage.—
Ducitur. "Is led along," *i. e.,* to the place where the body is to
be burned.—*Iratis amicis.* The friends are angry at him for not
having made a will.

131-135. *Nostris moribus.* "To our corrupt morals."—*Minores.*
"Our descendants."—*In præcipiti stetit.* "Has reached its highest
pitch." The additional idea implied in the phrase *in præcipiti* is
generally overlooked. Matters are now brought to the very brink
of a precipice, and no farther advance can be made in public corruption without the downfall and ruin of the state. Observe the

force of the perfect in *stetit*. Literally, "has been standing for some time back, and still stands on the very brink of a precipice.—*Utere velis*, &c. Addressed by the poet figuratively to satire, but in reality to himself as its representative. There is now a fair opportunity for satire to exert all its powers.—*Totos pande sinus.* "Unfold the whole bosom of thy canvass (to the winds)," *i. e.*, spread all your canvass.

134-138. *Dicas hic forsitan*, &c. The poet here anticipates the objections which some friend may be disposed to make to his writing of satires. These objections are stated from *unde* down to *arena* in line 141.—*Par materiæ.* "Equal to the subject," *i. e.*, able to grapple successfully with such a theme. Observe that there is apparently no elision of the diphthong in *materiæ*. In reality, however, one vowel of the diphthong is elided, and the remaining one is lengthened by the *arsis*.—*Priorum.* "Of the men of former days." He refers to Eupolis, Cratinus, and Aristophanes among the Greeks, and to Lucilius, Horace, and others of his own countrymen.—*Simplicitas.* "Plainness."—*Nomen.* "The true name." The true name was *libertas*, "freedom," a word dangerous to employ in imperial times.—*Quid refert*, &c. "What difference does it make (unto Lucilius, it is true) whether Mucius forgive the things said of himself or not? Do you, however, only put down Tigellinus (in your satire), you will shine," &c. Observe that *refert* is here the present for the past, to give animation to the narrative. The idea intended to be conveyed is this : The plainness of former days is over. Lucilius, in those good old times, might lash a Mucius with perfect impunity, caring not at all whether the latter forgave the attack or not. Do you, however, at the present day, select some Tigellinus, some powerful favourite, as the object of your satire, and you will soon be made to feel the difference.—*Mucius.* T. Mucius Albutius, who was satirized by Lucilius on account of his affecting, on every occasion, the Greek language and philosophy.

139-141. *Pone Tigellinum.* "Only put down Tigellinus in your verse," *i. e.*, some one as powerful as Tigellinus was. Tigellinus Sophonius was one who ministered to Nero's worst passions, and, of all his favourites, was the most obnoxious to the Roman people.—*Tæda lucebis in illa*, &c. "You will (soon) shine in that torch-like tunic, in which," &c. Literally, "in that torch," &c. The punishment here meant was commonly termed *tunica molesta*, and was the one inflicted by Nero upon the early Christians, on the false charge of having caused the great conflagration of Rome. A tunic, covered over with pitch and other combustibles, was put upon the victim,

and then lighted. Hence the term *tæda* applied here to the sufferer.—*Qui fixo gutture fumant.* "Who smoke with fixed throat."
The neck of the victim was fixed to the stake by an iron collar.—
Et latum media, &c. "And you draw a broad furrow in the middle
of the arena." The punishment of the *tunica molesta* commonly
took place in the amphitheatre. After life was extinct, the charred
corpse was dragged by a hook through the arena for the spectators
to gaze upon. Compare Pliny (*Pan.* xxxiii., 3): "*Nemo spectator
miseras voluptates unco et ignibus expiavit.*"

142-155. *Qui dedit ergo,* &c. Here the author indignantly replies.
Tigellinus is said to have poisoned off three uncles in order to inherit their property. Their signet-rings were taken from their fingers when dead, and the forged wills were sealed with them.—*Pensilibus plumis.* "On pensile feathers," *i. e.,* on downy bed suspended aloft. The reference is to the bed or mattress in the *lectica.*—
Quum veniet contra. "Ay, and when he shall come full in front,"
i. e., when he shall meet you. The friend now speaks.—*Accusator
erit,* &c. "There will be an accuser (ready for the one) who shall
only have uttered the remark, "That's he," *i. e.,* it will be dangerous even to say as much as "That's he." You will immediately be
informed against. How then can you seriously think of openly satirizing such a person. After *accusator* supply *ejus,* as the antece-
dent to *qui.*—*Securus licet committas.* "With perfect impunity may
you match in fight," *i. e.,* you may, without any fear of giving offence, handle some epic theme, such as the combat between Æneas
and Turnus, or the wounding of Achilles by Paris. Or you may select some mythological legend, such as that of Hercules and Hylas.
—*Nulli gravis est.* "Is troublesome to no one," *i. e.,* gives rise to
angry feelings in no one.—*Percussus.* "Wounded by Paris." Supply *a Paride.*—*Multum quæsitus.* Supply *ab Hercule.*—*Urnamque se-
cutus.* Beneath the waters of the fountain.—*Quoties Lucilius ardens.*
"As often, however, as some glowing Lucilius."—*Rubet.* "Red-
dens," *i. e.,* with mingled anger and shame.—*Frigida est criminibus.*
"Is chilled with the consciousness of many a crime."—*Culpa.*
"Guilt."—*Iræ.* "Angry feelings."—*Ante tubas.* Before the trum-
pets sound the signal for the conflict ; in other words, before you begin to write your satires, and make your onset upon the guilty.—
Galeatum. "One who has donned the helmet," *i. e.,* the soldier
when helmeted and ready for the fight. As appears from Trajan's
column, the soldiers, when not going into battle, wore the helmet
suspended from the right shoulder.—*Duelli.* Old form for *belli,* and
put here for *prælii.*

Experiar quid concedatur, &c. Concluding remark of the poet. Since it is dangerous, then, to attack the living, I will try how far it may be allowed me to satirize the dead. The poet, however, only adheres to this determination in appearance, since he still continues to attack the powerful, but does it under fictitious names.—*Quorum Flaminia*, &c. The laws of the Twelve Tables forbade all burials within the city. Places for burial, therefore, were usually by the sides of the great roads leading to Rome, and on some of these roads the tombs formed an almost uninterrupted street for many miles from the gates of the city.—*Latina*. The Flaminian Way has already been mentioned. The Latin Way led from Rome to Beneventum.

SATIRE III.

ARGUMENT.

Umbritius, an aruspex, and friend of the author, disgusted at the prevalence of vice and the disregard of unassuming virtue, is on the point of quitting Rome ; and, when a little way from the city, stops short to acquaint the poet, who has accompanied him, with the causes of his retirement. These may be arranged under the following heads : That Flattery and Vice are the only thriving arts at Rome. In these, especially the first, foreigners have a manifest advantage over the natives, and, consequently, engross all favour : that the poor are universally exposed to scorn and insult : that the general habits of extravagance render it difficult for them to subsist : that the want of a well-regulated police subjects them to numberless miseries and inconveniences, aggravated by the crowded state of the capital, from all which a country life is happily free ; and on the tranquillity and security of this last he dilates with great beauty. (*Evans.*)

1–9. *Confusus.* " Greatly troubled.—*Amici.* Umbritius.—*Quod destinet.* " Because he intends, as he tells me." Observe the force of the subjunctive. (*Madvig*, § 357, a.)—*Vacuis Cumis.* " In thinly-inhabited Cumæ." Literally, " empty Cumæ," *i. e.*, empty when compared with the overflowing population of Rome. Cumæ, now decayed, and with a scanty population, had been the ancient capital of Campania, and had contained at one time 60,000 inhabitants. It was celebrated as the residence of the earliest Sibyl.—

Atque unum civem, &c. "And to give at least one citizen to the Sibyl."—*Janua Baiarum est.* "It is the gate of Baiæ." The road leading to Baiæ passed through Cumæ, passengers going into Cumæ on one side, and coming out on the other, as through a gate. Baiæ was a celebrated watering-place in Campania, situate in a beautiful country, which abounded in warm mineral springs.—*Gratum litus amœni secessus.* "And a pleasing shore of delightful retirement." The allusion is to the entire shore between Cumæ and Baiæ.—*Prochytam.* Prochyta was a small rocky island off the coast of Campania, near the promontory of Misenum. It is now *Procida.—Suburæ.* The Subura or Suburra was one of the most frequented streets of Rome, inhabited by the lower classes, and containing a great number of shops and brothels.

Nam quid tam miserum, &c. Wretched and lonely as any place may be, yet it is better to be there than at Rome, where you have so many dangers and harassing disquietudes to apprehend.—*Ut non deterius credas.* "That you will not believe it worse."—*Sævæ urbis.* "Of this cruel city." Rome is here called *sæva,* from the constant alarms which it occasions.—*Et Augusto recitantes,* &c. There is much malicious humour, as Gifford remarks, in this climax : fires, falling of houses, and poets reciting their verses in the dog-days! In the hottest month, when every one who could ran away from Rome, those who remained behind were called upon to help make an audience for these incessant spouters.

10–11. *Sed dum tota domus,* &c. "But while his whole household is being stowed away in a single wagon," *i. e.,* all his family and furniture.—*Reda una.* This little touch marks very graphically the scanty means of Juvenal's friend. The *reda* was a travelling wagon or car on four wheels. It was the common conveyance used by the Romans for travelling, and was intended to carry both persons and baggage.—*Substitit.* "He stopped." Umbritius and Juvenal had walked in advance while the wagon was being packed, and Umbritius stops here with the poet to wait for the arrival of the vehicle.—*Veteres arcus.* The arches of an aqueduct are meant, the droppings from which kept the ground in this quarter constantly wet. — *Madidamque Capenam.* "And the moist Capenian gate." Supply *portam.* The epithet *madidam* has been explained in the previous note. The Capenian gate was one of the most celebrated of all the Roman gates, and from it issued the Appian Way, leading at first to Capua (whence the epithet *Capena* applied to the gate), but subsequently to Brundisium. It is now called *Porta di S. Sebastiano.*

12-16. *Hic.* Just without the Capenian gate began the vale of Egeria, containing the grove of Diana, in which Numa, according to the legend, used to have his interviews with the nymph Egeria. In this grove were the grotto and fountain of Egeria, and an old temple of the Camenæ.—*Nocturnæ constituebat amicæ.* "Used to make appointments with his nocturnal female friend." According to the legend, Numa received from the nymph Egeria, who was one of the Camenæ, his instructions respecting the forms of worship which he introduced. The grove in which the king had his interviews with the goddess was dedicated by him to the Camenæ. With *constituebat* we may here mentally supply *tempus colloquendi.* —*Delubra.* There were often more than one *delubrum* within the same τέμενος, or sacred inclosure.—*Locantur.* "Are let out." The Jews used to frequent woods near running water for sacred worship. —*Quorum cophinus,* &c. "Whose furniture is a basket and bundle of hay." The basket contained their stock of provisions, for they could not touch the food of Gentiles. The bundle of straw was intended to serve as a bed.—*Mercedem pendere.* "To pay a rent."— *Mendicat.* "Swarms with mendicants."

17-20. *Descendimus.* Umbritius and I.—*Dissimiles veris.* "All unlike the true ones," *i. e.,* to what they had been in their natural state. Art had so altered them, and decked them with ornaments, that their native beauty and simplicity were quite lost.—*Quanto præsentius esset,* &c. "How much nearer in influence would be the presiding deity of the spring," *i. e.,* how much more nearly should we feel the influence of that Egeria to whom the fountain is consecrated. We have given here the conjectural emendation *præsentius,* which is now adopted in the best editions. The common reading is *præstantius·* "How much better off would the deity of the spring have been."—*Herba.* "The herbage."—*Nec ingenuum violarent,* &c. "And no marble infringed the native limestone." There was now a marble basin where previously had been the native bed of stone.—*Tophum.* A species of coarse limestone, called by the Italians *tufa,* and formed by the deposition of springs holding carbonate of lime in solution.

21-28. *Artibus honestis.* "For virtuous practices."—*Nulla emolumenta laborum.* "No recompense for honest industry."—*Res.* "My property."—*Here.* Old form for *heri,* which latter would not be admissible into the verse.—*Deteret exiguis aliquid.* "Will lose something of the scanty portion that remains." Literally, "will wear away" or "diminish."—*Proponimus.* I and my family.—*Fatigatas.* "Wearied" with the long flight from Crete.—*Exuit.* According to some accounts, Dædalus first alighted in his flight at Cumæ, where he erected a temple to Apollo, in which he dedicated the wings that had enabled him to make his escape. Compare *Virg. Æn.*, vi., 14, *seqq.*—*Dum prima et recta senectus.* "While my old age is still fresh and erect."—*Quod torqueat.* "Something to spin." Clotho, Lachĕsis, and Atrŏpos were the three fates.—*Subeunte.* "Supporting." Literally, "going beneath."—*Bacillo.* Diminutive for the simple *baculo*, a characteristic of the Latinity of Juvenal's age.

29-33. *Artorius.* Artorius and Catulus are representative-names for a particular class of persons, who were neither over-nice nor scrupulous in their selection of means for the acquisition of gain.— *Qui nigrum in candida vertunt.* A proverbial form of expression, referring to those who are not deterred by the mean or dirty nature of any job, if it only promise to be a profitable one.—*Ædem conducere.* "To contract for the building of a temple." In this and what immediately follows, the allusion is to those who manage to get contracts for lucrative public works.—*Flumina.* "For the damming up of rivers," *i. e.*, confining to their beds rivers which have overflowed their banks. Some, less correctly, make the clearing of rivers to be meant; while others think that there is a reference to the monopolizing of the public fisheries.—*Portus.* "The cleansing of harbours." Here again the commentators are at variance. Some refer the term to the constructing or repairing of harbours; others to the farming of the harbour-dues, or *portoria.* It seems better, however, to make it mean the clearing of the mud and sand from harbours. — *Siccandam eluviem.* "The draining of some quagmire." This is generally supposed to refer to the cleansing of the public *cloacæ*, but such an explanation does not appear to suit the strict meaning of *siccare.* We have preferred, therefore, the interpretation of Heinrich, who mentions the Pontine Marshes as one instance of the kind.

Portandum ad busta cadaver. These men contracted also for the care and management of funerals, and in particular for the burning of the corpse. *Bustum* denotes the place where the dead body was burned, and the term was specially employed when this place was contained within the sepulchral inclosure. When the body was burned apart from such inclosure, the spot was called *ustrina* (or *ustrinum*), and meant, in fact, a public burning-ground. Considerable remains are still extant of a large burning-place on the Appian Way, about five miles from Rome.—*Et præbere caput*, &c. "And to set up for sale the (servile) head beneath the mistress-spear." Literally, "to offer the venal head," &c. The spear was set up in the forum to show that an auction was going on there.   Hence things so sold were said to be sold *sub hasta*.   The term *domina* implies the right of disposal of all things and persons there put up.   Hence the allusion in the text would appear to be a class of individuals who bought a drove of slaves on speculation, and then sold them again at public auction.   Heinrich makes the passage refer to persons who, when every other means of making money have failed, or, when they have squandered their all, put themselves up for sale. He changes the *domina* to *domino*, making this last indicate the purchaser, who obtains in this way the *dominium*, or right of ownership over them.

34–37. *Quondam hi cornicines*, &c.   These men, says Umbritius, once used to blow the horn at provincial exhibitions, and attend upon strolling companies of gladiatorial prize-fighters, led around by their *lanistæ* from town to town.   The horn was sounded to call the people together as at the shows in country fairs.—*Buccæ*.   Referring to the distended appearance of the cheek consequent upon the frequent blowing of the horn, or else to the force of the blast.—*Munera nunc edunt*.   "Now themselves exhibit public shows."   These were exhibitions given gratuitously to the people for the purpose of gaining public favour; hence the employment of *munera* for *ludos*.— *Verso pollice vulgi*.   "By means of the upturned thumb of the mob." At gladiatorial shows, the fate of a vanquished gladiator depended generally on the spectators.   If they wished him to be saved, they pressed down the thumb (hence *pollicem premere*, "to save" or "spare"); but if they wished him put to death by his antagonist, they turned the thumb upward (hence *pollicem vertere*, "to slay").— *Quem libet occidunt*, &c.   When the mob have signified their pleasure, the exhibitor of the show gives the death-signal in compliance with the wishes, and in order "to curry favour with the mob," which is the force here of *populariter*.

38–40. *Conducunt foricas*.   "They farm the public jakes."   The *foricæ* were a set of public privies, like the *cabinets d'aisance* of Paris, distributed in various parts of the city for the convenience of the population.   A small fee charged for the accommodation, together with the profits arising from the sale of the contents, induced individuals to take such premises on lease as a source of gain.   The old scholiast on Juvenal, however, quotes the opinion of some who make *foricæ* here to have a very different meaning, namely, shops adjacent to the forum : "*Alii tabernas dicunt foro vicinas*."—*Omnia*.   Supply *conducunt*.—*Magna ad fastigia rerum*.   "To a lofty pinnacle of greatness."—*Jocari*.   "To perpetrate a pleasant joke."   The elevation of such persons, according to Umbritius, is no proof whatever of any merit on their part, but merely a pleasant joke on the part of Fortune.

42–48. *Poscere.* " To ask the loan of it," *i. e.*, either for perusal, or in order to have a copy made of it at my own expense. A common piece of flattery.—*Motus astrorum ignoro.* I have no pretensions to skill in astrology, and cannot, therefore, make money by telling fortunes and calculating nativities, and, in particular, by informing some spendthrift son when he may expect the long-wished-ed-for death of a parsimonious parent.—*Ranarum viscera,* &c. " I have never peered into the entrails of frogs." *Rana* is here used for *rana rubeta,* as in *Plin., II. N.,* 32, 8, 29. Consult note on *Sat.* i., 70. Umbritius means that he has never searched the entrails of this kind of frog for poison, and in saying this he playfully uses the term *inspexi,* which belonged technically to his vocation as an inspector of entrails for purposes of augury. It is erroneous to suppose, as some do, that he actually alludes to a peculiar kind of *extispicium.*—*Me nemo ministro,* &c. He alludes to the extortion and plundering practised by the governors of provinces, and the aid afforded them in this by their followers, whom they were careful to select as their *ministri* and *comites,* with this special object in view. —*Et exstinctæ corpus,* &c. " And a useless trunk with its right hand completely disabled." Literally, " And the useless trunk of an extinct right hand." The employment of the genitive is very remarkable here, and *exstinctæ dextræ* must be regarded as equivalent to *cum exstincta dextra.* Markland, indeed (*Ad Stat.,* p. 95), recommends the ablative at once, *exstincta dextra,* to be substituted in the text for *exstinctæ dextræ,* but the MSS. all give the genitive, and, as being the more difficult reading, it ought, according to Porson's well-known rule, to be viewed as the true one.

49–57. *Quis nunc diligitur,* &c. A new ground of just complaint. No one but the confidant of a guilty secret is now taken into favour. —*Conscius.* " The confidant of crime."—*Æstuat.* " Is all in a ferment," *i. e.*, is agitated between telling and concealing what has been intrusted to its confidence. The metaphor in *fervens æstuat* is taken from the raging and boiling of the sea when agitated by stormy winds.—*Nil tibi se debere putat,* &c. No one will think himself under any obligation to you for concealing honest and fair transactions, or will think it incumbent on him to purchase your silence by conferring favours on you.—*Carus erit Verri.* " On the other hand, he will be dear to Verres," *i. e.*, will be Verres' dear friend and loaded with favours. The name of Verres, the notori-

ous oppressor of the Sicilians, is here figuratively employed to indicate the whole class of extortionate Roman governors.—*Tanti tibi.*
"Of so much value in thy eyes."—*Opaci.* "Shady." *Opacus* has
sometimes been rendered here as equivalent to *turbulenti,* "turbid
with gold," in reference to the auriferous sands of the river. But
Martial, himself a Spaniard, gives the true idea, when, in speaking
of the Tagus, he calls it *"obscurus umbris arborum." Ep.* i., 50, 16.
—*Somno.* "Your natural rest."—*Ponenda.* "That ought to be rejected." For *deponenda.* They are merely given as hush-money.
—*Tristis.* "With dejected brow."

58–61. *Quæ nunc divitibus,* &c. Umbritius now proceeds to mention a new reason for withdrawing from Rome, the influence namely exercised by foreigners, and more particularly the Greeks, over
the minds of the rich, and the consequent neglect of old and faithful retainers.—*Pudor.* Umbritius blushes for his country while making the disclosure.—*Non possum ferre,* &c. "I cannot endure, Quirites, Rome converted into a Grecian city." Literally, "I cannot
endure a Grecian city," *i. e.,* Græcised Rome. The term *Quirites*
contains a hit at the Romans, who are, in reality, no longer worthy
of the name.—*Quamvis quota portio,* &c. "And yet how small a
portion of its dregs are the Greeks themselves." With *Achæi,* which
is the nominative plural, supply *sunt.* Some editions give *Achææ,*
as an adjective, agreeing with *fæcis,* "And yet how small is the proportion of Græcian dregs." Observe the peculiar force of *quota,*
"how great comparatively," *i. e.,* how small.

62–65. *Jam pridem Syrus,* &c. Besides the Greeks, the Syrians
and other Asiatics have long been flocking to Rome, and introduc-
ing Eastern manners, and music, and corruption. The tide of these
new-comers pouring into the capital is as if the Orontes, the great
river of Syria, were joining its waters with those of the Tiber.—
Chordas obliquas. "The crooked harps." *Chordas,* the strings, is
put for the harp itself. The reference appears to be to the *sam-
buca,* a species of triangular instrument. The harp and flute were
very often played together; hence *cum tibicine* in the text.—*Gentilia
tympana.* "Its national tambourines." Chiefly used in the worship
of Cybele.

66–67. *Rusticus ille tuus.* "Thy rustic of former days." Observe
the force of *ille* as referring to what is now remote, and has long
since gone by.—*Rusticus.* A graphic term for the hardy and primitive Roman of the olden time.—*Sumit trechedipna.* "Puts on the
trechedipna." Juvenal means to lash not only the introduction of
effeminate Grecian manners and costume, but also the accompany-

ing inroad of Greek terms into the Roman tongue. We have, therefore, purposely retained here, in translating, the Greek form of the
word. What is meant by *trechedipna* is difficult to say. The term
is derived from τρέχω, "to run," and δεῖπνον, "supper," and the
scholiast explains it as "*Vestimenta parasitica currentium ad cœnam.*"
It would seem to have meant, therefore, not, as some suppose, the
thin supper-robe, but a garment like the *endromis*, worn by those
who were hastening to the banquet, parasites for instance, and of a
thick texture, to obviate the effects of sudden exposure when heated.
Some, however, make the *trechedipna* to have been a kind of dress
shoes.—*Et ceromatico*, &c. "And wears the niceteria on his neck
anointed with ceroma." The *niceteria* (νικητήρια) were rewards for
victory in gymnastic contests, such as collars, or chains of gold, rings,
&c. By the term *ceroma* (κήρωμα) is denoted an unguent for wrest-
lers, made of oil and wax.

63-71. *Alta Sicyone.* Sicyon, the capital of Sicyonia, in the Peloponnesus, lay in a northwestern direction from Corinth. The earlier city was situate in a plain, but was destroyed by Demetrius
Poliorcetes, who built a new one on the high ground close to the
Acropolis.—*Amydone.* Amydon was a town in Macedonia, on the
River Axius.—*Andro.* Andros was the most northerly, and one of
the largest of the Cyclades, and lay to the southeast of Eubœa.—
Samo. Samos was one of the principal islands of the Ægean, lying
off the coast of Ionia, and separated from it only by a narrow strait.
Observe that, in scanning this line, the third foot is | *mō hīc,* | the
long final vowel in *Samo* losing one of its component short vowels
by elision, and the remaining one being lengthened by the arsis.—
Trallibus. Tralles was a flourishing commercial city of Asia Minor,
reckoned sometimes to Ionia and sometimes to Caria, and lying on
the Eudon, a branch of the Mæander.—*Alabandis.* Alabanda was
an inland town of Caria, near the River Marsyas, to the south of the
Mæander. It was one of the most corrupt and luxurious towns of
Asia Minor.—*Esquilias.* The Esquiline and Viminal hills, two of
the seven on which Rome stood, are here put for the city itself.—
Viscera magnarum domuum, &c. "Destined to be the very vitals,
and the lords of powerful families."

72-80. *Ingenium velox,* &c. "Unto one and all are given a quick
wit, desperate impudence," &c. Supply *omnibus sunt,* equivalent to
omnibus ab ipsa natura data sunt.—*Isæo torrentior.* "More rapidly
fluent than Isæus." The ablative of the person instead of the ablative (*sermone*) of that which belongs to him. (*Madvig,* § 280, *Obs.* 2.)
The individual here meant is not the celebrated Attic orator, the

preceptor of Demosthenes, but a sophist and rhetorician of Assyria, who resided for some time at Rome in the days of Pliny the
younger, and of whom the latter speaks in terms of the highest
praise. (*Epist.* ii., 3.) He seems to have enjoyed a very great
reputation as a declaimer, and to have been particularly strong in
extempore speaking.—*Ede.* "Tell me."—*Putes.* Heinrich conjectures *jubes,* and thinks the indicative after the imperative more
animated.—*Quem vis hominem.* "Any character you choose." He
is a Jack of all trades ; nothing comes amiss to so universal a genius.—*Geometres.* To be pronounced here as a trisyllable, the first
and second syllables being contracted into one by synæresis (*gēo-
metres*).—*Aliptes.* "An anointer at the baths." The *aliptes* (ἀλεῖπ-
της) among the Romans was one who anointed the person of the
bather ; among the Greeks, however, he anointed the bodies of the
athletæ both before and after the exercises of the palæstra.—*Medicus, magus.* "A quack, a juggler."—*Græculus esuriens.* "Your
hungry Greekling."—*Jusseris.* For *si jusseris.*—*In cœlum ibit.* Some
think that there is an allusion here to a person who attempted the
experiment of flying in the presence of the Emperor Nero, but lost
his life in consequence.—*Mediis sed natus Athenis.* The allusion is
now to Dædalus, whom the ancient writers generally represent as
an Athenian, of the royal race of the Erechtheidæ.

81-84. *Horum conchylia.* "The purple finery of these fellows."
Conchylium properly means the shell-fish (*murex*) which yielded the
purple dye. The plural form here stands for "*vestes purpureas.*"—
Me prior ille signabit? " Shall one of this stamp affix his seal to
some document before me?" The allusion is in particular to the
witnessing of wills, in doing which a certain order was commonly
observed, and the more intimate friends took precedence of others.
—*Fultusque toro,* &c. Referring to a more honourable place at a
banquet. Not only the couches had their degrees of precedence,
but also the places themselves on each couch.—*Pruna et cottana.*
"His dried plums and little figs." The plums of Damascus, in
both their fresh and dried state, were very famous. *Cottanum* is a
Syriac word. Compare the Hebrew *Katán,* "small."—*Usque adeo
nihil est?* "Is it even so mere a nothing?" *i. e.,* is my being a native-born Roman a circumstance of no value to me?—*Bacca Sabina.* The olive is meant. The "Sabine berry" is here opposed
to the Syrian plum and fig.

85-88. *Quid, quod.* "Why need I tell how that?" Supply *dicam.* — *Prudentissima.* "Most adroitly versed." — *Longum collum.*
"The long scraggy neck."—*Cervicibus.* "To the brawny neck and

shoulders." *Cervix* is properly the back part of the neck merely, but here, from the force of the plural, it stands for the neck and shoulders combined.—*Antæum.* Antæus, son of earth, was invincible so long as he remained in contact with his mother earth. Hercules, discovering the source of his strength, lifted him up into the air, and crushed him while thus separated from his parent.

89–100. *Sed illis creditur.* "But credence is given to those fellows alone." Supply *tantum.*—*Nec tamen Antiochus,* &c. Antiochus, Stratocles, Demetrius, and Hæmus were all celebrated actors of the day, and natives of Greece. But, though famous at Rome, they would be nothing in their own country, since the whole Grecian nation is one pack of actors, and the representing of assumed characters is nothing new for them.—*Illic.* "There (in their own land)."—*Natio comœda est.* "The whole nation belongs to comedy," *i. e.,* it is all one broad farce; the people are all actors, without a particle of truth or sincerity in their nature.—*Rides.* What would have been the protasis if this had been expressed as a conditional sentence, is stated as a fact; and what would have been the apodosis is added as an independent clause.—*Meliore.* "Far more hearty."—*Lacrymas.* "A tear or two."—*Nec dolet.* "And yet he feels no real sorrow."—*Accipit endromidem.* "He puts on his great-coat." The *endromis,* as already remarked, was a thick, coarse cloak, worn after gymnastic exercises, and also in the winter, to prevent catching cold.—*Pares.* "Fairly matched."—*Melior.* "He is a better hand at the business," *i. e.,* of flattering.—*A facie.* We have adopted here the reading of one of the best MSS., as recommended by Markland, and given by Jahn. The parasite is represented as regulating his every expression of countenance by that of his patron. Athenæus (vi., 12, § 54, p. 249, A) makes mention of one Cleisophus, who used to make a wry face whenever Philip tasted any pungent dish. Plutarch compares such a flatterer to a polypus, or to a mirror which reflects all images from without. (*Plut., de Ad. et Am.,* 8, p. 53, A.) The common text reads *alienum,* placing a comma after *vultum,* and connects *A facie* with *jactare manus.* The reference will then be to what we call kissing the hand, and will denote respect and obsequious reverence. The superiority of the other reading, however, is manifest at first view. *Jactare manus* is "to throw up the hands in admiration." (*Mayor, ad loc.*)—*Laudare.* "To praise the other's every act."—*Scire volunt,* &c. This line is a feeble one, and regarded as spurious by some editors. Others consider it out of place.

101–106. *Transi gymnasia.* "Pass over to their very schools of philosophy." Some render this, "Pass by their gymnasia," *i. e.*, let us say nothing of their schools of exercise, and of the ordinary herd of Greeks, whom these may be said to represent, but let us turn to a graver crime. This explanation, however, has very little, if any thing, to recommend it.—*Facinus majoris abollæ.* "A crime of the larger cloak," *i. e.*, a crime committed by one of their philosophers himself. The ordinary *abolla* was a kind of short cloak, not differing materially from the *sagum*, and fastened by a brooch under the neck or upon the top of the shoulder. It was originally worn by the military, but subsequently by all classes. The *major abolla*, however, was a species of large cloak, or wrapper, worn more especially by philosophers, and hence is here taken figuratively for the philosopher himself, the garment for the person who wore it.—*Stoicus.* P. Egnatius Celer is meant, a follower of the Stoic sect in the time of Nero, who gave false evidence against Barcas Soranus, a most exemplary man, upon which the latter was capitally convicted. Egnatius received large rewards from the emperor. What made the conduct of Egnatius the more atrocious was, that he belonged to a sect which prided itself on its strict code of morals, and that he had been the client, and intimate friend, and philosophic teacher of his victim.—*Occidit.* "Killed," *i. e.*, by his false accusations.—*Discipulumque.* Ritter (*Philologus*, v. 567, *seq.*) conjectures *Discipulamque*, making the reference to be, not to Soranus, but to his daughter Servilia, who was put to death with her parent.—*Ripa nutritus in illa*, &c. "Though reared on that bank," &c., *i. e.*, though reared in the philosophic schools of Tarsus. The allusion is to the bank of the River Cydnus, in Cilicia, where stood the city of Tarsus, famed for its schools of philosophy. According to the legend, the winged horse Pegasus lost a hoof (ταρσός) here, whence the name of the city. Juvenal, following a different account from the ordinary one, makes Pegasus to have dropped here a "wing-feather" merely. Commentators find a great difficulty here, because Dio Cassius makes Egnatius to have been a native of Berytus, in Phœnicia, not of Tarsus; and hence, in order to reconcile Juvenal's account with that of the legend respecting the origin of this latter city, they make *ripa* in the text embrace the idea of the whole coast of southern Asia Minor and Phœnicia! Others, again, suppose the poet to be speaking, not of Tarsus, but of Thebes or of Corinth. The whole difficulty disappears, however, if we only bear in mind that *nutritus* does not necessarily imply *natus*, and that Egnatius, though born at Berytus, might very well have been reared and educated at Tarsus.

Gorgonei caballi. The winged horse Pegasus sprang from Medusa after her head had been struck off by Perseus. His sire was Neptune, who had appeared unto the Gorgon in the form of a horse or a bird. Juvenal shows his contempt for every thing Grecian by applying the term *caballus*, which properly means a pack-horse, to the winged steed of the Muses.

107–112. *Protogenes,* &c. These names are most probably fictitious. The common text gives the third one as *Erimarchus,* for which we have substituted *Hermarchus,* with the best recent editions, as a more genuine Greek form. The name *Hermarchus* occurs in Cicero, where the old editions, less correctly, give *Hermachus.*—*Gentis vitio.* "From the inherent vice of his race."—*Solus habet.* "Keeps him entirely to himself."—*Facilem.* "Too ready."—*De veneno.* The employment here of *de veneno* for the genitive *veneni* is meant to imply an abundant stock of venom, from which a portion is taken.—*Submoveor.* "I am gradually dislodged." Observe the force of *sub* in composition.—*Tempora.* "The recompenses." Put for *fructus temporum,* as Heinrich remarks.—*Servitii.* A very graphic term for the toilsome and ill-requited attendance of the client upon his haughty patron.—*Nusquam.* Supply *quam Romæ.*—*Minor.* "Of less account." The loss is soon supplied by some flattering Greek.

113–117. *Quod porro officium,* &c. "Besides, not to flatter ourselves, what service or what merit can come from the poor man here, even·though he make it his earnest care," &c., *i. e.,* to tell the plain and humiliating truth, what service can the poor man render, what merit can he plead, even though he be zealous enough, &c.—*Nocte.* "While it is still dark," *i. e.,* even before the break of day. The levees of the rich and powerful were held early in the morning.—*Togatus.* The clients were expected to wait upon their patron in full attire, of which the toga formed the most conspicuous part.—*Cum Prætor,* &c. The poor man stands no chance of being noticed, when even the higher magistrates are hastening on the same errand, and are treading, as it were, on the heels of the lictor, who cannot go fast enough to please them. The *Prætor Urbanus,* or City Prætor, is meant, and by *collega,* farther on, the *Prætor Peregrinus.*—*Lictorem.* The prætor originally had six lictors, but subsequently he was attended by two lictors within the city, and by six without.—*Dudum vigilantibus orbis.* "Childless matrons having long since been awake," *i. e.,* having long since been up and expecting morning calls.—*Ne prior Albinam,* &c. The contest between these two worthies is, which shall have the better chance of being named in the wills of these rich dowagers.

118-120. *Da testem Romæ.* "Produce me a witness at Rome."
We have here a new ground of complaint on the part of Umbritius.
The truth of a man's testimony is estimated at Rome, not by the
goodness of his character, but by the amount of his wealth.—*Hospes numinis Idæi.* "The host of the Idæan divinity," *i. e.*, of Cybele, who is here called "Idæan," from Mount Ida, an early seat
of her worship. The individual meant is P. Scipio Nasica. When
the Romans, during the second Punic war, brought the image of
Cybele from Pessinus to Rome, the oracle at Delphi directed them
to place the goddess in the hands of the most virtuous man (*optimus vir*) in the state; or, to adopt Livy's language (xxix., 11), "*Ut
eam, qui vir optimus Romæ esset, hospitio exciperet.*" The Senate
thereupon decided that Nasica was the most virtuous citizen in the
state, and he was therefore sent, along with the Roman matrons, to
Ostia, where the vessel lay that had conveyed the image to Italy.
Scipio, having received the statue from the priests who had charge
of it, conveyed it to the land, where it was placed in the hands of
the matrons, who brought it to Rome, and placed it in the temple
of Victory on the Palatine Hill. (*Liv.*, xxix., 14).—*Vel qui servavit,*
&c. L. Cæcilius Metellus, who, in B.C. 241, rescued the Palladi-
um when the temple of Vesta was in flames, but lost his sight in
consequence.—*Trepidam.* Trembling, not at the approach of the
flames, but at the defiling contact of mortal hands.

121-127. *Protenus ad censum.* "The question is first asked as to
his income." Supply *quæritur.* — *Jugera.* Commonly rendered
"acres," and this version will answer for ordinary purposes. In
strictness, however, the *jugerum* was less than two thirds of an English acre.—*Paropside.* "A side-dish." The *paropsis* was employed for serving up the smaller and more exquisite portions of a
meal, like the French *entrée.* Hence the inquiry in the text is the
same, in fact, as "What sort of table does he keep?"— *Fidei.*
"Credit as regards his oath."—*Samothracum et nostrorum.* "Of
the Samothracian and our own country's gods." The Samothracian
divinities were the Cabiri. Samothrace was a small island in the
northern part of the Ægean Sea, opposite the mouth of the Hebrus,
in Thrace.—*Dis ignoscentibus ipsis.* The gods, instead of punishing his perjury, excuse him on account of the temptations to which
he is exposed by his destitute condition.

129-140. *Hic idem.* This same poor fellow."—*Lacerna.* "His
cloak." The *lacerna* was a loose kind of cloak or mantle, open in
front, and fastened by a buckle or brooch under the throat. It was,
moreover, sufficiently ample to be worn over the toga or any other

garment, and had a hood, which could be raised over the head so as to conceal the features, or avoid the sight of any unpleasant object. — *Sordidula.* "Is somewhat soiled." — *Rupta pelle patet.* "Gapes with its upper leather burst."—*Vel si consuto,* &c. The poet's language here is humorously metaphorical. By *vulnere* is meant the rupture of the shoe, and by *cicatrix* the awkward "seam" on the cobbled patch, exhibiting to view the coarse thread in the new-made stitches. — *Inquit.* "Exclaims the superintendent of seats." Supply *designator.* This functionary was somewhat like the modern door-keeper of a theatre. Every seat was numbered, the space allotted to each being marked by a line drawn on each side of it, and the billet of admission (*tessera theatralis*) specified the number of the seat which the person was to occupy, and which was shown to him by the *designator* when he entered the theatre.— *Pulvino equestri.* In B.C. 68, the tribune L. Roscius Otho carried a law which regulated the places in the theatre to be occupied by the different classes of Roman citizens, and which enacted, in particular, that fourteen rows of benches should be assigned to the equestrian order.— *Cujus res legi,* &c. The amount of an equestrian fortune was 400,000 sesterces, and a person not having this was excluded from the fourteen rows. Bankrupts lost their seats. Many persons, moreover, belonging to the equites, whose estates were impaired, feared to take their seats, until Augustus ordained that no eques, whose father or himself had at any time possessed 400,000 sesterces, should be liable to the penalties of the law. (*Suet., Aug.,* 14.)—*Et sedeant hic.* The designator's speech is taken up by Umbritius, and continued with indignant irony.

Lenonum pueri, &c. Men of the vilest origin or character now take the equestrian seats, if they have but the requisite sum to constitute an equestrian fortune.—*Nitidi præconis.* "Of some spruce crier."—*Inter pinnirapi cultos juvenes,* &c. "Amid the smartly-dressed youths of some feather-snatcher, and the scions of some lanista." The term *pinnirapus* properly means any gladiator matched with a Samnite or Thracian, each of whom wore feathers (*pinnæ*) in their helmets, which it was the object of their opponent to "snatch away." Hence the name given them, from *pinna* and *rapio.*—*Lanistæ.* The *lanista* was the keeper of a gladiatorial school.—*Sic libitum vano,* &c. According to Umbritius, the law of Otho was prompted by mere caprice on the part of a vain and frivolous man.—*Qui nos distinxit.* "Who made distinctions between us."

141–144. *Quis gener hic placuit,* &c. Another evil attendant upon poverty at Rome, the disadvantages, namely, under which men of

G

small fortunes labour with respect to marriage.—*Atque puellæ sarcinulis impar.* " And if not a match for the money-bags of the young lady."—*Quis pauper scribitur heres?* Who, asks Umbritius, ever remembers a poor man in his will, so as to make him his heir?—*Quando in consilio,* &c. " When is he taken into consultation, even by the ædiles?" *i. e.,* when does he sit as assessor to an ædile? Under the republic, the ædileship was a highly honourable office, and was ranked among the *magistratus majores.* In the time of the empire, however, the powers of the ædiles were gradually diminished, and their functions exercised by new officers, and hence Dio Cassius (55, 24) remarks that, even in the days of Augustus, no one was willing to hold so contemptible an office, so that this emperor was reduced to the necessity of compelling persons to take it. By *ædiles* in the text, therefore, are meant, in fact, the lowest class of magistrates or public officers.—*Agmine facto,* &c. According to Umbritius, there is need of another secession to the *Mons Sacer,* in order to regain the lost rights of the lower orders, and restore once more political equality.—*Olim.* In the sense of *jamdudum.* A characteristic of the Silver Age of Latinity.—*Tenues Quirites.* " The Romans of slender means."

145–151. *Haud facile emergunt,* &c. Another evil. The expense of living at Rome. —*Virtutibus.* " Merits." — *Res angusta domi.* " Narrow means at home."—*Magno.* " Costs a large sum." Supply *constat pretio.*—*Ventres.* " The keeping." Supply *constant.*— *Pudet.* " One feels ashamed here." — *Quod turpe negavit,* &c. " Which he denied to be disgraceful, who was transferred on a sudden to the Marsi," &c. The reference is to Curius Dentatus, the conqueror of the Samnites and Sabines. The Marsi belonged to the Sabellian race. Many editions read *negabit,* making the remark of the poet a general one ; " which he will deny to be disgraceful, if transferred on a sudden," &c., *i. e.,* if he shall witness their plain and simple mode of life. But the ordinary reading is to be preferred. Juvenal is fond of deducing examples from the great and good men of earlier days.—*Contentusque illic,* &c. " And was there 'content with a bowl of blue and coarse earthenware." The *culullus* was a bowl or drinking-cup of earthenware. Some read here *cucullo,* the *cucullus* being a kind of hood or cowl attached to some other garment, such as the *lacerna, sagum,* &c.

152–157. *Pars magna Italiæ,* &c. Umbritius, wishing to show more clearly that one might live in other places much less expensively than at Rome, instances the article of dress. In many parts of Italy, as he remarks, where they lived in rustic simplicity, the people went dressed in the tunic, never wearing the toga, the ordinary habit of the men at Rome, during all their lifetime.—*Nisi mortuus*. The corpses of ordinary citizens, among the Romans, were arrayed in a white toga ; magistrates in their official robes.—*Herboso theatro*. The first permanent theatre even in Rome itself was that built by Pompey of hewn stone.—*Si quando*. "If at any time." *Quando* for *aliquando*. —*Majestas*. "The solemnity."—*Tandem*. At the expiration of the year, or at the conclusion of the serious piece. In either case it is meant to denote a previous eager longing. —*Redit*. Final syllable lengthened by the *arsis*. —*Pulpita*. "The stage." Strictly speaking, *pulpitum* is that part of the stage upon which the actors stood when they delivered their dialogues or speeches.—*Exodium*. "Interlude." The *exodium* was not a farce, as has commonly been supposed, but an old-fashioned and laughable interlude, deriving its name from ἐξ and ὁδός, and indicating something not belonging to the main representation.—*Personæ pallentis hiatum*. "The wide-distended mouth of the ghastly mask." The dramatic mask covered the whole head, having the mouth more or less open, in order to increase the volume of sound. On the present occasion, the unnaturally distended mouth indicates the *manducus*, a grotesque kind of masked character, with an enormous mouth set full of teeth, in order to excite merriment by his ugliness and voracious propensities, whence the name.

158-166. *Habitus*. "Costumes." Later Latin for *vestimenta*.— *Illic*. In the rural districts of Italy.—*Similes*. "Arrayed alike." —*Orchestram*. In the Greek theatres, the orchestra was the place where the chorus performed its evolutions. In the Roman theatres, on the contrary, as the Romans had no chorus to their dramatic representations, it was occupied by the senators and persons of distinction. In the present instance, therefore, the term is employed to denote, not only the *Decuriones*, or rural senate, but also the upper classes in the rural theatre, or, as we would say, the country gentlemen, who would occupy seats nearer the stage than the rest of the audience.—*Clari velamen honoris*. "As the attire of distinguished preferment." — *Ædilibus*. Put here for "magistrates" generally. The ædiles in the rural districts, though resembling in their functions and duties the ædiles at Rome, were, as might be expected, of more consequence than the latter.—*Hic*. "Here at Rome, on the contrary."—*Ultra vires*. "Beyond one's means."—*Interdum aliena*, &c. "Sometimes the money (for making this appearance) is obtained from another's strong-box," *i. e.*, by borrowing, &c.—*Vitium*. The living beyond one's means, in consequence of the ambition of the poorer classes to make a display and ape the wealthy.—*Quid das*, &c.   In the shape of a bribe to the domestics of the great man, in order that, after long dancing attendance, you may at length be admitted to his morning levee.   Observe the force of *aliquando.*— *Cossum.*   Cossus is here a fictitious name for some wealthy noble-man of the day.—*Te respiciat.*   "May look over his shoulder at you."   The great man merely deigns to give one glance of con-temptuous indifference, without uttering a syllable in reply to the morning salutation of his inferior.—*Veiento.*   Juvenal may possibly mean Fabricius Veiento, an infamous informer and flatterer under Domitian.

167-170.   *Ille metit barbam*, &c.   "That one lops off the beard, this one cuts the locks of some favourite minion."   The wealthier Romans, on arriving at early manhood, used to dedicate the first shavings of their beard and the pollings of their hair (worn uncut up to this time) to some deity, most commonly Apollo, and the day when this was done was celebrated as a festival.   The clients on such occasions were accustomed to bring presents.   In the present instance, the hair of some young favourite slave is lopped for the first time, and the presents consist of cakes, nominally as an offer-ing to the god, but in reality to be eaten by the guests.   So many of these complimentary cakes, moreover, are sent in honour of the event, that they are actually sold to get rid of them, thus forming an important perquisite for the slave.—*Libis venalibus.*   "Of venal cakes."   These cakes were a kind of gingerbread, made of flour, honey, and oil.—*Accipe, et istud*, &c.   "Listen still farther, and take this as a leaven unto your feelings," *i. e.*, and let it work like leaven within your spleen.—*Et cultis augere*, &c.   "And to increase the private gains of pampered slaves."   The *peculium* of a slave was the money or property which he could accumulate and hold with his master's consent.

171-173.   *Quis timet*, &c.   Another evil connected with the living at Rome, namely, the insecure state of the dwellings of the lower classes, and the constant danger of fires.—*Præneste.*   Either used here in the feminine, in imitation of the Greek (Πραίνεστος, ου, ἡ), or else having *urbe* understood, with which *gelida* is to agree.   Com-pare *Virg., Æn.*, viii., 561.   The ordinary gender of *Præneste* is neuter.   This was one of the most ancient towns of Latium, and was situate on a steep and lofty hill about twenty miles southeast of Rome.   In consequence of its lofty situation, it was a cool and healthy residence in the great heats of summer.   Its remains are to be seen at the modern *Palæstrina.*—*Ruinam.*   "The fall of a house."—*Volsiniis.* Volsinii, one of the most ancient and powerful of the cities of Etruria, was situate on a lofty hill at the northeastern extremity of the Lacus Vulsiniensis, now Lake of *Bolsena.* It was razed to the ground by the Romans, and the inhabitants compelled to settle on a less defensible site in the plain. On this latter site stands the modern *Bolsena.*—*Simplicibus.* Gabii is here called "simple," from the ease with which Sextus Tarquinius is said to have duped its inhabitants. It stood between Rome and Praeneste, and was in earlier times one of the most powerful of the Latin cities.—*Aut proni Tiburis arce.* "Or on the heights of sloping Tibur," *i. e.*, at Tibur, situate on sloping heights. Tibur, now *Tivoli*, lay on the slope of a hill, upon the left bank of the Anio, sixteen miles northeast of Rome.

174-177. *Tenui tibicine fultam.* "Supported on only a slender prop." In many parts of Rome, the dwellings of the lower orders were so ruinous as to require props or shores to keep them from falling. *Tibicen* has here a figurative meaning. The prop supports the building, just as the flute-player supports the singer in a public performance.—*Nam sic labentibus obstat,* &c. "For in this way the steward keeps up the falling inmates." Literally, prevents or opposes. With *labentibus* supply *incolis,* not *parietibus,* as some do. *Sic* refers to the propping up or shoring. Some editions read *si* for *sic,* and change *quum texit,* in the succeeding line, to *contexit,* but this wants force.—*Securos.* "Without apprehension."

178-183. *Illic.* In the country. If the houses in the city do not tumble down, still they are in constant danger of being burnt down. —*Jam poscit aquam,* &c. The repetition of *jam* three times is meant to denote the progress of the fire.—*Ucalegon.* A playful allusion to Virgil's "*proximus ardet Ucalegon*" (*Æn.*, ii., 310), and denoting here, not the next-door neighbour, as we might at first suppose, but the owner and occupant of the house itself in which the fire has broken out, and who has rented the upper stories to poor tenants.— *Frivola transfert.* "Is removing his furniture of inferior value." He has already removed the more valuable articles of property, and now is engaged in saving his less valuable chattels. This is meant to show how long the fire has been raging, and yet during all this while he has not bestowed a single thought upon his poor tenant up stairs.—*Tabulata tibi,* &c. "The third story now smokes for you." Heinrich makes *tibi* equivalent here to *in domo, in qua habitas.* It is much better, however, to give it the force of *in perniciem tuam.*— *Tu nescis.* You are sound asleep and unconscious of your danger.— *Nam si trepidatur,* &c. "For if the alarm begin from the bottom

of the stairs, he will be the last to be burnt," &c. The poor tenant
who occupies the garret.—*Tegula*. "The tiling."—*Molles ubi reddunt*, &c. The roof was used as a dove-cote.

184–189. *Lectus erat Codro*, &c. If a poor man is burnt out, no one
thinks of helping him. An instance of this is now given in the case
of an indigent poet named Codrus. Compare note on *Sat.* i., 2.—
Procula minor. "Too short even for little Procula." This is commonly supposed to be the name of his wife. It is better, however,
to regard the appellation *Procula* as a kind of proverbial one for a
dwarfish person. Perhaps it was the name of some dwarf well
known at Rome.—*Nec non et*. "And also both."—*Abaci*. "Of his
sideboard." This consisted of a marble slab, which was sometimes
inserted into the wall, but more commonly supported on a bracket or
a single foot.—*Infra*. "Beneath it."—*Cantharus*. This was a goblet
or drinking-cup of Greek invention, having two handles. It was the
cup particularly sacred to Bacchus.—*Chiron*. A reclining figure of
the Centaur under the marble abacus. Chiron was famed for his
skill in medicine, music, gymnastics, and the art of prophecy. His
acquaintance with the musical art recommends him here to the favour of the poet.—*Jam vetus*. "Now grown old."—*Opici*. Used here
in the sense of *barbari*. The Opici, or Osci, were an Ausonian tribe,
on the River Liris, from whom many barbarous innovations were introduced into Roman manners and language.

190–195. *Totum illud nihil*. "The whole of that nothing."—*Ultimus autem*, &c. "The crowning point, however, of his accumulated misery was," *i. e.*, the climax.—*Nudum*. "When stripped of
every thing." — *Frustra*. "Broken victuals." — *Hospitio tectoque*.
"With hospitable shelter." Hendiadys. Literally, "With hospitality and a roof."—*Cecidit*. "Has fallen a prey to the flames."—
Horrida mater. "Each Roman matron stands all dishevelled to the
view." In all public calamities, the Roman ladies took their part
in the common mourning by appearing in funereal garb, without ornaments, and with dishevelled hair. *Horrida*, in fact, implies all
this, being equivalent here to *sine cultu et incomta*.—*Pullati proceres*. "The nobles are clad in mourning." The *pulla vestis* was a
dark-gray garment of undyed wool, the dress of mourners. It was
also the attire of the lower orders, so that *pullati*, besides its meaning here, is sometimes employed as a general term to indicate the
common people.—*Differt vadimonia*. "Adjourns court." *Vadimo-
nium* properly means security, or a recognizance for one's appearing
in court on a certain day when the trial is to begin. Hence *differre vadimonia* signifies, strictly, "to put off the day of appearance,"

the plural indicating several law-suits. The closing of the courts was technically called a *justitium.—Tunc geminus*, &c. We now lament the fire as a national calamity.

196-202. *Ardet adhuc.* "The pile still blazes."—*Et jam accurrit.* "And already up runs one." *Accurrit* is the true reading here. *Occurrit,* "one meets him," wants force. — *Aliquid praeclarum.* "Some masterpiece."—*Euphranoris et Polycleti.* Euphranor, who flourished about B.C. 336, was a distinguished statuary and painter, and a native of the Corinthian isthmus, but he practised his art at Athens. Polycletus was one of the most celebrated statuaries of antiquity, but was also a sculptor, an architect, and an artist in toreutic. He was a native, probably, of Sicyon, and flourished about B.C. 452-412.—*Hic Asianorum,* &c. The common reading is *Hæc,* "this lady," but the change of gender is exceedingly awkward, and we have therefore given *Hic,* with Jahn and others. Some MSS. read *Phæcasianorum* instead of *Hæc Asianorum,* making the word equivalent to *Græcorum.* The term φαικάσιον, or φαικάς, means a species of white shoe worn by Athenian gymnasiarchs and Egyptian priests, and hence *Phæcasianus* will be *phæcasio indutus,* i. e., *Græcus.* This, however, is very far-fetched.

Forulos. "Cases." The *forulus* was a dwarf book-case, or cabinet for books, not permanently fixed to the walls like the *armarium,* but forming a small movable repository for a few favourite authors.—*Mediamque Minervam.* "And a bust of Minerva." The Greek προτομή.—*Modium.* "A whole peck." The *modius* was the Roman corn-measure, equivalent nearly to our peck, not, as some suppose, to our bushel. It contained sixteen *sextarii,* or the sixth part of a Greek medimnus, that is, nearly two gallons English.—*Meliora et plura reponit,* &c. "Persicus, now the most richly provided of the destitute, actually replaces what he has lost by better and more numerous things." Asturius is here called *Persicus* (i. e., "the Persian") in derision, on account of his luxurious style of living and the great wealth he had possessed.—*Orborum.* Incorrectly rendered by some, "Of childless men." The reference is to his losses by the fire, and *lautissimus orborum* is purposely meant as a pleasant oxymoron.

204-212. *Si potes avelli Circensibus.* "If you can tear yourself away from the Circensian games." Supply *ludis.* The Circensian games were so called from their being celebrated in the *Circus Maximus.* The Romans, particularly the lower orders, were passionately attached to them. Compare *Sat.,* x., 81. — *Soræ,* &c. Three small towns in Latium are here mentioned, where one might

live peaceably and happily.   Sora was on the right bank of the
Liris, to the north of Arpinum.   Fabrateria was on the right bank
of the Trerus, in the territory of the Volsci.   Frusino, originally a
town of the Hernici, was in the valley of the River Cosas.—*Paratur.*
"Is to be purchased."—*Quanti nunc,* &c.   "For as much as you
now hire some dark hole (in the city) for a single year."   Supply
tanti at the commencement of the clause.—*Hic.*   In these country
towns.—*Puteusque brevis,* &c.   The springs are so high that no rope
is required, but the bucket can be dipped at once into the well, a
matter of no little importance in a country where so much watering
was wanted as in Italy.—*Vive bidentis amans.*   Here pass your days
in cultivating your little spot of ground.   The *bidens* was a strong
and heavy two-pronged hoe, here put figuratively for husbandry in
general.—*Culti villicus horti.*   "And the dresser of a neat garden."
Villicus is properly a superintendent or overseer; here, however, it
stands for *hortulanus,* or *colonus* generally.—*Pythagoreis.*   The Pyth-
agoreans, in general, abstained from animal food, owing to their
belief, it is said, in the metempsychosis, and observed a vegetable
diet.   Such, at least, is the common account, and the one followed
in the text, though the best authorities contradict it.

Est aliquid.   "It is always something."   Compare the Greek,
ἐστι τι.—*Recessu.*   "Nook."—*Unius sese dominum,* &c.   "To have
made one's self the owner even of a single lizard."   The green
lizard is very abundant in the gardens of Italy.   Hence the text
means, to have made one's self owner of a spot of ground no larger
than that on which you may stand a chance of finding a lizard ; in
other words, a very small spot of ground.

213-219. *Vigilando.*   "From want of sleep."   Another evil attendant upon living at Rome is the perpetual noise in the streets,
occasioned by vehicles passing at all hours, so as to prevent one's
sleeping.   This, to people who are sick, is often attended with fatal
consequences.—*Sed illum languorem,* &c.   "Although (it must be
confessed) food imperfectly digested, &c., brought on that exhaustion
in the first instance."   A side hit, in passing, at the luxurious mode
of life pursued in the city, even by persons of limited means.   The
being kept awake, therefore, merely finishes what intemperance and
excess began.—*Meritoria.*   "Hired lodgings."   These were generally on the great thoroughfares, or in other noisy parts of the city,
and, moreover, next to the street.   None but the rich could afford
to live in houses in the retired parts of the city, or spacious enough
to have bed-chambers remote from the noise in the streets.   They,
therefore, who would sleep at Rome, must be at great expense, which
none but the opulent could afford.

Magnis opibus, &c. "One obtains sleep in the city only at a great outlay."—*Arcto vicorum in flexu.* "In the narrow curves of the streets." The streets of Rome, with the exception of the main avenues, were narrow and crooked. After the great fire in the time of Nero, they were enlarged and regulated, and the burnt district was laid out in a much better manner than before, and with better buildings.—*Stantis convicia mandræ.* "The revilings of the standing team," *i. e.*, the mutual revilings of the teamsters brought to a stand-still. *Mandra* is properly "a pen for cattle," and is then taken to signify the "cattle" themselves, as here a "team" of horses or mules.—*Druso.* "Even from a Drusus," *i. e.*, even from one as lethargic as the Emperor Claudius (Tiberius Claudius Drusus) is said to have been. Some editors are in favour of reading *urso* for *Druso*, and Jacobs recommends *vitulisve* for *vitulisque;* but the answer in both cases is the same: the poet, namely, by a stroke of wit, makes Drusus and the sea-calf, or seal, a creature proverbial for sluggishness, to belong to one and the same fraternity.

220-224. *Si vocat officium.* "If duty calls him." By *officium* is here meant attendance upon the levees of the great. Umbritius, having shown the advantage enjoyed by the rich in being able to afford themselves quiet repose, notwithstanding the constant noises in the city, which break the rest of the poorer classes, now proceeds to mention another privilege which they possess, in being able to travel rapidly along the crowded streets, lolling in their litters, while the poor are, with great difficulty and at great risk, slowly making their way on foot.—*Ingenti Liburno.* "By the aid of his strapping Liburnian." The tall and sturdy natives of Liburnia, whose country lay along the northeastern shore of the Adriatic, were much employed at Rome as litter-bearers.—*Super ora.* "Above their upturned faces." Observe the force of *ora.*—*Obiter.* "By the way."—*Clausa fenestra.* The windows were glazed with a kind of transparent stone, called *lapis specularis*, and were supplied with curtains.—*Ante tamen veniet.* He will lose no time, however, by all this, for, in whatever way he may employ himself on the route, he will be sure to arrive at his place of destination before us poor foot-passengers.

225-229. *Unda prior.* "The wave (of the multitude) that rolls on before."—*Magno agmine.* "In dense column of march."—*Assere duro.* "With the hard pole of a litter."—*Incutit.* "Knocks."—*Metretam.* "A nine-gallon cask." The *metreta* was an Athenian measure for liquids, containing 12 *congii* (χόες), and 144 κοτύλαι, or about nine gallons English.—*Pinguia crura luto.* Supply *mea fiunt.*—*Planta mox undique*, &c. "Presently I am trodden upon, on every side, by some huge splay-footed fellow."—*Clavus militis.* "The hob-nail of some soldier's shoe." The shoe worn by the Roman soldiery of the rank and file, including the centurions, but not the superior officers, was called *caliga.* It consisted of a close shoe, entirely cov-ering the foot, and having a thick sole studded with nails. It was bound by straps across the instep and round the bottom of the leg. —*In digito mihi hæret.* "Keeps sticking in my toe." With *digito* supply *pedis.*

230–234. *Nonne vides,* &c. Here the scene shifts. The difficult-ies of the morning are overpast, and the streets are cleared of the shoals of levee-hunters. New perils, however, arise, and the poor are obstructed by the crowd of clients returning with their slaves from the distribution of the dole at their patrons' houses.—*Celebre-tur.* "Is frequented."—*Sua culina.* The "kitchen" here spoken of was a large kind of chafing-dish, divided into two cells, in the up-permost one of which they put the meat, and in the lower fire, to keep it warm.—*Corbulo.* "A Corbulo," *i. e.,* even one as strong as Corbulo himself. Domitius Corbulo, remarkable for his great size and strength, was a distinguished general under Claudius and Nero. During the reign of the latter he carried on some very successful campaigns against the Parthians. But Nero, who had become jeal-ous of his fame, decoyed him to Corinth, where, on learning that orders had been issued for his death, he plunged his sword into his breast, exclaiming, "Well deserved!"—*Recto vertice.* "With up-right neck," *i. e.,* with his head upright, lest the gravy should be spilled.—*Servulus infelix.* "Some wretched little slave," *i. e.,* as op-posed to the gigantic and powerful Corbulo.

235–237. *Scinduntur tunicæ sartæ.* The patched tunics of the poor get torn in the squeeze.—*Modo longa coruscat,* &c. Now follows an indirect attack on the mania of the emperors for building, an evil, however, which Juvenal lived to see abated.—*Coruscat.* "Sways upon the view," *i. e.,* quivers, or keeps nodding up and down. Its swaying to and fro made it dangerous.—*Sarraco veniente.* There had been a law to prevent the nuisance of these loaded wagons passing and repassing after sunrise, or before four o'clock in the afternoon, when the Romans generally would be dining, unless it were for the construction or repairing of temples, public works, &c. Timber-carriages in the emperor's service would fall under this ex-ception.—*Altera plaustra.* "Another class of vehicles." Observe the employment of *altera* in the plural, to indicate one of two classes or kinds.—*Alte.* We have given *alte* here as superior to the common reading *altæ.*

238-244. *Saxa Ligustica.* "The blocks of Ligurian stone." Immense blocks of Ligurian marble were brought from Luna and its neighbourhood. As the quarries were near the sea, it was more used than any other. The white marble of Luna now takes its name from the neighbouring town of *Carrara.—Procubuit.* "Has sunk beneath the weight," *i. e.,* has given way.—*Et eversum fudit,* &c. "And has poured its overturned mountain-load upon the moving throng," *i. e.,* upon the troops of foot-passengers.—*Obtritum.* "Crushed to atoms."—*More animæ.* Because not a particle of it is visible.—*Interea,* &c. While the master (followed by his slave with the supper) has come to this untimely end, his unconscious domestics are making preparations for his meal, and his previous bath.— *Secura.* "Apprehensive of no evil."—*Foculum.* "A little fire." To warm the water for bathing before dinner.—*Et sonat unctis strigilibus.* "And are making a clatter with the well-oiled strigils."— *Striglibus* for *strigilibus.* The strigil (*strigilis*) was a kind of scraper for removing the moisture and impurities thrown out upon the surface of the skin by the heat of the vapor-bath or the violent exercise of the palæstra. It was made of iron or bronze, with a handle, into which the hand could be inserted, and a curved blade, hollowed into a channel, down which the moisture and perspiration would flow as in a gutter. When about to be used, the edge was lubricated with a few drops of oil, to prevent abrasion of the skin.—*Gutto.* The *guttus* was a "cruse" or flask with a very narrow neck, from which the liquid poured out flowed in small quantities, or drop by drop. On the present occasion it contains oil for rubbing over the body after bathing.

245-248. *Pueros.* The slaves. — *Ille.* "The master himself." Erroneously referred by most commentators to the *servulus infelix.* —*Sedet in ripa.* He takes a seat on the banks of the Styx, because he has a hundred years to wait, having been deprived of the rites of burial.—*Novicius.* "A novice," *i. e.,* newly arrived, and beholding for the first time so appalling a scene.—*Porthmea.* Charon. *Porthmeus* is a Greek form of expression for the ordinary Latin term *portitor.—Nec sperat.* Because unburied.—*Alnum.* "The bark." According to the poets, the alder (*alnus*), as growing on the banks of rivers, was the first tree the timber of which was used for navigation. Hence it is taken figuratively for the bark or vessel itself. Charon's boat is here meant.—*Cænosi gurgitis.* "Of the miry pool," *i. e.,* in which to cross the dark and troubled waters of the Styx.— *Trientem.* "The triens." A small copper coin, so called from its being the third of an *as.* It is put here, in reality, however, for the *obolus*, which, according to the Greek legend, was Charon's regular fare. The coin was always placed in the mouth of the corpse.

249–258. *Respice nunc alia,* &c. We have now a lively and faithful picture of the evils incident to the night, which will suit all large cities not sufficiently protected by a night-police.—*Quod spatium,* &c. "What a space it is from lofty roofs (to the ground)."—*Testa.* "The potsherd," *i. e.,* some piece of broken pottery. — *Curta.* "Chipped."—*Quanto percussum,* &c. "With what a weight they actually mark and indent the flinty pavement where stricken by them," *i. e.,* wherever they strike. From the force with which they strike the flinty pavement, you may judge, *a fortiori,* of the little chance which your head would have.—*Ignavus.* "Remiss."—*Casus.* "Accident."—*Adeo tot fata,* &c. "So clear it is that there are just so many chances of death," &c.—*Vigiles.* "Wakeful," *i. e.,* where the inmates are awake inside.—*Patulas defundere pelves.* "To pour down merely what the broad basins contain," *i. e.,* and not to throw down the basins along with it. There is a title in the Digest (ix., 3), "*De his qui effuderint vel dejecerint.*"

259–266. *Ebrius ac petulans,* &c. A vivid picture is now presented of the wanton insults to which the poor were exposed from the midnight frolics of drunken rakes and bullies. Nero was one of the first of these disturbers of the public quiet. Under shelter of his example, private persons took the opportunity of annoying passengers in the streets by night.—*Qui nullum forte cecidit.* "Who has chanced as yet to give no one a beating."—*Dat pœnas.* "Suffers the penalty for this," *i. e.,* by not being able to sleep. He accounts it a sad night's sport unless he has given some one a threshing, and therefore cannot sleep for pure vexation.—*Amicum.* Patroclus.— *Ergo non aliter,* &c. This must be regarded as a question on the part of the poet, not of Umbritius. But the whole line is probably spurious, and might be omitted without any injury to the sense.— *Improbus.* "Reckless."—*Coccina lœna,* &c. The scarlet cloak, the long train of attendants bearing torches, and the lamps, probably of Corinthian brass, carried immediately before him, all mark the rich nobleman, and teach the midnight brawler discretion.—*Multum præterea flammarum.* "Many a blazing torch too." — *Aënea.* A quadrisyllable, as required by the metre, unless we read *atque œnea.*

267–276. *Deducere.* "To escort on my way." The technical word for the clients' attendance on their patrons.—*Candelæ.* The candle consists of a rope dipped in wax or pitch.—*Dispenso et tempero.* "I parcel out and economize." Only a certain portion of the wick, and that a very small one, is to be allowed for going a certain distance.—*Prœmia.* "The prelude," *i. e.*, the way in which it begins.—*Stat contra.* "He takes his station full in front."—*Fortior.* "Stronger than yourself."—*Aceto.* "Vinegar," *i. e.*, sour wine.—*Conche.* Beans boiled in the shell, a common dish among the poorer people, and which was very filling.—*Sectile porrum.* "Chopped leek." There were two kinds of leek, the *sectile* and *capitatum*, of which the former was the coarser sort.—*Vervecis.* Sheep's heads were among the parts given away to the poor at the Saturnalia and other festivals.

277–281. *Ede, ubi consistas.* "Tell me where you take your stand." Implying that he was one of the regular fraternity of beggars.—*In qua proseucha.* "In what Jewish praying-house." This is said contemptuously, as if the poor man were not only a beggar, but (what was worse) a vagabond Jew. The *proseuchæ* (προσευχαί) were Jewish oratories, or houses of prayer, usually built without the walls of a city, by the river or sea side.—*Si tentes.* For *sive tentes.*—*Tantundem est.* "'Tis all one."—*Pariter.* "Equally in either event."—*Vadimonia faciunt.* "Make you give bail for the assault." They pretend to be the party aggrieved, and insist on your finding bail for the alleged assault. Consult, as regards *vadimonia*, the note on line 159.—*Pugnis concisus.* "Cut up with fisticuffs."—*Adorat.* "Supplicates."

283–288. *Nec tamen hæc tantum metuas.* Now come the dangers from robbers.—*Deerit.* To be pronounced as a dissyllable.—*Clausis domibus*, &c. All the houses being shut up, and the shops closed, there is no help to be had.—*Omnis ubique*, &c. "Every fastening of the chained shop has every where become fixed and silent." Literally, " every fixed fastening, &c., has become silent." The shutters were fastened by a strong iron chain running through each.—*Agit rem.* "Does your business."—*Armato quoties*, &c. When the banditti became so numerous in any spot as to render travelling dangerous, it was usual to detach a party of military from the capital to scour their retreats, the inevitable consequence of which was that they escaped in vast numbers to Rome, where they continued to exercise their old trade with probably more security than before. —*Pomtina palus.* "The Pontine marshes." This was the name of a low marshy plain on the coast of Latium, between Circeii and Terracina, said to have been so called from an ancient town Pontia, which disappeared at an early period. The plain is about 24 miles long, and from 8 to 10 miles in breadth. The marshes are formed chiefly by the rivers Nymphæus, Ufens, Amasenus, and some smaller streams, which, instead of finding their way to the sea, spread over this plain. Hence the plain is converted into a vast number of marshes, the miasma arising from which is exceedingly unwholesome in summer.

Gallinaria pinus. "The Gallinarian pine forest." A forest on the coast of Campania, occupying the sandy shore which extends from the mouth of the Vulturnus toward Cumæ. It was a favourite resort of banditti, and was, in consequence, often guarded by bands of soldiery. Strabo speaks of it as a forest of brushwood, but, from Juvenal's language, it is evident that there was also a wood of tall pine-trees, such as grow luxuriantly on many of the sandy shores of Italy.—*Tanquam ad vivaria.* "As unto some vast preserve." Observe here the force of the plural. *Vivarium* is a very general term for any place in which beasts, fowls, fish, or any kind of animals were kept alive, either for the purposes of gain or pleasure.

290–295. *Qua fornace graves,* &c. Though there is no forge or anvil but rings with the clank of chains, yet all is ineffectual for the suppression of crime. The regular prose order would be, *Qua fornace, qua incude, non graves catenæ?*—*Catenæ.* Supply *conficiuntur* or *fabricantur.*—*Modus.* "Quantity." Supply *consumitur.*—*Marræ et sarcula.* "Mattocks and hoes." The former of these words still exists in both Italian and Spanish; and in French, *marre* denotes the hoe used in vineyards. From *sarculum* comes, through the French, the English verb "sarcle," to weed corn.—*Proavorum atavos.* "Our forefathers of early times." The order is, *Pater, avus, proavus, abavus, atavus, tritavus.* He means, therefore, eight generations back at least.—*Tribunis.* The military tribunes with consular power were first appointed B.C. 444, sixty-five years after the abolition of the regal government; and the tribunes of the commons sixteen years after the same event.—*Uno carcere.* This prison was built by Ancus Martius (*Liv.,* i., 33). Servius Tullius added the dungeon, called from him *Tullianum.* The next prison was built by Appius Claudius the Decemvir. (*Liv.,* iii., 57.)

296–303. *His alias poteram,* &c. "To these I might have subjoined other and more numerous reasons (for leaving Rome)." Observe the employment of *poteram* here in the imperfect indicative, to denote what might have been done, but is not done (*Madvig,* § 348, *Obs.* 1).—*Sed jumenta vocant.* The wagon, as soon as it was loaded, set out and overtook Umbritius; and now it was waiting to depart.—*Nam mihi commota,* &c. "For the muleteer has long since been giving me a hint by smacking his whip."—*Tuo Aquino.* "To thy native Aquinum." Aquinum, Juvenal's native place, was situate in the territory of the Volsci, on the Via Latina, between Fabra-

teria and Casinum, and about four miles from the left bank of the
Liris. Ceres and Diana were especially worshipped here.—*Helvi-nam.* "The Helvine." Ceres was so called, from the "yellow (*hel-vus*) colour" of the ears of corn. *Helvus* is akin to *gilvus,* "dun,"
in etymology and signification. Compare the German *gelb,* "yel-low," and the Sanscrit *gaur.*—*Ni pudet illas.* "Unless they are
ashamed (of my poor aid)." Supply, with Ruperti, *auxilii mei.*—
Caligatus. "Fully equipped," *i. e.,* for a campaign against the vices
of the city. *Caligatus* literally means "wearing soldiers' shoes."
Compare note on line 229.—*Gelidos agros.* Aquinum was rendered
"cool" by its hills, woods, and streams.

SATIRE IV.

ARGUMENT.

No vicious man can be happy, least of all the profligate Crispi-nus, though his wealth be such that he can lavish the price of an
estate upon a fish, an instance of self-indulgence in the parasite
which prepares us for any extravagance on the part of the monarch
his patron.

In Domitian's reign, a rhombus of very large size, fully equalling
the Byzantine, was taken off Ancona. As such a prize would else
be seized by the informers, who swarmed even on the coast, the
fisherman destines it for Cæsar, and, though the season is winter,
hurries with it, as though afraid it may become tainted. At the
Alban villa he finds ready admission. He begs the emperor to ac-cept the fish as one reserved for his times, and eager for the honour
of being served up at his table. Gross as this flattery is, Domitian
welcomes it. But where find a dish capacious enough to contain
the fish? This is a point for a council of state to determine. A
council is accordingly summoned. The individuals called to con-sultation are then described, and the farce ends with the advice
of Montanus being followed, who recommends that a dish be made
for the purpose, since it were a dishonour to such a fish not to be
served up whole. The council is then dismissed, having been con-voked in as headlong haste as though some war had broken out.
Yet it had been well for Rome if, engrossed by such follies, Domi-tian had wanted time for the murder of her nobles, whom, more-over, he might have destroyed with impunity if he had not alarmed
also men of ignoble origin for their own safety.

From the concluding verses, we learn that this satire was composed after the death of Domitian, September 18, A.D. 96. —
(*Mayor.*)

———

1-9. *Ecce iterum Crispinus.* "See! Crispinus again makes his
appearance." Supply *adest.* He has already been mentioned in
Sat. i., 25.—*Ad partes.* "To play his part." A metaphor borrowed from the stage, where the actor is called when it is his turn to
appear.—*Nulla virtute.* "By not a single virtue." *Nulla* for *ne
ulla quidem.*—*Æger, solaque,* &c. "Enfeebled (by debauchery) in
body and mind, and strong in libidinous desire alone.—*Quantis porticibus.* "Beneath how large porticoes." The luxurious Romans
built long covered ways in their grounds, that they might not be
deprived of their exercise in bad weather.—*Quanta nemorum,* &c.
The allusion is now to the being borne along in a lectica through
shady groves.—*Vicina foro.* Land in the immediate vicinity of the
forum was of course exorbitantly dear.—*Ædes.* "Houses in the
same quarter." Supply, mentally, *vicinas foro.*—*Corruptor et idem
incestus.* "A seducer and one guilty at the same time of incest."
Such was the respect for religion, that the seducer of a Vestal vir-
gin was considered guilty of incest.—*Vittata.* Priests and priest-
esses wore fillets around the head.—*Jacebat.* "Forgot her vow."—
Sanguine adhuc vivo. "With the blood still living in her veins." A
Vestal who forgot her vow was buried alive in the Campus Scele-
ratus, just within the city walls, close to the Colline gate. Whether the Vestal alluded to in the text actually suffered is doubtful,
but Domitian did put Cornelia and some others to death in this
way.

10-13. *Sed nunc,* &c. "But now we are dealing with lighter
acts of delinquency." Supply *agimus.*—*Caderet sub judice morum.*
"He would have fallen under the cognizance of the judge of public
morals," *i. e.,* he would have been punished by an imperial censor.
The emperors were the *Magistri Morum,* or superintendents of public morals, discharging in this respect the functions of the earlier
censors. Domitian is here meant as the *judex morum.*—*Titio Seio-
que.* "A Titius and Seius, for instance." Titius and Seius (Lu-
cius Titus, Caius Seius) were fictitious personages, like our "John
Doe and Richard Roe," and, like them, inserted in all law processes.
Compare Plutarch, *Quæst. Rom.,* 30.—*Quid agas.* "What are you
to do with such a fellow?"—*Persona.* "His very person." The
idea appears to be this: What signifies satirizing such a wretch as

Crispinus, when his very person far exceeds in native loathsomeness his foulest deeds? One is at a loss how to treat him.

14–16. *Mullum sex millibus emit.* "He bought a sur-mullet for six thousand sesterces." Supply *sestertiorum.* This would amount to $234, the sestertius being equivalent to thirty-nine cents. The fish here meant is the red sur-mullet, or *mullus barbatus*, which was held in high estimation by the Roman epicures. Sur-mullets, in fact, were very plentiful and cheap, but seldom weighed above two pounds. In proportion, however, as they exceeded this, they grew valuable, until at last they reached the weight mentioned in the text, six pounds, and even went beyond it. At a later period they went out of fashion. In modern times they are but little esteemed, though their flesh is white, fat, and well-tasted.—*Æquantem sane,* &c. "Equalling, you must know, the sestertia to a like number of pounds." In 6000 *sestertii* there would be six *sestertia,* the *sestertium* (a sum of account, not a coin) being equivalent to 1000 *sestertii.* Observe the ironical force of *sane.—Ut perhibent.* Juvenal merely gives the story as he heard it, and refers for his authorities, in the present case, to the newsmongers of the day, who always make things greater than they really are. Some, however, think that the flatterers of Crispinus are here meant, who would, of course, magnify the size of the fish, and represent it as much larger than the truth.

17–20. *Consilium laudo artificis.* "I praise the cleverness of the contriver," *i. e.,* if he laid out this large sum upon the fish in order to make it a present to some childless old man, and thus secure, in return, the chief place in his will, or else to some powerful female friend, &c. But Crispinus, in truth, deserved no such praise, for, like a real glutton, he bought it for himself.—*Præcipuam in tabulis.* &c. "The principal place in the will of some childless old man," *i. e.,* the bulk of the property. The chief heir was named on the first tablet, or, as we would term it, the first page of the will. The tablets were frequently designated, as in the present instance, by the term *cera* alone ; thus *prima cera,* "first page ;" *altera cera,* "second page." Compare note on *Sat.* i., 56.—*Ulterior.* In the sense of *melior.—Magnæ amicæ.* "Some powerful female friend." —*Clauso latis specularibus antro.* "In some close cavern-like litter with its broad window-panes." The satire here is aimed at the affectation of the lady, who pretends to conceal herself in a vehicle which, from its splendour, must have attracted universal notice. Instead of glass, the Romans commonly used for the panes of their windows thin plates of mica, or Muscovy talc, called *lapis specularis.* None, however, but the rich could afford this.

21-26. *Multa videmus.* Supply *in Crispino.—Miser et frugi.* "Mean and thrifty compared with him."—*Apicius.* There were three notorious gluttons of this name. The first lived in the time of Sulla. The second and most renowned flourished under Tiberius. After spending a large fortune in gluttony, he destroyed himself. The third was a contemporary of Trajan. The treatise which we have at the present day, under the name of Apicius, and which is a sort of cook and confectioner's manual, was compiled at a later period by some one who prefixed to it the name of Apicius, in order to insure the circulation of the book.—*Hoc tu.* Supply *fecisti.* Some understand *pretio.—Succinctus patria,* &c. "Girt about in days of yore with your native papyrus," *i. e.,* you who were formerly an Egyptian slave, and girt round the loins with a garment made of papyrus. Some join *quondam* with *fecisti,* and render, "Did you do this in days of yore, when girt about," &c. The former, however, appears the more natural construction.—*Hoc pretium squamæ!* Supply *curuntur.* The term *squamæ* is contemptuously used instead of *pisces. — Provincia.* In some of the provinces which had become subject to Rome, one might purchase "a whole estate" (*agros*) for what was laid out on this sur-mullet.—*Appulia.* Land would be probably cheap in Apulia, from its barrenness and unwholesome air, and the prevalence of the wind Atabulus. Compare Horace, *Sat.* i., 5, 77.

27-32. *Glutisse.* "To have gorged." Hence our word "glutton," through the French. The low Latin verb is *glutto,* and the term is evidently derived from the sound made by the gurgling of liquor as it passes down the throat. He now proceeds to attack Domitian. — *Induperatorem.* Old form for *imperatorem,* applied here with laughable gravity. The form *induperator,* with its oblique cases, is used by Ennius and Lucretius, because *imperator,* &c., would be inadmissible in epic verse. *Induperator* obtains its first and second syllables from the Greek ἔνδον, old Latin *endo* or *indo.—Tot sestertia.* "So many sestertia," *i. e.,* a dish costing so many. The train of ideas is as follows : What kind of luxuries are we to suppose that the high and mighty Cæsar himself indulged in, when Crispinus, one of his court-buffoons, devoured so expensive a dish, and that not a principal one, but merely a side-dish, nor at a great banquet either, but an ordinary and moderate meal?—*Purpureus magni,* &c. "The purple-deck'd buffoon of the great palace devoured." Literally, "belched." The indigestion and crudities generated in the stomachs of those who fed on rich and high-seasoned food would occasion flatulence and nauseous eructations.—*Scurra.* The term "buffoon"

is here contemptuously applied to Crispinus instead of "courtier."
—*Magni palati.* Some keen-sighted commentators detect a pun
here.—*Princeps equitum.* "The leading man in the equestrian order," *i. e.,* in consequence of his wealth. Crispinus was also prefect
of the Prætorian guard, an office generally filled at this time by a
person of equestrian rank. We must not, however, confound the
title of *Princeps Equitum* with that of *Princeps Juventutis.* This latter was given to the probable successor to the throne.

Magna qui voce solebat, &c. "Who erst was wont in loud accents
to sell (about the streets), at retail, siluri from the same borough with
himself," *i. e.,* from Canopus or Alexandrea. The silurus (*Scheilan
Niloticus*) was a species of cured fish imported from Egypt, and
forming a common and cheap article of food for the lower orders.
Crispinus originally was a hawker of these. There is considerable
doubt about the true reading here. We have adhered, with Jahn, to
that of the MSS., which makes a very good sense. Some, however,
read *fricta de merce,* "from his stock of cured fish ;" others, *pacta
mercede,* "at fixed hire," *i. e.,* for fixed or regular wages, thus making Crispinus a hired hawker, not even the fish belonging to him ;
and others, again, give *Pharia de merce,* "from his Egyptian stock."
All these emendations, though ingenious, are quite unnecessary.
The reference is simply to selling by retail.

33-35. *Incipe Calliope.* A burlesque imitation of the usual mode
of invoking the Muses at the commencement of an epic poem. Calliope represents the whole nine, because presiding over heroic poetry, and the most distinguished one of the sisterhood. Compare
Hesiod., Theog., 79, where Calliope is called προφερεστάτη ἁπασέων.
—*Licet et considere.* "You may here even take a seat." A subject
of so much importance will require all the attention of the Muse,
and is not to be dispatched in a moment.—*Puellæ.* The poet calls
these antiquated deities young, just as in Lucian (*Icaromenipp.,* 28)
the question is sportively started why Apollo, though so very old,
has no beard : πῶς ἐν τοσούτῳ χρόνῳ ὁ Ἀπόλλων οὐ φύει πώγωνα.

36-43. *Semianimum.* To be pronounced here *sem'animum* for the
sake of the metre.—*Flavius ultimus.* "The last Flavius," *i. e.,* Domitian, the last of the Flavian line. The Flavian family was one
of no distinction before Vespasian's time. The emperors of this
line were Vespasian, Titus, and Domitian. — *Calvo Neroni.* "A
bald-headed Nero," *i. e.,* a second Nero, ay, and a bald one too.
Baldness was a very sore subject with Domitian, and was regarded
as unsightly by the Romans generally. On the stage it was one of
the distinguishing characteristics of parasites and other ridiculous

personages.—*Incidit.* Supply *in rete.*—*Adriaci spatium,* &c. For *Adriacus spatio mirabili rhombus.* Ravenna, in the Adriatic, was famous for its turbots, as Tarentum and the Lucrine Lake were for oysters; so also the Tiber for pikes, Sicily for *murænæ,* and Rhodes for the *elops.*—*Domum.* "The temple."—*Dorica Ancon.* Ancona, in the Picenian territory, was founded by a colony of Syracusans (who were of Doric origin), fleeing from the tyranny of Dionysius. —*Implevitque sinus.* "And filled its ample folds."

Neque enim minor, &c. "For neither had there stuck therein (on this occasion) a fish at all less in size than those which," &c., *i. e.,* the turbot caught on this occasion was fully as large as any of those which are produced in the Palus Mæotis, or *Sea of Azof.*—*Solibus.* "By the solar beams."—*Ad ostia.* "At the outlet." The Cimmerian Bosporus, now the Straits of *Jenikale,* connecting the Palus Mæotis with the Euxine.—*Desidia tardos.* "Slow of movement from previous inaction," *i. e.,* from having long lain torpid under the ice.

44–54. *Hoc monstrum.* "This prodigy of a fish."—*Pontifici summo.* All the emperors bore the title of chief pontiff (*Pontifex Maximus*). There is a covert allusion here to the striking discrepancy between the sanctity of the office and the viciousness of the present incumbent.—*Proponere.* "To offer for sale." Supply *venum.*—*Et litora.* "Even the very shores," *i. e.,* not merely the city.—*Dispersi protinus algæ,* &c. "The inspectors of sea-weed, scattered up and down, would immediately contest the point with the scantily-clad boatman." No particular class of officers are here meant, but merely prowling informers, who would pry into and turn up the very sea-weed; that is, would busy themselves about matters the most trifling and mean in their nature.—*Nudo.* "In his tunic only." Meant to indicate abject poverty.

Fugitivum dicere piscem. "To assert that the fish was a stray." This will give us some idea of the oppressive measures employed to fleece the people on the most groundless pretences, and yet under colour of legal claim.—*Vivaria.* Fish-ponds are here meant. Consult note on *Sat.* iii., 289.—*Palfurio.* Palfurius Sura, who had been a buffoon and parasite at the court of Nero; who was afterward expelled from the senate by Vespasian, but restored by Domitian. During his disgrace he applied himself to the study of the Stoic philosophy, and became distinguished for eloquence. He was conspicuous as one of the *delatores,* or public informers, under Domitian.—*Armillato.* Armillatus was another *delator* and sycophant, of much the same stamp with Palfurius.—*Conspicuum pulchrumque.*

"Remarkable and fine."—*Res fisci est.* "Belongs to the emperor's private purse." *Fiscus* here denotes the property which the emperor claimed as emperor. Compare *Dig.* xliii., 8, 2, § 4. "*Res fiscales quasi propriæ et privatæ Principis sunt.*"—*Donabitur ergo,* &c. "It shall be presented then (to the emperor), that it may not be utterly lost." The poor fisherman makes a merit of necessity, and resolves to carry the fish to Domitian, which he is otherwise sure of losing.

55–58. *Letifero autumno.* Acute and fatal diseases are frequent in autumn, more especially in Italy.—*Jam quartanam,* &c. "The sick now hoping for a quartan fever." The approach of winter was making the climate healthier, and those who had been labouring under a daily fever now began to entertain hopes of this being changed into a quartan one, which last, according to Celsus, kills off no patient : "*Nam quartana neminem jugulat.*" (*Cels., Med.,* iii., 15.) In accordance with this belief is the modern Italian saying, "*Febre quartana no far sonare campana,*" i. e., "a quartan fever does not make the bells toll," i. e., for a funeral.—*Deformis.* "Gloomy."—*Recentem.* "Fresh."—*Tamen hic properat.* Although the weather was so favorable for preserving the fish from being tainted, yet the poor fisherman made as much haste to reach the emperor's palace at Alba as if it had been now summer time.

59–60. *Utque lacus suberant.* "And when now the broad bosom of the lake lay beneath him." Observe the force of the plural in *lacus.* The reference is to the *Lacus Albanus,* lying at the foot of *Mons Albanus,* and now called *Lago di Albano.* It was about 14 miles to the southeast of Rome. On the side of the mountain, as it sloped upward from the lake, stood the villa of Domitian, his favourite place of residence, called *Arx Albana,* from its commanding situation, in line 144. The verb *suberant* denotes that the fisherman was ascending the high grounds towards the imperial villa, and that the bosom of the lake lay spread out below him. Some, less correctly, render the clause, "and when the lakes were near at hand." One MS. has *superant* for *suberant,* according to which *lacus* will be the accusative, and the reference will be to the fisherman and the *inquisitores* together : "And when now they are leaving the lake behind them." Heinrich, who condemns *suberant,* conjectures *properat* for *properant,* and refers it to the fisherman alone.—*Quanquam diruta.* Alba was destroyed, according to the Roman legend, by Tullus Hostilius, as a punishment for the treachery of its general, Metius Fufetius. The city was never rebuilt, but its temples were spared, and among them that of Vesta, containing a portion of the sacred fire brought from Troy to Italy.—*Vestam minorem.* "The lesser Vesta." Called "lesser" here, as compared with the splendour of her worship at Rome, which had been established there by Numa.

61-67. *Obstitit intranti.* "Impeded him on entering." This obstruction was occasioned by the *turba salutatrix* at the gates of the villa.—*Ut cessit.* "As they made way for him."—*Valvæ.* Most commonly used in the plural, like *fores,* because the doorway of every building of the least importance contained two doors folding together.—*Exclusi spectant,* &c. "The senators shut out behold the envied dainty let in." Observe the force of the plural in *opsonia.*— *Itur ad Atriden.* "He makes his way to (the Roman) Atrides." Another burlesque on the epic style. Domitian is the Roman Agamemnon, and the equal of the latter in imperious arrogance. *Itur* is taken impersonally.—*Picens.* "He of Picenum." Ancona, as before remarked, stood in the Picenian territory.—*Majora.* "What is too great.—*Genialis.* "As one peculiarly joyous." A *dies genialis* was one on which it was deemed right to give loose to festivity, and to offer to one's genius libations of wine, incense, flowers, &c. Hence to indulge in hilarity was not unfrequently expressed by "*genio indulgere,*" "*genium curare*" or "*placare.*"—*Propera stomachum laxare saginis.* "Hasten to relieve your stomach of the dainties with which it is now loaded." Literally, "from its crammings" or "stuffings." This relief was usually obtained by means of emetics.—*Tua in secula.* "For thy age," *i. e.,* for thy reign.

68-70. *Ipse capi voluit.* The very fish itself was ambitious of being taken, in order to gratify the palate of so renowned a monarch.— *Quid apertius?* &c. "What could be more fulsome? and yet the great man's crest arose." This piece of flattery, which some would have thought too transparent to have been received, yet pleased Domitian, and gratified his pride. The metaphor in *cristæ surgebant* is taken from the appearance of a cock when he is pleased, and struts and sets up his comb, just as the opposite idea is expressed by the word "crestfallen." Some commentators, however, make the words "*Quid apertius?*" to be uttered by the fisherman, not by the poet, and then refer "*et tamen illi,*" &c., not to Domitian, but to the turbot. The meaning will then be, "What is more evident (than that it actually did wish this to happen)? and yet (at the very moment when the fisherman said this) the fish (in anger at being taken) erected the fins on its back."

71-73. *Sed deerat pisci,* &c. The poet now goes on to inform us that they had no "dish" capacious and deep enough to contain this large turbot, so as to dress it whole. The *patina* was a deep dish, sometimes bowl, of earthenware, rarely of bronze. It was especially used in cooking when the articles of diet were to be accompanied with sauce or fluid.—*Vocantur ergo in consilium proceres.* There can not be a stronger instance of the capricious insolence with which the tyrants of Rome treated the servile and degenerate senate than their being summoned on such an occasion as this.—*Quos oderat ille.* He hated them from a consciousness of those feelings with which they could not but regard him.—*Miseræ magnæque pallor amicitiæ.* "The paleness engendered by wretched friendship with the great," *i. e.*, the paleness engendered by dread of his capricious cruelty.

74–79. *Clamante Liburno.* "The Liburnian making proclamation." The Liburnian here filled the office of an *admissionalis.* These *admissionales* were chamberlains at the imperial court, and introduced persons into the presence of the emperor. They were divided into four classes, the chief officer of each being called *proximus admissionum,* and the *proximi* being under a *magister admissionum,* or grand chamberlain. The *admissionales* were usually freedmen. On the present occasion, a native of Liburnia fills the office. The Liburnians also, as we have already seen, were usually selected at Rome as litter-carriers.—*Jam sedit.* "He has already taken his seat," *i. e.*, Domitian has already taken his seat on the throne, and awaits the presence of the Senate on important business admitting of no delay.—*Abolla.* The Roman lawyers, in the time of the empire, wore the larger *abolla,* in common with the philosophers of the day. (Consult note on *Sat.* iii., 102.) This reminds us of the modern form of expression by which the members of the legal profession are still called "the gentlemen of the long robe."—*Pegasus.* A Roman jurist under Domitian, one of the followers or pupils of Proculus. Nothing is positively known of any writings of his, though the *Senatus consultum Pegasianum,* passed in the time of Vespasian, when Pegasus was consul suffectus with Pusio, probably took its name from him. He was now *Præfectus Urbi.*

Attonitæ positus, &c. "Lately set as farm-bailiff over the astounded city." The *villicus* was a slave who had the superintendence in chief of all the stock and business of a farm, the supervision of the other slaves, &c. Rome is now regarded by Domitian, in his insolent despotism, as nothing but a large farm or domain, crowded with slaves, and the office of prefect of the city, so important under good emperors, now shorn of all its power, become, in fact, nothing more than that of superintendent of farm-slaves, &c. Hence the peculiar force of *attonitæ*, the city being lost in stupid amazement at the overbearing tyranny of Domitian.—*Tunc.* "In those days," *i. e.*, under a Domitian and others like him.—*Optimus.* Supply *erat.*—*Sanctissimus.* "Most conscientious."—*Omnia tractanda inermi justitia.* "That all things ought to be administered by justice unarmed." He was a time-server, not daring to wield the sword of justice with vigour; for, since it was impossible to punish the greater criminals, he thought it but fair to connive at petty offences.

80-92. *Crispi jucunda senectus.* "The pleasant old age of Crispus," *i. e.*, Crispus, that pleasant old man. Vibius Crispus was another worthy but cautious man, and remarkable for his numerous good sayings. Among these last was the well-known one, when he was asked whether there was any one with Domitian. "No," he replied, "not even a single fly." Crispus was an orator, of great wealth and influence, and a contemporary of Quintilian, by whom some fragments of his speeches are preserved. His orations were remarkable for their pleasant and elegant style.—*Cujus erant mores,* &c. "Whose character was, like his eloquence, all mildness of sentiment," *i. e.*, the mild and pleasing tone of his private character was like that of his mode of speaking in public.—*Regenti.* "To one ruling over," *i. e.*, Domitian.—*Quis comes utilior.* Supply *fuisset.*— *Clade et peste sub illa.* "Beneath that bane and pest of mankind." The reference is to Domitian, not, as some think, to the times themselves.—*Violentius.* "More swayed by wild and momentary impulse." Compare the explanation of Forcellini : "Iracundius, et offendi facilius." Gifford renders it by "ticklish."—*Loquuturi.* "Though only going to speak."—*Pendebat.* "Was all the while at stake."—*Vitam impendere vero.* "To spend life for truth," *i. e.*, to sacrifice life for truth. This was Rousseau's favourite maxim, excepting that with him *vero* meant the true in nature and in life, as opposed to what is untrue and deceptive. — *Octogesima solstitia.* "Eighty summers." Literally, "His eightieth solstices." *Solstitium* denotes "the summer solstice," as distinguished from *bruma,* "the winter solstice," but is here put, by synecdoche, for the summer itself. The Delphin editor makes *solstitia* here mean the *two* solstices (winter and summer) of each year, and equivalent, therefore, to *annos.*—*His armis.* He means the temporizing arts of dissimulation, taciturnity, and obsequiousness.

93-97. *Acilius.* M. Acilius Glabrio, of whom nothing more is known. — *Juvene.* M. Acilius Glabrio, son of the preceding, and who had been consul with Trajan in A.D. 91. To gain the favour of Domitian (some say at his command), he fought as a gladiator in the amphitheatre attached to the emperor's villa at Alba, and slew a lion of unusual size; but the applause which he received for this feat excited the envy of Domitian, who first banished him, and afterward put him to death.—*Olim.* "For a long time back." In the sense of *jamdudum.* (Consult note on *Sat.* iii., 144.)—*In nobilitate.* "In the case of our nobility," *i. e.,* in one of noble birth. They would be cut off by the reigning tyrant on the slightest suspicion.—*Fraterculus esse gigantis.* "The little brother of some giant." The giants (γηγενεῖς) were fabled to be the sons of Terra, and therefore their little brother would be a *Terræ filius* also, that is, an obscure person of the meanest origin, owing his existence, like a mere mushroom, to the earth. The term *fraterculus* also is meant to have a peculiar force, and to denote lowliness of size as superadded to lowliness of birth.

98-102. *Ursos figebat.* This he did in the hunting-matches frequently exhibited by Domitian. His combat with the lion, already referred to, would seem to have been prior to this, and it is probable that, in his bear-hunts, he counterfeited insanity in order to escape death at the hands of the emperor.—*Numidas.* For *Numidicos.* Pliny (*H. N.*, viii., 54) denies that bears are produced in Africa. But consult, on the opposite side, Herodotus (ii., 67; iv., 191) and Strabo (xvii., p. 828).—*Artes Patricias.* The artifices to which the Roman patricians disgracefully had recourse, in order to save their lives.—*Priscum illud,* &c. "That primitive cunning of thine." It is here called "primitive," because it would not pass current now, in the days of Domitian. The allusion is to the well-known story of Brutus having counterfeited idiocy in order to escape the fate of his elder brother, who had been put to death by Tarquin.—*Barbato imponere regi.* "To impose upon an old-fashioned king." Literally, "a bearded" one, *i. e.,* a king belonging to old and simple times, and therefore more simple and credulous than one of the present day. It was 444 years before barbers were introduced into Rome. They first came from Sicily.

103-105. *Nec melior vultu.* "Nor better of look," *i. e.,* equally dejected and pale of visage.—*Quamvis ignobilis.* He had no nobility of birth to bring him into danger, but then he had offences to answer for, which made the risk fully equal.—*Rubrius.* Rubrius Gallus is meant, who had assisted in suppressing the insurrection among the soldiers after the fall of Otho, and whom Vespasian had subsequently sent against the Sarmatæ.—*Offensæ veteris,* &c. The scholiast says that he seduced an imperial princess named Julia, the daughter of Titus.—*Et tamen improbior*, &c. "And yet more lost to shame than the satire-writing Nero," *i. e.*, more abandoned and profligate than even Nero himself had been, who was so hardened in guilt as to have written a satire on Quintianus Afranius, a senator of dissolute life, in which he taxed him with the very excesses of which he himself was guilty.

106-111. *Montani.* Curtius Montanus, described here as a corpulent epicure and parasite, enjoyed a fair reputation in early life. His unwieldy paunch prepares us here for the prominent part which he is to bear in the debate.—*Matutino sudans amomo.* "Reeking with morning unguent," *i. e.*, with perfume, though so early in the day.—*Amomo.* The amomum was a shrub, with a white flower, from which a very costly perfume was made. It grew, according to Pliny, in India, Armenia, Media, and Pontus. Its most common epithet, however, is *Assyrium.* This perfume was one of the ingredients used in embalming; hence the allusion in *funera.*—*Pompeius.* Of this individual nothing farther is known.—*Tenui jugulos*, &c. "In severing men's throats with insinuating whisper," *i. e.*, by means of the secret accusations against them, which he whispered into the imperial ear.—*Fuscus.* Cornelius Fuscus was slain with a great part of his army in an expedition against the Dacians. Domitian had intrusted him with the command. He had previously, however, distinguished himself under Vespasian.—*Dacis.* Dacia, after its boundaries had been fixed under Trajan, answered to what is now the *Banat of Temesvar; Hungary*, east of the *Theiss;* the whole of *Transylvania;* the *Bukowina;* the southern point of *Galicia, Moldavia* west of the *Pruth*, and the whole of *Wallachia.*—*Marmorea meditatus*, &c. After having studied the art of war in a marble villa, and not in a camp.

112-117. *Veiento.* Fabricius Veiento had been banished in the reign of Nero, A.D. 62, for having published several libels. He afterward returned to Rome, and became, in the reign of Domitian, one of the most infamous informers and flatterers of that tyrant.—*Catullo.* Catullus Messalinus had been governor of the Libyan Pentapolis under Vespasian and Titus, where he treated the Jewish provincials with extreme cruelty. He was, in consequence, recalled, but eluded the punishment due to his crimes through Domitian's interest with his father and brother. Under Domitian he became notorious as a *delator.* Josephus represents him as dying in extreme torments, aggravated by an evil conscience. Juvenal calls him "blind" (*cæcus*), and the younger Pliny also speaks of him as "*luminibus captus*," but he was probably not quite blind, other-

wise his praise of the turbot would have displeased rather than gratified the tyrant.—*A ponte.* "From the bridge," *i. e.*, from having
been once a common beggar. Beggars were accustomed to station
themselves on bridges, where they could ply their vocation more
effectually among the crowds that constantly passed by.—*Dignus
Aricinos*, &c. "A fit person to play the mendicant at Aricinian
axles." Aricia, an ancient city of Latium, was situated on ground
sloping upward from the Appian Way, at the base of Mons Albanus,
and sixteen miles from Rome. Mendicants were wont to frequent
this part of the road, since vehicles, in ascending or descending,
would have to move more slowly, and would therefore be more exposed to their importunities.—*Blandaque jactaret basia.* "And to
throw bland kisses," *i. e.*, to kiss his hand in coaxing style. Juvenal
means that he would have been a fit person to remain a beggar all
his life.

118-121. *Plurima.* "Very many things in its praise."—*At illi
dextra*, &c. "Whereas the enormous fish lay all the while on his
right." *Belua* and *bestia* both denote irrational animals, but *belua*
carries with it the additional idea of great size, indicating a large,
unwieldy animal, as the elephant, the whale, and principally sea-
monsters.—*Sic.* "In like manner," *i. e.*, without seeing them dis-
tinctly.—*Cilicis.* "Of the Cilician gladiator." Some skilful gladiator, a native of Cilicia, is here meant, and one who appears to
have been a favourite of Domitian.—*Pegma.* "The stage-ma-
chinery." A species of frame-work, raised or depressed at pleasure
by means of balance-weights. These machines always formed a
favourite exhibition, and persons were suddenly raised by them to a
great height. Slaves and malefactors were sometimes thrown from
them to the wild beasts.—*Ad velaria.* "To the awning." The
Roman theatres were open at the top. During the performance,
however, they were often covered with a large awning, made to
draw by means of ropes and pulleys attached to a number of masts
fixed into the outer wall.

122-124. *Non cedit.* "Does not yield to him in admiration."—
Ut fanaticus, &c. "Like one inspired, when smitten by thy stimulating influence." *Œstrus* properly means a species of stinging in-
sect, perhaps the *Œstrus Bovis*, or "Breeze," though some make it
merely a wasp or stinging-bee. It is here used figuratively for the
stinging or stimulating influence, as it were, of divine inspiration.—
Bellona. The main object for which Bellona was worshipped and
invoked was to grant a warlike spirit and enthusiasm which no enemy could resist. Her priests, when they offered sacrifices to her,

had to wound their own arms or legs, and either to offer up the blood or drink it themselves, in order to become inspired with a warlike enthusiasm. This, however, was afterward softened down into a mere symbolic act. These priests were called *Bellonarii*, and hence *fanaticus* is here the same in fact as *Bellonarius*.

125-128. *Regem aliquem*. Probably, as Gifford suggests, a sarcastical allusion to *Decebalus*, whose name could not be brought into verse, but whose exploits were the opprobrium of Domitian's reign. — *Temone*. The pole of the car put for the car itself. — *Arviragus*. This British monarch is otherwise unknown. Later legends tell of an Arviragus converted by Joseph of Arimathea. Another is introduced into Shakspeare's Cymbeline.—*Peregrina est bellua*. One thing was certain, that, .nasmuch as the fish was a foreign one, it denoted some foreign conquest.—*Sudes*. "The sharp fins." These sharp fins (literally "stakes") portended the spears which Domitian was to drive into the backs of his conquered foes.—*Hoc defuit unum*, &c. He was so diffuse in his language that nothing, in fact, was wanting to complete his history of the fish, except to tell where it had been produced, and how old it was.

129-134. *Quidnam igitur censes?* Domitian now speaks, and proceeds to put the question to the assembled senators individually. Observe the employment of *censeo*, the official term on such occasions.—*Conciditur?* "Is it to be cut up?" Present used for the future, in a case requiring immediate action. (*Madvig*, § 339., *Obs.* 2.)—*Testa alta*. "A deep dish."—*Quæ tenui muro*, &c. "Which shall inclose its spacious circumference with a thin wall," *i. e.*, it is to be a large and deep round dish, with thin sides. The thinness of the earthenware, according to Pliny, constituted its excellence.— *Prometheus*. The case urgently demands some potter no less cunning in his craft than was Prometheus of old, who gave proof of his skill by forming the first man out of clay.—*Argillam atque rotam*, &c. Clay is the material, and a solid wheel, revolving horizontally, the engine on which the potter forms his ware.—*Figuli tua castra sequantur*. To guard, not against the foe, but against large fish being spoiled by delay in cooking.

135-142. *Noverat ille*, &c. He was an old court-glutton, and well acquainted with the luxury of former emperors.—*Noctesque Neronis*, &c. "And the nights of Nero now half spent." Nero, according to Suetonius, used to prolong his banquets from midday to midnight. — *Aliamque famem*. "And a second appetite." Suetonius says that this was sought to be procured by warm baths in winter, and cold baths in summer. As already remarked, however, emetics were frequently employed for the purpose.—*Falerno.* The Falernian was a fiery, full-bodied wine of Campania.—*Usus edendi.* " Experience in eating." No one was a greater connoisseur in good eating than Montanus. — *Circeiis nata forent,* &c. All the localities mentioned in the text were famed for their oysters. Circeii was an ancient town of Latium, on the promontory Circeium, and was fabled to have derived its name from its having been the residence of Circe. The " Lucrine rock" indicates the *Lacus Lucrinus,* in Campania, between Baiæ and Puteoli. By the "Rutupian bed" is meant Rutupiæ or Rutupæ, now *Richborough,* a port-town of the Cantii, in the southeastern part of Britain.—*Et semel aspecti,* &c. " And he told the shore of a sea-urchin looked at but once," *i. e.,* at the first glance.

143–148. *Misso.* For *dimisso.* — *Albanam in arcem.* " Into his lofty Alban abode," *i. e.,* his villa situate on rising ground. Compare note on line 59.—*Dux magnus.* " The great chief." Said ironically of Domitian.—*Cattis.* The Catti were a powerful German tribe, occupying what answers now to *Hesse* and the adjacent countries.—*Sygambris.* The Sygambri were another powerful German tribe, dwelling at this period between the Lippe and the Sieg.— *Dicturus.* "In order to communicate." Both the Catti and Sygambri were troublesome enemies to Domitian. He appears, however, to have gained some advantages over the former in A.D. 84. —*Anxia præcipiti,* &c. " Some alarming dispatch had come on hurried wing." The words *præcipiti penna* are merely figurative, and do not refer, as some erroneously suppose, to any peculiar custom on the part of the Romans in transmitting intelligence. (*Casaub., ad loc.*)

149–153. *Tota illa tempora sævitiæ.* The last three years of Domitian's reign are especially meant, forming as they do one of the most frightful periods that occur in the history of man. We have given *illa* here as a more emphatic reading than the common *ille.*— *Sed periit.* Domitian was assassinated in A.D. 96, in the 45th year of his age, and the 16th of his reign. He was succeeded by Nerva. — *Cerdonibus.* " By men of lowly birth." Equivalent to *ignobilibus.* *Cerdo* properly means one who works for hire, a day-labourer, a low mechanic, and then a person of lowly condition generally. The assassins of Domitian were persons of lowly origin, officers of his court, whom he had intended to put to death himself; and hence the severe reflection on the pusillanimity of the patricians implied by the closing lines of the satire. The tyrant shed the blood of the noblest families with impunity; but when he began to single out victims from the lower orders, his own ruin ensued.—*Hoc nocuit.* " This proved fatal."— *Lamiarum.* The "Lamiæ" were a distinguished family of the Ælian gens, who claimed descent from the mythic hero Lamus. No member of this family is, however, mentioned till the end of the republic, but under the empire it was reckoned one of the noblest families in Rome. An individual of this ancient house was one of Domitian's victims; but here the Lamiæ stand for the Roman nobles in general.

SATIRE V.

ARGUMENT.

Under pretence of advising one Trebius to abstain from the table of Virro, a man of rank and fortune, Juvenal takes occasion to give a spirited detail of the insults and mortifications to which the poor were subjected by the rich at those entertainments to which, on account of the political connections subsisting between patrons and clients, it was sometimes thought necessary to invite them. (*Evans.*)

1–5. *Propositi.* "Of the course you have proposed to yourself," *i. e.*, of leading the life of a parasite.—*Bona summa.* "The chief good."—*Aliena quadra.* "At another's table," *i. e.*, at his expense. *Quadra* means properly a square table as distinguished from a round one, the former being the earliest model, the latter of most common usage.—*Sarmentus.* Originally a Tuscan slave, afterward taken into his train by Mæcenas, whom he had pleased by his buffoonery, and finally admitted into the household of Augustus, with whom he became a favourite. In the decline of life he was reduced to great destitution by his dissipation and extravagance.—*Iniquas Cæsaris,* &c. "At the unequal board of Augustus." Unequal, from the marked difference in the treatment of the different guests. —*Nec vilis Galba.* "Nor a Galba, contemptible though he was." The allusion is to Apicius Galba, a noted buffoon and parasite in the days of Augustus and Tiberius.—*Quamvis jurato,* &c. A parasite must be so lost to all sense of honour and gentlemanly feeling that one would hesitate to believe him even under oath.

6–11. *Frugalius.* "More easily satisfied."—*Hoc tamen ipsum,* &c. "Suppose, however, even this little itself to have failed," *i. e.*, suppose a man to want even this little that is absolutely needed.— *Nulla crepido vacat?* "Is there no raised footway vacant?" *i. e.*, where you can take your stand and beg. *Crepido* properly means

any raised basement upon which other things are built or supported,
as of a temple, altar, obelisk, &c. Here, however, it denotes the
trottoir, or raised causeway for foot-passengers on the side of a
Roman road or street. An illustration of this is given in the ruins
of Pompeii.—*Pons.* Consult note on *Sat.* iv., 115.—*Tegetis.* The
teges was a coarse rug worn by beggars.—*Dimidia brevior.* "Shorter by the half."—*Tantine injuria cœnœ?* "Do you set such a value
on a supper so insulting?" *i. e.*, will you endure for the sake of a
supper the gross contumelies that await you at the great man's table? Literally, "Is the insult of a supper of so much value (in
your eyes)?"—*Jejuna.* "Craving."—*Pol.* "I' faith." We have
adopted here the elegant emendation of Ruperti. Many of the
MSS. give *quum possis honestius,* which violates the measure, the
final syllable of *possis* being long. The Bipont edition reads *poscis*
in the sense of *mendicas.* Jahn and others prefer *possit,* making
fames the subject.—*Illic.* The beggar's stand, either on the foot-
pavement or the bridge.—*Tremere.* "To shiver."—*Et sordes farris,* &c. "And munch a filthy piece of dog's bread." The ancients were accustomed to make a coarse kind of bran-bread, which
they broke up and mixed with dog's-meat, as food for their animals.
(Compare the Latin term *canicœ.*)

12–15. *Fige.* "Bear it in mind." Supply *animo.* So in vulgar
English : "Regard it as a *fixed* fact."—*Discumbere jussus.* "When
invited to take a place at table." Literally, "to recline (at table),"
in allusion to the Roman mode of reclining at meals. We would
say, "When asked to dinner."—*Mercedem solidam.* "The entire
recompense," *i. e.*, payment in full.—*Veterum officiorum.* He means
"the services" rendered by the client in waiting upon and escort-
ing the patron. These are called *veterum,* "of long standing," as
having been rendered for so many days and months beforehand.—
Fructus. All you get by it.—*Imputat hunc rex.* "The great man
sets this down to your account." He makes a merit of it ; he claims
your gratitude for it.

16–23. *Si libuit.* "If it has come into his head." Expressive of
indifference.—*Adhibere.* "To invite." Supply *mensœ.*—*Tertia ne
vacuo,* &c. "Lest the third cushion should be unoccupied on the
unfilled couch." Literally, "should be idle." The third cushion
on the lowest couch is meant, the least honourable place at the banquet, and one only occupied by the client on the present occasion,
because there was no one else to fill it. *Culcita* properly means the
mattress placed on the frame-work of the couch, but it is taken here
for the pillow or cushion that separated the individual guests on

each couch, and against which they reclined.— *Una simus.* The words of the patron, inviting his client in a familiar way, in order to enhance the obligation.— *Trebius.* The parasite with whom Juvenal is remonstrating.— *Et ligulas dimittere.* "And to let his shoe-lappets hang down untied," *i. e.,* and to hurry away without stopping to tie his shoes. The *ligula* was the lappet on each side of the shoe, through which the strings (*corrigiæ*) that tied it on the foot passed.

Ne tota salutatrix, &c. "Lest by this time the whole saluting crowd may have completed their round," *i. e.,* lest he may be too late for the time of morning levee. The text does not mean that clients waited upon several patrons in succession, which would be directly contrary to Roman custom, but that clients were accustomed to *go round,* each to his particular patron. These visits combined form what is here called *orbem.* Compare Lucian, *Ni ...,* 22 : περιθέοντες ἐν κύκλῳ τὴν πόλιν.—*Sideribus dubiis.* "When the stars are now beginning to fade." This is intended to mark a very early period of the morning.—*Aut illo tempore,* &c. "Or else, at that time when the chill wains of slow Boötes are alone revolving." This marks a somewhat later period of the morning, though still quite early, when the other stars have disappeared, and only the most northern constellations are still seen moving around. In the language of poetry, the other stars have sunk beneath the ocean, but Boötes and the two Bears, inasmuch as they never sink below our horizon, still appear in the heavens, marking, therefore, the period immediately preceding the dawn. Compare Statius, *Theb.,* iii., 683, *seq.*—*Frigida.* Because so near the north pole. — *Sarraca.* In the plural, because both the Bears or Wains are meant.—*Bootæ.* The constellation of Bootes ("the herdsman") is frequently called Arctophylax ("the guard of the bear").

24-29. *Quod sucida nolit,* &c. "Which wool just shorn will refuse to imbibe," *i. e.,* too thick and worthless to be used even for washing out the grease from newly-shorn wool. Compare *Varro, R. R.,* ii., 11, 6. This is the common way of explaining the words of the text. It is better, however, to regard them as referring to the medical practice of antiquity, in which freshly-shorn wool was laid upon wounds after having been made to imbibe oil, or vinegar, or wine, according as a soothing or stimulating effect was sought to be obtained. Compare *Celsus,* viii., 3.—*De conviva Corybanta videbis.* The bad wine will disorder your head, and you will become as frantic as one of the Corybantes, or priests of Cybele.—*Proludunt.* "From the prelude of the fray." — *Mappa.* A table-napkin is meant. In ordinary cases, the host did not furnish his guests with napkins, but each person brought his own *mappa* with him, and occasionally carried away in it some of the delicacies which he could not consume at table, a practice of common occurrence also among the modern Italians.—*Inter vos*, &c. The contest will be between the clients, or parasites, on the one hand, and the freedmen on the other, the latter being sometimes admitted to the lower end of great men's tables.—*Saguntina.* The earthenware of Saguntum, in Spain, was in high repute. These earthen vessels, however, were only for the use of the guests. Compare line 38, *seq.* The *lagena* was a large earthenware vessel, two handled, and having a full and swelling body like a gourd, a short neck, and a foot to stand upon.

30–32. *Capillato diffusum consule.* "Drawn off (from the dolium into the amphora) under some consul with long hair." The date of the vintage was always marked on the amphora by the names of the consuls then in office. In the present instance a very old wine is meant, made, poetically speaking, many ages before, when the primitive Romans wore the hair uncut. (Consult the note on *Sat.* iv., 102.) In making their wine, the Romans first put the must into *dolia;* the choice kinds of wine were drawn off into amphoræ. The *dolia* were never of wood, hooped tubs of wood being, according to Pliny, employed in cold climates only.—*Tenet.* "Keeps to himself."—*Bellis socialibus.* The Social war occurred B.C. 90–88. But nothing more is meant here than a fine old wine. Although the ancients did keep their wines to a very great age. Thus, for instance, the famous Opimian wine could boast an antiquity of 200 years in Pliny's day. (*II. N.*, xiv., 14.)—*Cyathum.* "Even a small cup of it." The cyathus was properly the twelfth of a pint.—*Cardiaco amico.* "To a friend afflicted with the heartburn." This was termed *cardiacus morbus ;* in Greek, καρδιαλγία, and the only remedy for it was wine. Hence Seneca (*Ep.* 15) remarks: *"Bibere et sudare cardiaci vita est ;"* and also Celsus (3, 19): *"Cardiacis maximum remedium vinum esse putatur."*

33–37. *Albanis de montibus.* The Alban wine was produced from the hills that rise to the south of Rome, and which are in view from the city. It is ranked by Pliny as only a third-rate wine, but, from the commendation bestowed upon it by Horace and Juvenal, we must suppose it to have been in considerable repute, especially when matured by long keeping. It was sweet and thick when new, but became dry when old, seldom ripening properly before the fifteenth year.—*Setinis.* The Setine hills were in the vicinity of Setia, a town of Latium, in the east of the Pontine marshes. The Setine was a delicate white wine, and a favourite with Augustus, who prized it as being of all kinds the least apt to injure the stomach.— *Titulum.* "Date." The date of the vintage was either marked on the amphora, as we have already stated, or, when the jars were of glass, little tickets were suspended from them, indicating this.— *Multa fuligine.* "By the accumulated soot." The soot produced by the smoke of the apotheca, where the wine had been placed to ripen.—*Quale coronati,* &c. On days of particular rejoicing, the Romans wore garlands at their carousals, in imitation of the Greeks. Pætus Thrasea, and his son-in-law, Helvidius Priscus, from their hatred of tyranny, used to keep the birth-days of the great republican leaders of Rome. The former was put to death, and the latter banished by Nero.—*Brutorum.* Three of the name are in fact referred to : L. Junius Brutus, the expeller of the Tarquins ; M. Junius Brutus, the chief conspirator with Cassius against Julius Cæsar ; and D. Junius Brutus, who, in the attempt to uphold the cause of freedom against Antony, was put to death by the latter.

38-45. *Heliadum crustas,* &c. "Cups incrusted with the tears of the Heliades, and phialæ all rough with the beryl." Literally, "incrustations of the tears," &c. The reference is to cups set with amber, standing in shallower vessels studded with gems. The *crustæ* were exquisitely wrought in relief, either of amber, as in the present instance, or else of gold and silver, and were fastened upon the surface of the vessels they were intended to adorn. The *phialæ* were shallow circular vessels, like the modern saucer. The term *phiala,* in fact, is only the Greek word φιάλη Latinized, the genuine Latin term being *patera.* Amber was fabled to have been produced by the tears shed on the banks of the Eridanus (*Po*) for the loss of their brother Phaethon by his sisters the Heliades, or daughters of the Sun (Ἥλιος), who were transformed into poplars.—*Virro.* The wealthy host.—*Custos affixus ibidem.* "A guard is fixed in that same quarter," *i. e.,* a slave is stationed as a guard in the same quarter where you are reclining at table.—*Qui numeret gemmas,* &c. Lest any should be missing, and lest you should try to pick them out.—*Da veniam.* Such precautions are excusable ; you must not be offended at them.—*Illic.* "There, on that cup," *i. e.,* there is a particularly bright jasper, which is universally admired, set on that cup.—*Gemmas.* Supply *digitis.*—*In vaginæ fronte.* "On the outside of his scabbard." Compare Virg., iv., 261, *seq.* "*Atque illi stellatus iaspide fulva Ensis erat.*" The allusion is to Æneas.— *Zelotypo juvenis,* &c. Æneas, whom Dido preferred to her other suitor, Iarbas, king of the Gætuli. (*Virg., Æn.,* iv., 36, &c.)

46–48. *Beneventani sutoris.* "Of the cobbler of Beneventum." This was Vatinius, one of the vilest and most hateful creatures of Nero's court, equally deformed in body and in mind. He was originally a shoemaker's apprentice, next earned his living as one of the lowest kind of *scurræ*, or buffoons, and finally obtained great power and wealth by accusing the most distinguished men in the state. A certain kind of drinking-cup, having four *nasi*, or "nozzles," bore the name of this Vatinius, probably because he brought them into fashion.—*Siccabis.* "Will drain."—*Et rupto poscentem,* &c. "And asking sulphur for the fractured glass," *i. e.*, calling for the aid of sulphur-cement to make it sound again. Cracked and fractured glass was repaired by means of a composition in which sulphur formed the main ingredient. Some give a different explanation to this clause, and make the poet refer to a cup so much broken as to be only fit to be exchanged for sulphur-matches, it being customary at Rome to exchange broken glass for these. This latter explanation, however, though the livelier one, seems less correct than the first, since the poet, in that event, would rather have employed *fracto*.

50–55. *Decocta.* "Boiled water." The water was first boiled, and then cooled by means of snow. This means of treating water is said to have been first introduced by Nero. (*Plin., H. N.,* xxxi., 23.) The snow was preserved in pits, somewhat like our modern ice-houses. Snow was also brought on table, and used for cooling the wine. The epithet *Geticis* is employed in the text in a general sense, equivalent to *Scythicis.* The Getæ were originally a Thracian people, bordering on Scythia.—*Poni.* The wine was not circulated round the table, but was placed before each guest.—*Aliam aquam.* "A different kind of water," *i. e.*, neither boiled nor iced.—*Gætulus cursor.* "A Gætulian running-footman." The *cursor* was a slave, kept by the rich to precede their carriages on foot, similar to the running footmen of modern times. One of this class is turned into a waiter for the poor client. By Gætulia was meant the interior of northern Africa, south of Mauritania, Numidia, and the region bordering on the Syrtes, reaching to the Atlantic on the west, and of very indefinite extent toward the east and south.—*Nigri Mauri.* "Of some blackamoor."—*Et cui per mediam,* &c. Because you might take him for some frightful spectre out of the tombs.—*Latinæ.* Supply *viæ*, and consult note on *Sat.* i., 120.

56–66. *Flos Asiæ.* The master of the feast, on the other hand, has for his attendant and cup-bearer a young and beautiful Asiatic boy, blooming as a flower, and purchased for a sum exceeding the

whole revenue of one of the old Roman kings.—*Tulli et Anci.* The
third and fourth kings of Rome.—*Omnia frivola.* "All the poor
goods and chattels," *i. e.*, poor and trifling in comparison.—*Gœtulum
Ganymedem,* &c. "Look behind you for your negro Ganymede," *i. e.*,
when you want your cup replenished, look to the "*cursor Gœtulus*"
to do it for you, not to the "*Flos Asiæ.*"—*Millibus.* Supply *sestertiorum.*—*Miscere.* "To mix wine." It was the duty of the *pincerna*
or *pocillator* to mix the wine in the crater, fill the cups, and hand
them round to the guests. The wines of the ancients were not only
inspissated by being long kept, but also highly seasoned with various aromatic ingredients, both of which causes rendered them unfit
for use until they had been diffused in a large quantity of water.—
Digna supercilio. "Is worthy of his supercilious air," *i. e.*, justifies
his supercilious and disdainful look, as far as waiting on you is concerned.—*Calidæ gelidæqua minister.* "As a server of warm and cold
water." Supply *aquæ.* The Romans had both hot and cold water
at their feasts, that the guests might be served with either, as they
preferred. A favourite drink was warm water mixed with wine, with
the addition of spices.—*Quodque aliquid poscas,* &c. He thinks himself the more entitled to be a guest than you. *Quod,* with the indicative or subjunctive, is employed after verbs indicating wonder, indignation, &c., in place of the accusative with the infinitive, in order
to denote more the reason of the feeling. (*Madrig,* § 397.)—*Maxima quæque domus,* &c. The servants in the mansions of the rich and
great take their cue from their masters; or, in other words, "Like
master, like man."

67–72. *Quanto murmure.* "With what grumbling."—*Vix fractum.* "Scarce broken by the mill." Supply *mola.* The reference
is to a kind of very coarse bread, with the grains of corn almost
entire. This is explained immediately after by the words *solidæ
farinæ.* It is incorrect to refer *vix fractum,* as most do, to the hardness of the bread, and the difficulty of breaking it while eating.
The allusion is here to coarseness of material; the hardness is referred to in the succeeding line.—*Quæ genuinum agitent.* "Intended only to worry the jaw-tooth." Observe the force of the subjunctive.—*Mollique siligine.* "Of the finest wheat flour." The *siligo* was
a species of very white wheat, from which a fine flour was made. It
is indigenous to Italy, from which country it was carried into Greece.
The Greek term σιλίγνων is formed from the Latin.—*Dextram cohibere.* From the fine white bread of the host.—*Salva sit artoptæ
reverentia.* "Let the respect due to the bread-mould be unimpair-
ed," *i. e.*, let all due respect be shown by you to the distinction

which the bread-mould makes between the kind of bread meant for you and that intended for the master of the house. For *artoptœ* the ordinary text has *artocopi*, "the cutter of the bread," which is the reading also of several MSS. We have preferred, however, *artoptœ*, with Heinrich and Jahn. By *artopta* was meant a kind of bread-mould, or bread-pan, in which the finest bread was baked, and from which it was served up hot. In one of the bakeries discovered at Pompeii, several loaves have been found apparently baked in moulds. They are round, flat, and about eight inches in diameter.

73–79. *Improbulum.* "A little impudent." — *Vis tu impleri.* "Won't you fill yourself." *Vis tu* is for *annon vis tu.* Consult Bentley, *ad Horat., Serm.*, ii., 6, 92. — *Canistris.* The *canistrum* was a large, flat, open basket, made of wicker-work, and without handles, particularly employed as a bread-basket. — *Scilicet hoc fuerat*, &c. This is the client's indignant soliloquy : "So, then, it was this, forsooth, on account of which," &c. This is all the requital I get for my slavish attendance on a rich and haughty patron ! Observe the peculiar employment of the pluperfect. This end I *had* proposed to myself. — *Per montem adversum*, &c. "Up the steep ascent of the bleak Esquiline." A hendiadys. The Esquiline Hill had a very steep ascent, and was bleak and cold at the top, especially in bad weather. — *Pœnula.* "My cloak." The *pœnula* was a round frock, with a hood, but otherwise entirely closed down the front; or sometimes with a slit reaching half way up from the bottom of the skirt in front, so that the flaps might be taken up and turned over the shoulder. It was worn over the tunic, particularly on journeys, and in the city during very cold or wet weather. It had no sleeves.

80–85. *Distendat.* "Seems to distend." It was so large that it seemed to stretch the dish in which it was served up. — *Squilla.* "The lobster." There were two kinds of fish known by this name, one which formed a dish of itself, the lobster, as here; the other of a small size, serving as sauce to other fish, and answering to our shrimps and prawns. — *Septa.* "Garnished." Literally, "hedged around." — *Asparagis.* Under the general name of asparagus are here meant, in fact, the young shoots of various edible plants. — *Qua cauda.* He seems to look down upon the company as though proud of his noble tail, which is the choicest part. — *Quum venit*, &c. He is borne on high by the hands of some tall attendant. The servitors at table were generally selected by the rich on account of their size. So the *lecticarii*, or litter-carriers. — *Dimidio constrictus*, &c. "A common crab, hemmed in with half an egg," *i. e.*, scantily garnished with half an egg sliced. — *Feralis cœna.* The ancients were accustomed to give a feast in honour of the dead, generally on the ninth day after the funeral. It was done to appease their shades, and consisted of a little milk, honey, water, wine, and olives. These articles were placed commonly at the entrance of the tomb. "A funeral supper," therefore, came to mean a very scanty one.—*Exigua patella.* Observe that *patella,* although a diminutive itself, is made still more so by the epithet *exigua.*

86-91. *Venafrano.* Supply *oleo.* Venafrum, a town in the northern part of Samnium, near the River Vulturnus, and on the confines of Latium, was famed for its olives and oil.—*Pallidus.* "All sickly of aspect." The cabbage had turned yellow from long keeping, and had then been carelessly boiled. But, what is still worse, the oil to be poured over it is quite rancid, and fit only to be used for lamps.—*Illud.* Supply *oleum.*—*Vestris alveolis.* "'To your sauce-boats." *Alveolus* signifies any wooden vessel made hollow. Here it may be understood of wooden trays or sauce-boats, in which the oil was brought, that was to be poured over the cabbage. — *Canna.* "Some reed-boat," *i. e.,* some light vessel. *Canna* is properly a boat or small vessel, the framework of which is made of reeds or cane covered with skin.—*Micipsarum.* Put figuratively for *Numidarum.* Micipsa was king of Numidia, and the eldest of the sons of Masinissa.—*Cum Bocchare.* "With a native of Africa." Literally, "with a Bocchar." *Bocchare* for *Afro,* a name of an individual put again for a whole race. Bocchar or Bocchus was king of Mauritania, and father-in-law of Jugurtha, with whom at first he made war against the Romans, but whom he afterward delivered up to Sulla, the quæstor of Marius. Some, however, make Bocchar here to be the name of a certain Numidian living at Rome in the time of Juvenal.—*Quod tutos etiam,* &c. This line is deservedly regarded by many as spurious, not only on account of the awkward repetition of *quod,* but also because it does not appear in some of the best MSS. It was interpolated probably by one of the scholiasts, who wished to explain why no one would bathe at Rome with a native of Africa, because this oil, with which they anointed themselves, rendered their persons exceedingly offensive, so much so, in fact, that it even secured the Numidian snake-charmers from harm.

92-98. *Mullus.* Consult note on *Sat.* iv., 14.—*Tauromenitanæ rupes.* "The rocks of Tauromenium." This city was situate on the eastern coast of Sicily. The modern name is *Taormina.*—*Omne nostrum mare peractum est.* "All our own waters have been ransacked." Literally, "Have been gone through with." The sea on both sides of Italy is meant.—*Gula.* "Gluttony."—*Macello.* "'The market,"

i. e., those who supply the market.—*Proxima*. "The seas immediately adjacent." Supply *maria*.—*Crescere*. "To reach its full
growth."—*Instruit focum*. "Has to supply our kitchen."—*Illinc*.
From these foreign provinces of ours.—*Captator*. "The legacy-
hunter."—*Aurelia vendat*. "Aurelia may sell again." A rich childless widow, who had so many presents of fine fish made to her by
Lenas, and others of his tribe, that she could not use them all at her
own table, and therefore gratified her avarice by selling part of them
again.

99-106. *Murœna*. "A lamprey." A species of eel found in the
Mediterranean, and held in high estimation by the Roman epicures.
They were reared with the greatest care, and at an enormous expense, in artificial fish-ponds. This fish must not be confounded,
however, with the ordinary lamprey or *petromyzon*.—*Gurgite Siculo*.
"The Sicilian whirlpool," *i. e.*, the straits between Sicily and Italy,
now *Faro di Messina*.—*Dum se continet Auster*, &c. The fisherman
takes advantage of calm weather to fish in this dangerous locality.
—*Carcere*. The cave of Æolus.—*Mediam Charybdim*. "The very
centre of Charybdis."—*Longœ cognata colubrœ*. "A relation of the
long snake." Akin both in appearance and in name, *anguilla* being
the diminutive of *anguis*.—*Aut glacie adspersus*, &c. "Or a pike from
the Tiber, sprinkled with spots by the ice." Supply *lupus*. A common kind of river-fish is meant. For fish of this kind the Roman
epicures cared nothing, particularly when they were spotted. These
spots were commonly ascribed to the winter's cold.—*Vernula riparum*,
&c. "A native-born slave of the river's banks, fattened by the rushing sewer," *i. e.*, fed on the filth of the common sewer. Seven rapid
currents of water are said to have been introduced by Agrippa into
the sewers under the city. Hence the epithet *torrente* in the text.
The pike was esteemed in exact proportion to the distance it was
caught from the common sewers of Rome. Compare Horace, *Sat.*,
ii., 2, 31.—*Cryptam*. "Unto the dark-arched drain." The fish
was accustomed to explore these dark recesses in search of its loathsome food.—*Suburœ*. Consult note on *Sat.* iii., 5.

107-113. *Ipsi*. Supply *Virroni*.—*Facilem*. "An attentive."—
Nemo petit, &c. These words are addressed to Virro. No one expects from you such presents as used to be sent to their humble
friends in former days by patrons of known liberality.—*Seneca*. The
Stoic philosopher and preceptor of Nero, born at Corduba (*Cordova*),
in Spain.—*Piso bonus*. "The bounteous Piso." C. Calpurnius
Piso, leader of the well-known conspiracy against Nero, for which
he lost his life. He was famed for his wealth and liberality.—*Cot-*

ta. Aurelius Cotta, another munificent individual of Nero's time.
—*Titulis.* "Titles of ancestry," *i. e.*, a long line of ancestors. By
tituli are here meant the inscriptions on the images of ancestors, and
which marked the antiquity and nobility of a line.—*Fascibus.* The
higher offices of magistracy are meant. The *fasces* were the badges
of dictatorial, consular, and prætorian power.—*Ut cænes civiliter.*
"That you entertain at supper just as one citizen should another,"
i. e., as an equal with equals ; that when you give a supper-party,
you consider all your guests as fully on an equality with yourself,
and that you fare precisely as they fare, sharing in common with
them all that the banquet may afford.—*Dives tibi, pauper amicis.*
If you follow the rule just laid down, you may be as parsimonious
as you please when entertaining your friends, and as luxurious and
gluttonous as you choose when supping by yourself.—*Ut nunc multi.*
A hit at the richer class of the day.

114–119. *Anseris jecur.* This was reckoned a very great luxury,
and, in order to increase the size of the liver, the geese were shut up
singly in dark and extremely warm coops, too narrow to allow them
to turn, and their food was scientifically varied and regulated.
Dried figs, chopped fine, formed their principal aliment toward the
end of the process. Their drink consisted of water mingled with
honey. In the Strasburg mode, at the present day, the winter is the
season preferred, coolness being deemed important. Consult *St.
John, Hellenes,* vol. ii., p. 276.—*Anseribus par Altilis.* "A crammed
fowl, equal in size to geese." Supply *avis.* A fatted capon is probably meant.—*Flavi.* "Golden-haired." Imitated from the Homeric
ξανθὸς Μελέαγρος.—*Dignus ferro Meleagri.* Not inferior in size to
the one slain by Meleager at the famous Calydonian boar-hunt.—
Aper. Consult note on *Sat.* i., 125.—*Tradentur tubera.* "Truffles will
be served up." According to Pliny (*H. N.*, xix., 3), truffles were produced amid the rains and thunders of autumn, but were most in
season and tenderest in spring. This will serve to explain what
immediately follows in the text.—*Optata.* Devoutly wished for by
the epicure.—*Majores.* By affording a more abundant supply of
truffles.—*Tibi habe frumentum.* "Keep your corn to yourself." Africa Propria, or what had been the former territory of Carthage, was
remarkable for its fertility, and formed one of the granaries of
Rome. It is to this district that allusion in particular is made
under the appellation *Libye* in the text.—*Dum.* "Provided only."
The glutton cares little, if any thing, about the high price of bread
in case a scarcity of grain ensue ; all he wants is that Africa may
send his darling truffles.

120-124. *Structorem.* "The arranger of the feast," *i. e.*, the one who arranged the dishes on the tray or *ferculum* in which they were served up. We must suppose, with Heinrich, that the *structor* here discharges also the duties of carver or *scissor.* Carving was taught as an art, and frequently performed, as in the present instance, to the sound of music, and with appropriate gesticulations.—*Indignatio.* "Cause for indignation."—*Saltantem et chironomonta, &c.* "Caper-ing about and gesticulating with nimble knife." We have given *chironomunta,* as more in unison with the Greek χειρονομοῦντα than the *chironomonta* of the ordinary text. The object of the poet is to express a Greek fashion by a Greek term.—*Dictata magistri.* "The lessons of his instructor in the art." *Nec minimo sane, &c.* "Nor is it, I assure you, a matter of only very trifling import." More lit-erally, "Nor does it, in truth, bear upon the matter with only a very slight difference." It is by no means reckoned an indifferent matter in what manner or with what gesture a hare or a fowl is carved; this, as well as gluttony itself, is now become a regular science, and is taught by a master.

125-131. *Velut ictus ab Hercule Cacus.* Compare Virgil, *Æn.,* viii., 264, *seq.*—*Quid hiscere.* "To open your mouth about any thing." Not, as some understand the word, in the way of complaint at the treatment which you undergo, but rather as presuming to take part, even in the slightest degree, in the conversation going on among the other guests.—*Tanquam habeas tria nomina.* Free Roman citizens had three names, *prænomen, nomen,* and *cognomen.* Slaves had no *prænomen.* He means to imply that, by turning parasite, Trebius had virtually forfeited the privileges of a free Roman.—*Quando propinat Virro tibi?* "When does Virro drink wine with you?" Literally, "drink first for you." *Propinare* has here the strict meaning of the Greek προπίνειν, from which it is formed, and refers mainly to the Greek custom of first drinking one's self when pledging another, and then passing the cup to the person pledged.—*Sumitque tuis, &c.* This is the direct converse of the pre-ceding, and means, When does the great man condescend to answer your pledge, in case you should have the effrontery to ask him to drink wine with you?—*Perditus.* "So lost to all sense of shame." —*Bibe.* "Drink, sir!" Denoting familiarity, and equivalent some-what to the modern Bacchanalian phrase, "Put the bottle about." —*Pertusa læna.* "With a cloak full of holes," *i. e.,* out at the el-bows, in modern parlance.

132-136. *Quadringenta.* Supply *millia sestertiorum.* An eques-trian fortune is meant.—*Melior fatis.* Because they have been unkind to you in making you poor.—*Homuncio.* Though now a sorry mortal.—*Da Trebio,* &c. Virro now directs his attendant to help Trebius plentifully, and presses him to taste the delicacies of the table.—*Pone ad Trebium.* "Place before Trebius." The preposition *ad* has here the same force as in *ad pedes, ad manum.*—*Vis frater ab ipsis ilibus.* "My dear brother, will you take some of these dainty dishes." *Ilia* literally signifies "entrails," of which some very choice dishes were made. Under this head, however, many other dainty dishes may be comprehended.—*Frater.* This was a courteous appellation between equals.—*Vos estis fratres.* "You and he are brothers."

136–145. *Dominus et domini rex.* "A lord and a lord's lord." The meaning of the whole passage is this: If you wish to become not only a domineering patron over your own retainers, but even over the patron himself of other retainers, you must be childless; you must have neither son nor daughter to inherit your estate. Then all the legacy-hunters, whether poor or rich, will worship you.— *Nullus tibi parvulus,* &c. A parody on Virgil, *Æn.,* iv., 327, *seqq.*— *Jucundum et carum.* He means to legacy-hunters.—*Sed tua nunc Migale pariat,* &c. The case will be different, however, if the rich Trebius live with a female not united to him in lawful matrimony; for, even if she present him with three boys at a birth, Virro will not be afraid of being supplanted by these, since they are natural children; and he will even make them little presents in order to win over the father.—*Migale.* The common but less correct form is *Mycale.* Compare *D'Orville, ad Charit.,* p. 247, and *Heinrich, ad loc.* —*Ipse.* Virro.—*Viridem thoraca.* "A little green corslet." A mimic piece of armor, to be worn by children playing at soldiers. Some, less correctly, render *thoraca* by "stomacher."—*Minimas nuces.* "Filberts."—*Rogatum.* Which the little fellow begs for to buy playthings, cakes, or fruit.—*Ad mensam,* &c. Virro goes so far as to beg Trebius to bring one of the little darlings with him when he comes to dine at his house.

146–148. *Vilibus amicis.* "Before lowly friends," *i. e.,* his poor clients.—*Ancipites.* "Of doubtful character." There are several species of the mushroom kind, some of which are poisonous, and it is sometimes difficult to distinguish them.—*Boletus.* "A mushroom of the best sort."—*Sed quales.* He means such as were not poisoned. —*Ante illum uxoris.* "Before that one furnished by his wife," *i. e.,* by Agrippina, who poisoned him with it. The botanical name of this species of mushroom is *Agaricus Cæsareus,* or "imperial agaric." It is common in Italy, and is brought to the markets there for sale. The Romans esteemed it one of the greatest luxuries of the table. The notorious Locusta supplied the empress with the poison, which the latter introduced into this, her husband's favourite dish. —*Nil amplius edit.* Hence Nero jocosely called mushrooms "the food of the gods," in allusion to the apotheosis of Claudius. (*Sueton., Ner.*, 33.)

149–155. *Reliquis Virronibus.* "The rest of his brother Virros." —*Poma.* "Fruits." Pulpy fruits in general are indicated by this term, such as apples, pears, peaches, &c.—*Phæacum.* Homer describes the gardens of Alcinous, in the island of Phæacia, as filled with perpetual fruits. Hence an eternal autumn reigned there. The ancients sought, erroneously however, to identify Homer's fabled island of Phæacia with Corcyra.—*Sororibus Afris.* Alluding to the far-famed garden of the Hesperides, the daughters of Atlas, King of Mauritania.—*Scabie mali.* "A scurf-covered thing of an apple."—*In aggere.* "On the rampart." The *agger* of the Prætorian camp is meant, and the allusion is generally supposed to be to a monkey exhibited riding on a goat, chewing an unsound apple, and equipped as a soldier with shield and helmet. The animal, thus accoutred, is taught, under the terror of the lash, to hurl the javelin like a mounted horseman. The only objection to this mode of explaining the passage is, that strict Latinity requires *ex* (not *ab*) *hirsuta capella.* Some, however, think that a raw recruit is meant, and therefore read *hirsuto Capella*, making this latter term to be a proper name, and to indicate the *campidoctor*, or drill-sergeant, who taught the recruits their exercises. The difficulty here, however, is, that the instrument for correcting soldiers was not the *flagellum*, but the *vitis.* Hence Lobeck (*Aglaoph.*, p. 1325) supposes a barbarian recruit (*tirunculum barbarum*) to be meant. The first interpretation, however, appears to be the better one, and is given, moreover, by the scholiast, who, in reference to the apple, remarks, "*quale simia manducat.*"

156–165. *Forsitan impensæ*, &c. Juvenal now appears to be acting the rhetorician, and shifting his ground, in order to rouse the anger or excite the hatred of Trebius against Virro, by attributing the conduct of the latter not so much to meanness after all, as to a settled intention to insult and annoy.—*Hoc agit*, &c. "Why, he does this, in fact, that you may feel hurt."—*Plorante gula.* "Than deploring gluttony," *i. e.*, than a parasite in all the agonies of disappointed hunger.—*Effundere.* "To give vent to."—*Presso molari.* "With closely-pressed grinder." The teeth have no food between to keep them asunder.—*Tam nudus.* "So utterly destitute."—*Illum.*

"Him and his insolence."—*Etruscum vuero*, &c. "If the Etruscan gold fell to his lot when a boy, or else the knot merely, and the badge afforded by the leather band of the poor," *i. e.*, if born a Roman, whether of rich or humble parents. The allusion is to the *bulla*, as worn by the Roman boys up to the period of assuming the manly gown. The children of the rich wore one of gold, those of the poor one made of leather. The former consisted of two concave plates of gold, fastened together by an elastic brace of the same material, so as to form a complete globe, within which an amulet was contained. The bulla of the poor was made in a similar way, but of leather, and was worn attached to a thong or band (*lorum*) of the same material. The thong or band in both cases passed around the neck, and the bulla was suspended from it, hanging on the breast. Observe that *nodus* is employed here in the sense of "knob" or "boss," as "knot" often is in English.

166-173. *Spes bene cœnandi vos decipit.* Your love of gluttony gets the better of your reflection, and deceives you into a belief that, however ill-treated you may have been before, this will not happen again.—*Ecce dabit jam*, &c. The soliloquy of the expectant parasite.—*Clunibus.* "The haunch."—*Minor altilis.* "That diminished capon." After the great man has now helped himself from it.— *Inde.* "Hence," *i. e.*, owing to this constant state of expectation. —*Parato, intactoque*, &c. "With your bread clinched in your hand, ready for action, and yet still untouched (by the expected food)," *i. e.*, because you are still lying in silent expectation of the good things which are to come.—*Sapit.* "Shows his wisdom." — *Et debes.* "You ought also so to do."—*Quandoque.* "Some day or other." The meaning is, One of these days we may expect to see you playing the *morio*, or clown in a pantomime, with shaven head, or submitting to any servile indignities. You will prove yourself richly deserving of such scurvy fare as you are insulted with at Virro's table, and of just such a patron as Virro to give it to you.

SATIRE VII.

ARGUMENT.

This Satire contains an animated account of the general discouragement under which literature laboured at Rome. Beginning with poetry, it proceeds through the various departments of history, law, oratory, rhetoric, and grammar, interspersing many curious anecdotes, and enlivening each different head with such satirical, humorous, and sentimental remarks as naturally flow from the subject.

The date of this Satire is uncertain. The mention of the Thebais (v. 83), which was completed A.D. 94, forbids us to place it earlier than the last year of Domitian's reign. But the opening lines, which speak of the arts as reviving under Cæsar's smile after a period of neglect, will not apply to Domitian's time. It only remains for us, therefore, to inquire whether they may be best referred to Nerva, Trajan, or Hadrian. Hadrian may be left out of the account; for, though he was an encourager of learning, yet it cannot be said that it was neglected by his predecessor Trajan. Nerva is addressed by Martial in words very similar to those of Juvenal: *"Contigit Ausoniæ procerum mitissimus aulæ Nerva,"* &c. (xii., 6, 1, *seq.*). Most, however, fix upon Trajan as the Cæsar intended. For, if Nerva was a patron of letters, still, in two years (the length of his reign), he could do little to recover them from their decline; the *Camenæ* might be found *tristes* by his successor. Teuffel and C. F. Hermann think that this view is confirmed by the fact that Trajan had a favourite actor, Pylades, who they suppose may have been the actor who is said to have taken offence at verse 87, " *Quod non dant proceres, dabit histrio;*" but the whole story seems unworthy of credit. (*Mayor.*)

1-10. *Et spes et ratio studiorum*, &c. "Both the hope and the inducement of studies depend on Cæsar alone." Trajan is probably meant, not, as some suppose, Domitian, though the latter, in the beginning of his reign, affected the character of a patron of literature. Consult Introductory Remarks, where the question is briefly discussed. Observe that *studia* is here employed for *studia artium liberalium*, a meaning which it often has when thus standing alone in the Latinity of the Silver Age.—*Respexit.* "Casts a favouring eye upon." Present perfect, as some term it, or, in other words, continuance of action denoted by the perfect.—*Gabiis.* Gabii was at this period a poor and almost deserted country town. (Consult note on *Sat.* iii., 192.) In so small a place but little custom could be expected. Observe that, besides the public baths and those in private houses, there were also *balnea meritoria*, to which any one was admitted on payment of a small sum.—*Conducere.* " To hire," and thus obtain a livelihood.—*Furnos.* "Ovens," *i. e.*, a bake-shop. — *Tentarent.* "Would willingly try." — *Aganippes.* Aganippe was a celebrated fountain at the foot of Mount Helicon, sacred to the Muses.—*Esuriens.* "If starving."—*In atria.* "To the auction-halls," *i. e.*, would be willing to turn crier herself. The reference is to the *Atria Licinia*, and others of the kind, near the Forum, in which auctions were held, and not, as some think, to the halls of rich patrons.—*Umbra.* Some MSS. give *arca*, but this savours of the petty acumen of some sciolist.—*Ames nomen, &c.* "Be content with the name and calling of Machæra." This personage is generally supposed to have been a well-known crier of the day. Weber, however, from the name μάχαιρα, supposes him to have been a cook.—*Commissa quod auctio, &c.* "What the pitted auction sells to the standers-by." The epithet *commissa* here refers to the parties that bid being pitted (*commissi*) against each other like gladiators. Many, however, render *commissa* by "intrusted," and make the expression "intrusted auction" refer to the circumstance of the goods being intrusted to the auctioneer by the owner or some magistrate. This, however, is less spirited.

11–16. *Œnophorum.* "A wine-basket." The *œnophorum* was a basket or other contrivance for carrying small quantities of wine about from place to place, especially for the supply of persons on a journey, who preferred carrying their own wine with them to taking the chance of buying what they could upon the road.—*Tripodes.* Tables, seats, vases, &c., supported on three feet. Boissonade (*ad Herod., Epimeris.*) conjectures *ripidas*, "fans ;" but no Latin writer employs the word *ripis*, the regular term being *flabellum.*—*Armaria.* "Cabinets." By *armarium* is meant an armoire, cabinet, or cupboard for keeping domestic utensils, clothes, money, curiosities, or any articles in daily use. It stands also for a book-case.—*Alcithoen Pacci, &c.* "The Alcithoe of Paccius," &c. We have here the titles of three tragedies written by wretched poets, and which were sold along with the other lumber. The common but erroneous reading is *Alcyonen Bacchi.* Alcithoe, daughter of Minyas, king of Orchomenus, was changed into a bat for having refused to share in the worship of Bacchus.—*Thebas.* The scene of the tragedies of Œdipus Rex, the Seven against Thebes, and the Epigoni. (*Welcker, Griech. Trag.*, iii., 1490.)—*Hoc satius, &c.* This line of life, however, mean as it may appear, is still getting your bread honestly, and far better than hiring yourself out as a false witness.—*Faciant equites Asiani, &c.* Alluding to persons who do thus perjure themselves, fellows who were originally Asiatic slaves from Cappadocia, and Bithynia, and Gallo-Græcia, but who have now, by perjury and cheating, amassed equestrian fortunes.—*Quanquam et Cappadoces, &c.* Heinrich very justly regards this line as a mere interpolation.—*Altera Gallia.* "The other Gaul," *i. e.*, Galatia, or Gallo-Græcia.—*Nudo talo.* "With bare foot." Some refer it to chalked feet. Consult note on *Sat.* i., 96.—*Traducit.* "Brings over for sale."

17–21. *Nemo tamen,* &c. A compliment for the reigning emperor, from whom another golden age in literature was now expected.—*Studiis indignum.* Degrading to him as a literary man.—*Eloquium vocale.* "Melodious expression."—*Laurumque momordit.* "And has chewed the bay." Bards were called δαφνήφαγοι, from their chewing bay-leaves, by which they fancied that they became inspired.—*Hoc agite, O juvenes.* "On, then, with the work, young men!" This form of expression is always meant to call the attention of those addressed to a particular matter, sometimes as mere observers, in which case it is equivalent merely to our English term "*Attend,*" and sometimes, as in the present instance, inciting them to action. In the former sense it was used in solemn rites, and was also uttered by the crier when a magistrate was taking the auspices.—*Materiam.* "Objects for its exercise."—*Ducis indulgentia.* "The kindness of our emperor."

22–31. *Aliunde.* "From any other quarter than from him."—*Croceæ membrana tabellæ.* "Each parchment leaf of the saffron-coloured note-book." There is a great difference of opinion about the meaning of these words. We have followed Heinrich, who supposes that a species of memorandum-book is meant, with the leaves of parchment, and the two sides of wood coloured yellow, so that *tabella* will here be employed in the sense of *libellus.* Such a book would be used to contain the verses that might suggest themselves at the moment to the poet.—*Veneris marito.* Vulcan, *i. e.*, the fire.—*Telesine.* Telesinus may be the poet to whom this satire is addressed. The name is of frequent occurrence in Martial. The true form, however, is not *Thelesinus,* but *Telesinus,* as settled by inscriptions.—*Claude.* "Lock them up."—*Tinea pertunde.* "Perforate with the book-worm," *i. e.*, let the book-worm perforate.—*Positos.* "As they lie stored away."—*Vigilata.* "That have cost you many a sleepless night." More literally, "composed while wakeful." The allusion in *prælia* is to Epic composition.—*In parva cella.* "In your narrow garret."—*Venias.* "You may come forth."—*Hederis.* Poets were crowned not only with bay, but with ivy. Compare Horace, *Od.* i., 1, 29: "*Doctarum hederæ præmia frontium.*"—*Imagine macra.* "A meagre image." By this is meant not only a meagre recompense for the pains it costs to obtain it, but also a lank and lean representation of its half-starved prototype. Private and pub-

lic libraries were adorned with the busts of writers who had distinguished themselves.—*Spes nulla ulterior.* "You can hope for nothing more than this empty honour."—*Tantum admirari,* &c.   As
children admire and praise the beauty of the peacock, which is of
no service to the bird, so the rich patron gives you compliments
merely, but no substantial proofs of patronage.—*Junonis avem.* The
peacock came from India into Asia Minor, and thence into the
island of Samos, where it was consecrated to Juno.   The coins of
Samos bore the impress of a peacock.

32-35. *Ætas patiens,* &c.   "That period of life which is able to
endure," &c.   You little think that while you are thus spending
your time to little purpose, in composing verses, the most valuable
portion of your existence, in which you might lay up a provision for
the future, is passing rapidly away.—*Tædia tunc subeunt animos.*
"Then weariness creeps over the spirits," *i. e.,* as age approaches.
—*Facunda et nuda senectus.* "A tuneful and yet destitute old age."

36-37. *Artes.* "The devices resorted to," *i. e.,* by your supposed
patron, in order that he may have a plausible excuse for doing nothing for you.   He makes verses himself, and gives you poem for
poem, and expects praise for his own compositions.—*Quem colis,* &c.
"To whom you now pay reverence, having abandoned both the
temple of the Muses and that of Apollo," *i. e.,* whom you, having
abandoned your fealty to the Muses and Apollo, are now reverenc-
ing and offering homage to as a mere present deity.   The temple
of the Muses (or, rather, of Hercules Musagetes) was dedicated by
Fulvius Nobilior, and restored by Marcius Philippus ; that of Apollo was erected by Augustus on the Palatine Hill.   These edifices
were used both as libraries and as places where men of letters might
assemble for the purpose of conversation or recitation.   They are
both deserted here by Telesinus for the hall of his wealthy but nig-
gardly patron.

38-47. *Propter mille annos.*   On the score of his priority merely
by a thousand years.   In other words, he judges of poetry as of
wine, by its age, as if Homer had little else save his antiquity to
recommend him.—*Aut si dulcedine,* &c.   If, however, you are particularly anxious to recite your poems, and care more for fame than
money, he will lend you some untenanted mansion for the purpose,
which has long been barred up, and is full of dirt and cobwebs.
He will furnish you also with an applauding audience of his freedmen and clients, but as for contributing any portion of the expense,
that is quite out of the question ; all this will fall to you.—*Maculosas ædes.* "Some mansion all soiled with dirt."   The common

text has *Maculonus* as a proper name. But this is evidently a corrupt reading.—*Ferrata.* "Barred up."—*Servire.* "To be at your service."—*Sollicitus imitatur portas.* "Is like the anxious gates (of some besieged city)."—*Extrema in parte ordinis.* "At the farthest end of the row." He places his freedmen in the back rows, that they may give the cue, unobserved, for frequent plaudits.—*Disponere.* "To place in different parts of the room." His clients he distributes over the benches, that their loud plaudits may appear to come from all parts of the room.—*Regum.* "Of these great lords."—*Subsellia.* The "benches" in the body of the room.—*Et quæ conducto, &c.* "And the side seats which hang supported by the hired beam." The *anabathra* were temporary wooden seats, rising one above another like a flight of stairs, and placed round the sides of a room. They were supported by timbers from below.—*Quæque reportandis, &c.* "And the orchestra which is placed there with its seats to be carried back," *i. e.*, carried away and paid for when the performance was over. By *orchestra* is here meant the row of chairs in front for the accommodation of the higher class of company, just as the *orchestra* in the Roman theatre was reserved for the Senate and persons of distinction.—*Reportandis cathedris.* To be returned, after the recitation, to the person from whom they were hired.

48–62. *Nos tamen hoc agimus.* "Yet still we ply this (unprofitable) task." Compare note on line 20. — *Sterili.* "Sterile," because affording us no prospect of any return for our trouble.—*Si discedas.* "Even if you try to draw off," *i. e.*, to abandon the pursuit of writing.—*Ambitiosi consuetudo mali.* Evil ambition, which it is so customary for poets to be led away by.—*Scribendi cacoethes.* "Itch for scribbling."—*Ægro.* "Distempered."—*Non publica vena.* "No vein that marks the common herd."—*Nihil expositum deducere.* "To spin out no vulgar theme."—*Nec qui communi, &c.* "And who strikes off no hackneyed productions of the common stamp." *Moneta* is here employed in the sense of a stamp or die for coining.—*Qualem nequeo monstrare, &c.* "Such a one as I cannot point to, and only feel in soul," *i. e.*, the poet such as I can conceive, but cannot point out among living men. Observe that *monstrare* is not, as some suppose, equivalent here to *describere* ("describe in words"), a signification that does not belong to it, but means "to point to." (Compare *Sat.* viii., 45.) Juvenal here touches on the inquiry *whether the idea can be adequately realized*, which has been warmly discussed, not only in ancient times, but by different schools, philosophical and theological, in our own day. (*Mayor, ad loc.*)—*Omnis*

I

acerbi impatiens. "Exempt from every thing embittering," *i. e.*, every thing that can embitter existence.—*Aonidum.* "Of the Aonian maidens," *i. e.*, the Muses. By both the Greek and Roman poets Bœotia is often called *Aonia*, from the Aones, an ancient people of the land, and the adjective *Aonius* is in like manner used as synonymous with Bœotian. Hence the Muses, who frequented Mount Helicon in Bœotia, are styled *Aonides*, and also *Aoniæ sorores.* — *Pierio.* "Pierian," *i. e.*, sacred to the Muses, who were called *Pierides* from *Pieria*, near Mount Olympus, where they were first worshipped.—*Thyrsumve contingere.* "Or to handle the thyrsus," *i. e.*, to feel poetic inspiration. The thyrsus of Bacchus was believed to communicate inspiration generally. Compare the Greek ϑυρσοπλῆγες.—*Sana.* "When of sober mood," *i. e.*, cowed down, and rendered tame and spiritless by the wants and troubles of life.—*Æris.* "Of that pelf."—*Satur.* "Full of good cheer." If Horace ever felt what it was to want, it was but for a short time. He was in comfortable circumstances before the battle of Philippi, and three years after it he was taken into the favour of Mæcenas. —*Euæ!* Consult *Hor.*, *Od.* ii., 19, 5 : "*Euæ! recenti mens trepidat metu*," &c.

64–71. *Feruntur.* "Are hurried onward." The "lords of Cyrrha and Nysa" are respectively Apollo and Bacchus. Cyrrha was the port of Crissa, on the Crissæan (a bend of the Corinthian) Gulf, and Crissa itself lay to the southwest of Delphi, and on the route pursued by pilgrims to the latter place. Nysa, in India, was the legendary scene of the nurture of Bacchus. The name indicates both a place and a mountain, particularly the latter.—*Duas curas.* "Two sources of care," *i. e.*, poetry and the providing of necessaries.—*Nec de lodice paranda attonitæ.* "And of one not bewildered about procuring a blanket," *i. e.*, how to get enough to buy one. The *lodix* was a coarse and rough sort of blanket, chiefly manufactured at Verona, used sometimes as an outside wrapper, at others as a counterpane for a bed, and also as a rug for the floor.—*Currus et equos*, &c. In this and the following line Juvenal alludes particularly to *Æn.*, 2, 602, *seqq.*, and 7, 445, *seqq.* The latter is the splendid passage where Alecto discovers herself to Turnus.—*Nam si Virgilio*, &c. Had not Virgil been in easy circumstances, the energy of his genius would have flagged. Virgil, by the bounty of his patrons, lived in comparative affluence.—*Puer.* "A slave."—*Tolerabile.* "Comfortable."—*Deesset.* To be read as a dissyllable. Observe that *deesset* and *caderent* are for *defuissent* and *cecidissent.* So *gemeret*, in line 71, for *gemuisset.* (*Zumpt*, § 525.)—*A crinibus.*

"From the locks of Alecto."—*Surda nihil gemeret*, &c. "The silent trumpet would have sent forth no dread re-echoing sound," *i. e.*, the trumpet starved to silence. The adjective *surdus* signifies "mute" as well as "deaf." So κωφός in Greek. Juvenal alludes to the fine passage in *Æn.*, 7, 511, *seqq.*, where Alecto arouses with the horn the rustic population of Latium. The *buccina* originally was a particular kind of horn, formed in spiral twists; afterward, when made of metal, it had a bent form, with an enlarged mouth, and was one of the three wind instruments with which signals were made, or the word of command given to the soldiery.

72–78. *Poscimus.* "And yet we require." More forcible without the interrogation. We require that a poor, starving poet equal the best efforts of former days.—*Cothurno.* The cothurnus, or buskin of the tragic actor, put for tragic composition itself.—*Cujus et alveolos*, &c. "Whose Atreus obliges him to pawn both his sauceboats and cloak." Atreus is the title of a tragedy which he is composing, and, while engaged on this, he has to pawn his very table utensils and clothing to keep himself from starving. Observe that *pignerat* here literally means "gives to pawn," being equivalent to *pigneri dat.*—*Non habet infelix Numitor*, &c. Ironical. Numitor is the name of some rich patron, who, of course, is quite poor when his friends want aid, and very unhappy at not being able to give them any thing, but who, at the same time, has money enough to squander upon his pleasures, or wherewith to purchase some useless curiosity, such as a tame lion, the keeping of which entails a heavy expense.—*Quintillæ.* Some female friend.—*Leonem.* For his vivarium. This was no uncommon fancy among the rich Romans.—*Constat leviori*, &c. Irony again.—*Bellua.* "The huge beast." Consult note on *Sat.* iv., 120.—*Nimirum.* "No doubt."—*Capiunt plus.* "Hold more."

79–81. *Lucanus.* M. Annæus Lucanus, the celebrated poet, and author of the Pharsalia, who inherited a large fortune from his father. He was at first a favourite with Nero, but excited at length that emperor's literary jealousy, and, having subsequently joined the conspiracy of Piso, was put to death in the 26th year of his age.—*Jaceat.* On a *lectus.* Compare line 105.—*Marmoreis.* "Adorned with marble statues."—*Serrano.* Sarpe assigns to this Serranus the Eclogues which have come down to us under the name of Calpurnius Siculus. (*Quæst. Philol.*, Rostoch, 1819.) — *Tenuique Saleio.* Salcius Bassus, poor in purse, but rich in merit and poetical talents. On one occasion he received a present of five hundred sesterces from **Vespasian**, and this sum, though small, was sufficient perhaps to

make Domitian neglect him. — *Gloria quantalibet quid erit?* " Of
what avail will glory be, however great?"

82-89. *Curritur.* " People run in crowds."—*Ad vocem jucundam.*
To the modulation of the voice great attention was paid in recitations. — *Amicæ Thebaïdos.* "Of the favourite Thebais." The subject of the Thebais of Statius is the war between Eteocles and Poly-
nices, sons of Œdipus, for the crown of Thebes.—*Promisitque diem.*
" And has fixed a day for reciting it." Notice was given publicly
in such cases by a *programma* or *edictum*, or what we would term " a
bill." Pressing invitations were also sent to the author's friends.—
Statius. P. Papinius Statius, a native of Neapolis. He was famed
for the brilliancy of his extemporaneous effusions, and gained the
prize three times in the Alban contests. From Juvenal's language
we might infer that, in his earlier years at least, he had to struggle
with poverty; but he appears to have profited subsequently by the
patronage of Domitian, whom he addresses in strains of the most
fulsome admiration. He may justly claim the merit of standing in
the foremost rank among the heroic poets of the Silver Age.—*Tanta
libidine vulgi.* "With so much eager desire on the part of the multitude."—*Fregit subsellia.* A figurative form of expression to indicate loud and oft-repeated applause.—*Esurit.* "He starves."—*Paridi.* This Paris was the celebrated pantomime, and the favourite
of Domitian, and these lines of Juvenal upon him are commonly,
though perhaps not very correctly, supposed to have been the cause
of the poet's banishment. — *Intactam Agaven.* "His unpublished
Agave," *i. e.*, as yet unexhibited on the stage. Heinrich supposes
this to have been a pantomimic ballet on some tragic subject.—*Militiæ honorem.* "High military preferment."—*Semestri vatum*, &c.
" He encircles the fingers of poets with the gold conferring six
months' rank," *i. e.*, the equestrian ring. *Semestris* here refers to an
honorary military commission, conferred on favourites, even though
not in the army, and called " *Semestris tribunatus militum.*" It lasted
for six months only, but conferred the privilege of wearing the equestrian ring, with perhaps others.

90-97. *Tu Camerinos*, &c. The Camerini and Bareæ are put here
for rich nobles generally. If the poet wishes to succeed, he must
not go to them. He must pay court to the actor Paris, who, by his
performances on the stage, and more particularly in the two pieces
entitled Pelopea and Philomela, has so won the favour of Domitian
as to be allowed to bestow high offices, not only on the authors of
these pieces, but on whomsoever else he may please.—*Pelopea.* A
piece turning on the legend of Pelopea, daughter of Thyestes, and

mother of Ægisthus.—*Philomela.* A piece having for its subject
the story of Philomela, metamorphosed into a nightingale.—*Haud
tamen invideas vati,* &c. The train of ideas is as follows : Though,
however, in some instances, great things have been done for some
individuals through the influence of Paris, yet, in general, those
who have nothing else to depend on but writing for the stage are
left to starve, and therefore are not to be envied.—*Pulpita.* "The
stage." The sale of his dramatic productions. — *Proculeius.* A
contemporary of Mæcenas, and, like him, a liberal patron of literary men. He is the same individual to whom Horace alludes in
Od. 2, 2, 5.—*Fabius.* Fabius Maximus also was a noble patron, and
Ovid addressed to him several of his Epistles from Pontus.—*Cotta.*
Aurelius Cotta, as well as Fabius, joined to great liberality the rarer
quality of fidelity in distress. — *Lentulus.* P. Lentulus Spinther,
who was mainly instrumental in the recall of Cicero from exile.—
Par ingenio pretium. "Talent met with a suitable reward."—*Et
vinum toto,* &c. That is, to be a stranger to wine, lest it might im-
pede their studies, and to refrain from it even during the whole
month of December, when the celebration of the Saturnalia would
allow one to indulge himself more freely.

98-104. *Fecundior.* "More profitable." He now speaks of the
writers of history, whose labour is much greater than that of poets,
and yet they are equally neglected.—*Petit.* "Demands." — *Olei.*
Figuratively for nocturnal toil.—*Oblita modi.* "Forgetful of all
limit," *i. e.,* exceeding all ordinary bounds.—*Surgit.* In the sense
of *incipitur.*—*Et multa crescit,* &c. "And grows in bulk, ruinous by
reason of the abundant papyrus," *i. e.,* which is consumed by the
work. Writing a history is a ruinous undertaking, and does not
pay for the paper. Papyrus was a very expensive article, and hence
the bulk of many histories made a complete transcript very costly.
Epitomes, therefore, such as those of Florus, Eutropius, Aurelius
Victor, &c., took the place of the larger works. Hence the loss of
many of the latter, or else the imperfect state in which they have
come down to us.—*Rerum.* "Of facts."—*Operum lex.* "The law
that regulates such works," *i. e.,* the rules of historic composition,
which compel the writer to be particular in his narration of facts,
and, consequently, to be more diffuse than in other departments of
composition.—*Apertæ.* "Even after it has been opened up," *i. e.,*
upturned, as it were, by the plough.—*Acta legenti.* "To one reading the public register." By *acta* is here meant a kind of gazette
or public chronicle, published daily at Rome by the authority of the
government, during the latter times of the republic, and also under

the empire, and corresponding in some degree to a modern news-paper. It contained an account of the proceedings of the Senate, the edicts and decisions of the magistrates, births, deaths, marriages, accidents, &c. By *legenti* is here meant the *actuarius*, who made a transcript of the *acta*, and used to read them aloud for the amuse-ment of the company at table. Compare Petronius, 53: "*Actua-rius, qui tanquam urbis acta recitavit.*"

105–107. *Sed genus ignavum*, &c. "But (historians, you will re-ply, are) a lazy race, who delight in the couch and the shade," *i. e.*, in a life of literary leisure, away from the bustle of public life. This is the excuse on the part of the rich for neglecting them.— *Lecto.* The ancients had couches made purposely for writing and studying. Hence the historian is called an idle and lazy fellow, who writes lolling on a couch.—*Umbra.* A sedentary life is meant, what Cicero calls "*vita umbratilis.*" (*Tusc. Disp.*, ii., 27.) This kind of life is often spoken of with contempt by both Greeks and Romans, who daily devoted some time to athletic exercises in the open air, and whose institutions (those of Athens and republican Rome at least) required all citizens to take part in public affairs.— *Dic igitur quid causidicis*, &c. The poet now takes up the case of the lawyers, and proceeds to show how little they also make by their profession.—*Præstent.* "Bring in." On the legal restrictions upon the fees of the *causidici*, consult *Dict. Ant.*, § v., *Lex Cincia.*—*Et magno comites*, &c. "And the briefs that accompany them in a big bundle." By *libelli*, however, which we have here rendered freely, are meant, in fact, depositions of witnesses, extracts from laws, &c.

108–114. *Ipsi magna sonant.* "They themselves talk grandly enough (of their gains)," *i. e.*, they boast of their extensive and lu-crative practice in the law courts. This they do particularly on two occasions : first, before a creditor of their own, whom they are anxious to impress with a high opinion of their professional gains, in order that he may be less solicitous about repayment of his debts ; and, secondly, before some rich litigant, who comes to them with an important and doubtful case, and from whom they wish to squeeze a larger fee by leading him to entertain a very lofty notion of their professional standing. (*Madvig, ad loc.*)—*Vel si tetigit la-tus*, &c. "Or if one still more urgent than he has nudged their side, who comes with his great account-book to sue for a doubtful debt."—*Nomen.* This word was of extensive use in money transac-tions. Properly, it denoted the name of a debtor registered in a banker's or any other account-book, and hence it came to signify the articles of an account, a debtor, or a debt itself.—*Cari folles.*

"The hollow bellows," *i. e.*, of cheeks and lungs.—*Conspuiturque sinus.* "And each bosom is all bespattered with foam." They talk about themselves till they foam at the mouth and bespatter the *sinus*, or bosom of the toga.—*Veram messem.* "The actual harvest," *i. e.*, of their professional labours.—*Hinc.* "In the one scale."—*Solum russati Lacernæ.* "The single fortune of the red-clad Lacerna." Supply *patrimonium.* Lacerna was a favourite charioteer of Domitian's, and belonged to the "Red party." The parties or factions of the Circus were distinguished by the colours which they wore.

115–121. *Consedere duces*, &c. A parody on Ovid's account of the dispute between Ulysses and Ajax for the armour of Achilles. (*Met.*, xiii., 1, *seq.*) It is here humorously introduced to describe the proceedings in a court of justice. The *duces* in the present instance are the judges.—*Pallidus Ajax.* "A pallid Ajax." Ajax stands here for the barrister, sallow from confinement at the desk, and not bronzed by the sun like the weather-beaten hero in Homer. Some, however, refer *pallidus* to anxiety for success. — *Dubia pro libertate.* "In behalf of freedom called in question," *i. e.*, in behalf of a client whose title to freedom is disputed.—*Bubulco judice.* "With a neat-herd for a juryman." The allusion is to the court of the *centumviri.* There were, in all, 35 city and country tribes, from each of which were chosen three *judices* or jurymen. These were called, in round numbers, *centumviri*, though the whole amounted to 105. Owing to this arrangement, it often happened that ignorant rustics had to decide upon knotty points. After the changes introduced by Augustus, the office of *judex* was no longer an honour, but a burden. Any free male adult who had not been condemned for a criminal offence might, it would seem, now sit as *judex.* ‐ (*Dict. Ant.*, *s. v.*)—*Jecur.* Some suppose that a blood-vessel in the lungs is meant, as the ancients in general were but indifferent anatomists.—*Figantur.* "May be fixed up." When advocates gained an important case, the triumph was made known by the entrance of their houses being decorated with palm-branches.—*Scalarum.* "Of your staircase." These poor lawyers here referred to lived in garrets, and could, therefore, only deck with evergreens the staircase leading up to their apartments. — *Quod.* "And what, after all." Put for *quale.* What do you get for all the noise you have been making?—*Siccus petasunculus.* There seems to be no reason for distinguishing *petaso*, as the shoulder of ham, from *perna*, as the leg. Rather the *perna* was a part of the *petaso*, although Forcellini thinks otherwise. The important distinction is that the *per-*

na was smoked or salted, whereas the *petaso* was eaten fresh. Our pleader receives one small of size and musty (*siccus*) besides. (*Mayor, ad loc.*)—*Pelamidum.* "Of young thunnies." These were salted and brought to Rome, where they afforded a cheap diet. The name *palamyde* is still given them at Marseilles.—*Aut veteres, Afrorum*, &c. "Or some shrivelled onions, the monthly allowance of African slaves." The allusion appears to be to the monthly rations of onions allowed to African slaves, who were accustomed to plenty of them in their own country.—*Tiberi devectum.* Poor wine, brought down the Tiber from the northern vineyards, such as those of Veii and Etruria generally, and not up the river, from the southern ones of Campania.—*Lagenæ.* Consult note on *Sat.* v., 29.—*Si quater egisti.* There must be a full stop after *egisti*, and a comma after *lagenæ.* The fee consists of five jars of wine for pleading four times.

122-124. *Aureus unus.* "A single gold piece." If you have been lucky enough to touch a gold piece for a fee, you cannot pocket any thing until you have satisfied the claim of the attorneys. The *aureus* varied in value. It was, at this time, worth about sixteen shillings sterling.—*Inde cadunt partes.* &c. "The shares of the attorneys, fixed by previous agreement, are deducted therefrom." In Cicero's time these *pragmatici* (attorneys or solicitors) were confined to Greece. The Roman advocates were then in the habit, if ignorant of a point of law, of referring to learned men of rank, such as the Scævolæ, &c. Under the successors of Augustus, however, there was not the same encouragement for the leading men to study that science, and therefore the advocates were obliged to adopt the Grecian method. Quintilian forcibly depicts the embarrassment of those *causidici* who, themselves ignorant of law, rely for all legal arguments on these attorneys. (*Inst. Or.*, xii., 3, 1, *seq.*)—*Quantum licet.* "As much as the law allows." The *Lex Cincia de Muneribus* forbade any one to take any thing for his pains in pleading a cause. In the time of Augustus it was confirmed by a senatus consultum, and a penalty of four times the sum received was imposed on the advocate. In the time of Claudius, however, the law was so far modified that an advocate was allowed to receive ten sestertia; but in Trajan's time this permission was so far restricted that the fee was not to be paid till the work was done.—*Et melius nos egimus.* Observe that *et* is here for *et tamen*, "and yet," as in Greek, καί for καίτοι. The pronoun *nos* is emphatic : "We, poor lawyers."

125-133. *Hujus.* Depending on *vestibulis.*—*Currus Æneus*, &c. Indicative of the triumphs gained by his ancestors.—*Bellatore.*

"Charger." Supply *equo.*—*Curvatum hastile minatur.* "Aims the bending spear." So exquisitely is the statue wrought, that the spear seems to tremble as it is poised.—*Statua lusca.* Æmilius was represented as closing one eye to take better aim. This vagary of Æmilius, which is here ridiculed, namely, in choosing, though a man of peace, to be represented on a war-horse, seems to have taken mightily at Rome, and to have had a great many imitators. —*Sic.* "In this same way," *i. e.,* by foolishly imitating Æmilius, and wanting to appear rich in order to draw clients.—*Conturbat.* "Becomes involved." Supply *rationes.* A legal form of expression. So *deficit* immediately after, "fails," *i. e.,* becomes insolvent. —*Magno cum rhinocerote.* "With a huge rhinoceros' horn of oil." Such a horn would be very expensive, and Tongilius, therefore, does this in order to appear rich. The animal is put for its horn; so *elephas* for ivory.—*Vexat.* He annoys the people at the baths, not only by the condition of his retinue, who have followed him through the miry streets, and are themselves muddy and dirty, but also by the numbers (*turba*) comprising his train.—*Juvenes longo premit,* &c. "Presses down with long litter-pole upon the Median youths that bear him," *i. e.,* both with his own weight and with that of a litter having longer poles than ordinary, as if intended to bear some very important burden.—*Medos.* The Medes were not subjugated by the Romans, but Media is sometimes taken in a wider sense, so as to include Assyria, Persia, and other countries of Asia.—*Murrhina.* Murrhine vases. Supply *vasa.* These were extremely costly, and came from the East. Most recent writers are inclined to think that they were true Chinese porcelain. Some, however, are in favour of fluor spar (*Derbyshire spar*). Consult *Becker's Gallus,* ii., 277.— *Emturus.* "To bid for," though not to buy.—*Argentum.* "Plate."

134–138. *Spondet enim Tyrio,* &c. "For it is his foreign purple with its Tyrian tissue that gains him credit," *i. e.,* causes him to appear a wealthy man. *Stlataria* is an old Latin form, derived from *stlata,* itself an old form for *lata,* just as they said, in early Latin, *stlis* for *lis,* and *stlocus* for *locus;* according to some of the best commentators, it means here "imported," or "foreign;" the term from which it is derived, namely *stlata,* signifying, according to Festus, "a broad-beamed" merchant ship. Others take the word to mean "deceitful," and refer it to the attempt to impose on the public by an unreal display of wealth. Lobeck (*Aglaoph.,* p. 1318, *n.*) is in favour of this latter explanation.—*Vendit causidicum.* The purple cloak is said "to sell" the lawyer, because it recommends him to notice, and makes him, as it were, fetch more money.—*Amethysti-*

na. "His violet-coloured garments." Supply *vestimenta.—Convenit illis.* "It suits these people," *i. e.,* such pretenders as Pedo and the rest.—*Majoris.* "Greater than they really possess."—*Sed finem impensæ,* &c. "But prodigal Rome sets no limit to her extravagance." We have here the reason given why so many wished to appear rich, because no one was held in any estimation who was not deemed able to live extravagantly; and this same extravagance finally ruins them.

139–149. *Fidimus eloquio?* "Do we trust in our eloquence?" *i. e.,* to bring us professional emolument. Such is the importance of fashionable and expensive appearance, that even Cicero himself, if he could return from the dead, would not receive even the smallest fee, unless he appeared with a ring of great value glittering upon his finger. Several MSS. read *Ut redeant veteres,* "Even though the old (orators) return to life." But this is less forcible.—*Ducentos nummos.* "Two hundred sestertii." Between seven and eight dollars of our currency.—*Servi octo.* To carry your litter. The litters were more or less respectable as to their appearance from the number of bearers. Consult note on *Sat.* i., 53. — *Decem comites.* Clients are meant.—*Post te sella.* This refers to what was termed the *sella gestatoria,* a kind of portable chair in which the occupant sat upright, and which was entirely open, and must not be confounded with the lectica. The sella here comes after him, in order that he may enter it whenever he pleases. The empty lectica, with its eight bearers, if present, precedes.—*Togati.* "Friends arrayed in the toga."—*Conducta.* "Hired for the occasion." He was too poor to buy one.—*Agebat.* "Used to plead."—*Sardonyche.* The sardonyx is a reddish-yellow or orange-coloured gem, nearly allied to the onyx.—*Pluris.* "For a higher fee."—*Rara.* "Rare" in the opinion of the day, not in reality.—*Quando licet Basilo,* &c. When will Basilus, or any pleader of mean appearance, be employed in a case of great importance, as when Cicero appeared for Fonteius, who had been accused of extortion, and be able to bring into court the near relatives of the defendant, in order to excite the compassion of the judges ?—*Bene dicentem.* "Though pleading with great ability." Who would not resent it as presumption if Basilus should plead a cause with eloquence ?—*Accipiat te Gallia,* &c. The lawyer is recommended to go to Gaul, and more particularly Africa, in which countries eloquence still flourished, by reason of the multiplicity of lawsuits.—*Mercedem ponere linguæ.* "To set a reward upon your tongue," *i. e.,* to let your tongue for hire.

150–154. *Declamare doces?* He now proceeds to show that the

teachers of rhetoric, who instructed young persons in the art of
declamation, are, if possible, still worse off than the lawyers.—*O
ferrea pectora Vetti.* "Oh, bosom of Vettius, steeled against fa-
tigue!" Vettius Valens, an eminent professor of rhetoric, is supposed by some to be meant here. The correct form of the name is
Vettius, not *Vectius.*—*Quum perimit,* &c. Alluding to the declamations of the pupils against tyranny.—*Numerosa.* In this sense the
word belongs to the Silver Age. The Augustan writers use it in no
other than "rhythmical," "harmonious," &c.—*Nam quæcunque,* &c.
Whatever the class learn by reading over at their seats, this they
repeat standing, the very same lines in the same sing-song tone and
twang. The instructor, it would appear, first taught them the pronunciation and utterance while they were sitting, and then gave
them directions about the gesture and action, at which time they
stood up, and repeated the same things over and over again, the
master all the while exerting himself to show them the best method
of speaking and action.—*Perferet.* "Will rehearse from beginning
to end."—*Occidit miseros,* &c. "It is the cabbage continually re-
produced that kills the wretched masters." An allusion to the
Greek proverb, δὶς κράμβη θάνατος. The poet means that the hearing of the same things constantly (like cabbage warmed up and
served at table many times to the same person) must be surfeiting
and disgusting enough to wear out and tire the poor masters to
death.

155–160. *Quis color.* "What is the plea to be urged?" *Color* is
a rhetorical term, analogous to the χρῶμα of the Greeks, and indicates the mode in which a speech is to be dressed up, and its arguments brought forward in extenuation, mitigation, &c. In other
words, it means the *colouring* which is to be given to it. Hence
colorare is often employed in the same way, in a rhetorical sense, to
signify "to gloss over," "to give a false colouring to." Among the
Declamations of Quintilian, forty-three are distinguished from the
rest as *coloratæ;* and in the *Controversiæ* of Seneca the *color* regularly follows the *divisio.* The term *color* will also apply to accusations, as, for instance, where matters are urged in aggravation of a
crime, &c. (*Mayor, ad loc.*)—*Et quod sit causæ genus.* Causes were
variously classified, as, for instance, into the *demonstrative* (where
some certain person is praised or blamed), the *deliberative* (where
the speaker advises or dissuades), and the *judicial* (where he accuses or defends). This classification is borrowed from Aristotle
(*Rhet.,* 1, 3, 3).—*Summa quæstio.* "The main point." The *gist,* or
that on which the whole case hinges.—*Sagittæ.* "Shafts." Fig-

uratively for arguments.—*Mercedem solvere.* "To pay the teacher's
fee."—*Mercedem appellas?* &c. "Pay do you ask for?" The common construction is *appellare aliquem de pecunia.*—*Quid enim scio?*
"Why, what do I know (more than before)?" The language of
the dull or inattentive scholar, who lays the whole blame of his ig-
norance upon the teacher.—*Culpa docentis,* &c. "The fault of the
teacher, it seems, is alleged (as a reason for non-payment)."—*In
læva parte mamillæ.* Some of the ancients made the seat of wisdom
and understanding to be in the heart.—*Nil salit Arcadico juveni.*
"There is not a spark of energy in this scion of Arcadia." Arcadia was famed for its breed of asses, which were in request in every
part of Greece (*Varro, R. R.,* ii., 1, 14 ; *Plin., H. N.,* viii., 43, 68);
hence *Arcadicus juvenis* is here the same as "blockhead." Perhaps, however, it is better to make the reference to be to the low
reputation for intelligence which the Arcadians had among the other Greeks.

161-164. *Sexta quaque die.* We would say, regularly once a
week. It appears from Quintilian (x., 5, 21) that it was customary
to hear classes on stated days ("*Consuetudo classium certis diebus
audiendarum*").—*Dirus Hannibal,* &c. No themes were more common in the Roman schools of declamation than those drawn from
the movements of Hannibal.—*An petat Urbem,* &c. The question
was often mooted in the schools whether Hannibal ought not to
have marched to Rome immediately after the battle of Cannæ.
This was Maharbal's advice.—*An post nimbos,* &c. This usage of
an....an is only poetical, and does not properly belong to classical
prose. (*Zumpt,* § 554, *sub fin.*) The allusion in *nimbos,* &c., is to
the storm, which, according to Livy (xxvi., 11), discouraged Hannibal, when, in the fifth year after the battle of Cannæ (B.C. 211), he
did march upon the Roman capital, and which induced him to draw
off his forces into Apulia. Livy's account, however (which may be
compared with those of the deliverance of Delphi from the troops
of Xerxes and of Brennus), would seem to be a mere fable. It was
unknown to Polybius (ix., 6, 5).—*Circumagat.* In the sense of *ab-
ducat.*

165-170. *Quantum vis stipulare.* "Bargain for as much as you
please," *i. e.,* ask any sum you choose. The teacher is here supposed to be addressing some third person, and declares himself
ready to give the latter any sum he may choose to ask, on condition
that he get this stupid boy's father to hear him declaim and go
through his school exercises as often as he has done. Parents were
accustomed to visit occasionally the Roman schools, with their con-

nections and friends, and listen to the exercises of their sons.—
Quod do. "What I am perfectly willing to give." The present in
a future sense.—*Ut.* "On condition that."—*Ast alii sex,* &c. The
connection is as follows: Not one instructor merely complains thus,
but many do. Several, indeed, have abandoned the profession of
teaching, and have betaken themselves to that of the law, where
they now declaim in loud accents (*conclamant*), and plead real instead of imaginary causes.—*Sophistæ.* Professors of rhetoric and
belles-lettres are meant. That the word *sophist* originally denoted
a teacher, chiefly of rhetoric, such as Gorgias was, has been shown
by Mr. Grote in his chapter on the Sophists.—*Raptore relicto.* "The
abductor (of Helen) being abandoned by them." They have now
abandoned all fictitious declamations about Paris.—*Fusa venena silent.* No more declamations now are heard about poison " poured
into another's cup." Some think that the allusion here is to the legend of Medea and Creusa, but it is more likely to be a general one.
—*Malus ingratusque maritus.* A general case of ill-treatment on
the part of a husband. Some suppose Jason to be meant, others
Theseus. We have an imaginary case, however, in Seneca (ii.,
Contr., 13), that would seem to apply best.—*Et quæ jam veteres,*
&c. "And the drugs that heal the now aged blind." This is generally supposed to allude to the story of Æson, the father of Theseus, restored to youth by Medea. Some, however, more correctly
make the reference to be to an imaginary case, where a step-mother discovers her step-son preparing a medicament for the purpose
of curing his father's blindness, and accuses him of mixing poison
for his parent.—*Mortaria.* Literally, " mortars," and then, figuratively, medicines brayed in a mortar, &c.

171–175. *Sibi dabit ipse rudem.* " Will discharge himself." Literally, "will give himself the *rudis.*" This was a stick with a knob
at the end, or else blunted at the point, employed by gladiators and
soldiers while learning the art of attack and defence, and usually
presented to a gladiator when he received his discharge. Juvenal
advises the teacher of rhetoric, who has now turned lawyer, to abandon this latter profession also, as being no better than the one which
he has left, and to pursue some totally different vocation.—*Ad pugnam.* " To real conflicts," *i. e.,* to the actual collisions of the bar.
—*Rhetorica ab umbra.* " From the retirement of the rhetorician's
school." *Umbra* is here put for the *vita umbratilis,* the retired life,
spent, as it were, in the shade, that is, led by those who pursue
such studies. Consult note on line 105.—*Qua vilis tessera venit,* &c.
" From which the miserable corn-ticket has come," *i. e.,* with which

it has been purchased. The poorer citizens were furnished month-ly, on the nones, by the magistrates, with a small tablet of lead (*tessera*), which, on being presented to the keepers of the public granaries, entitled the bearers to a certain quantity of corn. These tallies, as appears from the text, were transferable ; those who were not in want of corn disposed of them for a trifling sum. Consult *Dict. Ant., s. v. Frumentariæ Leges.—Quippe hæc merces lautissima.* " Since this is their most splendid reward," *i. e.*, this is all they can expect to make by their labours. Ironical.

176-177. *Chrysogonus quanti doceat*, &c. He now proceeds to the teachers of music, and shows how much better they were paid than those who gave instruction in the more solid branches of education. Chrysogonus was a favourite singer, and Pollio a favourite musician, but both of them men of very loose principles. The wealthy nobles placed their sons, at an enormous expense, under the tuition of these two worthies, from whom they learned every thing that was bad.— *Artem scindes Theodori.* "You will tear up the ' Art' of Theodo-rus." Theodorus of Gadara was an eminent rhetorician in the time of Tiberius, and wrote several works, of which a few fragments are preserved by Quintilian. His " Art of Rhetoric" is here particularly referred to, and the meaning of the passage is this : Make but a trial of the gains of music-masters, and you will tear up your " Elements of Rhetoric," *i. e.*, will abandon the schools of declamation for this more lucrative employment. The common reading is *scindens*, which some explain by " going into all the details of the treatise of Theodorus." But this will make Chrysogonus and Pollio teachers of rhetoric themselves. Heinrich, on the other hand, considers *scin-dens* to be for *proscindens*, in the sense of " deriding" (*cutting up* for the amusement of their pupils). The true reading, however, is the one which we have given in the text.

178-185. *Balnea.* The Roman baths, both public and private, were remarkable for their magnificence.—*Sexcentis.* " Will cost six hundred thousand sestertii." Supply *millibus sestertiorum constabunt.* The sum here given would be equivalent to $23,400.—*In qua geste-tur dominus*, &c. Consult note on *Sat.* iv., 5.—*Anne serenum exspec-tet ?* "Is he to wait, forsooth, for fair weather ?" No : let him drive about under cover, where there is no fear of splashing the mules.—*Hic potius.* " Here rather does he wish to take his exer-cise." Supply *gestari vult. — Numidarum.* The Numidian marble was in high repute. It had a dark surface variegated with spots.— *Cœnatio.* " A banqueting-hall." The *cœnatio* in rich houses was fitted up with great magnificence.—*Algentem rapiat solem.* " Catch the cool sun." The rich had dining-rooms facing different quarters, according to the season of the year, with a southern aspect for the winter, and an eastern one for the summer. The former is here probably meant.—*Quanticumque domus.* Supply *constabit.* However expensive the house may have been, money will be forthcoming for the purchase of a *structor* and a cook; but only a small pittance, grudgingly given, for the education of a son. — *Qui fercula docte componat.* An artiste, or arranger of the dishes, technically called *structor.* Compare note on *Sat.* v., 120. — *Qui pulmentaria condat.* "To prepare the food." The cook is meant. *Pulmentaria* is a general term for victuals, and is derived from *puls,* a thick pap or pottage made of meal, pulse, &c., and which the Romans long used as food before they became acquainted with bread. The true reading here is *condat* (from *condĕre*), not *condit* (from *condīre,* "to season"). The subjunctive is required by the context, not the indicative. Lachmann conjectures *condiat,* to be pronounced as a dissyllable.

186–188. *Sestertia duo.* About $78. — *Quintiliano.* The celebrated rhetorician.—*Ut multum.* "As a great deal."—*Filius.* "His son's education." Here intrusted to Quintilian.—*Unde igitur tot,* &c. Juvenal instances Quintilian as a rich man, whereas the younger Pliny, in a letter which does, as Gifford remarks, equal honour to himself and his master (for such Quintilian was), talks of his moderate fortune, and makes him a present of 50,000 sesterces ($1950) as a contribution toward the outfit of a daughter about to be married. It must be borne in mind, however, that Juvenal here employs a tone of declamatory exaggeration, and that he speaks with evident, though suppressed bitterness of the good fortune of Quintilian, probably in consequence of the flattery lavished by the latter on the hated Domitian. It must be observed, also, that though the means of Quintilian may not have been so ample as to render an act of generosity on the part of a rich and powerful pupil in any way unacceptable, still the handsome salary which he received from the state (100,000 sestertii = $3900) must have appeared boundless wealth when compared with the indigence of the troops of half-starved grammarians who thronged the metropolis, and whose miseries are so forcibly depicted by Juvenal.—*Saltus.* "Forests." Put figuratively for acres or landed property.

189–196. *Exempla novorum fatorum transi.* "Pass by instances of unprecedented good fortune (like Quintilian's)," *i. e.,* Quintilian's case, however, is only to be regarded as an instance of rare good luck, and must not be mentioned as an example for others. The idea, therefore, intended to be conveyed by the text, when freely

expressed, will be this : "Do not instance Quintilian unto me as a
proof of the incorrectness of my remarks respecting the miserable
compensation of rhetoricians.   He is only an instance of great good
luck, and an instance, too, that very rarely occurs."—*Felix et pulcher
et acer.*   "He who has luck is both handsome and talented."   Juvenal means that luck is every thing.   Observe that *acer* here is
equivalent to *acris ingenii.—Generosus.*   "Well-born."—*Appositam
nigræ lunam*, &c.   He becomes also a senator, and wears the crescent on his foot.   Senators wore a kind of high shoe, like a buskin,
of soft black leather, having the letter C woven or embroidered on
the top of the foot.   This C (compared to a crescent, *luna*) is supposed to have referred to the original number of 100 (*Centum*) senators.—*Alutæ.*   The material taken for the boot itself.   The term
properly means a kind of leather softened by means of alum.—*Jaculator.*   "Debater."   So called facetiously from his hurling arguments, as it were, against his opponents.—*Et si perfrixit.*   "Even
though he has a bad cold."   From *perfrigesco.—Distat.*   "It makes
all the difference."—*Te excipiant.*   "Welcome you," *i. e.*, preside
over your natal hour.—*Rubentem.*   A new-born infant looks red,
owing to its thin and tender skin.

199-202. *Ventidius.*   Ventidius Bassus is meant.   He was a native of Picenum, and was taken prisoner in the Social War by Pompeius Strabo (B.C. 89), and carried captive to Rome.   When he
grew up to man's estate, he got a poor living by undertaking to furnish mules and vehicles for those magistrates who went from Rome
to administer a province.   In this humble employment he became
known to Julius Cæsar, whom he accompanied into Gaul.   In the
civil war he executed Cæsar's orders with ability, and became a favourite of his great commander.   In B.C. 43 he was made prætor.
After Cæsar's death he sided with Antony, and the same year with
his prætorship was made consul suffectus.   He subsequently was
sent by Antony against the Parthians, over whom he gained a brilliant victory, for which he obtained a triumph.—*Tullius.*   Servius
Tullius, born of a slave, but who became the sixth king of Rome.—
Servis.   Alluding to Servius Tullius.—*Captivis.*   Ventidius is meant.
—*Felix ille tamen.*   The reference is now again to Quintilian.—
Corvo quoque rarior albo.   The Latinity of *tamen. . . . quoque* is somewhat harsh.

203-206. *Vanæ sterilisque cathedræ.*   "Of this fruitless and barren profession," *i. e.*, the teaching of rhetoric.—*Cathedra.*   The instructor's seat is here put for the profession itself of a teacher.—
Thrasymachi exitus.   Thrasymachus of Chalcedon was one of the

earliest cultivators of the art of rhetoric, and a contemporary of Gorgias. Suidas very erroneously makes him a pupil of Plato and Isocrates. He opened a school of rhetoric at Athens, but, meeting with no encouragement, hung himself.—*Secundi Curinatis.* Secundus Carinas was a rhetorician of the time of Caligula, by whom he was expelled from Rome for having, by way of exercise, declaimed on one occasion against tyrants.—*Hunc.* Socrates is meant, not, as some erroneously think, Carinas.—*Ausæ conferre.* " You who had the heart to bestow upon him." Socrates was condemned to death by the Athenians, and compelled to drink hemlock.

207–214. *Di.* Supply either *date* or *dent.*—*Tenuem et sine pondere terram.* This was a common wish on the part of survivors toward their friends, and was generally indicated on monuments by the letters S. T. T. L., an abbreviation for *Sit tibi terra levis,* " Light lie the earth on thee."—*Spirantesque crocos,* &c. The ancients used to strew fragrant flowers annually on the tombs of their departed friends, and they even believed that flowers grew spontaneously on their graves, so that the shades of the deceased enjoyed a perpetual spring.—*Metuens virgæ jam grandis.* " In awe of the rod, though now grown up," *i. e.,* regarding, even when large of size, his preceptor Chiron with respectful deference.—*Cantabat.* "Learned to sing," *i. e.,* to sing and to accompany his voice on the lyre.—*Patriis in montibus.* Mount Pelion in Thessaly, the abode of the Centaurs. —*Citharœdi cauda magistri.* " The tail of his master, the harper." Chiron, being a Centaur, was half man, half horse.—*Sed Rufum atque alios,* &c. Times are now changed, and so far are the masters from meeting with reverence from their pupils, that it is a common practice for the scholar to beat the master. The Rufus here referred to was, according to the scholiast, a native of Gaul. He is represented in the text as charging Cicero with barbarisms or provincialisms. Jahn reads *quem toties* for *qui toties,* making his own scholars to have nicknamed Rufus " the Allobrogian Cicero." We have followed the common text with Heinrich.—*Allobroga.* "The Allobrogian." The Allobroges were a Gallic people, dwelling between the Rhodanus (*Rhone*) and Isara (*Isère*), as far as the Lacus Lemannus, or Lake of *Geneva,* and, consequently, in the modern *Dauphiné* and *Savoy.*

215–221. *Quis gremio,* &c. The grammarians come next, and are shown to be no better off than the others. As regards *gremio,* observe that money was usually carried in the *sinus* of the toga.— *Celadi.* Of this Celadus nothing is known. The common text has *Enceladi,* but the true form is *Celadi,* as confirmed by inscriptions.

—*Palæmonis.* Q. Remmius Palæmon was a celebrated grammarian in the reigns of Tiberius, Caligula, and Claudius, but a man of very profligate character. The scholiast on Juvenal (vi., 451) makes him to have been the master of Quintilian.—*Grammaticus labor.* "Their grammarian labours."—*Rhetoris æra.* "The pay of a rhetorician."—*Discipuli custos,* &c. "Acoenonetus, the one who has the pupil under his care, takes the first nibble." By *custos* is here meant the same as *pædagogus,* namely, the slave who had the care of the boy from his sixth or seventh year until he attained the age of puberty, and who, among other duties, went with him to and from school or the gymnasium.—*Qui dispensat.* "The steward." The *dispensator* is meant, a kind of steward or account-keeper, through whose hands the money passes, and who will also deduct something for himself.—*Cede.* "Yield to their demands."—*Inde.* For *ex hoc.*—*Aliquid decrescere.* "Some abatement to be made."—*Institor.* "The salesman." This was a salesman, factor, or manager, who was placed over an establishment or shop to manage its concerns. Sometimes also he travelled about with goods for the manufacturer.—*Cadurci.* "Cadurcian bed-linen." So called from the Cadurci, whose district is now *Querci* in *Guyenne,* and who were famous for its manufacture.

222-232. *Dummodo non pereat,* &c. Provided only you do not utterly lose the fruits of your labour.—*Mediæ quod noctis,* &c. The Roman schools opened very early, long before daybreak. The master is here represented sitting in his cathedra, awaiting the arrival of his pupils, at an hour when the meanest artisan would be unwilling to commence his daily toil.—*Totidem olfecisse lucernas.* Each boy had his lamp, as it was not yet daylight. They brought these to school with them.—*Quot stabant pueri,* &c. During recitations the master sat, the scholars stood.—*Quum decolor esset Flaccus,* &c. From this passage we learn that Horace (as he himself predicted, *Ep.* i., 20, 17, &c.) and Virgil were the standard books in the schools of those days. Compare *Quintilian,* i., 8, 5.—*Fuligo.* Soot from the smoky lamps.—*Rara tamen merces,* &c. Seldom, however, small as the sum is, can the amount be recovered without a recourse to law.—*Cognitione tribuni.* "The cognizance of the tribune." The tribunes of the commons, under the empire, presided in a court for the recovery of small debts.—*Vos.* "You parents." The remaining verses are ironical.—*Ut præceptori,* &c. "That the rule of words be clear to the preceptor," *i. e.,* that the teacher be never at fault in his syntax, but be perfect in the rules of grammar for each word.—*Historias.* Not only regular histories, but also legendary tales. — *Omnes.* To be taken with both *historias* and *auctores.* — *Tanquam ungues*, &c. We would say, to have all these things at his fingers' ends.

232–241. *Thermas.* "The thermæ." Hot water and vapour baths. — *Phœbi balnea.* Cold baths. Phœbus was the name probably of some bath-keeper. The scholiast says, "*Privatæ balneæ, quæ Daphnes appellantur.*" — *Dicat nutricem Anchisæ.* Her name, according to the scholiast, was Tisiphone. — *Nomen patriumque*, &c. The step-mother of Anchemolus, who fought on the side of Turnus (*Æn.*, x., 389), was Casperia. (*Serv. ad Virg., l. c.*) She was the wife of Rhœtus, king of the Marrubii, in Italy. This absurd curiosity about trifles was common among the ancients. Tiberius was very fond of propounding such questions to the grammarians of the day, with the view of puzzling them, and then enjoying their confusion. — *Acestes.* The Sicilian monarch mentioned in the Æneid. Virgil calls him "*ævi maturus*" (*Æn.*, v., 73). — *Siculus.* Alluding to the wine bestowed by Acestes on the Trojans, as related by Virgil (*Æn.*, i., 195), "Vina bonus quæ deinde cadis onerarat Acestes." — *Urnas.* "Vessels." Here used generally. Strictly speaking, however, the *urna*, as a liquid measure, contained four *congii*, or half an *amphora*, which last was about six gallons. — *Ut ducat.* "That he would." The moral education of the pupil must be equally attended to. — *Cera.* Thus Horace speaks of the youth as being "*cereus in vitium flecti*" (*Ep. ad Pis.*, 163). — *Facit.* "Models." — *Hæc inquit cures.* The father insists on having all these points carefully attended to. — *Se verterit.* "Shall have come round again." The school year, according to Macrobius (*Sat.* i., 12), ended in the month of March, at which time teachers were paid. — *Accipe victori*, &c. "Receive as much gold as the people demand for the victor in the chariot-race." The victorious charioteer in the Circensian games is meant. He was not allowed to receive more than five *aurei*. The *aureus*, as before remarked, was worth at this time about sixteen shillings sterling. The yearly income of a grammarian, therefore, does not exceed what a jockey is presented with for a single race.

SATIRE VIII.

ARGUMENT.

Juvenal demonstrates, in this Satire, that distinction is merely personal; that, though we may derive rank and titles from our ancestors, yet, if we degenerate from the virtues by which they obtained them, we cannot be considered truly noble. This is the main object of the Satire, which, however, branches out into many collateral topics—the profligacy of the young nobility; the miserable state of the provinces, which they plundered and harassed without mercy; the contrast between the state of debasement to which the descendants of the best families had sunk, and the opposite virtues to be found in persons of the lowest rank and humblest descent.

1-5. *Stemmata quid faciunt?* "What do pedigrees avail?" The images of ancestors in the *atrium*, or hall of the dwelling, were connected together by festoons (*lineæ*), so that the descent from father to son could be readily traced. The images themselves, together with the connecting *lineæ*, constituted what the Romans termed the *stemma*, or "pedigree." (*Becker, Röm. Alt.*, ii., 1, p. 220.)—*Longo sanguine censeri*. "To be ranked by a long descent," *i. e.*, to take rank by or in proportion to one. *Censere* is the term properly applied to the exercise of their official functions, on the part of the censors, in estimating or valuing the property of individual citizens, so far as it was subject to the *census*, and is then taken to denote valuing or ranking generally.—*Pictos vultus*. The images of their ancestors were merely busts made of wax (hence the term *vultus*), coloured so as to represent life. They were therefore, in fact, a collection of family portraits. We learn from Polybius (vi., 53) that at funerals the ancestors of the deceased were personated, and their *imagines* worn, by persons resembling them in stature and bearing.—*Stantes in curribus*. Triumphal statues are meant.—*Æmilianos*. The son of Paulus Æmilius, when adopted by the son of Scipio Africanus the elder, received the name of P. Cornelius Scipio Æmilianus Africanus Minor.—*Curios*. M'. Curius Dentatus, the celebrated opponent of Pyrrhus.—*Dimidios*. "Diminished one half," *i. e.*, mutilated from the effects of time.—*Humeros minorem*. A Græcism. The common text was *humero*.—*Corvinum*. Compare *Sat.* i., 93.—*Galbam*. The Emperor Galba traced his pedigree up to Jupiter! (*Suet.*, *Galb.*, 2.) One of his ancestors is here meant.

6-9. *Generis tabula.* A genealogical table is meant. The Roman nobles had these in addition to the *stemmata.* Schneider (*ad Vitruv.*, vol. ii., p. 458) thinks that the reference here is to the *tablinum,* an apartment immediately adjoining the *atrium,* and in which the family archives were kept. But the epithet *capaci* is opposed to this.— *Corvinum posthac,* &c. Several MSS. omit this verse. It certainly cannot have followed upon verse 6th, for two reasons: first, because Corvinus has been mentioned just before; and, secondly, because the genealogical table need not be *capax* to contain merely a single name. (*Mayor, ad loc.*)—*Multa contingere virga.* "To reach after travelling along many a branch," *i. e.,* along many a *linea* or *ramus,* connecting together the different *imagines.* We would say, along many a branch of the genealogical tree. This is certainly the most natural explanation. The scholiast, however, makes *multa virga* equivalent to *multis fascibus;* while K. F. Hermann thinks that *virga* means the rod which the noble lord holds, and with which he points to (*contingit*) the images of his ancestors. He also retains verse 7, but strikes out verses 5th and 6th. (*Rhein. Mus.,* 1848, p. 454, *seqq.*)—*Fumosos.* "All dingy with smoke," *i. e.,* from the *atrium.* This, of course, would be an indication of high antiquity. —*Si coram Lepidis male vivitur.* "If one leads an evil life under the very eyes of the Lepidi." A noble family of the Æmilian gens. He means in the presence of their *imagines.*

9-15. *Quo.* Supply *pertinent.* "Whither tend," *i. e.,* of what real value are?—*Si luditur alea pernox.* "If the dice are played with all night long." In prose, *alea pernox* would be in the ablative, and *luditur* would be an impersonal.—*Numantinos.* Scipio Africanus the younger, who forced Numantia to surrender, B.C. 133, received for this the surname of *Numantinus.*—*Luciferi.* The planet Venus was called *Vesper* or *Hesperus* in the evening, and *Lucifer* or *Phosphorus* in the morning.—*Duces.* "Those leaders of old," *i. e.,* your martial forefathers.—*Cur Allobrogicis,* &c. "Why shall Fabius, though born in an Herculean home, plume himself on many an Allobrogicus, and on the great altar of his line." *Lare* is here for *domo.* Fabius, the founder of the Fabian *gens,* was said to have been a son of Hercules by Vinduna, a daughter of Evander; and by virtue of this descent, the Fabii claimed the exclusive right of ministering at the altar consecrated by Evander to Hercules. It stood in the *Forum Boarium,* near the Circus Flaminius, and was called *Ara Maxima.* Q. Fabius Maximus Æmilianus, the consul in the year B.C. 121, defeated the Allobroges in southern Gaul, at the junction of the Isara (*Isère*) and the Rhone, and received for this the surname of *Allobrogicus*, which he transmitted to his descendants.—*Euganea*. The Euganei originally inhabited Venetia on the Adriatic, but were driven toward the Alps and the Lacus Benacus by the Heneti or Veneti. They possessed numerous flocks of sheep, the wool of which was very celebrated.

16–23. *Catinensi pumice*. The pumice found at Catana, now *Catania*, at the foot of Mount Ætna, was used by the effeminate and luxurious to rub the body with and make it smooth, after the hairs had been removed by resin.—*Squalentes traducit avos*. "He shames his rugged sires." *Squalentes* is put for *incomptos*. The literal meaning of *traduco* here is "to expose to ridicule," "to disgrace." The metaphor is taken from offenders being *led around* through the public places of the city, with the name and nature of their misdeeds inscribed on a tablet suspended from the neck. Hence to expose to public derision generally.—*Frangenda*. The busts and statues of such as had been guilty of any capital crime were delivered up to the common executioner, to be destroyed, that they might not disgrace the name by being exhibited in the funeral processions of the family.—*Ceræ*. For *imagines cereæ*.—*Unica*. "The only real."—*Paullus*. "A Paullus." Such, for instance, as the conqueror of Perseus, king of Macedonia.—*Cossus*. Such as Cornelius Cossus, who won the *spolia opima* from Lar Tolumnius, king of Veii.—*Drusus*. Such as one of the many eminent members of this distinguished family of the Livian *gens*.—*Hos*. Referring to *mores*. He means, Rank virtue above high birth, and let it take precedence even of the consular fasces.

24–29. *Prima mihi debes*, &c. "You owe me first the noble qualities of the mind." If you look for respect from me, I will tell you what I exact first from you, namely, the noble and virtuous qualities of the bosom, duly cultivated and brought into exercise.—*Sanctus*. "A man of spotless integrity."—*Agnosco procerem*. "Then I recognize the true nobleman." Charisius (i., 13, § 3, p. 16, *ed. Lind.*) and Servius (*ad Virg., Æn.*, ix., 309, where one MS., however, acknowledges a genitive singular *proceris*) reckon this noun among the *pluralia tantum*. Capitolinus, however, uses *procer*, and Paulinus of Nola *proceris*. (*Gesn., Thes.*—*Mayor, ad loc.*)—*Gœtulice*. Cn. Cornelius Lentulus Cossus received the surname of *Gœtulicus* from his victory over the Gætuli, A.D. 6, in the reign of Augustus. He had been consul in B.C. 1.—*Seu tu Silanus*. Supply *es*. Silanus was a cognomen of the Junian *gens*. The reference here is particularly to the son-in-law of the Emperor Claudius, who, as Tacitus says (*Ann.*, xvi., 7), "*Claritudine generis, et modesta juventa præcel-*

lebat."—*Patriæ contingis ovanti.* "Thou fallest to the lot of thy rejoicing country." *Contingere* is said of good fortune, *accidere* of misfortunes. — *Osiri invento.* Osiris was the great Egyptian divinity,
and husband of Isis. The allusion in the text is to the great festival
of the finding the scattered remains of the god, who had been dis-
membered by Osiris. The cry of the populace on this occasion was
Εὑρήκαμεν, συγχαίρωμεν.

30–38. *Qui indignus,* &c. Observe the omission of *est* in a relative
sentence, and compare Horace, *Epist.* ii., 2, 139 : " *Cui sic extorta
voluptas."* — *Præclaro nomine tantum insignis.* Panegyric then becomes irony, and can only be applied by antiphrasis, as in the instances cited immediately after. — *Nanum.* Νάννον. The older
Latin term was *pumilio* (*Gell.,* xix., 13). Dwarfs often formed part
of the household of the rich. Domitian was fond of these deformed
specimens of humanity, and the poet may possibly allude to that
emperor here.—*Æthiopem.* Such slaves were much used at Rome,
and always commanded a high price. — *Europen.* "Ἁ Europa."
Daughter of Agenor, and sister of Cadmus.—*Scabie vetusta.* "With
long-standing mange."—*Siccæ lambentibus,* &c. "Licking (in their
hunger) the edges of the lamp, now dry."—*Si quid adhuc est.* An
asyndeton for *seu quid* (scil. *aliud*) *adhuc est.* Compare the Greek
καὶ εἴ τι ἄλλο. (*Toup, Emend. in Suid.,* p. 207.) — *Ergo.* Since a
great name is sometimes ironically applied.—*Ne tu sic Creticus,* &c.
"Lest you in this same way be a Creticus," &c., *i. e.,* lest it may be mere
irony in him who thus addresses you. The common reading is *ne
tu sis,* for which we have not hesitated to give *ne tu sic,* the conjecture of Junius and Schrader. Supply *sis.* — *Creticus.* "A Creticus." Q. Cæcilius Metellus, consul B.C. 69, in the two following
years completed the conquest of Crete, for which he received the
surname of Creticus. — *Camerinus.* Servius Sulpicius Camerinus
was consul B.C. 500, and in the early period of the republic other
members of the family filled high offices. Under the empire the
Camerini again appear in history. (*Dio Cass.,* lxiii., 18.)

39–43. *Rubelli Plaute.* C. Rubellius Blandus married (A.D. 33)
Julia, daughter of Drusus, the son of Tiberius. By her he had a
son, Rubellius Plautus. The latter was thus the great-grandson of
Tiberius, and the great-great-grandson of Augustus, in consequence
of Tiberius having been adopted by Augustus. Descended thus from
the founder of the Roman empire, Plautus incurred the jealousy of
Nero, and was put to death by him. He is the individual alluded
to in the text. The common reading is *Blande,* for which we have
given *Plaute,* the conjectural emendation of Lipsius. It is evident

that the son, not the father, is meant, since the words *tumes alto
Drusorum stemmate* can only apply to the former, who was descended from the Drusi through his mother Julia.—*Et te conciperet*, &c.
"And a mother should conceive you who shines resplendent with
the blood of Iulus," *i. e.*, and on account of which you should deserve to be born of a Julia. We have given *et te*, the conjecture of
Heinrich, in place of the common reading *ut te*, and which makes
the connection plainer. If, however, *ut* be retained, it must be regarded as equivalent to *et ut*, and even then makes an awkward
construction. The Julian *gens*, it will be remembered, claimed descent from Iulus, the son of Æneas.—*Non quæ ventoso*, &c. "Not
one that weaves for hire beneath the shelter of the windy rampart."
The reference is to the *agger*, or rampart of Servius Tullius (completed and enlarged by Tarquinius Superbus). This was a mound
on the eastern side of the city, on which were raised a wall and
towers, and which extended from the Colline gate to the Esquiline.
(*Fabretti, ap. Græv.*, t. iv., p. 1751.) The height of the mound and
wall exposed the place to the winds, whence the epithet *ventosus*.
At the base of the mound were establishments for weaving, &c.,
where the poorer classes worked for daily wages, and in the vicinity
of which they dwelt.

44–50. *Inquit*. Says Rubellius. — *Quorum nemo queat*, &c. Of
such obscure parentage as to be unable to trace out the birth-place
of your parents.—*Cecropides*. "A descendant of Cecrops." Cecrops
was a hero of the Pelasgic race, and the first king of Attica. The
patronymic, therefore, is here employed, not in its literal sense, but
figuratively, merely to denote a person of royal and ancient lineage.
—*Vivas*. "Long life to you." Ironical. Sir, I wish you long life
and much joy of your noble descent.—*Tamen*. Though you scorn
the poor.—*Quiritem*. Not used in the singular by good prose writers. It is found in poets and in some legal formulæ.—*Nobilis indocti*. "Of some ignorant noble." *Nobilis* is here employed as a
substantive. Compare *Sat.* vii., 170: " *Veteres cæcos ;*" and *Cic.,
Lœt.*, 54: "*Insipicus fortunatus.*"—*De plebe togata*. "From the
gowned crowd," *i. e.*, from this herd of low-born civilians. *Togata*
is opposed to *armis industrius*, the *toga* being the garb of peace and
of the law-courts. The general idea is this: Among low-born civilians will be found great lawyers, among low-born soldiers great
captains.—*Qui juris nodos*, &c. "One that shall solve the knotty
points of the law and the enigmas of the statutes." Students of
law in their fourth year were termed *Lytæ* (λύται), or *solutores*, because they were then occupied with the "*Responsa Pauli*," which
were regarded as so many λύσεις, or *solutiones*.

51-60. *Hic.* Another plebeian. — *Petit Euphraten.* He serves
against the Parthians and Armenians. — *Domitique Batavi*, &c.
" And the eagles that keep watch over the conquered Batavi."
Aquilas put for *legiones*, the main standard of the legion being the
eagle.   The Batāvi, or Batăvi (*Lucan*), were a German people, who
occupied the country between the rivers Rhenus, Vahalis, and Mosa.
They made an unsuccessful attempt, under Claudius Civilis (A.D.
69), to shake off the yoke of Rome.—*Industrius.* " Ever active."—
Truncoque simillimus Hermæ. "And most like a Hermes-trunk."
The Hermæ (or *Mercuries*) were a particular kind of statues, in
which only the head, and sometimes the bust, was modelled, all the
rest being left as a plain four-cornered post, a custom which descended from the old Pelasgic style of representing the god Mercu-
ry.   The noble, therefore, who has nothing but his birth to recommend him, is as useless as if he had neither hands nor feet.—*Discrimine.* " Point of difference."—*Illi.* The Hermes-trunk.—*Tua
vivit imago.* "Whereas thy image is endowed with life," *i. e.*, thou
art a breathing statue.—*Teucrorum proles.* Alluding to the descent
of the Julian gens from Iulus and the regal line of Troy.—*Generosa.*
" Highly bred."—*Fortia.* " Spirited."—*Nempe sic.* " It is on this
score surely."   After an interrogation the Latins often give an affirmative reply by *nempe* when the case is too clear to admit of any
doubt. (*Hand, ad Turs.*, iv., p. 161.)—*Facili.* " Conquering with
ease."—*Fervet.* "Glows," *i. e.*, with frequent clapping. — *Rauco.*
" Hoarse with many a shout."

61-65. *Fuga.* " Speed." — *Primus.* " Foremost." — *Sed venale
pecus Coryphæi*, &c. " But the brood of Coryphæus and the posterity of Hirpinus are put up for sale, if victory has but rarely perched
on their yoke."   For a literal translation, supply *venalis* with *posteritas.* Coryphæus and Hirpinus are the names of two horses celebrated for their speed.   The former of these appellations is of
Greek origin, Κορυφαῖος, and means "leader."   The other appears
to be derived from the country of the Hirpini, in Central Italy,
which was famed for its breed of horses.   Both Coryphæus and
Hirpinus were celebrated for their victories in the Roman Circus.
The grandsire of Hirpinus was Aquilo, who had won the first prize
130 times; the second, 88 times; the third, 37 times.   Hirpinus
himself was victorious 114 times as the first winner, 56 times as the
second, and 36 times as the third.   These particulars are obtained
from ancient inscriptions. (*Lips., Epist. ad It. et Hisp.*, 26.)   The
names of several horses are given by Orelli, (*Inscr.* 2593, 4322).
—*Coryphæi.* The common text has *Corytha*, which offends against

K

the metre, the first and second syllables being both short.—*Ibi.* "In their case."—*Majorum.* The pedigree of the steed.—*Gratia nulla umbrarum.* "No favour is shown on account of their departed sires."—*Dominos pretiis,* &c. The horse of highest pedigree is sold for a small sum, to draw a cart, if he wins no palms in the course.

66–70. *Epiredia.* "Carts." *Epiredium* is a hybrid word, compounded from the Greek preposition ἐπί and the Gallic term *reda.* The true meaning, however, is not settled. Schaffer and Ginzrot believe it to have been a square or oblong cart, inclosed with four sides in the same manner as the *reda.* Others, however, consider the word to have reference only to the ornamental decorations of a *reda,* or that it designates the harness of the horses which drew it. The scholiast gives both opinions : " *Ornamenta redarum, aut plaustra.*" We have followed Ginzrot.—*Trito.* " Galled."—*Segnipedes.* This word seems to occur nowhere else.—*Molam.* Mills were commonly worked by asses or mules, sometimes by horses. Above the upper mill-stone a horizontal beam projected, to which the animal was fastened by a trace (*helcium*), and thus, as he was driven round the mill, turned the upper stone on a pivot.—*Nepo'is.* A well-known miller at Rome, who kept his mill at work night and day.— *Te, non tua.* "You, not yours," *i. e.,* you personally for your own sake, and not merely for your family, or fortune, or title.—*Privum aliquid da.* "Exhibit something of your own." Literally, "give (forth to the view)." The common text has *primum,* for which we have substituted *privum,* the excellent emendation of Salmasius (*ad Solin.,* p. 61.)—*Titulis.* The titles marked either on a tomb or on the pedestal of a statue.—*Honores.* The honorary titles of forefathers.—*Dedimus.* Markland (*ad Stat.,* p. 48) conjectures *dabimus.* This, however, weakens the meaning.

71–78. *Juvenem.* Rubellius Plautus.—*Fama.* " Report."—*Plenumque Nerone propinquo.* Consult note on line 39.—*Ferme.* " In general." Generally speaking, it is only now and then that you will meet with an example of due consideration for others in that rank of life.—*Sensus communis.* "The courtesies of good breeding." Not to be rendered by our phrase "common sense," which means something quite different. The idea of Juvenal is well given in Sir W. Hamilton's Reid, p. 759, *a,* as cited by Mayor: "An acquired perception or feeling of the common duties and proprieties expected from each member of society, a gravitation of opinion, a sense of conventional decorum," &c.—*Fortuna.* "Condition of life."—*Censeri laude tuorum.* "To be valued for the renown of your ancestors." Compare line 2.—*Noluerim.* "I don't think I would like." The subjunctive elegantly employed to denote a modest and friendly expression of opinion. (*Madvig*, § 350, *b.*)—*Futuræ laudis.* "Worthy of the praise of posterity." Observe the peculiar employment of the genitive.—*Ruant.* "Fall in ruins."—*Stratus humi.* "Strowed on the ground," *i. e.*, that trails along the ground. Vines were commonly trained on trees, especially on the elm. The idea is: If you owe the support of your fame entirely to that of others, let the latter be removed, and you will be like a vine which has been deprived of the aid of the elm, along which it was wont to climb, and now trails along the ground.—*Viduas.* The training of the vine along the tree is termed, by the Latin poets, marrying the former to the latter.

79-86. *Esto.* "Strive by your own merits to become."—*Arbiter.* The *arbiter* decided according to equity, the *judex* according to strict law.—*Phalaris.* This most cruel of all the Sicilian tyrants seized upon the government of Agrigentum about 570 B.C. His brazen bull passed into imperishable memory. This piece of mechanism was hollow, and sufficiently capacious to contain one or more victims inclosed within it, to perish in tortures when the metal was heated. The cries of these suffering prisoners passed for the roarings of the animal. The artist was named Perillus, and was said to have been himself the first person burnt in it by order of the despot. Consult *Grote, Hist. of Greece*, vol. v., p. 274.—*Admoto.* "Brought near," *i. e.*, placed before your eyes.—*Animam præferre pudori.* "To prefer life to honour."—*Vivendi perdere causas.* "To part with the true motives for existing," *i. e.*, to sacrifice life's true and only end. The only causes that make life truly valuable, the only motives to existence are, according to the heathen view, however, truth, and surviving fame.—*Dignus morte perit*, &c. "He who is deserving of death is dead, even though he sup," &c. He who prefers existence to honour deserves to lose existence; and he who deserves to lose it is already dead, even though he indulge in all manner of luxurious and sensual excesses. To live is to live virtuously and worthily. An opposite course of life is only moral death.—*Gaurana.* Gaurus, or, rather, *montes Gaurani*, was the name given to a volcanic chain of hills between Cumæ and Neapolis, which produced excellent wine. At their foot lay the oyster-beds of Baiæ and of the Lucrine lake.—*Cosmi toto aheno.* "In a whole cauldron of (the perfume of) Cosmus." This was the name of a celebrated perfumer of the day, mentioned repeatedly by Martial.

87-97. *Exspectata diu*, &c. He now proceeds to advise Ponticus as to his government of the province which he has long been waiting for.—*Iræ.* "To vindictive feelings."—*Sociorum.* The inhabitants of the province are meant, according to Ruperti. It is better, however, to suppose, with Heinrich, that actual allies are here spoken of, unto whom the Romans had left kings only in name.—*Vacuis exsucta.* Hypallage for *vacua exsuctis.*—*Fulmine.* The figure turns not so much on the severity of the punishment as on its being a sudden and unexpected one amid so much public corruption.—*Capito.* Cossulianus Capito, a Roman advocate in the reigns of Claudius and Nero. In A.D. 56 he obtained Cilicia as a province, and in the year following was accused by the Cilicians of extortion. Having been condemned, he lost, in consequence, his senatorian rank. But he afterward received this back through the mediation of Tigellinus, his father-in-law, and subsequently came forward as the accuser of Thrasea Pætus, who had supported the cause of the Cilicians against him, and had been instrumental in bringing about his condemnation. Capito was rewarded by Nero with an immense sum of money.—*Numitor.* No governor of Cilicia bearing this name is mentioned in history.—*Piratæ Cilicum.* "Pirates of the Cilicians," *i. e.,* robbers of those who had once been robbers themselves. The Cilicians in former days had been notorious for their bold piracy, and were put down at length by Pompey. —*Quum Pansa eripiat,* &c. Since what one governor leaves you, his successor plunders. This line, in many MSS. and editions, is erroneously placed after the 96th.—*Præconem, Chærippe,* &c. "Chærippus, look around for a crier to sell your patched clothes at auction." The idea is, Waste no more time or money in endeavouring to bring oppressive governors to justice. Sell at auction the little that remains of your impoverished property, and when you have placed the proceeds of the sale out of the reach of extortionate governors, give over complaining.—*Furor.* "Downright madness."—*Naulum.* "The passage-money to Rome." Do not waste the little remnant of your fortunes in an unprofitable journey to Rome to accuse your plunderer.

98–104. *Neque vulnus erat par,* &c. They could better afford then to be deprived of superfluities, than to be stripped of necessaries now.—*Sociis.* The dative.—*Modo.* "But recently." Some give *modo* here the force of *tantummodo,* and make *modo victis* mean "only subdued, not yet plundered." The former, however, is the more natural explanation.—*Spartana chlamys.* "The Spartan military scarf." The epithet *Spartana* here refers to its purple colour, one of the localities where the *murex* was obtained being the promontory of Tænarus, in Laconia. The chlamys was not, as some suppose, a mantle or cloak, but a species of scarf worn by youths, soldiers, hunters, &c. The usual mode of wearing it was to pass one of its shorter sides round the neck, and to fasten it by means of a brooch, either over the breast, in which case it hung down the back, reaching to the calves of the legs, or over the right shoulder, so as to cover the left arm, as is seen in the well-known example of the Belvidere Apollo.—*Conchylia Coa.* "The purples of Cos." The shell-fish put for garments coloured with the dye which it yielded. The island of Cos was famed for its purple dye.—*Par-rhasii.* Parrhasius, the celebrated painter, was a native of Ephesus, and contemporary with Zeuxis. He flourished about B.C. 400.— *Myronis.* Myron, one of the most famous of the Greek statuaries, and also a sculptor and engraver, was born at Eleutheræ, in Bœotia, about B.C. 480.—*Phidiacum vivebat ebur.* "The ivory of Phidias seemed instinct with life." Literally, "the Phidian ivory lived." Phidias, the greatest sculptor and statuary of Greece, was a native of Athens, and was born about the time of the battle of Marathon, B.C. 490. He constructed the Propylæa and Parthenon. His chief works were the statue of Minerva in the Parthenon, and that of Jupiter at Olympia. Many of his productions were in gold and ivory, or chryselephantine.—*Polycleti multus labor.* "Many an elaborate work of Polycletus." Consult note on *Sat.* iii., 198.— *Raræ sine Mentore mensæ.* "Few were the tables without a Mentor," *i. e.*, without a cup of Mentor's chasing. Mentor, the most celebrated silver-chaser among the Greeks, must have flourished before B.C. 356. His works were vases and cups, and were most highly prized by the Romans. Cicero describes the efforts made by Verres to possess himself of a Mentor, the property of one Diodorus (*Verr.*, iv., 38, *seqq.*).

105-112. *Dolabella.* There were three depredators of this name. (1.) Cn. Cornelius Dolabella, impeached by Cæsar for extortion as proconsul of Macedonia, but acquitted. (2.) Cn. Dolabella, prætor of Cilicia, accused by M. Scaurus, and found guilty of a like offence. (3.) P. Cornelius Dolabella, Cicero's son-in-law, and governor of Syria, who seems to have been the worst of the three.— *Antonius.* C. Antonius Hybrida, younger son of Antonius the orator, uncle and father-in-law of the triumvir. After his consulship, in which he was Cicero's colleague (B.C. 63), he received Macedonia as his province, and grievously oppressed it. He was afterward condemned and banished, probably on a charge of *repetundæ.*—*Sacrilegus.* This epithet is purposely reserved for Verres, as pre-eminently worthy of it. Verres was prætor of Sicily, impeached by

Cicero, and condemned. It is satisfactory to find that at last he fell a sacrifice to the same detestable rapacity for which he is here stigmatized, being proscribed by M. Antony, who took a fancy to his Sicilian rarities, and could not obtain them by fair means.—*Navibus altis.* "In their deeply-laden ships." — *Occulta spolia.* They called them " spoils," and yet dared not show them.—*Plures de pace triumphos.* "More triumphs from peace (than were ever won from war)," *i. e.*, more plunder and ornamental works, such as usually grace a triumph.—*Et pater armenti*, &c. So that there is no longer any possibility of making good their losses.—*Spectabile.* " Worth looking at."—*In ædicula.* "In a niche." By *ædicula* is properly meant a shrine, niche, or canopy, with a frontispiece suspended by columns constructed within the cella of a temple, and under which the statue of the divinity was placed.—*Hæc etenim*, &c. "For these are the highest prizes (they can seize upon), since these are the most valuable things (the others have)." *Summis* is to be taken absolutely, *maxima* relatively. The whole clause, however, savours of an awkward interpretation. If we reject it, and read *unus* in line 111 for *unicus*, we can connect this latter line with *Despicias tu* in the 112th, and make a very desirable change. Manso recommends that lines 111 and 112 be both entirely omitted.

113–124. *Unctam.* "Essenced." Equivalent to *unguentis madenten.* Corinth, from its commercial advantages, acquired immense wealth, and became, in consequence, notorious for every species of luxury and debauchery. — *Resinata juventus.* " A resin-smeared youth." A species of resin dissolved in oil was used to clear the skin of superfluous hairs. (*Plin., H. N.*, xiv., 20.)—*Levia.* "Depilated." Opposed to *horrida* in the following line. — *Horrida.* "Shaggy," *i. e.*, rough and uncombed, and of hairy frame.—*Gallicus axis.* "The Gallic sky," *i. e.*, the climate of Gaul, as colder than that of Rome, and breeding fierce men. *Axis* is here put poetically for *cælum.* Some render *Gallicus axis* "the Gallic axle," *i. e.*, war-chariot.—*Latus.* "Coast."—*Messoribus.* The " reapers" here meant are the Africans, from whom Rome derived her principal supply of corn.—*Vacantem.* "Having leisure only." It was the policy of the Roman emperors to amuse the people with shows, &c. Compare *Sat.* x., 80 : " *Duas tantum res anxius optat, Panem et Circenses.*"—*Quanta autem inde*, &c. But if you do commit this foul wrong, what will you gain by it, seeing that Marius lately stripped the impoverished Africans of their all?—*Diræ.* Because by plundering Africa you starve Rome.—*Marius.* Consult note on *Sat.* i., 47.—*Discinxerit.* " Stripped." *Discingere* properly means to remove the girdle, ungird. This, in the case of a thinly-attired race like the Africans, passes very easily into the cognate meaning of to strip, &c.—*Fortibus et miseris.* "Unto those who are bold as well as wretched."—*Spoliatis.* "Unto them, even though plundered of every thing else."

125-134. *Quod modo proposui,* &c. "What I have just set forth is no mere opinion of my own."—*Verum est.* The common text has *verum* the adverb, without *est,* connected in construction with *credite.*—*Folium Sibyllæ.* The Cumæan Sibyl wrote her predictions on palm leaves.—*Si tibi sancta cohors comitum.* "If you have an upright retinue of followers." The *cohors comitum* were the persons composing the governor's suite.—*Nemo Acersecomes.* "No minion with unshorn locks," *i. e.,* no favourite youth, with flowing locks like Bacchus or Apollo. Acersecomes is a Greek term, ἀκερσεκόμης, derived from ἀ priv., κείρω, "to cut short," and κόμη, "the hair."—*Tribunal.* "Your decisions as magistrate."—*Conjuge.* The avarice and rapacity of the women, who followed their husbands to their governments, had long ere this become a serious subject of complaint. Before the time of Augustus, the women rarely, if ever, went abroad. That uxorious emperor took Livia with him in most of his expeditions, and his example seems to have had a pernicious effect; for, in the succeeding reign, the custom was grown so common, and so oppressive to the provinces, that Severus Cæcina made a motion against it in the Senate. (*Tac., Ann.,* iii., 34.)—*Per conventus.* "Through the circuits," *i. e.,* the judicial districts. In order to facilitate the administration of justice, a province was divided into a number of districts or circuits, each of which was called *conventus, forum,* or *jurisdictio.*—*Celæno.* "Like another Celæno," *i. e.,* Harpy-like. Celæno was one of the Harpies, the daughters, according to Hesiod, of Thaumas by the Oceanid Electra.—*Tunc licet a Pico,* &c. Then you are welcome to boast of your nobility, and may derive it from as early a source as you choose.—*Pico.* Picus was a Latin prophetic divinity, and the father of Faunus. In some traditions he was called the first king of Italy.—*Omnem Titanida pugnam.* "The whole host of the Titans." Literally, "the whole Titan conflict," *i. e.,* every Titan that engaged in the conflict with Jove. The contest was between Jove and Saturn for the supremacy of the skies. The Titans fought for Saturn, who was one of their number.—*Promethea.* Prometheus was one of the most distinguished among the Titans, and the moulder of primæval man.—*De quocunque voles libro.* He means any book or work whatsoever, in which fabulous names and legends are set forth.

136-145. *Virgas.* "Your fasces."—*Sociorum in sanguine.* "In the blood of our allies," *i. e.*, on their bloody backs. Persons condemned to death were first scourged by the lictors and then beheaded.—*Hebetes.* "Blunted by constant use."—*Contra te stare.* "To stand up against you," *i. e.*, to rise in judgment against you.— *Pudendis.* "Your shameful deeds." The nobility of your line only serves to make your shameful deeds more conspicuous, and to expose them in a clearer light.—*Conspectius crimen.* "The more glaring criminality."—*Major habetur.* That is, in exact proportion to the rank in life of him who offends.—*Quo mihi te solitum,* &c. "Why vaunt yourself to me, accustomed as you are to affix your seal to forged wills in the very temples which your grandsire erected," *i. e.*, why vaunt your pedigree to me? you that are accustomed, &c. Supply *jactas.* The sealing and witnessing of wills was usually performed in temples, in the morning, and fasting, as the canon law afterward directed. A forged will is here substituted for the true one, which the degenerate noble has abstracted. Wills, after being executed, were kept in temples, like other valuables.—*Santonico cucullo.* "With a Santonic cowl." This was the same as the *Burdocucullus,* namely, a cloak of coarse materials, with a hood attached to it, made and worn by the Santones, who occupied the coast of Gaul to the north of the Garumna or Garonne. The name of this people still survives in *Saintes,* the capital of the old province of *Saintonge.*

146-149. *Præter majorum cineres,* &c. The sepulchres of the higher classes were erected along the great roads leading forth from Rome, such as the Appian, Flaminian, and Latin Ways. Compare *Sat.* i., 155. The poet here inveighs against the low and depraved taste of the Roman nobility as exhibited in their passion for charioteering. The fashion was introduced in compliment to Nero.—*Carpento.* The *carpentum* was a species of covered chariot, with two wheels, used by females and by the luxurious.—*Pinguis Lateranus.* "The bloated Lateranus." Plautius Lateranus is meant. He was condemned to death by the Emperor Claudius (A.D. 48) in consequence of an intrigue with Messalina, but pardoned on account of the brilliant services of his uncle, Aulus Plautius, the conqueror of Britain. He was deprived, however, of his rank as senator, but was afterward restored to this on the accession of Nero in A.D. 56. Ten years subsequently, though consul elect, he took part in the conspiracy of Piso, and was put to death. The greater part of the MSS. have *Damasippus* here in place of *Lateranus,* but others, and among them one of the best, give the latter reading, which we have adopt-

ed with Heinrich, Jahn, and others, and so again in line 151. The
Damasippus mentioned in line 185 is a quite different character.—
Multo sufflamine. " With the frequent drag-chain." The introduction of the drag-chain, as Badham remarks, has a local propriety:
Rome, with its seven hills, had just so many necessities for the frequent use of the sufflamen.—*Sed sidera testes*, &c. "But the stars
strain on him their attesting eyes." Some prefer making *testes* here
a nominative.

150–155. *Honoris.* "Of elevated office," *i. e.*, the consulship.—
Nusquam. Not even in the most public place.—*Trepidabit.* Takes
an accusative here by a poetic and rare usage. Compare *Sat.* x.,
21.—*Ac virga prior annuet.* "And will be the first to give him the
salute with his whip." This is called in Greek προσκυνεῖν τῇ μάσ-
τιγι, an expression employed by Dio Cassius, in speaking of Cara-
calla, when that emperor appeared as a charioteer, and saluted the
umpires (lxxvii., 10). The term *prior* implies that he does not turn
away his head in shame, but tries to catch his friend's eye by the
movement of his whip.—*Infundet.* Theophrastus makes it a characteristic of the ἄγροικος, or boorish man, τοῖς ὑποζυγίοις ἐμβαλεῖν
τὸν χόρτον. (*Charact.*, 4.)—*Hordea.* Horses in Italy are fed on
barley, not on oats.—*Lanatas.* "The woolly victims." Used substantively, like *laniger, bidens,* &c.—*Robumque juvencum.* "And the
red steer." Red oxen were most highly valued. We have given
robum here, with Orelli, Madvig, Jahn, and Mayor. The common
text has *torvum.* The epithet *robus* is an archaic one, and purposely employed here to harmonize with *more Numæ* in the succeeding line. As regards its meaning, compare the words of Paulus Di-
aconus (*ed. Lind.*, p. 134): "Robum *rubro colore et quasi rufo sig-
nificari, ut bovem quoque rustici appellant, manifestum est....Hinc et
homines valentes et boni coloris* robusti."

156–162. *More Numæ.* Numa was the founder of the Roman
ritual. The consuls offered an ox to Jupiter Capitolinus on entering upon their office, and also to Jupiter Latiaris on the Alban
Mount. — *Eponam.* Epona was the patron-goddess of grooms and
horses. Images of her, either statues or paintings, were frequently
seen in niches of stables. Various inscriptions in honour of her are
given by Orelli (402, 1792, *seqq.*). Some MSS. give *Hipponam*, according to the Greek form Ἵππωναν, omitting *solam.* Gifford prefers this latter form on account of the tameness, as he thinks, of
the epithet *solam.* But *solam* is by no means tame here. It shows,
on the contrary, that, even amid the most solemn rites, he thinks
of her alone, and that all his thoughts are engrossed by horses and

stables. — *Facies olida*, &c. Referring to rude representations of
Epona and other deities painted on the stalls. — *Olida.* "Rank." —
Pervigiles instaurare popinas. "To repeat his visits to the taverns
open all night long." — *Obvius assiduo*, &c. "The Syro-Phœnician,
wet with his constant perfumes, runs to meet him, the Syro-Phœnician that dwells at the Idumæan gate." Under the Romans, Phœ-
nice, which was included in the province of Syria, received the
name of Συροφοινίκη, to distinguish it from Syria proper. It comprised the narrow strip of land between Mount Lebanon and the
Mediterranean, from Aradus in the north to Carmel in the south.
— *Amomo.* Compare *Sat.* iv., 108. — *Idumeæ portæ.* The gate at
Rome, near the arch of Titus, through which Vespasian and Titus
entered the city in triumph after their victories in Palestine. — *Hospitis affectu.* "With all the studied courtesy of a host." That the
caupones invited passers-by to enter appears from Cicero, *pro Cluent.*,
§ 163. The Syro-Phœnicians were famous for their insinuating address. — *Cyane.* A *Copa Syrisca* (a Syrian female castanet-dancer)
accustomed to exhibit in taverns. — *Succincta.* "With gown tucked
up," *i. e.*, nimble, active. This was done by tightening the girdle.
The opposite term is *discinctus.*

164-172. *Desisti nempe.* "You have given it up, you mean to
say." — *Ultra.* "Beyond that period." — *Breve sit quod turpiter
audes.* To err is human, but to persist in error is gross folly. —
Crimina. "Faults." — *Thermarum.* These *thermæ* were connected
with and formed part of the *popinæ.* After coming out of the bath,
they often staid and drank hard. — *Inscripta lintea.* "The inscribed linen signs." These were linen curtains, having inscribed
or painted on them what was for sale within. — *Armeniæ.* Compare
line 51. — *Præstare Neronem*, &c. Lateranus is in the prime of life;
he has vigour enough to secure Nero from all fear of foreign enemies. — *Mitte ostia*, &c. "Pass by his own doors, Cæsar," &c.
Most commentators render this, "Send to Ostia, Cæsar," *i. e.*, send
your legatus to Ostia, at the mouth of the Tiber, to take command
of the troops for foreign service, waiting for embarkation there.
But if this were the meaning, then, as Heinrich remarks, *ad* should
be expressed, and either *Tiberina* added, or *Ostia* made of the first
declension. The true idea, therefore, appears to be, "Don't inquire for your general at his own abode of the Ostiarius, but seek
for him in some drinking establishment.

173-182. *Percussore.* "Cut-throat." — *Fabros sandapilarum.*
"Cheap coffin-makers." The rich were carried out to burial on a
lectus, or *lectica funebris*; the poor in a coarse and common kind of

open coffin or bier, called *sandapila*. This was used also for the bodies of gladiators who had been slain in the amphitheatre, and also for malefactors.—*Galli resupinati*. " Of some priest of Cybele, lying drunk upon his back." The worship of Cybele was of an orgiastic character, and her rites became closely connected with those of Dionysus or Bacchus. At Rome the Galli were her priests.—*Lectus non alius*. " No different couch." No couch is more honourable than the rest, as at private banquets. — *Remotior*. " Set more aloof from the herd." — *Nempe*. " Doubtless." — *Lucanos*. Slaves were sent into the country as a punishment, and were kept there at hard labour. In Lucania and Etruria, as well as other parts of Italy, many of the Roman nobility had extensive estates worked by large gangs of slaves. — *Ergastula*. " Work-houses." The *ergastulum* was a private prison attached to most Roman farms, where the slaves were made to work in chains. It appears to have been usually under ground. The slaves confined in an *ergastulum* were also employed to cultivate the fields in chains. Slaves who had displeased their masters were punished by imprisonment in the *ergastulum;* and in the same place all slaves who could not be depended upon, or were barbarous in their habits, were regularly kept. —*Trojugenæ*. The Roman nobles of ancient families are meant. Compare *Sat.* i., 85.—*Cerdoni*. " Unto a low mechanic." Compare *Sat.* iv., 152.— *Volesos*. The Volesi were sprung from one of the three noble Sabines who settled at Rome with King Tatius, in the reign of Romulus. The name was afterward changed to Valerii, who are here, in fact, meant.

183–187. *Quid, si nunquam*, &c. The idea is, What will you say if, after the examples which I have produced, though so foul and shameful, there should remain still worse ones?—*Damasippe*. A fictitious name.— *Vocem locasti sipario*. " You hired out your voice to the stage." The *siparium* is commonly supposed to have been a piece of tapestry stretched on a frame, which rose before the stage of the theatre, and consequently answered the purpose of a drop-scene with us, although, contrary to our practice, it was depressed when the play began, so as to go below the level of the stage, and was raised again when the performance was concluded. It is here taken figuratively for the stage itself. Some, however, make it a kind of folding screen.—*Clamosum ageres*, &c. " To act the noisy Phasma of Catullus." *Phasma*, or the " Apparition," was the Greek title of a mime, composed by Q. Luctatius Catullus. The scholiast says that Damasippus appeared in it as a *præco*, or crier. Others suppose that the character personated by him raised a loud cry at the sight of the apparition.—*Laureolum velox*, &c. " Lentulus, light of heel, also acted well the part of Laureolus." This is supposed to be uttered by Damasippus in self-defence. He cites the instance of another noble who appeared on the stage in a mime, the principal character in which was a captain of a band of robbers named Laureolus, who was represented as affixed to a cross, and torn to pieces by wild beasts.—*Dignus vera cruce.* Richly deserving to be crucified in earnest for turning actor upon a public stage. Those who appeared on the stage became *infames.*

188–194. *Nec tamen ipsi*, &c. Lentulus and other nobles, who thus degrade themselves, may be most to blame, yet even the spectators are not to be excused. If they had any shame they would not sit out such plays. For the people themselves are degraded in the voluntary degradation of their superiors.—*Durior.* " Is still more hardened."—*Triscurria.* " The gross buffooneries." The prefix *tri* has a superlative force. Compare *trivenefica.*—*Planipedes audit Fabios.* " Who listen to the bare-footed Fabii." The epithet *planipes* is applied to an actor in the mime, who received this designation because he came upon the stage with naked feet ; that is, without either the *cothurnus* or *soccus.*—*Mamercorum alapas.* " The slaps on the faces of the Mamerci." The Mamerci were a noble family of the Æmilian *gens.* The whole *gens* traced its descent from Mamercus, a son of Numa.— *Quanti sua funera*, &c. " What difference does it make at how high a price they sell their own obsequies." Commentators generally refer the words *sua funera* to gladiatorial exhibitions, and hence the usual translation is, " at how high a price they sell their lives." The explanation given by Madvig, however, is far preferable. When these nobles sell, that is, hire out their services to the public stage, they not only give the death-blow to the glory of their own line, but, being themselves dead, as it were, to all sense of shame, their appearance as actors amounts virtually to a celebration of their own obsequies. Nor does the circumstance of their receiving high theatrical wages afford any palliation ; the act on their part is voluntary, and not brought about by compulsion from any tyrant.—*Nullo cogente Nerone.* According to Suetonius (*Ner.*, 12), Nero, on one occasion, compelled 400 senators and 600 equites to exhibit in the arena of the public amphitheatre. Lipsius, however, with great probability, conjectures that the true numbers are 40 and 60 respectively.—*Nec dubitant*, &c. This line is generally regarded as an awkward interpolation. —*Celsi prætoris.* " Of the prætor seated on high." The prætor now, as formerly the ædile, superintended the games of the circus and the theatrical representations. The person who exhibited the games, &c., sat on a place elevated like a pulpit or tribunal.

195–199. *Finge tamen gladios*, &c. "Imagine, however, on the one hand, the swords (of a tyrant), and place, on the other, the stage. Which is the better alternative?" To show how utterly disgraceful is this appearing on a public stage, the poet says that even death itself, in case you refused to obey an order so to appear, would be infinitely preferable. Some commentators refer *gladios* here to gladiatorial exhibitions, and make the meaning to be that even to lose one's life as a public gladiator is better than to appear as an actor. We have followed Madvig's interpretation, which is the only true one.—*Mortem sic quisquam exhorruit*, &c. The idea is, Who would be such a craven as not rather to forfeit existence than to appear as an actor, and associate with so vile a crew as the performers of the day?—*Zelotypus Thymeles*, &c. "The jealous husband of Thymele, the fellow-actor of the stupid Corinthus." Two actors are here given as a fair specimen of the whole histrionic fraternity, with whom it would be such degradation to associate. The first of these is Latinus, of whom mention is made in *Sat.* i., 34; the other is Corinthus, a sort of theatrical buffoon or harlequin.—*Res haud mira tamen*, &c. No wonder, however, that a nobleman in the reign of Nero, who turned harper himself, should be influenced by and follow the example of that emperor. The object of the poet here is to show the mischief which results from the example of princes.—*Cithærœdo principe.* "When a prince turns harper." The allusion is to Nero, and his public appearance as a cithærœdus.—*Hæc ultra, quid erit*, &c. What will there be beyond this but a gladiatorial exhibition?" *i. e.*, to crown all this, what is left but some disgraceful exhibition, on the part of our nobles, as gladiators in the amphitheatre? *Ludus* properly means the gladiatorial school, in which the gladiators were trained by the lanista. Compare *Cic. in Cat.*, ii., 9.—*Et illud dedecus*, &c. "And that disgrace of the city you (already) have." There is no futurity about it, but it is actually present.

200–210.—*Mirmillonis.* The *Mirmillones* were a class of gladiators usually matched in combat with the *Thraces* or the *Retiarii.* They wore the Gallic helmet, with the image of a fish ($\mu o \rho \mu \acute{v} \lambda o \varsigma$, whence their name) for the crest. Gracchus did not appear as one of these, because the face was concealed by a vizor, and his unblushing impudence courted notoriety.—*Nec clypeo*, &c. "Nor (as a Thracian) fighting with shield or uplifted faulchion." A second class of gladiators are here meant, distinct from the first, and called

Thracians from their being armed like the natives of Thrace. They had the small Thracian shield, and a short sword with a curved blade and sharp point. Gracchus did not appear either as one of these, for the same reason as already given.—*Damnat tales habitus*. Because they conceal the visage.—*Nec galea faciem abscondit.* He appears as a *Retiarius.* This name was given to a gladiator who wore no helmet nor any body-armour, but was equipped with a net (*rete*, whence his name) and a heavy trident, or three-pronged fork. His art consisted in casting the net over the head of his adversary, generally a *Secutor*, with whom he was matched; and then, if he succeeded in his throw, he attacked his opponent with his trident. Gracchus appeared as one of these because there was no covering for the head, and the face was fully exposed to view.—*Nequidquam effudit.* "He has cast without effect." If the Retiarius failed in his throw, having no defensive armour, he immediately took to flight, and endeavoured to collect his net for a second cast before he could be overtaken by his adversary, who pursued him round the arena, and hence was called *secutor.*—*Spectacula.* "The spectators."—*Agnoscendus.* "Easy to be recognized."—*Credamus tunicæ.* If any one still entertain doubts whether the personage thus moving in the arena be Gracchus, a Roman nobleman, and is not satisfied with the view of his visage, let him give credence to his tunic. Gracchus was one of the priesthood denominated *Salii,* or priests of Mars, and, as such, wore an embroidered tunic with a gold fringe around the border, and also a tall conical cap, fastened under the chin by a gold band of twisted work.—*De faucibus aurea,* &c. "Since the golden band of twisted work reaches upward from his chin, and is tossed to and fro from his tall cap."—*Sequutor.* "The Secutor." Compare note on *nequidquam effudit.*

212–220. *Senecam præferre Neroni.* There is generally supposed to be an allusion here to the plot of Subrius Flavius to assassinate Nero by the aid of Piso, and then to cut off Piso and make Seneca emperor. It was believed that Seneca was privy to it. Compare *Tac., Ann.,* xv., 65.—*Non debuit una parari,* &c. The punishment of parricides was to be scourged till they bled, and then to be sewn up in a sack (*culeus*) with a dog, cock, viper, and ape, and to be thrown into the sea if the sea was at hand, and if not, by a constitution of Hadrian they were exposed to wild beasts, or, in the time of Paullus, to be burned. The ape would appear to be a late addition. Among the Romans, the crime of parricide was extended to the killing of a brother, sister, uncle, aunt, and many other relations enumerated by Marcianus. (*Dig.* 49, tit. 9, s. 1.) Nero murdered his mother Agrippina, his aunt Domitia, both his wives, Octavia and Poppæa, his brother Britannicus, and several other relations. Hence the propriety of Juvenal's language, " non *una*," &c.—*Par Agamemnonidæ crimen.* Alluding to Orestes, who slew his mother Clytemnæstra. There was a well-known verse current at Rome in Nero's days : Νέρων, Ὀρέστης, Ἀλκμαίων, μητροκτόνοι.—*Causa.* "The motive."—*Deis auctoribus.* Orestes acted by direction of Apollo.—*Inter pocula.* Juvenal follows the Homeric account, according to which Ægisthus invited Agamemnon, on his return home, to a repast, and had him and his companions treacherously murdered during the feast. In Æschylus, a bath is the scene of the murder. —*Sed nec Electræ,* &c. He never imbrued his hands in the blood of a sister or a wife. Orestes married his cousin Hermione, daughter of Menelaus and Helen.—*Conjugii.* For *conjugis.*—*Aconita.* Nero poisoned Britannicus, Domitia, and Antonia ; he twice attempted to poison his mother, but she was secured by antidotes. He thought of poisoning the whole Senate. (*Suet., Ner.,* 43.)—*In scena.* Before singing on the stage in the public theatres, Nero practised in a private theatre.

221-223. *Troica non scripsit.* "He never wrote a poem on Trojan events." Among his other follies, Nero composed an epic poem entitled *Troica,* which he recited publicly in the theatre. (*Dio Cass.,* lxii., 29.) On Nero's poems, consult Tacitus, *Ann.,* xiii., 3 ; xiv., 16, &c. Some affirmed that he was not the author of the works which went by his name, but Suetonius (*Ner.,* 52) had seen some originals, with erasures and corrections, all in his handwriting.— *Quid enim Verginius,* &c. Ironical. What crime, of all that Nero committed in his cruel tyranny, more called for vengeance than the having composed so stupid a poem?—*Verginius.*—L. Verginius Rufus, consul A.D. 63, was governor of Germania Superior A.D. 68, when Julius Vindex, proprætor of Gaul, rose against Nero. Vindex having offered Galba, governor of Hispania Tarraconensis, the empire, Galba also revolted. Verginius marched against Vindex. At Vesontio (*Besançon*) the two generals had a conference, and, it was said, agreed to unite against Nero. Owing to a mistake, however, their armies joined battle, and Vindex, being defeated, fell by his own hand. Verginius afterward repeatedly refused the empire. He lived until A.D. 97, when his funeral oration was pronounced by Tacitus, who was consul that year. Pliny the younger, his neighbour and ward, speaks of him in the highest terms of praise.—*Galba.* Successor to Nero in the empire.—*Quod Nero,* &c. The common text ends the previous line with a mark of interrogation, and has here *Quid Nero,* commencing a new interrogative sentence.

224–230. *Generosi principis.* "Of a high-born prince." Ironical.
—*Gaudentis fœdo*, &c. "Delighting to have his high rank prosti-
tuted by disgraceful singing on a foreign stage, and to have earned
the parsley of the Grecian crown." We have adopted *cantu*, with
Jahn and Mayor, as preferable to *saltu*, the more common reading.
Nero was in Greece A.D. 67, into which year he crowded all the
Grecian games. He received no less than 1800 crowns, partly in
compliment, and partly for his so-called victories at these games;
and on his return to Rome he entered the city in triumph, wearing
on his head an Olympic crown of wild olive, and bearing in his
hand a Pythian crown of bay, while he had the catalogue of his
victories borne before him. The parsley crown mentioned in the
text had special reference to the musical contests connected with
the Nemean games, in which games a crown of parsley was the
prize.—*Insignia.* "The trophies." Ironical. The Romans used to
hang their *insignia* around the pedestals of their ancestors' statues,
or, if there were no statues, they appended them to the *imagines* in
the *atrium.*—*Domiti.* Domitius was the name of both the father and
grandfather of Nero. His father was Domitius Ahenobarbus, governor of Transalpine Gaul.—*Thyestæ.* Vindex also charged Nero
with appearing in this character (*Dio Cass.*, lxiii., 9). — *Syrma.*
"The long trailing robe." The *syrma* (σύρμα) was a long robe,
trailing on the ground, more particularly worn upon the tragic stage
by actors who performed the parts of divine or heroic personages.
It was intended to give grandeur and dignity to the person, and at
the same time to conceal the unsightly appearance of the high-soled
buskin, or *cothurnus*, at the back of the actor.—*Antigonæ.* Nero
himself wrote a tragedy named *Antigone.—Personam Menalippes.*
"The mask of Melanippe." Melanippe, daughter of Æolus and
Eurydice, bore to Neptune twins, Æolus and Bœotus. Two of the
tragedies of Euripides bore her name.—*Et de marmoreo*, &c. Not
the colossal statue (120 feet high) of Nero himself, which stood in
the vestibule of the *golden house* (*Suet.*, *Ner.*, 31), for this was of
brass, but most probably the statue of a Domitius. Some commentators, misled by a passage in Suetonius (*Ner.*, 12), suppose the statue
of Augustus to be meant, but the reference there is to a crown, not
to the lyre itself.

231–236. *Tuis natalibus.* "Than thy lineage." Catiline was the
descendant of an ancient patrician family, which had sunk into poverty. His great-grandfather and his great-great-grandfather both
bore the name of M. Sergius Silo, and were both distinguished men.
—*Cethegi.* Cethegus also was descended from an old patrician line.

Compare Horace (*Ep. ad Pis.*, 50), "*cinctutis Cethegis.*"—*Arma tamen*, &c. Compare *Plut., Cic.,* 18 ; *Cic., Cat.,* iii., 14, &c. ; *Sall., Cat.,* 43, &c.—*Ut Braccatorum pueri*, &c. "As though you had been the sons of the braccæ-wearing Gauls and the descendants of the Senones," *i. e.*, of the hereditary and inveterate enemies of Rome. The Latin term *braccæ* is the same as the Scottish "breeks" and the English "breeches." They were a kind of trowsers or pantaloons worn by the Gauls and many other ancient nations. *Braccata*, however, was a name specially given by the Romans to what was afterward the *Provincia Narbonensis*, and the allusion in the text appears to be particularly to the Allobroges, a Gallic people in this quarter, who had been invited, through their ambassadors, to join in the conspiracy of Catiline. — *Senonum.* The Senones in Gaul were bounded by the Parisii on the north, and the Ædui on the south. Their name still survives in that of the town *Sens.* A band of them settled on the Adriatic, between Ravenna and Ancona. This was the nation which took and burned Rome, B.C. 390.—*Tunica molesta.* "With the tunic of torture." Consult note on *Sat.* i., 140.—*Sed vigilat consul.* On the night of the 1st of November, B.C. 63, Catiline had planned an attempt on Cicero, who, however, frustrated his purpose. Compare *Cic., Cat.,* 1, 8 : "*Intelliges multo me* vigilare *acrius ad salutem, quam te ad perniciem reipublicæ.*"

237–243. *Hic novus Arpinas.* "This 'new man' of Arpinum." Cicero was a native of Arpinum, and of equestrian, not patrician origin. The appellation "*novus homo*" was applied by the Romans to a plebeian who first attained a curule office, and was the founder of his family's *nobilitas.* Metellus Nepos, in a debate with Cicero, often asked, "Who is your father?" (*Plut., Cic.,* 26).—*Municipalis.* A term applied to a native of a *municipium.* There were various kinds of *municipes*, some enjoying the full rights of Roman citizens, others only a portion of such rights. The natives of Arpinum belonged to the former class. The term *municipalis* would be employed by a Roman noble with a sneer.—*Galeatum ponit*, &c. The Roman knights, under Atticus, were stationed by Cicero in the Capitol. Sestius also brought troops from Capua. (*Cic., Ep. ad Att.*, ii., 1, 6 ; *pro Sest.*, 11.)—*Attonitis.* "For the bewildered citizens."—*In omni monte.* This is the reading of the scholiast, and is adopted by Jahn. The common text has *in omni gente*, which commentators explain by *de omni populo.* Our reading, however, is far superior, and is the same as *in tota urbe.* Another reading is *in omni ponte*, in allusion to the arrest of the ambassadors of the Allobroges at the Mulvian bridge. — *Toga.* "The peaceful toga."

The *toga* was the robe of peace, the *sagum* the cloak of war. The reference is to Cicero in his civil capacity as magistrate.—*Leucade.* "From Leucadia." The reference is to the battle of Actium. Leucadia, now *Santa Maura*, an island off the western coast of Acarnania, was in reality 240 stadia distant from Actium, but is here put poetically for the scene of the conflict itself.—*Thessaliæ campis.* The battle of Philippi is meant; but there is either an error in geography here, by which Philippi is confounded with Pharsalia, or else Thessaly is put by a bold poetic license for Thrace. Merivale (*Hist. Rom. Emp.*, iii., 214) charges the Roman writers with direct error in making the battle of Philippi to have been fought on the same spot as the battle of Pharsalia.—*Abstulit.* Supply *non*, from the previous clause.—*Udo cædibus assiduis gladio.* These words are supposed by some to refer to the brutal cruelty of Augustus after the battle.

244-253. *Patrem Patriæ.* This title was first given to Cicero by Catulus, in the Senate (*Cic. pro Sest.*, 121).—*Arpinas alius.* The celebrated Caius Marius. Cicero often names him as his fellow-townsman. Marius was born at the village of Cereatæ, near Arpinum, B.C. 157.—*Volscorum.* Arpinum belonged originally to the Volsci, afterward to the Samnites, from whom it was wrested by the Romans.—*Poscere mercedes.* "To ask for his wages." So indigent is the family represented to have been from which the future saviour of Rome arose, that young Marius is said to have worked as a common peasant, for wages, before he entered the ranks of the Roman army.—*Nodosam frangebat*, &c. "He broke the knotted vine-sapling with his head," *i. e.*, he had it broken about his head. The vine-sapling was the centurion's baton of office, as well as his instrument of punishment.—*Cimbros.* Alluding to the famous inroad of the Cimbri and Teutones. They defeated successively six consular armies, until, in the end, they were conquered by Marius, B.C. 101, in the Campi Raudii, near Vercellæ.—*Excipit.* "Sustains," *i. e.*, braves.—*Stragem.* The Cimbri are said to have lost in the battle with Marius 100,000, or even 140,000 men.—*Majora cadavera.* The Cimbri, like the Germans, were remarkable for their stature. —*Nobilis collega.* "His nobly-born colleague." Q. Lutatius Catulus, consul with Marius B.C. 102. Juvenal follows the popular opinion, which gave to Marius the whole merit of having saved Rome. Another version, however, derived confessedly from the commentaries of Sulla, and probably also from the historical work of Catulus himself, gives the whole honour of the victory to the latter. The testimony of these two authorities, however, cannot be received with confidence, since they were bitter enemies of Marius.

254-260. *Plebeia fuerunt nomina.* "Their very names were plebeian."—*Pro totis legionibus,* &c. The father, son, and grandson all bore the name of *P. Decius Mus,* and all devoted themselves for their country, the first in a war with the Latins, the second in one with the Gauls, the third in that with Pyrrhus. Compare Arnold, *Hist. Rom.,* ii., 509.—*Pro totis legionibus,* &c. The legions were Roman, the auxiliaries were the forces of the allies, the Latin youth were the flower of Latium.—*Sufficiunt dis infernis,* &c. Juvenal comes very near the formula of self-devotion given in Livy (viii., 6) : "*Exercitum Diis Manibus matrique terræ deberi.*" It was believed that if a leader would consent to this sacrifice of himself, the misfortunes which impended over the combatants would all, by this pious and patriotic act, be transferred to the foe.—*Pluris enim Decii,* &c. "For the Decii were more highly valued by them." Supply *erant.*—*Ancilla natus,* &c. The allusion is to Servius Tullius, who was the son of Ocrisia or Ocriculana, a captive from Corniculum. His mother became a female slave of Tanaquil, the wife of Tarquinius Priscus.—*Trabeam.* The trabea was a white robe with a border, and broad horizontal stripes (*trabes*) of purple, worn by the Roman kings, and afterward by the consuls. Servius (*ad Æn.,* vii., 612) mentions three kinds of trabea ; one wholly of purple, which was sacred to the gods ; another of purple and white, worn by the kings and consuls, and also by the equites ; and another of purple and saffron, which belonged to augurs. The consuls wore the trabea in public solemnities, such as opening the temple of Janus. The equites likewise wore it at the *transvectio,* and on other public occasions. Hence the trabea is mentioned as one of the badges of the equestrian order.—*Diadema.* The *diadema* of the ancient kings was a fillet or ribbon, not a crown.—*Meruit.* "Won."—*Regum ultimus ille bonorum.* "That last of good kings." He was succeeded by Tarquinius Superbus.

261-268. *Laxabant.* "Attempted to loosen." Observe the force of the imperfect.—*Juvenes ipsius consulis.* The sons of Brutus, put to death by their own father's sentence for this nefarious conspiracy against the new-born liberties of their country.—*Magnum aliquid.* "Some glorious achievement."—*Coclite.* Horatius Cocles kept the troops of Porsena at bay while the bridge was broken down behind him, and, when this was done, he plunged into the Tiber and rejoined his comrades.—*Mucius.* Mucius Scævola, having assassinated the secretary of King Porsena instead of the monarch himself, thrust his right hand into the fire on the altar, and held it there without flinching.—*Et quæ,* &c. Clœlia, who had been given as a hostage to the Tuscans, made her escape, and swam, on horseback, across the Tiber, which then divided the Etrurian and Roman territories.—*Imperii fines.* After the surrender of the city (*dedita urbe,* *Tac., Hist.,* iii., 72) to Porsena, the Romans lost their territory on the right bank of the river. (*Niebuhr, R. H.,* i., 546.)— *Servus.* A slave of the Aquilii, who were among the conspirators to restore the Tarquins.—*Matronis lugendus.* When Brutus died, the Roman matrons mourned a whole year for him, as for a parent. Of like honour this slave was deemed worthy. But the sons of Brutus died by public execution, after having been flogged like slaves.—*Legum prima securis.* The first legal, as opposed to arbitrary execution.

269-275. *Malo pater tibi,* &c. The concluding idea of the Satire is given as follows by Holyday : It were better to be the son of an unworthy Thersites, so that one's self were an Achilles, than to be a Thersites, though one were the son of an Achilles. But, says he, by way of jeer, to the noblest Roman, thou canst not properly derive thyself better than from the company which assembled at Romulus's asylum. — *Æacidæ.* A Homeric name of Achilles, son of Peleus, the son of Æacus. Achilles is contrasted with Thersites as being not only the bravest, but the fairest of the Greeks.—*Vulcania arma.* Made by Vulcan, at the request of Thetis, to supply the place of those lost with Patroclus.—*Et tamen,* &c. If you were indeed nobly born, it would avail you little ; in fact, however, your pedigree, be it as long as it may, ends at last in a shepherd or a bandit of the asylum. (*Mayor, ad loc.*)—*Ut longe,* &c. "However far you go back, and however far you trace your name." Supply *ut* with the second *longe.*—*Deducis.* "You do but derive."—*Infami asylo.* Romulus, according to the legend, in order to augment the number of his subjects, established an asylum or sanctuary for the reception of all who would fly thither from servitude, from debt, or from justice.—*Pastor.* Romulus and Remus were shepherds, and so were their immediate followers.—*Aut illud quod dicere nolo.* As we say in English, Or some one no better than he should be.

SATIRE X.

ARGUMENT.

The subject of this inimitable Satire is the vanity of human wishes. From the principal events in the lives of the most illustrious characters of all ages, the poet shows how little happiness is promoted by the attainment of what our indistinct and limited views represent as the greatest of earthly blessings. Of these he instances wealth, power, eloquence, military glory, longevity, and personal accomplishments, all of which he shows have proved dangerous or destructive to their respective possessors. Hence he argues the wisdom of acquiescing in the dispensations of Heaven; and concludes with a form of prayer, in which he points out, with great force and beauty, the objects for which a rational being may presume to approach the Almighty. There is a celebrated imitation of this poem by Dr. Johnson. (*Evans.*)

1-6. *Gadibus.* Gades (now *Cadiz*) is here regarded as the western limit of the earth. It stood on a small island, separated from the main land by a narrow channel. It was a colony of the Phœnicians, and their chief commercial settlement outside the Pillars of Hercules. Its Phœnician name was *Gaddir*, "a fortified inclosure." —*Usque Auroram.* "Even to the farthest east." Aurora had her abode in the farthest east, and came forth in the dawn of morning from the eastern Oceanus. Observe that *usque* without *ad*, except in the names of cities, is of rare occurrence even in the poets.— *Dignoscere.* "To discriminate between."—*Remota erroris nebula.* "The mist of error being removed from the mental view."—*Ratione.* "With reason as our guide," *i. e.*, on rational grounds.—*Quid tam dextro pede concipis.* "What do you so auspiciously enter upon." Observe that *dextro pede* is for *fausto pede*, i. e., *feliciter* or *fauste.*— *Ut te non pœniteat.* "That you will not, in all likelihood, repent of." Observe the force of the subjunctive.—*Peracti.* "Accomplished."

7-15. *Optantibus ipsis.* "Themselves desiring it," *i. e.*, they pray for what, when granted, involves their own ruin.—*Di faciles.* "The too easy gods," *i. e.*, turning too ready and indulgent an ear to the foolish prayers of their votaries.—*Nocitura.* "Calculated to harm." —*Toga.* "In the robe of peace," *i. e.*, in civil life.—*Multis.* As, for instance, to Demosthenes, Cicero, &c.—*Ille.* Milo of Crotona, the celebrated athlete. There were different accounts of his death.

The common one makes him to have been devoured by wolves, while his hands were wedged in the trunk of the tree, which he in vain endeavored to rend. According to another, when a pillar of the house in which he was gave way, he supported the roof until all the rest who were present had made their escape, and was himself then crushed by the falling timbers. (*Strab.*, vi., p. 263.)—*Periit.* Last syllable lengthened by the arsis.—*Strangulat.* "Chokes out of existence," *i. e.*, causes to be strangled. They are strangled on account of their riches.—*Patrimonia.* "Ordinary patrimonies." —*Quanto.* Not preceded by *tanto*, which latter, however, is presupposed.—*Balæna.* The Greek φαλαίνα, our whale. After the conquest of Britain by the Romans, it is not improbable that they may have acquired some knowledge of the *balæna mysticetus*, or great Greenland whale, and that this may be "the whale of Britain" to which Juvenal alludes. — *Temporibus diris igitur.* When Nero used to plunder the rich.

16–18. *Longinum.* C. Cassius Longinus, the celebrated jurist, governor of Syria A.D. 50, in the reign of Claudius. He was banished by Nero in A.D. 66, because he had among his ancestral images one of Cassius, the famous conspirator against Cæsar. He was recalled, however, from banishment by Vespasian.—*Egregias Lateranorum ædes.* This palace, on the site of the modern Lateran, stood, amid many splendid mansions, on the east of Mount Cœlius. Under Nero it belonged to the illustrious Plautii Laterani ; but after the consul elect, Plautius Lateranus, had, from patriotic motives, engaged in Piso's conspiracy, and had been condemned and put to death, it seems to have been forfeited to the Cæsars. On the gift of the palace to the popes, who have held it since the fourth century, consult *Tillemont, Emp.*, iv., 141.—*Cænacula.* "The garrets of the poor." *Cænaculum* properly means "an eating-room," and as this was usually in the upper part of the house, the word came to be used much more commonly in our sense of "a room up stairs," and the plural *cænacula* to designate the whole suite of rooms contained in an upper story. As the upper stories at Rome were chiefly occupied by the poorer classes, a sense of inferiority is frequently implied by the term, and hence our words "attics" or "garrets" would, in such cases, furnish the most appropriate translation.

19–27. *Pauca licet*, &c. Even though you may not be so rich as to become an object of the emperor's avarice and cruelty, yet you cannot travel by night with the paltry charge of a little silver plate without fear of your life from robbers, who will either dispatch you with the sword or knock you down with a pike.—*Umbram.* "The shadow." As regards the accusative here, compare note on *Sat.* viii., 152.—*Vacuus*. "With empty purse."—*Prima fere vota.* "The prayers that are generally the first put up."—*Divitiæ, crescant ut opes.* "Are that riches, that political influence may increase." *Ut* is to be supplied in the first clause. As regards the distinction between *divitiæ* and *opes*, compare the remark of Cicero (*Læl.*, 6.): "*Expetuntur* divitiæ *ut utare;* opes, *ut coluris.*"—*Ut maxima toto,* &c. The idea is, that we may have a larger capital than any one else at interest in the banker's hands.—*Fictilibus.* "From earthenware." Supply *vasis.*—*Gemmata.* "Jewelled." Compare *Sat.* v., 41.—*Setinum.* Compare *Sat.* v., 34.—*Lato ardebit in auro.* "Shall flash in the wide gold," *i. e.*, in the capacious goblet of gold.

28–35. *Jamne igitur laudas,* &c. "Do you not now, then, commend the fact, that of the two sages, one used to laugh," &c. The two sages are Democritus of Abdera and Heraclitus of Ephesus, and the idea intended to be conveyed is as follows: Since, then, men are so blind and unhappy as thus to pray for their own ruin, do you not, accordingly, agree with Democritus in deriding their folly, and with Heraclitus in lamenting their misery? *Jam* is here equivalent to *quum hoc sit* (*Hand, ad Tursell.*, iii., p. 147), and *ne* is used where we might have looked for *nonne*, as ἆρα for ἆρ᾽ οὐ. (*Mayor, ad loc.*)—*Flebat contrarius auctor.* "While the teacher of views directly opposite was accustomed to weep." *Auctor* is here employed in the sense of *doctor.* Compare Cicero, *de Off.*, ii., 2: "*Cratippus auctor;*" and Horace, *Od.* i., 28, 14: "(Pythagoras) *auctor naturæ verique.*"—*Sed facilis cuivis,* &c. "But the harsh censure of a sneering laugh is easy enough for any one." Observe that *rigidi*, though belonging in construction to *cachinni*, refers in fact to *censura.*—*Unde.* "From what fountain-head."—*Urbibus illis.* "In the cities of those regions." Abdera, his native place, is particularly meant.—*Prætexta.* The robe of magistracy, white, with a broad border of purple.—*Trabeæ.* Consult note on *Sat.* viii., 259.—*Tribunal.* The court of the prætor and judices in the basilica. The *tribunal* was a raised platform at one extremity of a law court, upon which the curule seats of the judges and other persons of distinction who wished to attend the proceedings were placed. It was sometimes of a square form, and constructed within the external wall of the court. At other times it consisted of a semicircular absis or alcove (*hemicyclium*) projecting beyond the external wall of the edifice.

36–37. *Quid si vidisset,* &c. The idea is, What food for laughter would not Democritus have discovered in our Circensian games, where the prætor presides in triumphal insignia, and needs a slave to remind him that he is a man!—*Curribus altis.* Driving through the city was only allowed to triumphant generals, to the higher magistrates, and to priests on solemn occasions. The prohibition, however, though often renewed, was not well observed. (*Becker, Gallus,* iii., 8.)—*Circi.* A detailed account of the Circensian procession is given by Dionysius (vii., 72). The procession moved from the Capitol into the arena of the circus, and was intended as the opening of the games. All those who meant to exhibit in the circus, as well as persons of distinction, bore part in it. The prætor, who was to preside at the games, rode in a triumphal car, arrayed in triumphal gown and tunic. In describing this procession, however, Juvenal has mixed up with it many things that were strictly confined to a triumphal celebration, as, for instance, the crown, the sceptre, and the eagle surmounting this last. But a trifling inconsistency like this would not deter our author from stepping out of the way in order to make his ridicule more poignant. The consul, too, is mentioned farther on instead of the prætor, to mark the contrast more strongly between the high public functionary and the slave.

38–42. *Tunica Jovis.* This was otherwise called *tunica palmata,* from its being adorned with embroidery representing palm leaves. It was termed *tunica Jovis* because taken from the temple of Jupiter Capitolinus, where it was kept along with the *toga picta.* This last was a robe embroidered with gold on a purple ground.—*Pictæ Sarrana ferentem,* &c. "Wearing the Tyrian hangings of the embroidered toga." The *toga picta* is meant. With *pictæ* supply *acu.* Its cumbrous folds, resembling curtained drapery, are satirically called "hangings," or tapestry.—*Sarrana.* The earlier Latin name for Tyre was *Sarra.* The Oriental form was *Tsor* or *Sor,* from which the Carthaginians adopted *Tsar* or *Sar* as a dialectic variation; and the Romans, receiving the term from these last, made out of it *Sarra,* and the adjective *Sarranus* equivalent to *Tyrius.*— *Magnæ coronæ.* The triumphal crown of gold, originally of bay.— *Quippe tenet sudans,* &c. The commander, who triumphed, originally wore merely a crown of Delphic bay around his brows. Afterward, when the gold crown was introduced, the chaplet of bay was retained, while behind him stood a public slave, holding over his head a golden Etruscan crown ornamented with jewels.—*Et sibi consul ne placeat,* &c. "And in order that the consul may not please himself (too much), the slave is borne along in the same chariot," *i. e.,* may not be too much elated. The presence of a slave in such a place at such a time seems to have been intended to avert "*invid-*

ia" and the influence of the evil eye ; and for the same purpose, a fascinum, a little bell, and a scourge were attached to the vehicle. Tertullian tells us that the slave ever and anon whispered in the ear of the general the warning words, "*Respice post te, hominem memento te.*"

43-55. *Da nunc.* "Add now." — *Sceptro quæ surgit eburno.* "Which is in the act of rising from the ivory sceptre." The general bore in his right hand a branch of bay, and in his left a sceptre, surmounted by an eagle in the act of soaring.—*Præcedentia longi agminis officia.* "The long array of clients marching before his car to do him honour."—*Niveos.* "In snow-white togas." On public occasions a brighter white than ordinary was given to the toga by rubbing it with argillaceous earth.—*Ad fræna.* "By the bits," *i. e.,* walking by his horses' heads.—*Defossa.* "Buried deep." A hit at both stingy patrons and mercenary clients.—*Tunc quoque.* "Even in those days."—*Ad omnes occursus hominum.* "At all meetings of his fellow-men," *i. e.,* in every place where human beings met. — *Prudentia.* "Acute sagacity."—*Vervecum in patria.* "In the native country of mutton-heads," *i. e.,* blockheads. Literally, "of bell-wethers," or "of wether-sheep." Abdera, in Thrace, the native place of Democritus, was proverbial for the stupidity of its inhabitants.—*Crassoque sub aere.* "And beneath a thick (Bœotian) atmosphere." Bœotia had a thick and heavy atmosphere, in consequence of the vapours rising from the valleys and lakes. Hence the Athenians, who lived in a pure and transparent atmosphere, ascribed dullness to their Bœotian neighbours.—*Mandaret laqueum.* "Would consign a halter," *i. e.,* would bid her go and hang herself. —*Mediumque ostenderet unguem.* "And would show her his middle nail," *i. e.,* would point his middle finger at her in scorn. This was regarded as an act of gross insult, the other fingers being at the same time contracted and bent downward. Hence the middle finger was often called "*digitus infamis.*" — *Ergo supervacua,* &c. In the common text and in all the MSS., *supervacua* is followed by *aut* or *et,* thus making an awkward hiatus. Some editions insert *vel* after *aut.* We have preferred following, however, the reading given by Achaintre.—*Fas est.* "It is right (in our eyes)," *i. e.,* it is deemed right by us. Ironical. — *Genua incerare deorum.* "To cover with wax the knees of the gods," *i. e.,* to hang wax tablets to them. They used to fasten wax tablets, containing their vows written on them, to the knees or thighs of the gods. When their wishes were granted, these tablets were replaced by the offerings which they had vowed. Madvig, who thinks *fas est* inconsistent with *su-*

L

pervacua and *perniciosa*, places a period after *petuntur*, and reads *in-cerate* in the imperative. But this is too abrupt. (*Madvig, Opusc.*, ii., p. 201; *Mayor, ad loc.*)

56–64. *Subjecta.* "Exposed."—*Pagina.* "List." A brass plate attached to the statues of eminent persons, and containing a pomp-ous enumeration of their titles and honours. With *mergit* supply *alios.*—*Descendunt.* "Descend from their pedestals."—*Restemque sequuntur.* They "follow the rope," which was used to pull them down from their elevated position, and afterward to drag them through the streets.—*Bigarum.* Triumphal statues are meant.—*Impacta.* "Driven home."—*Cædit.* "Hacks."—*Jam stridunt ig-nes.* Many statues of bronze had been erected in honour of Sejanus. These were melted down as soon as he was disgraced.—*Crepat.* "Crackles in the flame."—*Sejanus.* A most happily-chosen in-stance of the instability of imperial as well as popular favour. No subject ever ascended to such a height of power, none ever fell from it so rapidly into disgrace and ruin. Sejanus was put to death, Oct. 18, A.D. 31, having been in favour with Tiberius for the space of sixteen years.—*Toto orbe secunda.* Sejanus, as prefect of the præ-torian guard, almost rivalled the imperial power and authority. (Compare *Becker, Röm. Alt.*, ii., 3, *n.* 1278.)—*Sartago.* "A frying-pan." This was a sort of pan used in the Roman kitchens for a variety of purposes, such as roasting, melting fat or butter, cook-ing, &c.

65–71. *Pone domi lauros*, &c. To understand, as Gifford remarks. the little drama which follows, we must suppose one of those who had witnessed the commencement of Sejanus' punishment hasten-ing home to announce the intelligence, and prepare his public dem-onstrations of loyalty and joy. The dialogue passes between him and his neighbours.—*Cretatum.* If an ox perfectly white could not be found, any dark spots in the victim selected were rubbed over with chalk.—*Unco.* The hook by which the bodies of the condemn-ed were drawn to the *scalæ Gemoniæ*, or to the Tiber. Compare note on line 71.—*Quæ labra, quis illi vultus erat!* The exclamation of one of the neighbours. What a haughty curl of the lip he had, what a proud and contemptuous look!—*Crimine.* "Charge."—*Qui-bus indiciis?* "On what information (was the charge preferred)?" —*Probavit.* Referring to Tiberius.—*Nil horum.* The reply of an-other neighbour. — *Verbosa et grandis epistola venit.* Sejanus had long aimed at imperial power. Tiberius probably had suspected him for some time, but had duplicity enough to conceal his suspi-cions. Josephus, however, states that Antonia, his sister-in-law, informed him, by letter, of the ambitious views of the prime minister. The emperor, accordingly, while seeking to delude Sejanus by an appearance of friendship, took measures secretly for his ruin. Sertorius Macro was sent to Rome with a commission to assume the command of the prætorian cohorts. Macro, after assuring himself of the troops, and depriving Sejanus of his usual guard, produced a letter from Tiberius to the Senate. In this Tiberius expressed himself in his usual perplexed way, when he wished his meaning to be inferred without being declared in explicit terms. The meaning, however, was clear enough ; he was afraid of Sejanus, and wished to be secured against him. Sejanus, who was present, had received the usual fawning submission of the servile Senate so long as they thought that the letter of Tiberius was going to announce new honours for him. When it was read, there was not a man among them to give him a word of consolation, or show him a sign of respect. The consul Regulus conducted him to prison, and the people, who would have declared him emperor if the word had been given to them, loaded him with insult and outrage. His statues were pulled down before his face. The Senate on the same day decreed his death, and he was immediately executed. His body was dragged about the streets, and finally thrown into the Tiber, or, rather, says Seneca, there scarcely remained a fragment of it for the executioner to drag to the river.

72–80. *Capreis.* Capreæ, now *Capri,* an island in the bay of Naples, lay immediately opposite the Surrentine promontory, from which it was separated by a strait only three miles in width. Tiberius spent here the last ten years of his life, and here he gave himself up to the grossest debaucheries.—*Bene habet.* " 'Tis all right," *i. e.,* that's enough. Compare the Greek εὖ ἔχει.—*Turba Remi.* Compare Catullus (58, 5), " *Remi nepotes ;*" and Propertius (ii., 1, 23), "*Remi regna.*"—*Nursia Tusco.* That is, *Fortuna Sejano.* Nursia (called also Nyrtia, Nortia, and Nurtia) appears to have been the Etrurian goddess of Fortune. Sejanus is here called "the Tuscan" because born at Vulsinii, now Bolsena, in Etruria.—*Secura senectus principis.* "The secure old age of the prince (as he thought it to be)." *Tuta* would have been too strong here.—*Augustum.* "As Augustus," *i. e.,* as emperor.—*Ex quo suffragia nulli vendimus.* The last blow was given by Tiberius. Compare the language of Tacitus (*Ann.,* i., 15): "*Tum primum e campo comitia ad patres translata sunt.*" The election of all the magistrates now passed over from the people to the Senate.—*Effudit curas.* "They have thrown off all (public) cares." A metaphor taken from emptying a vessel by pouring out

the liquor.—*Imperium, fasces.* Dictatorships, consulships, prætor-
ships.—*Legiones.* Perhaps the command of armies, or the military
tribuneships, two thirds of which were assigned in the comitia (*Liv.*,
vii., 5; ix., 30. *Mayor, ad loc.*)—*Omnia.* In apposition.—*Panem et
Circenses.* Largesses of corn monthly, and the sports of the circus,
are all that the once sovereign people now require. Compare note
on *Sat.* vii., 174. At a later period, instead of distributing corn
every month, wheaten bread (*annona civica*) was given to the people.

81–90. *Perituros audio multos.* His children, and Livia the widow
of Drusus, were put to death, the latter by starvation. His relations,
friends, and flatterers were all condemned, the mere fact of having
been a friend of Sejanus standing in lieu of any proof of guilt.
Many of the accused laid violent hands on themselves before condemnation, in order to secure their estates from confiscation; the
rest, men and women, knights and senators, were cast into prison,
and either there dispatched or thrown from the Tarpeian rock. The
bodies were then exposed in the Forum, and lastly flung into the
river. (*Dio Cass.*, lviii., ii., 12, 15.)—*Magna est fornacula.* "It is
a large furnace." It is capable of holding many an image besides
Sejanus's.—*Brutidius.* Brutidius Niger, the rhetorician and historian, was an intimate friend of Sejanus, and involved in his ruin.
The controversy between Ajax and Ulysses for the arms of Achilles,
a favourite theme with the ancient rhetoricians, appears to have furnished Brutidius also with the subject of a *declamatio*, in which he
espoused the side of Ajax, but in a very frigid and feeble manner.
The speaker, therefore, whom Juvenal here introduces, sneeringly
expresses his fears lest Ajax, whose side has been so badly advocated by him, and who has, in consequence, lost his cause, now exact atonement from him by involving him in the downfall of Sejanus. (*Madvig, ad loc.*) Some, with much less propriety, refer *Ajax*
to the Emperor Tiberius.—*Martis Aram.* From *Liv.*, xxxv., 10, and
xl., 45, the altar of Mars would appear to have been not far from
the polling-place (*ovile*), in the Campus Martius. (*Becker, Röm.
Alt.*, i., p. 269.)—*Sed videant servi*, &c. But let our slaves see us
insulting the traitor's body, lest they accuse us as not having given
this proof of our loyalty. The rule of Roman law (*Cod.*, x., 11, 6,
seq.) was, that no slave should give evidence against his master except in cases of high treason, when they could be examined by torture in order to elicit information. Tiberius, however, evaded the
rule by ordering that the slaves should be purchased by the *actor
publicus*. (*Tac., Ann.*, ii., 30.)—*Cervice obstricta.* "With fettered
neck." A figurative expression merely for an arrest, and not to be
taken in a literal sense.

91-98. *Illi*. The Latinity of *illi . . . illum*, instead of *huic . . . illum*, is worthy of notice. Compare Ovid, *Her.*, 3, 28 : "*Ille gradu propior sanguinis, ille comes.*"—*Summas curules*. "The highest curule seats," *i. e.*, honours. Supply *sellas*. The *sella curulis* was reserved for dictators, censors, consuls, &c.—*Tutor*. Alluding not only to Sejanus' being actual regent, but also to Tiberius being completely under his control.—*Cum grege Chaldæo*. These were the astrologers and calculators of nativities. Tiberius had studied astrology under Thrasyllus in Rhodes (*Tac., Ann.*, vi., 20), and yet he was so jealous of the influence of the *mathematici* upon others that he expelled them from the city. (*Suet., Tib.*, 36.)—*Vis certe pila*, &c. "You wish at least for javelins, cohorts, a brilliant train of equestrian attendants, and a domestic camp," *i. e.*, you wish at least to be attended by a guard, as Sejanus was. The *equites egregii*, otherwise styled *insignes*, *illustres*, and *primores equitum*, consisted of young men of the first families. They formed a distinct order from the common equites, and had special privileges. Even these Sejanus had at his disposal. By *domestica castra*, on the other hand, is meant a body-guard quartered in the house, not, as some think, the Prætorian camp, of which Sejanus was prefect.—*Posse volunt*. "Wish to possess the power so to do," *i. e.*, even though they do not exercise it.—*Tanti*. "Are of so much value (in the eyes of any one)." Supply *alicui*.—*Ut sit*. "That there shall be," *i. e.*, that he is willing there shall be. Well explained by Madvig : "*Tantum habent pretium, ut propter ea parem quis esse velit mensuram malorum? sive; ut parem aliquis simul malorum summam suscipere velit?*" (*Madvig, Opusc.*, ii., p. 189.)

99-102. *Hujus*. Sejanus. Compare verse 66.—*Prætextam*. Compare verse 35.—*An Fidenarum*, &c. "Or to be some village authority of Fidenæ or Gabii." *Potestas* for *magistratus*. Compare *Cic., Tusc.*, 1, 30. Fidenæ, now *Castel Giubileo*, was forty stadia northeast of Rome, near the confluence of the Tiber and Anio. After having been an important city, and frequently brought into collision with Rome, it dwindled subsequently into an insignificant village.— *Gabiorum*. Gabii lay half way between Rome and Præneste, and was originally a colony of Alba Longa. Like Fidenæ, it fell into complete decay, though its cold, sulphurous waters would seem at one time to have made it again a source of considerable attraction. Gabii was noted in ancient times for its stone, known as the *lapis Gabinus*, a hard and compact variety of the volcanic tufo or *peperino*, extensively employed by the Romans as a building stone from the earliest ages down to that of Augustus.

Et de mensura, &c. In little municipalities the ædiles probably

were the only magistrates. Like their namesakes, the plebeian
ædiles at Rome, they took cognizance of weights and measures, of
markets and provisions, &c. In the Italian villages they still subsist at the present day, as ragged, says Gifford, and as consequential
as ever, under the name of *Podesta*, a corruption of the ancient
term *potestas.—Ulubris.* Ulubræ was a small town of Latium, in
the neighbourhood of the Pontine Marshes. It corresponds to the
modern *Cisterna.*

103–107. *Ergo quid optandum foret*, &c. The connection in the
train of ideas is as follows: You allow, then, that Sejanus mistook
the nature of true happiness; you must admit the same of Crassus,
Cæsar, and Pompey.—*Parabat.* "Was all the time only preparing." Observe the force of the imperfect. — *Tabulata.* Compare
Sat. iii., 180.—*Et impulsæ præceps immane ruinæ.* "And dreadful
the headlong descent of his ruin once set in motion." *Præceps* is
here used substantively. Compare Statius, *Sylv.* i., 4, 51: "*Subiti
præceps juvenile pericli."—Impulsæ.* A metaphor, taken from one
who is pushed forward to his fall.

108–113. *Crassos.* The allusion is to M. Licinius Crassus, who
fell in the Parthian war. The plurals *Crassos* and *Pompeios* refer
to Crassus and Pompey, and others like them, not, as some maintain, to others of the same name. Compare note on *Sat.* i., 94.—
Illum. Julius Cæsar.—*Ad sua deduxit flagra.* "Brought down under his lash," *i. e.*, enslaved.—*Nempe.* Very frequently used in replies, where it corresponds to our colloquial "why." — *Nulla non
arte.* "By every possible device."—*Magna.* "Ambitious."—*Generum Cereris.* Proserpina was daughter of Ceres.—*Sicca.* "Bloodless."

114–117. *Eloquium ac famam*, &c. The train of thought is as follows: The youngest schoolboy burns to emulate the eloquence of
Demosthenes and Cicero, and yet that eloquence was their ruin.—
Totis Quinquatribus. "Through all his Quinquatrian holidays."
The *Quinquatrus* (or *Quinquatria*) was a festival sacred to Minerva,
which was celebrated on the 19th of March (*a. d.* xiv. *Kal. Apr.*),
and was so called, according to Varro, because it was the fifth day
after the Ides. It originally lasted only one day, but was afterward
extended to five days. These five days were the schoolmasters'
holidays, and on the first day they received their pay, or entrance-
fee; hence called *Minerval*, though Horace seems to imply that the
fees were paid every month. There was another festival, called the
lesser Quinquatrus, on the ides (13th) of June, when the Tibicines
went through the city in procession to the temple of Minerva.—

Quisquis adhuc uno, &c. "Whoever pays court to Minerva, purchased as yet with only a single *as*," *i. e.*, the youngest boy, at the bottom of the school, who has not as yet paid his fee to the master more than once. Some read *parcam* for *partam*, which Heinsius explains as follows: "*Qua puer parce adhuc est imbutus.*" The common lection is preferable.—*Custos*. The *capsarius* is meant, the slave who carried the box or *capsa* containing the young master's schoolbooks.

118-128. *Perit*. Contracted form of the perfect. Not used by writers of the Augustan age. (*Madvig, Opusc. Alt.*, p. 225, *seq.*)—*Exundans*. "Outpouring." — *Ingenio manus*, &c. Popilius Lenas, who cut off Cicero's head and hands, carried them to Antony, who rewarded him with a civic crown and a large sum of money, and ordered the head to be fixed between the hands to the Rostra.—*Causidici pusilli*. "Of an inferior pleader."—*O fortunatam natam*, &c. "O fortunate Rome, really born when I was consul," *i. e.*, whose natal day may date from me as consul. This is a verse of Cicero's, which has been often ridiculed for its unfortunate jingle. It belonged to a poem on Cicero's consulship, the third book of which he quotes in a letter to Atticus (ii., 3). Cicero, however, was not ashamed of the sentiment, for he repeats it in prose, " *O Nonæ Decembres! quæ me consule fuistis, ego diem vere natalem hujus urbis*," &c. (*Or., pro Flacc.*)—*Antoni gladios*, &c. Quoting Cicero's own words, " *Contempsi Catilinæ gladios, non pertimescam tuos.*" (*Phil.* ii., 46.) The idea conveyed in the text is, He might have braved the anger of Antony also if his speeches had been as tame as his poems.—*Potuit*. Not *potuisset*. (*Madvig, L. G.*, § 348, *e.*)

Quam te conspicuæ, &c. Alluding to the second Philippic, which cost Cicero his life. Cicero called his fourteen orations against Antony, not *Antonians*, but *Philippics*, after those of Demosthenes against Philip of Macedon. The first Philippic was delivered in the Senate on the 2d of September, B.C. 44. Antony replied on the 19th, when Cicero was not present. Cicero, on this, wrote, but never spoke, except before his private friends, the scurrilous second Philippic. (*Drumann*, i., 199, *seq.*; vi., 344. *Mayor, ad loc.*)—*Volveris a prima*, &c. "Which art rolled up (in the scroll) next after the first."—*Illum*. Demosthenes.—*Torrentem et pleni*, &c. "Rushing along torrent-like, and controlling (at pleasure) the reins of the crowded theatre."—*Theatri*. Where the popular assemblies were held, according to Grecian custom.

129-132. *Dis adversis*. "With adverse gods."—*Quem pater ardentis*, &c. The father of Demosthenes was not a blacksmith, as Juvenal here represents, but a man of substance, as appears from his son's speeches against Aphobus and Onetor. He was owner of a sword factory, it is true, but that was only one item in the sum of his fortune. Nor did he send his son to a rhetorician. When he died the orator was only seven years of age. Lucian (*Rhet. Præc.*, 10; *Somn.*, 12), Valerius Maximus (iii., 4; *Ext.*, § 2), and others, have fallen into the same error as Juvenal. A truer account is given by Libanius (*Vit. Demosth.*, p. 2, ed. *Reiske. Mayor, ad loc.*). —*Luteo Vulcano.* "Dingy Vulcan." A humorous designation of a smith.—*Rhetora.* It is probable that, during the latter years of his minority, Demosthenes privately prepared himself for the career of an orator, and that, during the first years after his attaining the age of manhood, he availed himself of the instruction of Isæus. His having been, however, a pupil of Isocrates also is exceedingly doubtful.

133-146. *Bellorum' exuviæ*, &c. The train of ideas is as follows : Many wish for military renown, and the honours connected with military achievements. Mere empty pageantry! Witness Hanni-bal, Alexander, Xerxes.—*Truncis.* "Trunk-formed." Equivalent to *e trunco factis.*—*Buccula.* "The cheek-piece." The Greek παραγναθίς. The helmet had one on each side, attached by hinges, so as to be lifted up and down at pleasure. In active exercise the *bucculæ* were fastened under the chin.—*Curtum temone.* "Shorn of its pole," *i. e.*, with pole broken short off.—*Aplustre.* "The stern-ornament." This was an ornament answering to the Greek ἄφλασ-τον, made of wooden planks, somewhat resembling that of the feath-ers of a bird's wing, commonly placed on the stern of a ship.—*Sum-mo tristis captivus*, &c. The statues of captives taken in war, sculp-tured on a triumphal arch.—*Induperator.* Old form for *imperator.* Compare *Sat.* iv., 28.—*Causas habuit.* "Has he derived the incen-tives."—*Quis enim virtutem*, &c. The idea is, Who embraces virtue for its own sake, or would embrace it at all if you should take away its rewards. On the subjunctive *tollas*, consult *Madvig, L. G.*, § 348, *b.*—*Tituli.* "An honorary title." Alluding to the inscriptions on marble monuments. — *Ad quæ discutienda*, &c. "When for the bursting asunder of these the mischievous strength of the barren fig-tree is all sufficient." The sturdy growth of the wild fig-tree, which forces its way through walls, is often alluded to by the poets.

147-158. *Expende Hannibalem.* "Weigh the ashes of Hannibal." —*Capit.* "Contains," *i. e.*, is not large enough to satisfy.—*Admota.* "Extending to." Some of the ancient writers regarded the Nile as the boundary between Asia and Africa. Compare Herodotus, ii.,

16.—*Rursus.* "Again in another direction stretching." Supply *admota*, from the previous clause.—*Altos.* Some MSS. give *alios*, referring to the elephants of Africa as well as Asia.—*Transilit.* "He bounds over." — *Diducit scopulos*, &c. "He cleaves asunder the rocks, and rends the mountain with vinegar." This fable is not to be found in Polybius. It is given by Livy (xxi., 37).—*Frangimus ....pono.* Observe the change of number. The gates are broken open by a crowd; whereas the standard may be planted (in token of occupation) by one. (*Mayor, ad loc.*)—*Subura.* The most thickly-settled part of Rome; in other words, the very heart of the city. Compare *Sat.* iii., 5.—*Gœtula.* Put here for *Afra.* Strictly speaking, Gœtulia was the name given to the interior of Northern Africa, lying to the south of Mauritania, Numidia, and the region bordering on the Syrtes.—*Luscum.* When Hannibal broke up from the winter-quarters which he had occupied after his descent from the Alps, he proceeded to march through a swamp on the banks of the Arnus (*Arno*), where he lost the sight of one eye by a violent attack of ophthalmia.

159-167. *Ergo.* "Then," *i. e.*, after all his victories.—*Vincitur.* At Zama, by Scipio, B.C. 202.—*Nempe.* Consult note on verse 110.—*Exsilium.* Hannibal first fled to Antiochus (B.C. 193), who, however, consented, after the battle of Magnesia, to give him up to the Romans (B.C. 190). On this, he took refuge with Prusias, king of Bithynia, who would have delivered him up at the demand of the Romans; but Hannibal escaped his enemies by taking poison, B.C. 183.—*Prœtoria.* By *prœtorium* is properly meant a general's or provincial governor's head-quarters; often, however, as here, "a palace." Compare *Sat.* i., 63.—*Vigilare.* "To awake." As a client, Hannibal went early in the morning to pay his respects to his royal patron. Compare *Sat.* i., 112. — *Cannarum vindex.* "Atoner for Cannæ." After the battle of Cannæ, two or three *modii* of rings, taken from equites who had fallen in the battle, were sent to Carthage.— *Annulus.* Hannibal destroyed himself with poison, which he always carried in a ring.—*Declamatio.* "The theme for a declamation," *i. e.*, the subject of a school exercise. Compare *Sat.* vii., 160.

168-172. *Pellœo juveni.* Alexander of Macedon, born at Pella, an ancient town of Macedonia, made the capital of the country by Philip his father.—*Æstuat.* "He pants." The world is too close for him; he cannot breathe in it.—*Gyari.* Compare *Sat.* i., 61.—*Seripho.* Scriphus, now *Serpho*, one of the Cyclades, between Cythnus and Siphnus. Like Gyarus, it became a place of exile under the Cæsars. — *Figulis munitam.* "Fortified by the brick-makers." Babylon is meant, whose walls were constructed of brick. Here Alexander ended his days.—*Sarcophago.* "With a simple sarcophagus." Σαρκοφάγος was the name of a kind of limestone, found at Assus, in Troas, remarkable for consuming the flesh of corpses laid in it. Hence coffins were often furnished with or made of it; and hence, also, the term became a general one for any coffin or receptacle of the dead.—*Fatetur.* "Discloses," *i. e.*, clearly shows. Equivalent to *declarat* or *significat.*— *Quantula sint hominum corpuscula.* "How little are the puny bodies of men."

173-178. *Olim velificatus.* "To have been sailed through of yore." Mount Athos, at the extremity of the peninsula of the same name, projecting from Chalcidice, in Macedonia, rises abruptly from the sea to a height of 6349 feet. There is no anchorage for ships at its base, and the voyage round it was so dreaded by mariners that Xerxes had a canal cut through the isthmus, which connects the peninsula with the main land, to afford a passage for his fleet. The isthmus is about a mile and a half across, and there are most distinct traces of the canal to be seen at the present day, so that we must not imitate the scepticism of Juvenal expressed in the text. —*Græcia mendax.* The fondness of many of the Greek historians for the marvellous is here made a ground for a sweeping charge against the entire class. — *Constratum.* "To have been bridged over." More literally, "to have been strewed or covered over." The allusion is to the bridge of boats over the Hellespont made by order of Xerxes. — *Amnes.* Drunk dry by the myriad hosts of Xerxes. (Compare *Herod.,* vii., 21, 2 ; 43, 1.) Namely, the Scamander, the Melas, the Onochonus, and Epidanus (*Id. ib.,* 196, 3). —*Prandente.* "Lunching."—*Et quæ.* "And what else." —*Sostratus.* Of this poet nothing is known.—*Madidis alis.* "With pinions moist with wine." Hence the extravagance of his flights.

179-187. *Ille.* Xerxes.—*In Corum,* &c. Herodotus says nothing of this.—*Barbarus.* Ironical.—*Æolio carcere.* Alluding to the description given in Virgil, *Æn.,* i., 51, *seqq.* — *Ennosigæum.* The Greek Ἐννοσίγαιον Latinized. An Homeric epithet of Neptune. "The earth-shaker."—*Mitius id sane.* "It was, it must be confessed, an act of more than ordinary clemency," *i. e.*, it must be allowed that the punishment was slight.—*Quid? non et,* &c. We have adopted here the emendation of Weber, as given by Jahn. The common reading is *mitius id sane, quod non et stigmate,* &c., which directly contradicts the statement of Herodotus, who says expressly that he branded the Hellespont. (*Herod.,* vii., 35.)—*Huic quisquam*

rellet, &c. The idea is, Would any god be willing to serve so hard
a master?—*Nempe una nare*, &c. Herodotus (viii., 115, *seqq.*) believed that Xerxes, having left a part of his forces with Mardonius,
marched to the Hellespont, which he crossed with the remnant of
his troops. Another account, however (c. 118), stated that he fled
in a Phœnician ship from Eion, in Thrace, on the River Strymon,
and that, in a storm, many of the passengers threw themselves overboard to lighten the vessel. Juvenal, however, seems to say that
Xerxes fled at once from Salamis in a single ship, the course of
which was impeded by floating bodies.

188-191. *Da spatium vitæ*, &c. The train of ideas is as follows :
All pray for long life, yet old age brings with it deformity, and decay, and dotage. At the best, however hale and hearty the aged
may be, they must be often pained by seeing their nearest kin
struck down around them. So Nestor, Peleus, and Laertes mourned for their sons. Happy had it been for Priam had he died before
the rape of Helen ; yet Priam's fate was not so hard as Hecuba's.
So, too, Mithradates, Crœsus, Marius, and Pompey, all proved the
truth of Solon's saying, that "no man is to be counted happy before
death."—*Recto vultu.* "With the erect look of health."

192-205. *Dissimilemque sui.* "And unlike its former self."—
Pellem. "Hide."—*Tabraca.* Now *Tabarca*, on the coast of Numidia. Strabo (xvii., p. 827) and Herodotus speak of the mountains and woods of this coast as swarming with apes.—*Plurima sunt
juvenum*, &c. The idea is, Youths differ one from another in features or in strength ; the old, on the contrary, are all alike feeble
and ill-favoured.—*Madidique infantia nasi.* Compare the scholiast,
"*Ita nam senibus humor de naso ut infantibus pendet.*"— *Ut captatori
moveat*, &c. The idea is, Loathsome even to the fortune-hunter,
who will stay by your side when wife and sons are driven away.

206-220. *Citharœdo.* A better reading than the *citharœdus* of
the common text.—*Seleucus.* A musician, apparently a citharœdus. Such artists were highly paid. Their professional costume,
too, was exceedingly splendid. Compare *Auct. ad Herenn.*, iv., 60.
—*Et quibus aurata*, &c. "And one of those whose custom it is to
glitter in gold-bedecked robe." As regards the *lacerna*, compare
Sat. iii., 129.—*Qua parte.* Whether in the orchestra (*Sat.* iii., 135)
as a senator, or in the fourteen rows as an eques.—*Qui vix cornicines*, &c. Trumpeters were employed to give the signal in the theatre. (Compare *Seneca*, *Ep.* 84, § 10.)—*Quem dicat venisse*, &c.
The slave must bawl in his master's ear the name of a visitor or
the hour of the day. Sun-dials, as well as clepsydræ, were found

in private houses. More commonly, however, slaves watched the public dials on the temples or basilicæ, and reported the hours to their masters. (*Mayor, ad loc.*)—*Gelido jam in corpore.* "In his now chilled frame."—*Themison.* Not to be confounded with the physician of Laodicea, who flourished in the first century B.C., and founded the sect of the *Methodici.* — *Basilus.* Some fraudulent member of a *societas* or partnership.—*Socios.* "Partners in business."—*Quo tondente,* &c. Repeated from *Sat.* i., 23.

221-232. *Ille humero,* &c. He now returns to his description of the old.—*Pallida.* "Bloodless."—*Diducere rictum suetus.* "Once accustomed to open widely his distended jaws." — *Mater jejuna.* "The parent bird, herself fasting."—*Dementia.* "That idiocy."—*Quos eduxit.* "Whom he has brought up." *Eduxit* for *educavit.*—*Codice sævo.* "By an unfeeling will." If a man had disinherited his own children, or passed over his parents, or brothers, or sisters, the will was in form a good will; but if there was no sufficient reason for the inheritance, the persons aggrieved might have an action, entitled *"Inofficiosi testamenti querela."*—*Phialen.* Some female of loose character.—*Artificis oris.* "Of an artful mouth."

233-238. *Ut.* "Even supposing, however, that." The idea is, Even though the old man's mind should retain its vigour, still he must see his family die around him. — *Ducenda sunt.* "Are to be led forth."—*Sororibus.* "Of sisters' ashes."—*Clade domus.* "The death-blow in their house."

239-250. *Rex Pylius.* Nestor, king of Pylos, in the Peloponnesus, who, according to Homer, had outlived two generations of men, and was reigning at the period of the Trojan war over a third. If we reckon, with Herodotus, three generations to a century, Nestor would have been at this time seventy or eighty years old. Others, however, understand by a generation (γενεά) a century.—*Cornice.* The crow is fabled by Hesiod to live nine generations of men.—*Nimirum.* "No doubt."—*Distulit.* "Put off."—*Suos jam dextra,* &c. This the Greeks expressed by ἀναπεμπάζεσθαι. They counted on the left hand as far as a hundred, then on the right up to two hundred, and then again on the left for the third hundred, and so on. — *Novum mustum.* "The new-made wine." — *Nimio stamine.* "The too-prolonged thread of existence."—*Antilochi.* Antilochus, son of Nestor, slain by Memnon, son of Aurora. Compare Horace, *Od.* ii., 9, 14.—*Cur hæc in tempora duret.* "Why he himself lingers on to this period."—*Raptum.* "Prematurely snatched away."—*Alius.* Laertes.—*Ithacum natantem.* "The swimming Ithacensian," *i. e.,* the shipwrecked Ulysses.

251-265. *Incolumi Troja.* "Troy remaining safe the while," *i. e.*, with Troy still standing.—*Assaraci.* Electra, daughter of Atlas, bore to Jupiter Dardanus, father of Erichthonius, father of Tros, father of Ilus, Assaracus, and Ganymede. Priam was son of Laomedon, son of Ilus ; Capys, son of Assaracus, was father of Anchises. (*Apollod.*, iii., 12.) — *Funus.* "His corpse." Put for *cadaver.*— *Cassandra.* Both Cassandra and Polyxena survived their father, but they could not lament at his burial.—*Longa dies.* "Length of days."—*Tunc miles tremulus*, &c. Compare Virgil, *Æn.*, ii., 509, *seq.*—*Jovis.* Hercæan Jove is meant, Ζεὺς ἑρκεῖος, the household god, so called because his statue stood in the ἕρκος, or front court. Priam was slain before his altar by Pyrrhus, son of Achilles.—*Bos.* In Greece it was only in exceptional cases that oxen from the plough were sacrificed.—*Jam fastiditus.* "Long since scorned."— *Ab aratro.* The preposition is here employed with the ablative, instead of the simple ablative only, on account of the personification. — *Utcunque.* "However." The idea is, However it may have been, he died the death of a human being, not that of a dog, as Hecuba did.— *Canino rictu.* "With a canine distention of the jaws." Alluding to the well-known metamorphosis of Hecuba.

266-276. *Regem Ponti.* The celebrated Mithradates.—*Cræsum.* It has been shown by Grote that the visit of Solon to Cræsus (*Herod.*, i., 30, *seqq.*) is unhistorical.—*Ultima spatia.* "The closing scenes." Literally, "the last heats." A metaphor borrowed from the Roman circus. The competitors had to run seven times round the *spina*, and each course round was called a *spatium* or "heat."— *Minturnarum.* Minturnæ was a town of Latium, near the mouth of the Liris. In the marshes in the vicinity of this place Marius endeavoured to conceal himself from the cavalry of Sylla, but was discovered, and dragged to prison at Minturnæ.—*Mendicatus victa*, &c. Alluding to the well-known story of Marius sitting on the ruins of Carthage.—*Hinc causas habuere.* "Had all their origin from this." —*Circumducto captivorum agmine*, &c. Juvenal means after his triumph over the Teutones and Cimbri had been ended.—*Animam opimam.* "His soul glutted with glory."

277-282. *Provida.* "In her foresight," *i. e.*, foreseeing the misfortunes that would befall him if he continued to live.—*Optandas.* "To be really wished for by him," *i. e.*, for which he should actually have prayed, in order that it might have cut life short, and saved future trouble.—*Multæ urbes.* The people of Neapolis first offered sacrifices for his restoration to health. The neighbouring people followed their example, and the thing thus going the round of Italy, every city, small and great, celebrated a festival for several days. (*Plut., Vit. Pomp.*, 57.)—*Fortuna ipsius.* The good fortune of Pompey was no less celebrated than that of Sulla.—*Servatum.* "Spared by disease," *i. e.*, by the fever.—*Caput abstulit.* Pompey, after his flight from Pharsalia, sought refuge in Egypt, but was put to death before he came to land, being fifty-eight years of age. His head was cut off and brought to Cæsar, who had come to Egypt not long after, but he turned from it with horror.—*Hoc cruciatu.* "This torment," *i. e.*, the degradation of being beheaded.—*Lentulus.* This individual and Cethegus were accomplices in the conspiracy of Catiline, and were strangled in the *Tullianum*, or prison at Rome, on the night of the 5th of December.—*Catilina.* Catiline fell on the field of battle, against the forces of Antonius the proconsul, at Pistoria in Etruria. According to Dio Cassius, however, his head was cut off and sent to Rome (xxxviii., 40).

283–290. *Formam.* "Beauty."—*Modico (murmure).* "In subdued tone."—*Majore murmure.* "In louder accents."—*Usque ad delicias votorum.* "Even unto the delight of vows," *i. e.*, offering up vows so splendid as to prove delightful even unto a god. Some, less correctly, render it, "Carrying her fond wishes even to the verge of trifling."—*Corripias?* "Are you to chide me for this?"—*Lucretia.* Wife of Collatinus.—*Rutilæ.* Unknown.—*Virginia.* The intended victim of Appius Claudius.—*Concordia.* "The union."

291–304. *Sanctos licet*, &c. "Though the house, austere in virtue, and imitating the Sabines of old, may have handed down the uncorrupted morals (of earlier days)." The Sabines were a people of simple and virtuous habits, faithful to their word, and imbued with deep religious feeling.—*Non licet esse viros.* "It is not allowed them to attain unto unsullied manhood." Literally, "to be men." *Viros* is here emphatic.—*Parentes.* The parents of the youth.—*Sed casto*, &c. But if he be chaste, asks the mother, what harm can beauty do him? Nay, replies the poet, what did their resolute purity avail Hippolytus or Bellerophon?—*Grave propositum.* "His virtuous resolve."—*Hippolyto.* The story of Hippolytus, son of Theseus, falsely accused by Phædra.—*Bellerophonti.* The story of Bellerophon and Sthenoboea, wife of Prætus, king of Argos.—*Hæc.* Phædra.— *Et se concussere ambæ.* "And both aroused themselves to vengeance."—*Cressa.* Phædra was daughter of Minos, king of Crete.— *Quum stimulos odio*, &c. "When shame sets goads to hatred," *i. e.*, sets sharper spurs to her hate.

305–311. *Quidnam suadendum*, &c. "What course you think should be recommended to him." The allusion is to the marriage of Messalina with C. Silius, as related by Tacitus, *Ann.*, xi., 12. This happened A.D. 48, when her husband, the Emperor Claudius, was at Ostia.—*Gentis patriciæ.* Not exactly correct. Silius was the son of a general distinguished by his victories over the Gauls and Belgæ; but the gens was plebeian.—*Flammeolo parato.* "With the bridal veil all ready." The marriage veil, worn by Roman brides, was of a deep and brilliant yellow colour, like a flame, from which circumstance the name arose. Observe that *flammeolum* is a diminutive of *flammeum;* not, however, meaning small in size, but of a very fine and thin texture, and, consequently, of greater value.—*Hortis.* The gardens of Lucullus are probably meant; although, from Tacitus (*Ann.*, xi., 12, 27) and Dio Cassius (lx., 31), it would seem that the marriage was celebrated in the house of Silius.—*Ritu antiquo.*—Among other formalities, a dowry too is brought, according to ancient rite.—*Decies centena.* "A million of sesterces." Equal to $39,000.—*Signatoribus.* "Witnesses to the settlement."

312–320. *Tu.* Silius is meant. — *Legitime.* "In due form of law."—*Quid placeat.* "Which alternative is to please."—*Lucernas.* "The evening lamps," *i. e.*, nightfall. — *Sciet ultimus.* It was with great difficulty, after all, that Narcissus prevailed on Claudius to order Messalina's execution; and she was put to death at last without his knowledge.—*Obsequere imperio.* "Obey her behests."—*Si tanti,* &c. The idea is, If it is worth while, for a few more days of life, to commit such a crime.—*Gladio.* To the sword either of Messalina or of Claudius.

321–332. *Nil ergo optabunt homines?* The poet here anticipates a natural objection that might be made. If all that has been just said be carefully considered, the consequence would seem to be that it is wrong to wish or pray for any thing.—*Consilium.* "My advice."—*Expendere.* "To consider."—*Jucundis.* "Merely pleasing things."—*Partum uxoris.* "Issue by a wife."—*Ut poscas aliquid.* The idea is, That you may not merely acquiesce in the divine appointments, but *also* prefer some petition.—*Divina.* "Sacrificial." —*Tomacula.* "Sausages." The liver and other parts cut out of the pig, minced up with the fat. The *tomacula* were eaten hot, and hence were carried about the streets for sale in small tin ovens.— *Ut sit mens sana,* &c. The famous prayer of philosophic antiquity, namely, for a sound mind to judge, determine, and act aright; and for a sound and healthy frame as essential to true enjoyment.

333–341. *Spatium extremum.* "The closing scene," *i. e.*, the last heat in the race of existence. Compare note on verse 000.—*Munera.* "The privileges." Compare Dryden: "And count it nature's privilege to die."—*Potiores.* "Far preferable."—*Herculis.* Hercules is often put forward as a paragon of virtue. The Cynics and Stoics in particular so esteemed him.—*Venere.* "The lust."—*Pluma.* "The downy couch."—*Sardanapali.* The allusion is to Sardanapalus, the last king of the Assyrian empire of Ninus or Nineveh, noted for his luxury, licentiousness, and effeminacy. Rawlinson reads the name as Assardanbal; Hincks as Ashmakhbal; and others, again, as Assur-banipal. There would seem, from the researches of Layard, to have been more than one monarch of the name.—*Nullum numen habes*, &c. "Thou hast no divinity if man possess wise foresight," *i. e.*, no power or control over us as a deity; or, in other words, no existence as a deity. Another but inferior reading is, *Nullum numen abest.* "No deity is absent," *i. e.*, all the gods are present with and favour us.

SATIRE XI.

ARGUMENT.

Under the form of an invitation to his friend Persicus, Juvenal takes occasion to enunciate many admirable maxims for the due regulation of life. After ridiculing the miserable state to which a profligate patrician had reduced himself by his extravagance, he introduces the picture of his own domestic economy, which he follows by a pleasing view of the simplicity of ancient manners, artfully contrasted with the extravagance and luxury of the current times. After describing, with great beauty, the entertainment he proposes to give his friend, he concludes with an earnest recommendation to him to enjoy the present with content, and await the future with calmness and moderation. (*Evans.*)

1-6. *Atticus.* Put for any man of wealth and rank. So Apicius, on the other hand, for any poor one.—*Eximie.* "Sumptuously." — *Lautus.* "A splendid fellow." — *Demens.* "Lost to all judgment."—*Pauper Apicius.* "An Apicius reduced to poverty." By Apicius here is meant any extravagant glutton. The name, however, particularly indicates the noted gourmand in the time of Tiberius. Consult note on *Sat.* iv., 22.—*Omnis convictus*, &c. "Every dinner-party, the baths, the knots of loungers." *Convictus*, in the Latinity of Juvenal's time, was equivalent to *convivium.* As regards the *Thermæ*, consult note on *Sat.* vii., 233; and in illustration of

the term *stationes*, compare the language of Pliny (*Ep.* i., 13 ; xi.,
9): "*Locus ubi otiosi in urbe degunt, et variis sermonibus tempus ter-
unt.*"—*De Rutilo.* Supply *loquuntur.*—*Juvenalia.* Earlier and rarer
form for *juvenilia.*—*Sufficiunt galeæ.* Supply *portandæ.* Alluding
to his being fit to bear arms.—*Ardens.* Supply *est.* A much better
reading than *ardent*, a mere conjectural emendation, without MS.
authority.

7–11. *Non cogente quidem*, &c. The tribune has not, indeed, assigned over Rutilus's estate to his creditors, and so driven him to
engage himself to the *lanista* for his bread, but yet he has not in-
terposed to save him from a degradation worse than slavery. By
the tribune is here meant the *tribunus plebis*, who appears to have
had a kind of judicial authority under the empire.—*Scripturus leges,*
&c. Gladiators had to write out the rules given by their trainer,
and also the words of command, in order to learn them by heart.—
Regia verba. "Imperial commands," *i. e.*, commands requiring im-
plicit obedience.—*Multos porro vides*, &c. The idea is, There are
many spendthrifts over head and ears in debt, whom the often-
eluded creditor is sure to meet at the market.—*Macelli.* The *ma-
cellum* was an inclosure or building which served as a market. It
differed, however, from the *forum*, which was an open area surrounded by colonnades, and in which the market was held upon
stated days in each week.—*Vivendi causa.* "Inducement to live."

12–20. *Egregius.* Comparative adverb. Lucretius (iv., 469) uses
a similar form, but the reading there is uncertain.—*Et cito casurus,*
&c. The ruined spendthrift, just on the point of becoming bankrupt, is compared to a building about to fall, with cracks and fis-
sures in its walls, through which the daylight is streaming.—*Interea
gustus*, &c. "Meanwhile they seek after delicacies through all the
elements," *i. e.*, they ransack earth, air, and water for them. The
gustus, or *promulsis*, after all, however, was only the first course, intended to whet the appetite, consisting of such vegetables as the
lactuca or lettuce, shell and other fish, with piquant sauces, mul-
sum, &c.—*Animo obstantibus.* "Standing in the way of their gratification."—*Ergo haud difficile est*, &c. Therefore, since they like
expense for its own sake, they make no conscience of pawning the
family plate.—*Perituram.* To be squandered on their appetite.—
Oppositis. "Pawned."—*Matris imagine fracta.* He defaces a silver statue of his mother, and pawns it as old silver.—*Quadringentis
nummis.* Four hundred sesterces, or $15.60.—*Condire gulosum fic-
tile.* "To load with dainties an earthen dish." More literally, "to
render savoury an earthen dish containing many a dainty."—*Mis-*

cellanea ludi. "The mixed food of the gladiatorial school." This was a mixture of cheese and flour, probably a kind of macaroni. With *ludi* supply *gladiatorii.*

21–26. *Refert ergo,* &c. "It makes all the difference, therefore, who it is that procures these same things." The idea is, Since so many are ruined by luxury, men give it a bad name in those of narrow means, while in the rich it is extolled as generosity.—*A censu famam trahit.* "Derives credit from his fortune."—*Libya.* The continent of Africa is meant.—*Hic tamen idem ignoret,* &c. The poet despises him, because, although he has sense enough to see the difference in size between Atlas and inferior mountains, he is foolish enough not to distinguish between his own narrow circumstances and the fortunes of the rich, so as to regulate his manner of living accordingly.—*Ignoret.* The subjunctive is used because the *qui,* which is the common subject to *scit* and *ignoret,* before the former means *who,* whereas before the latter it expresses the ground of the contempt, namely, *because* he is ignorant. (*Mayor, ad loc.*)

27–31. *E cœlo descendit,* &c. This precept has been assigned to Socrates, Chilo, Thales, Cleobulus, Bias, and Pythagoras. It was inscribed in golden letters over the portico of the temple at Delphi. Hence, perhaps, the notion afterward that it was derived immediately from heaven.—*Tractandum.* "To be carefully cherished." *Conjugium.* The poet means that, in seeking for a wife, a man must keep to his line. Compare Ovid, *Heroid.,* ix., 32: "*Siqua voles apte nubere, nube pari.*"—*Vel sacri in parte,* &c. The idea is, If you wish to be a senator, you ought to know yourself, and be able to judge whether you are fit for such an office ; for not even Thersites, with all his impudence, had the audacity to put in a claim to the armour of Achilles, which even Ulysses, with all his wisdom, made himself ridiculous by wearing.—*Se traducebat.* "Exposed himself to ridicule."

32–45. *Ancipitem seu tu,* &c. "Or whether you aim at defending a doubtful cause, involved in great risk," *i. e.,* a cause of great moment, with heavy risk accompanying. Some, less correctly, connect *ancipitem* with *se* in the previous line. Observe that the connection, having been interrupted by the parenthesis (*nec . . . . Ulixes*), a new sentence follows here with *affectas* in the indicative.—*Te consule.* "Consult your own powers."—*Buccæ.* "Mere talk," *i. e.,* mere spouters. Literally, "mere cheeks."—*Spectandaque.* "And it must be kept in view."—*Mullum.* Compare *Sat.* iv., 14.—*Gobio.* "The price of a gobio." A fish of small value, probably the gudgeon.— *Ære paterno,* &c. "Your patrimony and whole fortune having been upon your belly, capable of holding, &c.—*Post cuncta novissimus*, &c. "Last of all the ring goes forth," *i. e.*, the last thing sold is the equestrian ring. *Exit* is a well-selected term here, indicating that the property is taken out of the house for sale.—*Non præmaturi cineres*, &c. "The ashes of the funeral pile are not premature, nor is the end of existence bitter to luxury," *i. e.*, their aim is a short life and a merry one; they fear an old age of privation more than an early death.

46–51. *Gradus.* "The steps," *i. e.*, the degrees by which they proceed.—*Coram dominis.* "Before the very owners' faces," *i. e.*, under the very eyes of the lenders.—*Fenoris auctor.* "The usurer." —*Qui vertere solum.* "They who have made off." Literally, "who have changed their soil," *i. e.*, have given their creditors the slip.— *Baias.* Baiæ was the Brighton of Rome, and was situated on the coast of Campania, on the southwest side of the Sinus Baianus. It was famed for its beautiful situation, its warm springs, and its shellfish. Some read *Ostia* for *ostrea*, but this is far inferior.—*Cedere foro.* "To withdraw from the forum," *i. e.*, to abscond from 'change, or to become bankrupt.—*Deterius.* "More discreditable." The idea is, To run away from Rome and one's creditors is so common that there is no more discredit in it than to change the hot air of the Subura for the cool and healthy atmosphere of the Esquiline Hill. As regards the Esquiline, compare Horace, *Sat.* i., 8, 14 : "*Nunc licet Esquiliis habitare salubribus.*"—*Subura.* Compare *Sat.* v., 106 ; x., 156.

52–55. *Ille dolor solus*, &c. Both in Greek and Latin, a pronoun, when the subject of a sentence, takes by attraction the gender of the predicate. Hence we have here for *illud solum* the masculine *ille solus* by attraction to *dolor*, and *illa* by attraction to *mæstitia*. (*Zumpt*, § 372.)—*Circensibus.* Supply *ludis*, and compare *Sat.* x., 81.—*Sanguinis in facie*, &c. They have lost all sense of shame, they cannot blush.—*Morantur pauci*, &c. The virtue of modesty is laughed at and ridiculed. She is, as it were, taking her flight from the city, and few are for stopping her or delaying her departure.

56–63. *Hodie.* "This day (when you are to dine with me)."— *Pulcherrima dictu.* "Those things that are very fine to be talked about."—*Non præstem.* "I do not exhibit."—*Et re.* "And in deed."—*Pultes.* "Pottage." By *puls* is meant a thick pap or pottage, made of meal, pulse, &c. It was the food of the primitive Romans.—*Puero.* For *servo.*—*Habebis Evandrum.* "You will find in me an Evander," *i. e.*, you will be received by me with homely and simple hospitality, as Hercules was by kind Evander. Compare

Virgil, *Æn.*, vii., 100, *seqq.*—*Hospes.* Æneas.—*Et ipse tamen*, &c. "And yet himself also akin to heaven." Æneas was the son of Anchises and the goddess Venus.—*Aquis.* Æneas was drowned in the Numicius. Hercules was burned on Mount Œta.

64–76. *Fercula nunc audi*, &c. "Listen now to the several courses, prepared in no market." *Ornata* is here equivalent to *instructa.* Jacobs (*Anthol.*, iii., 2, p. 18) suggests *corrasa*, but at the market all things would be in abundance.—*Macellis.* Compare verse 10.—*Tiburtino agro.* Juvenal probably had a country-house near Tibur.—*Inscius herbæ.* "Ignorant of (the taste of) grass," *i. e.*, unweaned. —*Montani asparagi.* The wild asparagus is still very common on the Italian hills.—*Posito quos legit*, &c. "Which my farm-steward's wife has gathered, her spindle having been laid down."—*Tortoque calentia fœno.* Fresh eggs were carried about in hay.—*Matribus.* The same hens that laid them.—*Servatæ parte anni.* The various modes of keeping grapes, in an air-tight cask, in sawdust, &c., are described by Pliny (*H. N.*, xv., 18) and Varro (*R. R.*, i., 54).— *Quales fuerant in vitibus.* Looking quite as fresh as when they were on the vines.—*Signinum.* The Signian pear came from Signia, now *Segni*, a town of Latium, east of the Volscian hills.—*Syriumque pyrum.* By the Syrian pear is meant the Bergamot, said to have been originally brought from Syria.—*Picenis.* Horace says that the apples of Tibur were inferior to those of Picenum. It is a high commendation, therefore, of Juvenal's apples to say that they rivalled those of the latter country.—*Siccatum frigore*, &c. "Since they have lost their autumnal moisture dried up by the cold, and the dangers to be feared from their juice if crude." They are now mellowed by the cold of winter, and have lost the acid and unripened juice which they had in autumn when newly gathered.

77–88. *Jam luxuriosa.* "Already luxurious," *i. e.*, when compared with the frugal diet of Curius.—*Curius.* Curius Dentatus, the conqueror of the Samnites, Sabines, Pyrrhus, &c., and a noble specimen of old Roman frugality.—*Compede fossor.* Slaves, as a punishment, were put in irons, and made to dig in the fields, &c.— *Sicci terga suis.* "Flitches of the smoked swine."—*Rara pendentia crate.* "Hanging from the wide-barred rack." The rack here stands in the kitchen.—*Natalicium lardum.* "Bacon as a birth-day treat."—*Accedente.* "Being added."—*Quam dabat.* "Afforded any." A part of the victim was burnt, and the remainder was eaten by the offerer, or sold.—*Solito maturius.* He left his work betimes for so rare a treat.—*Domito a monte.* Where he had been at work, digging and subduing the soil.

89–99. *Quum tremerent autem,* &c. "When men, however, trembled at the Fabii." The most famous censor of the *Fabia gens* was Q. Fabius Maximus Rullianus, colleague of P. Decius, B.C. 304. — *Severos censoris mores,* &c. The censors here alluded to were M. Livius Salinator and C. Claudius Nero, B.C. 204. These individuals had long been enemies, and their long-smothered resentment now burst forth, and occasioned no small scandal in the state. Juvenal's view of the matter is not correct. — *Nemo inter curas,* &c. "No one thought that it was to be ranked among subjects of anxious care and serious concern."—*Qualis testudo.* Namely, whether great or small. In Juvenal's time, however, when tortoise-shell was used by the rich and luxurious for inlaying the couches at entertainments, no expense was spared to procure the largest and finest pieces. — *Fulcrum.* "Couch-foot." Decorated with sphinxes and other figures.—*Nudo.* "Bare of ornament."—*Parvis lectis,* &c. The regular form of expression would have been *lectus parvus nudo latere et fronte ærea.* But *frons ærea,* as the main point to be attended to, is made the subject. (*Heinrich, ad loc.*)—*Vile.* "Of rude and cheap workmanship." — *Ad quod lascivi,* &c. "Near which the playful country boys were accustomed to sport." The bed stood in the atrium, opposite the entrance, and near it the children were wont to play. Compare *Sat.* xiv., 160. Some incorrectly render this, "at which, &c., they were accustomed to laugh," *i. e.,* to make it a matter of wanton jest.—*Tales ergo cibi,* &c. This line comes in very tamely, and rather spoils the picture. Heinrich regards it as spurious.

100–109. *Prædarum in parte reperta.* "Found in his share of the booty." — *Ut phaleris gauderet equus.* He broke them up to make trappings for his steed. Florus, however, says that the *phaleræ* were introduced from Etruria. — *Cælataque cassis,* &c. The rest of the precious metal thus obtained was employed to adorn his helmet and arms with embossed work.—*Romuleæ feræ.* The she-wolf.—*Geminos Quirinos.* Romulus and Remus.—*Sub rupe.* According to the common legend. Compare Virgil's "*Mavortis in antro*" (*Æn.,* viii., 630).—*Dei.* Mars is meant. — *Ponebant farrata omnia.* "They used to serve up all their preparations of meal," *i. e.,* all their food.—*Quibus invideas,* &c. The idea is, If we had lived then, we should have been ready to envy their plain and wholesome fare, if we had had even a spark of envy in our disposition.—*Lividulus.* "Only in the slightest degree envious."

110–125. *Præsentior.* "Was more present," *i. e.,* came home more to the bosoms of men. Compare *Sat.* iii., 18.—*Vox.* Alluding to the story of M. Cædicius, a plebeian, who informed the tribunes that, as he was going along by the temple of Vesta, he heard, amid the silence of the night, a voice louder than human, bidding him tell the magistrates that the Gauls were coming. — *Audita.* Supply *est.*—*Peragentibus.* "Performing."—*Fictilis.* "While still of earthenware." Referring to the primitive statues of the god.— *Violatus.* "Profaned."—*Domi natas.* Of home-growth. Not, for instance, the foreign *citrus.* Compare *Sat.* i., 63.—*Mensas.* The extravagance of the Romans in their tables is almost incredible.— *Nucem.* "Nut-tree." The walnut is meant.—*Rhombus.* Compare *Sat.* iv., 38.—*Dama.* "The doe," *i. e.,* the venison.—*Orbes.* Circular tables, called also *monopodia,* because supported upon a single foot and stem, which, in the present instance, is of ivory.—*Grande ebur.* "A huge mass of ivory."—*Sublimis pardus.* "A tall leopard." The ivory is cut into the figure of a leopard, supporting the table. The leopard belonged to the legends of Bacchus, hence the figure of one supports here the convivial table.—*Dentibus ex illis.* "Made of those tusks."—*Porta Syenes.* Syene, now *Assouan,* a frontier town in southern Egypt, was held by three cohorts. Hence *porta* may be taken strictly for the gate of the place, through which all traffic from Æthiopia must pass. Others, however, since the valley of the Nile is greatly narrowed below Syene, understand by *porta* the pass thus formed. Syene is the place to which, according to the common account, Juvenal was subsequently banished. (*Mayor, ad loc.*) — *Celeres.* "Active." — *Obscurior.* "Of duskier hue."—*Deposuit.* "Has shed." The elephant changes its tusks only once in its life ; but not then, as Juvenal says, "*nimios, capitique graves.*" (*Mayor, ad loc.*)—*Nabathæo.* The Nabathæi were an Arabian people, whose original settlements were in the northwestern part of the peninsula, and who became subsequently very powerful by inland traffic. Their capital was the celebrated rock-hewn Petra.

126–140. *Orexis.* "Appetite." The costly table gives an edge to the appetite.—*Nam pes argenteus,* &c. A table with legs of silver is as vulgar and shabby in the opinion of our voluptuaries (*illis,* i. e., *divitibus*) as a ring of iron.—*Caveo.* "I shun."—*Res exiguas.* "My scanty means."—*Adeo.* "In so much that."—*Tessellæ.* "My dice." Of six sides, not to be confounded with the *tali* of four.— *Calculus.* A counter, used for playing the *ludus latrunculorum* and *duodecim scriptorum,* a sort of draughts. *Calculi* were commonly of glass.—*His.* "By means of these." The bone-handled knives will not taint the dishes carved.—*Pejor.* "Any the worse."

Structor, "a carver." Compare *Sat.* v., 120. — *Omnis pergula.*

"Every carving-school." *Pergula*, literally and in a general sense, meant any kind of building added on to the side of a house or other edifice beyond the original ground-plan. Then, among other special meanings, it indicated a lecture-room or school, in which any art or science is taught.—*Trypheri.* Compare the Greek τρυφερός, "effeminate," "voluptuous," &c.—*Sumine.* By *sumen* is meant the "udder of a sow," with the paps and part of the belly cut from her the day after she has farrowed.—*Pygargus.* A sort of "antelope," with white buttocks, whence the name.—*Scythicæ volucres.* Pheasants are meant. The pheasant (ὄρνις Φασιανός, *Phasiana avis*) takes its name from the Phasis, a river of Colchis, on the confines of Scythia, at the mouth of which these birds congregated in large flocks.—*Phœnicopterus.* The flamingo, the tongue and brain of which were most esteemed.—*Oryx.* A species of wild goat.—*Ulmea cæna.* Trypherus and other professors of the art of carving employed wooden models of the various dishes to be carved. The parts of these were slightly fastened together, so that the pupil could separate them with a blunt knife.

141-157. *Subducere.* "To filch."—*Afræ avis.* Probably our Guinea-fowl. (*Becker, Gallus,* 1, 97.)—*Noster tirunculus.* "My little fellow, who is a mere novice." He is not like the older slaves of great houses, an expert thief.—*Imbutus.* "Initiated."—*Furtis.* Some read *frustis*, and make *subducere* mean "to take off neatly by the carving-knife." But *furtis* is much more playful.—*Incultus.* "Plainly clad."—*A frigore tutus.* Wearing warm and coarse clothing, and not, like a favourite page in a great house, rustling in silks.—*Phryx aut Lycius.* The Asiatic slaves were in high request. —*A mangone petitus.* "Purchased from the slave-dealer."—*In magno*, &c. "When you shall ask for wine in a large cup." Supply *poculo.* Another reading is *et magno*, "and at a great price," which must then be taken with what precedes.—*Latine.* Not in Greek, for he knows nothing of that language.—*Tonsi rectique.* "Close-cropped and straight." *Recti* refers to their not being curled.— *Suspirat.* "He sighs after."—*Ardens purpura.* "The glowing purple."—*Diffusa.* Compare *Sat.* v., 30. Home-made wines are meant, not Chian or Falernian.

158-161. *Multos.* We have purposely substituted this for *alios*, the common reading, after having omitted a part of the text.—*Conditor Iliados cantabitur.* A *lector* was employed to read during meals.—*Dubiam facientia palmam.* "Rendering the palm doubtful," *i. e.*, contesting the prize with the Homeric poems.—*Quid refert, tales versus,* &c. Juvenal here contrasts the poems which need a skilful reader to make them endurable, with Virgil's, which have an intrinsic merit of their own.

162–174. *Averte negotia.* "Lay aside serious employments."— *Cessare.* "To be idle."—*Fenoris.* "Of money out at interest."— *Exue.* "Divest yourself of."—*Pone.* "Banish from your thoughts." —*Interea Megalesiacæ,* &c. The idea is, You may just as well make it a holiday : all the world is at the Circus, and you would find no one with whom to transact business of any kind.—*Megalesiacæ spectacula mappæ.* "The spectacles of the Megalesian napkin." The Megalesian games were celebrated in honor of Cybele, called also *Magna Mater* (Μεγάλη θεά). The consul or prætor, by dropping a napkin, gave the signal for the commencement of the games.—*Idæum sollemne, colunt.* "Grace the Idæan solemnity." Compare *Sat.* iii., 129.—*Triumpho.* For *trumphanti.*—*Præda.* Eaten up, as it were, by horses. Falling a prey to the ruinous expenses of the games.— *Pace.* "With the permission."—*Totam Romam capit.* Indicating the eagerness with which all ranks flocked to these games, as well as others of the kind.—*Fragor.* "A burst of applause."—*Eventum viridis panni.* "The success of the green uniform." Four chariots generally contended, the drivers being distinguished by four colours.

175–184. *Si deficeret.* "If it should fail."—*Cannarum in pulvere.* In the battle of Cannæ the Roman army faced the south, and the Carthaginian the north, and Hannibal thereby gained the advantage of having the wind called the Vulturnus behind him, which drove clouds of dust into the face of the enemy, from the parched fields around. Cannæ was in Apulia, on the south bank of the Aufidus, about six miles from its mouth.—*Consulibus.* Æmilius Paullus and Terentius Varro.—*Sponsio.* "Betting."—*Cultæ puellæ.* "Some neatly-dressed maiden."—*Contracta cuticula.* "Let our skin, wrinkled with age."—*Togam.* "The toga-wearing crowd."—*Jam nunc in balnea,* &c. The usual time for bathing was the eighth hour (2 o'clock). The tenth hour is also named. That some bathed at the sixth hour (noon) appears from Martial (x., 48, 1, *seqq.*). Here Juvenal proposes to bathe at once, though it wants a whole hour of noon. (*Mayor, ad loc.*)—*Salva fronte.* "With unblushing brow."— *Talis vitæ.* "Even of such a life as this." Frequenting feasts and indulging in idleness may be occasionally pleasant enough ; but a continuance of this mode of life, for many days in succession, would prove a source of great weariness.—*Rarior usus.* "A more moderate use."

SATIRE XII.

ARGUMENT.

Catullus, a valued friend of the poet, had narrowly escaped shipwreck. In a letter of rejoicing to their common friend Corvinus,
Juvenal describes the danger that his friend had incurred, and his
own hearty and disinterested delight at his preservation, contrasting
his own sacrifices of thanksgiving at the event with those offered by
the designing legacy-hunters, by which the rich and childless were
attempted to be ensnared. (*Evans.*)

1-9. *Natali die.* "Than my own natal day." The birth-day
was sacred to the Genius, to whom they offered wine, incense, and
flowers, abstaining from bloody sacrifices.—*Festus cespes.* "The
festal altar of turf." The altar of green turf which the poet had
erected on the present occasion, thus suiting his devotion to his circumstances.—*Reginæ.* Supply *divûm.* Temples were built in honour of *Juno Regina* by Camillus and M. Æmilius (*Liv.*, v., 23; xxxix.,
2). The title is frequent in inscriptions. (*Mayor, ad loc.*)—*Gorgone.* Ablative of the instrument. As Minerva bore the Gorgon's
head on her shield, the term *Gorgo* is here used for the shield. The
Gorgons, according to one legend, dwelt in Africa, near the confines
of Mauritania.—*Extensum.* It was esteemed a very bad omen if the
victim did not go willingly to the sacrifice. It was always led,
therefore, with a long, slack rope.—*Tarpeio Jovi.* To Jupiter, Juno,
and Minerva belonged separate *cellæ* in the Capitoline temple, and
hence they are frequently invoked together.—*Coruscat.* "Sways
to and fro." Compare the scholiast, "*Movet, sicut telum.*"—*Ferox
vitulus.* "It is a spirited calf."—*Ducere.* "To drain."—*Vexat.*
"Buts." Literally, "teases."

10-16. *Similisque affectibus.* "And equal to my wishes."—*Hispulla.* A female of disreputable character, alluded to by the poet in
Sat. vi., 94.—*Piger.* "Slow-paced." —'*Ostendens.* "Giving evidence of."—*Clitumni.* The Clitumnus (now *Clitumno*) falls near
Mevania, in Umbria, into the Tinia, a tributary of the Tiber. It
was celebrated for the clearness of its waters and the beauty of the
cattle that pastured on its banks.—*Sanguis iret*, &c. The blood
and neck would go to the altar, *i. e.*, the ox chosen for his fulness
of blood and for his thick neck. (*Mayor, ad loc.*)—*A grandi ministro.* "By the strong assistant." *Grandis* here is meant to imply .

M

full physical development. The victim was, in most cases, not killed by the priests who conducted the sacrifice, but by an assistant,
termed *popa* (for which *ministro* is substituted in the text), who
struck the animal with a hammer before the knife was used.—*Amici*. Catullus.

17-28. *Et*. "Also."—*Evasit*. Some read *evasi*, "escaped from,"
giving *et* the ordinary force of "and," and continuing the sentence with
densæ, but this makes an awkward tautology.—*Nube una*. "In one
dense cloud."—*Subitusque antennas*, &c. "And a sudden bolt smote
the sail-yards." *Ignis* is here what we would term "the electric
fluid."—*Conferri posse velis ardentibus*. "Could be compared with
blazing sails," *i. e.*, with a ship on fire.—*Omnia fiunt talia*, &c. The
storm realized the most fearful inventions of poetry.—*Genus ecce
aliud discriminis*. Besides the wind and lightning, Catullus had to
endure the loss of his property.—*Iterum*. "A second time."—*Sortis ejusdem*. That is, of shipwreck.—*Et quam votiva*, &c. Persons
in peril of shipwreck often vowed to some deity a painting of their
dangers and escape in case they got safe to land. — *Pictores quis
nescit*, &c. The Romans made so many vows to the Egyptian goddess Isis, whom the traders and mariners regarded as their patron-
ess, that many painters got their bread by drawing votive paintings,
which were hung up in her temples.

30-40. *Quum plenus*, &c. The hold was half full, or full up to the
middle. — *Evertentibus*. "Trying to lay low." The idea is this :
When now, the ship pitching from side to side, the helmsman could
not save the tottering mast. We have given *arbori*, Lachmann's
conjecture, in place of the common *arboris*, which affords no intel-
ligible meaning. (*Mayor, ad loc.*)—*Decidere jactu*, &c. "He began
to compound with the winds by throwing overboard." — *Fundite.
*"Throw overboard."—*Mæcenatibus*. Compare *Sat*. i., 54.—*Atque
alias*, &c. "As well as others, the very fleece of which the quality
of the generous pasture has tinged," *i. e.*, other attire, dyed on the
sheep's back by the nature of the herbage. — *Ipsum vestium pecus.
*The very sheep that yield the cloth. The pastures spoken of were
on the banks of the Bætis, or *Guadalquiver*, the waters of which river
also, together with the surrounding atmosphere, were said to add to
the effects of the pasture, all combined giving a golden tinge to the
fleeces of the sheep.—*Fons egregius*. "The excellent water." *Fons*
for *aqua*.—*Bœticus aer*. Bætica is now *Andalusia*.

41-49. *Mittere*. "To cast into the sea." For *demittere*.—*Parthenio*. Parthenius must have been a silversmith, since *lances* and
cratera are in apposition with *argentum*. (*Mayor, ad loc.*)—*Urnæ*

cratera capacem. "A mixer that would hold three gallons." The *urna* contained 24 sextarii, nearly three gallons.—*Pholo.* Pholus, the centaur, is meant. Compare *Virg., Georg.,* ii., 455.—*Conjuge Fusci.* Noted for her intemperate habits.—*Bascaudas.* "Baskets." *Bascauda* means a British basket. This term, which remains with very little variation in the Welsh "basgawd" and the English "basket," was conveyed to Rome together with the article denoted by it.—*Escalia.* "Chargers." Supply *vasa.* — *Cœlati.* "Of chased work." Consult *Smith's Dict. Ant., s. v. Cœlatura.* — *Callidus emtor Olynthi.* Philip of Macedon is meant, who bribed Lasthenes and Eurycrates to betray Olynthus to him. Olynthus was a city in Chalcidice, at the head of the Toronaic Gulf.—*Quis alius.* "Who else," *i. e.,* besides Catullus.—*Non propter vitam,* &c. This and the succeeding line are condemned by Bentley (*ad Hor., A. P.,* 337) as mere interpolations. — *Faciunt patrimonia.* "Make fortunes." Bentley condemns this Latinity, and terms it "*scabies locutionis.*"—*Propter patrimonia.* "For the sake of money-getting." Suspicious Latinity again.

50–59. *Rerum utilium.* "Even of necessary things," *i. e.,* provisions and furniture.—*Sed nec,* &c. "But not even these sacrifices afford any relief." Literally, "lighten," *i. e.,* the danger.—*Adversis.* "Adverse affairs."—*Illuc recidit.* "It came to that pass."— *Ac se explicat angustum.* "And extricates himself at length when reduced to narrow straits."—*Discriminis ultima,* &c. "The last degree of danger is come, when we apply helps that will only cripple the vessel." Literally, "make the vessel less." With *ultima* supply *adsunt.* The idea is, Distress is desperate when the help only serves to injure the vessel.—*Dolato confisus ligno.* "Trusting to a hewn plank," *i. e.,* chipped smooth with the axe.—*Si sit latissima tœda.* "If the pine be of the thickest."—*Mox.* When on board. —*Cum reticulis et pane.* "Along with your net-bags of bread." Hendiadys.—*Aspice.* "Look after," *i. e.,* provide.

60–72. *Jacuit planum.* "Lay all level to the view," *i. e.,* had subsided into a calm.—*Tempora postquam,* &c. The construction is *postquam tempora vectoris* (erant) *propitia, fatumque* (ejus erat) *valentius Euro.* — *Meliora pensa ducunt.* "Draw kindlier tasks." The phrase *ducere pensa* alludes to the action of the spinster who "draws" the wool or flax from the distaff as she spins it, and this she continues until the "task" assigned her is finished.—*Et staminis albi lanificæ.* "And are spinsters of a white thread." The white or black threads of the Parcæ were supposed to symbolize the good or bad fortune of the mortal whose yarn Clotho was spinning.

—Inopi miserabilis, &c. " In piteous plight ran along by a poor contrivance."—*Vestibus.* The garments of the crew.—*Atque novercali,* &c. Alba Longa is meant, founded by Iulus, who left Lavinium to his stepmother Lavinia. Though twenty miles from the coast, it formed a conspicuous landmark.—*Candida scrofa.* Compare *Virg., Æn.,* iii., 390.—*Et nunquam visis,* &c. " And famous for thirty dugs, never seen before." With each a pig sucking at it. A sight never seen before.

73-80. *Intrat.* Supply *navis.*—*Positas inclusa,* &c. " The moles built through the waters inclosed within them." The harbour of Ostia is meant. This massive work was planned and begun by Julius Cæsar, executed by Claudius, and repaired by Trajan. A Pharos was erected here in imitation of the celebrated one at Alexandria in Egypt.—*Porrectaque brachia rursum.* " And the arms extending back again." Breakwaters stretching far into the sea, and then bending again toward the land.—*Occurrunt.* " Meet," *i. e.,* jut out into.—*Longe.* " Far behind."—*Non sic igitur,* &c. No mere harbour formed by the hand of nature will excite so much admiration as this.—*Baianœ pervia cymbœ.* " Pervious even to a Baian wherry," *i. e.,* which even a light skiff, accustomed to ply on the smooth waters of the harbour of Baiæ, could enter in safety.—*Vertice raso.* It was the custom in storms at sea to vow the hair to some god, most commonly Neptune.—*Garrula.* " The theme of many a garrulous tale." Observe that *garrula pericula* is put by a species of hypallage for *pericula quæ nautas garrulos reddebant.*

81-86. *Ite igitur pueri,* &c. Addressed by Catullus to his slaves. —*Linguis animisque faventes.* The idea is, Help on the solemnity by observing a profound silence and paying the closest attention to the rites. This was always recommended during a sacrifice, that there might be no ill-omened disturbance and interruption.—*Farra imponite cultris.* The salted meal *(mola salsa),* here called *farra,* was sprinkled on the sacrificial knives, as well as on the head of the victim.—*Molles focos,* &c. Alluding to the turf altars mentioned in verse 3.—*Sacro quod præstat,* &c. " The sacred business, which is most important, being gone through with in due form." Alluding to the sacrifices mentioned in the beginning of the Satire, namely, to Juno, Pallas, and Tarpeian Jove, and therefore more important than those to the Lares.—*Parva simulacra.* The little images of the Lares.—*Fragili nitentia cera.* " Shining brightly with brittle wax." They were covered over with a kind of varnish, of which wax formed the main ingredient.

87-90. *Nostrum Jovem.* He means his domestic Jove, or the

Jove who was the tutelary deity of his abode. So Cicero had a household Minerva.—*Jactabo.* " I will scatter." Put for *spargam.* Compare the Greek φυλλοβαλεῖν.—*Omnes violæ colores.* Put for *violas omnis coloris.* " Violets of every hue."—*Erexit.* " Has set up."—*Et matutinis,* &c. " And celebrates the festivities with lamps lighted in the morning." It was customary on any joyful occasion to adorn the gates of the house with branches of bay, and with lamps even in the daytime. By the term *matutinis* the poet means to convey the idea that he will light them early, out of zeal toward his friend, so that they might burn from morn to night.

91–108. *Nec suspecta tibi,* &c. The general idea is this: Wonder not, then, Corvinus, at my rejoicings, nor question their sincerity. He for whom I raise so many altars is no childless person, that a fortune-hunter should pay him court. Even those who would sacrifice their own children to gain the favour of the childless rich would think any the smallest attention thrown away upon the father of three sons. (*Mayor, ad loc.*)—*Libet exspectare,* &c. " You may wait long enough for one who will expend upon so unproductive a friend," &c. — *Verum hæc nimia,* &c. " A hen, did I say? No, even this is too great an outlay."—*Pro patre cadet.* " Will fall for one who is a father," *i. e.,* will be killed and offered up.—*Sentire calorem.* " To feel the approach of fever."—*Capit.* Agreeing in the singular with the nearer noun, as indicating the more important personage of the two.—*Gallita et Paccius.* Fictitious names.—*Legitime fixis.* " Affixed in due form." If votive offerings fell from the walls, it was deemed an evil omen.—*Tabellis.* Votive tablets. Some prefer *libellis,* as more satirical, and denoting little books, as it were, written full of vows.—*Hecatomben.* The hecatomb properly consisted of oxen, 100 being sacrificed simultaneously on 100 different altars. But sheep or other victims were also offered.—*Quatenus.* " Since." They vow, indeed, a hecatomb of oxen, since they cannot vow one of elephants, the latter animal not being produced among us.—*Sidere.* " Climate."—*Arboribus Rutulis,* &c. Turnus was king of Ardea, among the Rutuli. Here there were stables for the elephants which the emperors kept for exhibition in the theatre or amphitheatre.—*Tyrio.* Carthage being a colony of Tyre.—*Nostris ducibus.* The Romans first employed elephants in battle in the war against Philip, B.C. 200. — *Regi Molosso.* Pyrrhus, king of Epirus, of which country the Molossi were a people. — *Cohortes.* " Whole cohorts." Exaggeration, of course. In *Maccabees,* 1, 6, 35, *seqq.,* each elephant carries thirty-two soldiers in a tower, besides the Indian driver.—*Partem aliquam.* " No mean portion."

109-112. *Nulla igitur mora*, &c. "It is no fault, therefore, of Novius, &c., that that ivory is not led," &c. More literally, "There is no delay, as far as Novius is concerned," &c. The idea is, As elephants are not procurable in Italy, it is no fault of Novius's or Pacuvius's if those victims are not at once obtained for the health of Galita. Novius and Pacuvius were two fortune-hunters.—*Illud ebur.* The elephant.—*Gallitæ.* To be taken with *Lares.*—*Deis.* The Lares.—*Captatoribus horum.* "Those who hunt after these," *i. e.*, after the rich and childless.

113-125. *Alter.* "One of these two fellows." He means Pacuvius.—*Si concedas mactare.* "If you give him license thus to immolate."—*De grege servorum*, &c. It was a common belief, as we see from the legend of Alcestis, that the sacrifice of one life might redeem another. (*Mayor, ad loc.*)—*Vittas.* The head of the victim intended for sacrifice was always encircled with a fillet.—*Nubilis.* Just as Iphigenia was led to the altar, "*nubendi tempore in ipso.*" (*Lucret.*, i., 99.)—*Etsi non sperat*, &c. Pacuvius will devote his daughter, though he cannot hope that a stag will be suddenly substituted for her, as for Iphigenia in Euripides. — *Laudo meum civem.* I highly commend my fellow-citizen Pacuvius for his wisdom and address. Agamemnon sacrificed his daughter to release the fleet, but how unworthy an end is that in comparison with a rich inheritance!—*Libitinam evaserit.* "Shall have escaped Libitina." *Libitina* was properly an epithet of Venus (the goddess who presides over *deaths* as well as births), in whose temple all things belonging to funerals were sold.—*Delebit tabulas.* "He will cancel his former will." If he recovers, he will ascribe it all to the vow of Pacuvius, and revoke in his favour his former will.—*Inclusus carcere nassæ.* "Inclosed within the prison of the weel." *Nassa* is a weel or basket for snaring fish, made of wicker-work, with a wide, funnel-shaped mouth, long body, and narrow throat, constructed in such a way that the fish could enter it, but could not get out again.—*Meritum.* "A service."—*Breviter.* "In one brief line."—*Incedet.* "Will strut." *Incedo* generally denotes a stately, consequential movement.—*Quam grande operæ pretium*, &c. "How great a recompense the Mycenean maid intended for immolation gains for him." Agamemnon was king of Mycenæ in Argolis, and hence *Mycenis* would be an appellation for Iphigenia. The term, however, is here applied to the daughter of Pacuvius, just as she was styled, in line 117, his Iphigenia.

126-128. *Vivat Pacuvius*, &c. The idea is, May Pacuvius be cursed by the fulfilment of his desires! may he have long life and riches, but know nothing of that friendship which he dishonours by an unworthy counterfeit. (*Mayor, ad loc.*)—*Vel Nestora totum.* "Even to the full age of Nestor." Compare *Sat.* x., 240, *seqq.* Wittenbach compares the expression *vivere Nestora* with *Cyclopa moveri*, &c. (*ad Plut., Mor.*, p. 150, B). Mayor, on the other hand, thinks that *Nestora* is equivalent here to *Nesteream ætatem.*—*Rapuit Nero.* On Nero's wholesale robberies in Greece and elsewhere, compare Tacitus, *Ann.*, xv., 45; xvi., 23, &c. More than five hundred statues were removed from Delphi alone.

SATIRE XIII.

ARGUMENT.

Calvinus had left a sum of money in the hands of a confidential person, who, when he came to re-demand it, forswore the deposit. The indignation and fury expressed by Calvinus at this breach of trust reached the ears of his friend Juvenal, who endeavours to soothe and comfort him under his loss. The different topics of consolation follow one another naturally and forcibly, and the horrors of a troubled conscience were, perhaps, never depicted with such impressive solemnity as in this Satire. (*Evans.*)

1–5. *Exemplo malo.* "Fraught with bad example unto others," *i. e.*, that will furnish a precedent for crime. Heinrich, less correctly, explains these words by "*malo modo*," "*male*," and to the same effect Mayor.—*Improba quamvis*, &c. "Though the corrupt influence of the prætor may have gained his cause for him by means of the false-speaking urn." From the *Judices Selecti* (a kind of jurymen chosen annually for the purpose) the Prætor Urbanus, who sat as chief judge, chose by lot about fifty to act as his assistants or assessors. To each of these were given three tablets : one inscribed with the letter A, for "*absolvo;*" one with the letter C, for "*condemno;*" and the third with the letters N. L., for *non liquet*, "not proven." After the case had been heard, and the judices had consulted together privately, they returned into court, and each judex dropped one of these tablets into an urn provided for the purpose, which was afterward brought to the prætor, who counted the number, and gave sentence according to the majority of votes. In all these various steps there was plenty of opportunity for a corrupt prætor to frustrate the ends of justice. (*Evans, ad loc.*)—*Fallaci.*

Some read *fallacis* agreeing with *Prætoris*, and *urnam* for *urna*, but this is prosaic and inferior.

6–17. *Et fidei violatæ crimine.* "And the charge you bring of violated faith," *i. e.*, breach of trust.—*Sed nec*, &c. The idea is, It is a gross act of dishonesty, to be sure, but, at the same time, &c. Before Juvenal enters upon the guilt of the offender, he endeavours to moderate the passionate transports of his friend.—*Te mergat.* A metaphor taken from a ship's sinking by being overloaded.—*Rara.* "To be of unfrequent occurrence."—*Tritus.* "Worn threadbare." —*Et medio*, &c. That is, drawn at random.—*Flagrantior æquo esse.* "To blaze forth more than is just."—*Quamvis levium.* "However light."—*Sacrum.* "Sacred," on account of the oath to which the gods were witnesses. — *Stupet hæc*, &c.   The idea is, Does my friend Calvinus, now turned of sixty, and consequently well acquainted with the nature of mankind from many years' experience, stand astonished at such a common transaction as this?—*Fonteio Consule*, &c. Of four consuls of this name (B.C. 33; A.D. 12, 59, 67), the last two alone come here into question. Clinton (*Fast. Rom. ad Ann.* 118) and Lipsius (*Quæst., Epist.* iv., 20) assume that L. Fonteius Capito, consul A.D. 59, is here intended. If so, the date of the Satire will be A.D. 119. (*Mayor, ad loc.*)

18–31. *An nihil in melius*, &c. The idea is, Have you learned no wisdom from your long experience ? The philosopher's victory over fortune is indeed the highest, yet it is no slight thing to be taught submission in the school of life. (*Mayor, ad loc.*)—*Ducimus.* "We deem."—*Jactare.* "To try to shake off," *i. e.*, to fret under. —*Quæ tam festa dies*, &c. The idea is, What day, no matter how holy, is not profaned by bringing to light instances of all sorts of crime ?—*Pyxide.* "Poison." The box put for the poison contained in it. *Pyxis* is properly a coffer or casket of boxwood, πυξίς.— *Thebarum portæ.* Egyptian Thebes had one hundred gates; Bœotian Thebes seven. The latter is here meant. The mouths of the Nile were also seven.—*Nona ætas*, &c. "The ninth age of the world is now being passed through by us, and times worse than the days of iron." There is considerable doubt about the true reading here. One of the best MSS. has *nunc* for *nona*, so that the meaning will then be, Now we live in an age and times worse than the Iron Age. This latter reading is adopted by Jahn, Mayor, and others. We have preferred, however, the common text, regarding, with Heinrich, the epithet "*nona*" as a species of satiric hyperbole. —*Et posuit.* "And has imposed one."

32–37. *Quanto Fæsidium*, &c. "As the vocal sportula praises

Fæsidius when he pleads," *i. e.*, as that with which the sportula, that gives them tongues, makes his clients applaud him. Compare *Sat.* i., 103 ; x., 46.—*Senior bulla dignissime.* "Man advanced in years, and yet most worthy of the bulla," *i. e.*, most fit to wear the bulla of boyhood, and to be regarded as a mere child. The *bulla* was worn until the *toga virilis* was assumed. Compare *Sat.* v., 164. The meaning of Juvenal is, Well, my old friend, are you at sixty years of age such a child as not to know? &c.—*Veneres.* "Charms." —*Vulgo moveat.* "Will in all likelihood excite amid the crowd." —*Esse.* "Is really present."—*Rubenti.* "Red with the blood of victims." The blood was poured on the altar from a vessel, termed in Greek σφάγων or σφαγεῖον.

38–45. *Quondam.* In the Golden Age.—*Indigenæ.* "The aborigines."—*Sumeret.* "Took up," *i. e.*, assumed as his symbol after having fled from the skies.—*Virguncula.* "Was a little maid."— *Privatus adhuc.* "Was as yet in a private station." Compare the scholiast, "*nondum rex cœli.*"—*Idæis antris.* The Cretan Ida is meant, in the caves of which mountain the youthful Jove was concealed by his mother Rhea, that Saturn might not devour him.— *Puer Iliacus.* Ganymedes. —*Herculis uxor.* Hebe.—*Ad cyathos.* Supply *erat* or *stabat.* "Officiated as cup-bearer."—*Et jam sicca- to nectare,* &c. "Nor did Vulcan (but not till he had drained the nectar) wipe his arms, rendered all sooty by his workshop in Lipara," *i. e.*, by the smoke of his forge. With *Vulcanus* supply *aderat* for a literal translation. *Nec* would have been more regular than *et.*

46–58. *Sibi.* "By himself."—*Talis ut est hodie.* The poet is covertly satirising the apotheoses of the Cæsars.—*Urgebant.* "Pressed upon."—*Aliquis sortitus.* "Had any one obtained for his share." Alluding to the division of the universe between Jupiter, Neptune, and Pluto.—*Aut Sicula torvus,* &c. "Nor was there the grim Pluto with his Sicilian bride." Pluto had not as yet obtained the empire of the lower world, nor carried off his spouse, Proserpina, from the Sicilian fields of Enna.—*Nec rota,* &c. The term *rota* contains an allusion to the legend of Ixion, *saxum* to that of Sisyphus, and *vulturis atri pœna* to the punishment of Tityos.—*Sed infernis hilares,* &c. "For there being at that time no crimes, there was no need of laws, or of any king to enforce them ; of course, no punishments in the lower world."—*Admirabilis.* "Was an object of wonder," *i. e.*, a prodigy or marvel.—*Quo.* "When." The common text has *hoc.* —*Vetulo non assurrexerat.* On the reverence for old age in early times, consult *Aul. Gell.,* ii., 15 ; *Val. Max.,* ii., 1, 9 ; *Ovid, Fast.,* v. 65, *seqq.*—*Cuicunque.* For *cuilibet.*—*Licet ipse videret,* &c. Money did not then make the man as now. Strawberries, acorns, and the like are here supposed to have been the first food of mankind in the Golden Age, and stores of these the first wealth.—*Tam venerabile erat*, &c. "So strong a claim to deference was it to be older than another by only four years, and so entirely equal was," &c. *Quatuor annis* means, in fact, "by only a few years."

61-70. *Veterem cum tota*, &c. "The old leathern bag, together with all its rust," *i. e.*, with all its contents, even to the rust. The money has been kept so long that the bag has grown old and its contents have become rusty.—*Prodigiosa fides*, &c. "It is a very prodigy of good faith, and worthy of (being recorded in) the Tuscan books." The marvellous events of the year were registered by the Etruscans in their sacred records, in order that, if they portended the displeasure of the gods, they might be duly expiated.—*Coronata.* "Crowned for sacrifice."—*Bimembri.* "Half human, half brute." Compare Livy, xxxvii., 11: "*Cum elephanti capite puerum natum.*" The epithet *bimembris* is also applied to the Centaur. —*Miranti.* Personification. The common reading *mirandis* is less poetical and less in the spirit of Juvenal. Theophrastus speaks of certain kinds of fish which had been dug up in Paphlagonia and elsewhere. (*Op. ed Schneid.*, vol. i., p. 825.)—*Fetæ.* "With foal."—*Lapides.* Showers of stones are frequently mentioned in Livy. The descent of acrolites probably gave rise to those accounts.—*Longa uva.* "In a long cluster." Compare Virgil (*Georg.*, iv., 558): "*Uvam demittere ramis.*"—*Et lactis vortice torrens.* "And rushing impetuous with a stream of milk." Compare *Liv.*, xxxiv., 45: "*Nuntiatum est, Nare amni lac fluxisse.*"

71-85. *Decem sestertia.* Equivalent to $390.—*Arcana.* "Deposited without any witness."—*Quam patulæ vix ceperat*, &c. "Which (each) corner of his capacious strong-box had with difficulty contained," *i. e.*, his money-chest filled in every corner.—*Tam facile et pronum*, &c. The idea is, So prone are mortals to despise the gods, who are witnesses to all their actions, if they can but hide them from the eyes of men.—*Ficti constantia vultus.* "The unshaken firmness of the look put on by him."—*Tarpeia fulmina.* The thunderbolts of Capitoline Jove are meant.—*Frameam.* The *framea* was properly the "pike" used by the ancient Germans.—*Cirrhæi spicula vatis.* "The darts of the phophet-god of Cirrha." Apollo is meant. Compare *Sat.* vii., 64. — *Puellæ.* Diana. — *Pater Ægæi Neptune.* At Ægæ, in Eubœa, Neptune dwelt beneath the sea (*Hom., Il.*, xiii., 21), and between Imbros and Tenedos he had a grotto. (*Ib.*, 33.) —*Armamentaria.* "The arsenals." — *Comedam*, &c. The father pledges himself to eat (like Thyestes) his son's head if he breaks his faith.—*Phario aceto.* The vinegar of Egypt was more celebrated than its wine.

86–94. *Casibus.* "The accidents." — *Nullo rectore.* "With no one to guide it." Ablative absolute.— *Volvente vices.* "Bringing round the revolutions."—*Intrepidi.* "They are fearless as to consequences." — *Et pejerat.* Observe that *et* has here the force of "and yet."—*Secum.* "He reasons with himself." Supply *cogitat.* —*Isis.* Blindness, the most common of Egyptian diseases, was supposed to be the peculiar infliction of Isis. The worship of this goddess was introduced into Rome in the time of Sulla, and, though the Senate made many attempts to suppress it, yet the new religious rites took deep root at Rome, and became extremely popular. Under the early Roman emperors the worship of Isis became firmly established.—*Lumina.* On which a curse may have been invoked. —*Sistro.* The sistrum was a sort of rattle used by the Egyptian priests in the religious ceremonies of Isis. It consisted of a number of metal rods inserted into a thin oval frame of the same material. To this a short handle was attached, by which it was held up and rapidly shaken, so as to make the rods give out a sharp and rattling noise. Isis herself was described as holding a sistrum in her right hand.—*Abnego.* "I disown."

95–99. *Tanti.* "Of so much importance," *i. e.*, such mighty matters as to counterbalance the joy of possessing a large sum of money.—*Pauper locupletem, &c.* "Neither let Ladas, if poor, hesitate to wish for the gout that waits on wealth, if he needs not Anticyra nor Archigenes," *i. e.*, a poor man, though swift as Ladas, unless he be crazy (needing, therefore, the hellebore of Anticyra, or the aid of the physician Archigenes), will pray for riches even with the gout.—*Ladas.* A victorious runner at the Olympic games in the time of Alexander the Great.—*Anticyra.* There were two places of this name, both famous for producing hellebore, the great remedy with the ancients for madness. One was in Phocis, on a bay (*Sinus Anticyranus*) of the Corinthian Gulf; the other on the Maliac Gulf in Thessaly, near the mouth of the River Spercheus.—*Archigene.* Archigenes was an eminent Greek physician, born at Apamea, in Syria, and who practised at Rome in the time of Trajan.— *Quid enim præstat.* "For what avails." — *Esuriens Pisææ, &c.* "The hungry branch of Pisa's olive," *i. e.*, the branch that will afford no food to the gainers of it. Pisa was a city of Elis, giving name to the district of Pisalis, and lying to the east of the Olympian plain. The poets confound it with Olympia.

100–111. *Ut.* "Though."—*Curant punire.* "They concern themselves about punishing."—*His.* "Such perjuries as these."—*Diverso fato.* "With a different fate," *i. e.*, with results widely different.
—*Confirmant.* "They strive to encourage."—*Præcedit.* He leads
the way before you, as if in the utmost haste to clear himself by
oath. Observe the change of number here, which is frequently
found when a class is spoken of.—*Immo.* "Or rather."—*Vexare.*
"To worry you to put him to the test."—*Nam quum magna*, &c.
He is thus eager to appeal to the gods, because effrontery is mistaken by many for the security of innocence.—*Superest.* "Abounds."
—*Mimum agit ille*, &c. "He acts as good a farce as the runaway
buffoon-slave of the witty Catullus," *i. e.*, the acting of the false
swearer is quite as good a farce as the buffoonery of the runaway
slave in the Phantom of Catullus. Compare *Sat.* viii., 186. The
runaway slave, in this play, "*dominum traxit*," as the scholiast says,
perhaps to the altar, to receive his oath that he was free-born.
(*Mayor, ad loc.*)

112–119. *Stentora.* Stentor was a herald of the Greeks in the
Trojan war, whose voice was as loud as that of fifty other men together.—*Gradivus.* Mars, when wounded by Diomede, roared, according to Homer, as loudly as ten thousand men. (*Il.*, v., 859.)—
Vel marmoreus. "Even though formed of marble."—*In carbone tuo.*
"On thy coal," *i. e.*, in thy censer.—*Charta soluta.* "From the
loosened wrapper."—*Ut video.* For *quantum video.*—*Vagelli.* Vagellius was a desperate fool, to whom, nevertheless, a statue had
been erected. He is the same with the one mentioned in *Sat.* xvi.,
23. Some read *Bathylli.* The reference will then be to the pantomime Bathyllus, no very reputable character.

120–123. *Accipe.* "Hear." Supply *auribus.*—*Solatia.* He means
"consolations" derived, not from the doctrines of philosophy, but
from the dictates of common sense. The individual who can offer
these is the poet himself.—*Tunica.* "By a tunic alone." The tunic
was not worn by the Cynics, whereas the Stoics wore both the tunic
and the pallium or cloak over this.—*Non Epicurum suspicit.* "Who
has no reverence for Epicurus."—*Exigui lætum*, &c. The garden
of Epicurus, says Gifford, was a school of temperance, and would
have afforded little gratification, and still less sanction, to those
sensualists who, in turning hogs, flatter themselves that they are
becoming Epicureans.

124–134. *Dubii ægri.* "The sick whose cases are desperate."
Observe that *ægri* is here used substantively.—*Vel discipulo.* "Even
to an apprentice." The idea is, A philosopher might be required

to console one suffering from a more serious calamity; a less skilful practitioner may heal your wound.—*Philippi*. Philippus must
have been an inferior practitioner of the day.— *Tam detestabile factum*. Alluding to the conduct of his false friend.—*Plana palma*.
"With the flat palm," *i. e.*, with open palm.—*Quandoquidem accepto,*
&c. When a man has had losses, he closes his house as for a funeral.— *Vestem diducere*, &c. "Content with merely tearing the
upper edge of the tunic," *i. e.*, in order to bare the breast.—*Humore
coacto*. "With moisture got together for the occasion."

135–142. *Sed si cuncta vides*, &c. This is the nature of the consolation that is offered by the poet, who represents to his friend the
frequency, not only of the same, but of much greater injuries than
what he has suffered, and that he is only sharing in this the common lot of mankind.—*Si decies lectis*, &c. "If, when the obligation
has been read over ten times on the opposite side," *i. e.*, has been
read over by the creditor's advocate time after time. We have followed the explanation of Madvig, who makes *diversa parte* equivalent here to *a parte contraria adversarii*. (*Mayor, ad loc.*)— *Vana supervacui*, &c. "They, whom their own handwriting, and the sardonyx, their principal signet-ring, that is carefully kept in its ivory
casket, openly convict, assert (nevertheless) that the signature of
the invalid tablet is a forgery," *i. e.*, of the tablet or obligation thus
rendered nugatory. *Ligni* is for *tabellæ*, the tablets having been
made of thin deal.—*Gemma princeps*. Literally, "the principal
gem." Pliny says (*H. N.*, xxxvii., 6) that the sardonyx was the
principal gem employed for seals.—*O delicias !* "My choice sir !"
—*Gallinæ filius albæ*. Equivalent to *feliciter natus*, white being the
lucky colour. "The son of a white hen" was a proverbial expression, as it still is in French, "*le fils de la poule blanche*." (*Mayor, ad
loc.*)— *Viles pulli*. "A worthless brood."

143–161. *Bile*. "Choler."—*Confer*. "Compare (with what has
befallen you)." The general idea is, You might have been assailed
by a hired robber, or have seen your house burned down by an in-
cendiary. (*Mayor, ad loc.*)—*Primos quum janua*, &c. So as to pre-
clude all possibility of escape.—*Adorandæ robiginis*. "Of venerable
rust," *i. e.*, of venerable antiquity. *Robigo* is not to be taken here
in its strict sense.—*Populorum dona*. It was customary for communities and kings to send cups, and crowns, and other valuable offerings to the temple of Capitoline Jove, and those of other deities.—
Minor sacrilegus. "Some sacrilegious wretch on a smaller scale."
—*Bracteolam*. "His leaf-gold." — *An dubitet*, &c. The idea is,
Should he shrink from these petty thefts, who has often melted

down Jupiter? (*Mayor, ad loc.*)—*Artifices.* "The compounders." —*Deducendum.* "The one deserving of being launched." The parricide. The first who underwent this punishment was P. Malleolus, convicted of murdering his mother. (*Liv.* lxviii., *Ep.*)—*Hæc quota pars.* "How small a portion is this." Compare *Sat.* iii., 61. —*Gallicus.* Rutilius Gallicus, *Præfectus Urbis* under Domitian.— *Una domus.* That, namely, of Gallicus. Spend a few days in his court, and then, if you can, when you have learned what others suffer, complain of your own lot.

162-173. *Quis tumidum,* &c. Crimes are not more wonderful in Rome than goitres amid the Alps.—*Meroe.* The great island of the Nile, formed by the Astapus and Astaboras. Its chief town, Meroe, was a city of priests, and had a temple of Hammon. Ritter supposes it to have comprised the whole of *Sennaar.* (*Mayor, ad loc.*) —*Cærula quis stupuit,* &c. The Germans are described as having light blue eyes, and fair or red hair, which they rendered still more bright by a peculiar kind of soap.—*Et madido,* &c. "And at him twisting his horns with moistened curl, *i. e.,* having his moistened curls twisted into horns. The epithet *madido* refers to the use of the soap mentioned in the previous note.—*Nempe quod.* "Why, because."—*Ad.* "To meet." (*Hand, Tursell.,* i., 84; *Mayor, ad loc.*)—*Volucres.* The cranes. They were believed to come from the country around the Strymon, in Thrace. Compare *Virg., Georg.,* i., 120.—*Pygmæus.* Alluding to the warfare between the pigmies and cranes. Compare *Stat. Sylv.,* i., vi., 57, from which it appears that Domitian exhibited a spectacle of pigmy gladiators. —*Quanquam eadem,* &c. Though the combat, so ridiculous to us, is often witnessed.—*Pede uno.* The legendary height of the pigmies would be thirteen and a half inches, that being the measure of the Greek πυγμή, whence the term Πυγμαῖοι is derived.

174-186. *Nullane perjuri,* &c. The train of ideas is as follows: Shall perjury, asks Calvinus, go unpunished? Suppose, is the reply, the criminal to be given over to execution at our will; his death will not repair your present loss, nor secure you against a like wrong for the future; but you will encounter, if you shed only a few drops of blood, the detestation of mankind. Yet, it may be retorted, revenge is sweet, &c. (*Mayor, ad loc.*)—*Sospes erit.* Equivalent to *reddetur.*—*Sed corpore trunco,* &c. Incorrectly supposed by some to be uttered by Calvinus. It is, in fact, a continuation of Juvenal's remark, and *invidiosa* is not to be rendered "enviable," as some give it, but "calculated only to produce odium."—*At vindicta.* The reply of Calvinus.—*Nempe hoc indocti.* "Ay, fools think

so." The rejoinder of the poet. Supply *consent.—Chrysippus.* The
Stoic, a pupil of Zeno and Cleanthes, the latter of whom he suc-
ceeded as head of the Stoic school.—*Thaletis.* Thales of Miletus, a
celebrated Ionic philosopher, and one of the seven wise men.—
Dulcique senex, &c. Socrates. Mount Hymettus was not far from
Athens. It is here called "sweet," because famous for its honey.—
Qui partem acceptæ, &c. Socrates was condemned to die by drinking the juice of the hemlock.—*Accusatori.* Meletus is meant, who
in Plato appears more prominently than the other two accusers,
Anytus and Lycon.—*Nollet.* With the force of *noluisset.* So mild
and gentle was the character of the sage, that he would have refused his very accuser a portion of the contents of the cup, if the
latter, in a fit of repentance, had wished to die either for him or
along with him.

187–198. *Felix.* "Blessed power!" With the eulogium here
pronounced on philosophy, compare the language of Cicero (*Tusc.
Quæst.,* 5, 5): "*Vitæ Philosophia dux, virtutis indagatrix, expultrixque
vitiorum.*"—*Prima docet rectum.* To know what is right is first necessary, in order to do it.—*Continuo sic collige quod.* Infer this at once
from the fact that.—*Evasisse.* "To have escaped unpunished."—
Habet attonitos. "Keeps in constant terror." *Attonitus* well represents here the bewildering effect of a guilty conscience.—*Surdo verbere cædit.* "Lashes with an unheard thong." *Surdo* is here used
passively for *tacito.—Occultum quatiente,* &c. "Conscience, as their
tormentor, brandishing a scourge unseen by human eyes."—*Cædicius.* A courtier of Nero's, and a most cruel minister of that tyrant.
—*Rhadamanthus.* Compare *Virg., Æn.,* vi., 566, *seq.—Suum testem.*
"A witness against one's own self."

199–210. *Spartano cuidam,* &c. The story is told at large in Herodotus (vi., 86). A Milesian had intrusted a sum of money to one
Glaucus, a Spartan, who, when the Milesian's sons claimed it, denied all knowledge of it, and went to Delphi to learn whether he
could safely retain it ; but, terrified at the answer of the oracle, he
sent for the Milesians and restored the money. Leotychides relates the story to the Athenians, and leaves them to draw the infer-
ence from the fact which he subjoins, namely, that the family of
the offender had become totally extinct in Sparta.—*Quondam.* "In
time to come."—*Mens.* "The opinion."—*Moribus.* "From principle."—*Tamen.* Though he returned it.—*Adyti.* "That issued from
the shrine," *i. e.,* the innermost part of the sanctuary, whence the
prophetic sounds issued, and where was the fissure over which the
tripod of the Pythoness was placed.—*Et quamvis longa,* &c. "And,

though derived from a widespread clan, with all his kin," *i. e.*, all relatives, however remote their common ancestor.— *Facti crimen habet.* "Has all the criminality of an actual commission."

210–221. *Cedo, si conatu peregit?* "Tell me, then, (what) if he has accomplished his designs?"—*Nec.* Equivalent to *ne quidem.*— *Interque molares,* &c. "And the food, difficult to swallow, swelling between his teeth." From the dryness of the throat the food is swallowed with uneasiness, and wanting the saliva to moisten it and make it into a paste, it breaks into pieces between the teeth, and, taking up more room than when in one mass, it fills the mouth as if it had increased in quantity. (*Madan, ad loc.*)—*Setina.* Supply *vina,* and compare *Sat.* v., 33. The common reading *sed vina* is far inferior.—*Albani.* Compare *Sat.* v., 33.— *Velut acri ducta Falerno.* "As if called forth by harsh Falernian." Falernian wine, when new, was harsh and unwholesome. (*Mayor, ad loc.*)—*Indulsit.* "Has granted him."—*Versata.* "After having been tossing to and fro." — *Te videt in somnis,* &c. Thee, the man whom he has injured.—*Tua sacra et major imago,* &c. The ancients regarded apparitions as sacred, and (as fear magnifies its objects) they were always supposed to appear greater than the life.

223–235. *Ad omnia fulgura pallent.* Cicero does not use *ad* thus to denote the occasion of fear. *Hand, Tursell.,* i., 101. — *Primo quoque murmure cæli.* "Even at the first rumbling of the sky."— *Fortuitus.* Trisyllable. Compare *pituita (Horat., Ep.* i., 1, 108; *Sat.* ii., 2, 76). Horace has *fortuïtus* with the long penult, as a quadrisyllable (*Od.* ii., 15, 17). That thunder was fortuitous was the opinion of the Epicureans. — *Ventorum rabie.* Some believed that the violence of the winds caused a collision of the clouds, and thus produced thunder.—*Judicet.* "Is fraught with retributive justice." — *Velut hoc dilata sereno.* "As if merely deferred by this brief calm," *i. e.*, as if delayed by one fair day, on purpose afterward to fall the heavier.—*Laribus cristam,* &c. On recovery from illness, it was customary to offer a cock to Æsculapius. But these guilty ones are so far from promising a cock to Æsculapius, that they have not the courage to vow even a cock's comb as a sacrifice to their household gods. (*Madan, ad loc.*)—*Non dignior vita.* Does not more deserve to live than they.

236–249. *Natura malorum.* "The character of bad men."—*Superest constantia.* "They have resolution enough and to spare."— *Ad mores damnatos.* "To her depraved courses." Custom becomes second nature.—*Ejectum semel,* &c. "Once banished from his now hardened brow."—*Dabit in laqueum,* &c. "This false friend of ours will fall into the snare of temptation."—*Uncum.* Compare *Sat.* x., 66.—*Rupem.* Compare *Sat.* x., 170.—*Surdum, nec Tiresiam.* You will confess that the gods have an ear for your prayers and his perjuries, and an eye from which no crime can escape. Tiresias was the blind soothsayer of Thebes.

SATIRE XIV.

ARGUMENT.

The whole of this Satire is directed to the one great end of self-improvement. By showing the dreadful facility with which children copy the vices of their parents, the poet points out the necessity as well as the sacred duty of giving them examples of domestic purity and virtue. After briefly enumerating the several vices which youth imperceptibly imbibe from their seniors, he enters more at large into that of avarice, of which he shows the fatal and inevitable consequences. Nothing can surpass the exquisiteness of this division of the Satire, in which he traces the progress of that passion in the youthful mind, from the paltry tricks of saving a broken meal to the daring violation of every principle human and divine. Having placed the absurdity as well as the danger of immoderate desires in every point of view, he concludes with a solemn admonition to rest satisfied with those comforts and conveniences which nature and wisdom require, and which a decent competence is easily calculated to supply. (*Evans.*)

1–9. *Fuscine.* Nowhere else mentioned.—*Fama digna sinistra.* "Deserving of a bad name," *i. e.*, disgraceful or disreputable in their nature.—*Nitidis rebus.* "To things otherwise bright," *i. e.*, to a condition in life otherwise brightly prosperous. — *Damnosa.* "Ruinous."—*Bullatus.* "While yet wearing the bulla," *i. e.*, while yet a mere boy. Compare *Sat.* v., 164.—*Arma.* "Weapons." The dice.—*Parvo fritillo.* "In his own little dice-box." The *fritillus* was of similar construction to those still in use, with graduated intervals on the inside to give the dice a rotatory motion during their descent. — *Melius.* Better than the *hæres.* — *Radere tubera terræ.* "To peel truffles." Compare *Sat.* v., 116.—*Boletum condire.* "To season a mushroom."—*Eodem jure.* "In the same sauce" with the mushroom, truffle, and other similar dainties.—*Ficedulas.* "Beaficos." A small bird is meant, which fed on figs. It was the only bird of which epicures allowed the whole to be eaten. It was considered a piece of high luxury to have these birds dressed and served up at table in the same sauce with truffles, &c.—*Nebulone parente*, &c. "His epicure parent, and hoary gluttony pointing out the way." Gourmands could not trust the cook to prepare the choicer dishes.

10-14. *Quum septimus annus*, &c. After the completion of the sixth year, Plato directs that boys and girls be separately educated. (*Leg.*, vii., 4, p. 794.)—*Nondum omni dente renato.* "All his teeth being not as yet renewed," *i. e.*, before all his second teeth have as yet come. Compare Pliny (*H. N.*, vii., 16): "*Editis infantibus primores dentes septimo gignuntur mense: iidem anno septimo decidunt, aliique sufficiuntur.*"—*Barbatos magistros.* Philosophers, to instil abstinence and temperance. — *Lauto paratu.* "In sumptuous style."—*Magna culina.* Of his sire.

15-25. *Mitem animum*, &c. For *mitemne animum*, &c. "Does Rutilus inculcate a merciful disposition?" &c., *i. e.*, teach his son forbearance.—*Modicis erroribus æquos.* "Indulgent to venial faults." —*Nostra materia constare.* "Are formed of matter like our own." Construe *nostra* with *materia*, not with *corpora.*—*Et nullam Sirena*, &c. "And compares no Siren to scourges," *i. e.*, and thinks no Siren's song can equal the sound of scourges.—*Antiphates.* King of the cannibal Læstrygones. — *Trepidi Laris.* "Of his trembling household."—*Duo propter lintea.* "On account of two towels," *i. e.*, for stealing a couple of towels.—*Quid suadet juveni.* "What kind of advice does that man give to his own son?" *i. e.*, what kind of doctrine does he preach to him?—*Mire.* "With strange delight." —*Inscripta ergastula.* "The work-house full of branded slaves." Literally, "branded work-houses." The abstract for the concrete, the place of correction for those contained in it. Compare *Sat.* viii., 180.—*Carcer rusticus.* The country prisons, for the confinement of slaves, were generally under ground.

26-40. *Sic natura jubet.* "Such is nature's law."—*Magnis quum subeunt*, &c. "When they insinuate themselves into our minds from those who have great influence with us," *i. e.*, when vice is recommended by a parent's authority.—*Hæc.* "These practices." —*Quibus arte benigna*, &c. "Whose hearts the Titan has formed with kindly art, and moulded out of a better clay." Prometheus is meant.—*Fugienda.* "That ought to be shunned."—*Et monstrata diu*, &c. "And the routine of inveterate depravity, that has long been before their eyes, attracts them on." *Orbita* is properly "the track of a wheel," then "a beaten track" generally, and hence, figuratively, a course or routine of life. — *Hujus enim vel una*, &c. "For there is one powerful motive, at least, to this."—*Quocunque in populo*, &c. The idea is, We all readily imitate what is evil; you may find a Catiline in any clime, but a Brutus or Cato (of Utica, brother of Servilia, mother of Brutus) nowhere.

41–52. *Maxima debetur puero reverentia.* "The greatest reverence is due to a child." Reverence the young, and beware lest they hear or see you saying or doing any thing evil; for where the old have no shame, there the young will be most unabashed. (*Madan, ad loc.*) —*Contemseris.* The perfect subjunctive is invariably used by Cicero after *ne.* The imperative or subjunctive present are poetical. (*Madvig*, § 386.)—*Dignum Censoris ira.* The punishments inflicted by the censor were either expulsion from the Senate, or taking away the horse of an *eques*, or degradation from some tribe, or reducing one to the condition of an *ærarius.*—*Quandoque.* "One day." For *quandocunque.* — *Et qui omnia,* &c. Construe *omnia* with *vestigia.* The meaning is, Such a one as to follow and outstrip you in every path of sin.—*Nimirum.* "Doubtless." Ironical.—*Tabulas mutare.* "To alter your will," *i. e.*, to disinherit him.—*Unde tibi.* Supply *parabis.* How will you be able to assume the severe front and the license of a parent's speech?—*Vacuumque cerebro,* &c. "And when the exhausted cupping-glass has long since been looking out for your brainless head," *i. e.*, and when you have for a long time been acting as if you were mad. *Cucurbita* properly means a kind of gourd; and then, from the shape, the term is used to denote a cupping-glass. It was employed in cases of derangement. Some of these instruments were of brass, others of horn. In those of brass lighted linen was placed, and the instrument then applied to the skin. The pressure of the external air would force the nearly exhausted *cucurbita* with a strong draught against the part to be cupped, and hence the epithet *ventosa* in the text, by which name a cupping-glass was known in the mediæval Latin. (Ital. *ventosa;* Fr. *ventouse.*) In those of horn, the air was drawn out by suction through a small orifice, which was afterward closed with wax. (*Mayor, ad loc.*).

53–63. *Hospite venturo,* &c. When you expect a friend to make you a visit, you set all hands to work in order to prepare your house for his reception. — *Verre pavimentum,* &c. The language of the master. The pavements were of costly marble or mosaic. They were swept with a broom of palm twigs, or cleaned with a sponge. —*Arida.* "Shrivelled."—*Leve.* "Smooth" or "plain," opposed to *aspera,* "embossed."—*Furit.* "Blusters forth."—*Ergo miser trepidas, &c.* Are you ashamed lest your friend may see any thing offensive about your abode, and do you take no pains to prevent any moral filth or turpitude from being beheld in your house by your own son?—*Scobis.* Sawdust was left on the floor during a feast. Heliogabalus used gold dust.—*Illud non agitas.* "Do you not bestir yourself about this."—*Omni sine labe.* "Without any stain."

64–79. *Gratum est.* "It is a source of gratitude."—*Si facis.* "If you bring it to pass."—*Agris.* "To her fields."—*Plurimum intererit.* "It will prove a matter of the highest importance." — *Artibus.* "Pursuits."—*Maribus.* "Moral habits." — *Crucibus.* The dead body was left hanging on the cross.—*Hic est ergo cibus, &c.* From being supplied with this kind of food by the parent bird, the young vulture, when grown up to be a large bird, feeds upon the same.— *Propria arbore.* "In a tree of its own."—*Famulæ Jovis.* "The ministers of Jove." The eagles.—*Generosæ aves.* "Birds of noble breed." Not only eagles, but falcons, &c.—*Inde.* "Thence," *i. e.*, from the nest.—*Rupto ovo.* When they broke the shell.

80–89. *Ædificator erat Cetronius,* &c. The general idea is, If the father impair his estate by building villas of costly marble in fashionable localities, no wonder that his son yet more prodigally wastes what remains. If the father observes the Sabbath, and abstains from meats forbidden by the Jewish lawgiver, no wonder that the son, having been early trained to neglect his country's laws, becomes a proselyte, bound to the observance of the whole Mosaic law.— *Caietæ.* Caieta, now *Gaeta*, was situate on the Sinus Caietanus, in Latium.—*Tiburis.* Tibur, now *Tivoli*, lies twenty miles northeast of Rome, chiefly on a rocky hill, on the left bank of the Anio.— *Prænestinis.* Consult note on *Sat.* iii., 190.—*Græcis marmoribus.* The marbles of Paros, Pentelicus, Hymettus, Carystus, Tænarus, and Sparta were celebrated.—*Longeque.* From Synnada in Phrygia, or from Numidia.—*Fortunæ ædem.* The splendid temple of Fortune at Præneste.—*Herculis.* That of Hercules at Tibur.—*Posides.* A freedman of the Emperor Claudius, who amassed immense wealth. He must have built a mansion in Rome rivalling the very Capitol. —*Sic habitat.* "Is thus lodged," *i. e.*, so magnificently.—*Totam hanc.* Namely, the part that still remained.—*Turbavit.* "Squandered." *Turbare* is here for *conturbare* or *decoquere.*—*Attollit.* For *in altum tollit.*

90–98. *Sortiti metuentem,* &c. "Having obtained for their lot a father fearing Sabbaths," *i. e.*, whose lot it is to have a father that fears, &c.—*Metuentem.* The heathen conceived the God of the Jews to be a malignant being.—*Nil præter nubes*, &c. This gross conception of the Romans arose from the Jews having no visible representation of Deity. They thought, therefore, that they worshipped merely the clouds and the material heaven or blue sky.—*Nec distare putant*, &c. They think it as abominable to eat the one as the other.—*Arcano volumine.* The Pentateuch or Five Books of Moses, especially the one containing the Levitical law. A copy of the Pentateuch was kept in every synagogue, locked up in a press or chest (*arca*), and never exposed to view unless when brought out to be read at the time of worship. At the conclusion of the service it was returned to its place and again locked up.—*Ignava.* "One of sloth."—*Et partem vitæ non attigit ullam.* "And came into contact with no part of life," *i. e.*, and was kept distinct from the ordinary duties of life.

99–113. *Sponte tamen juvenes*, &c. The train of thought is as follows: To other vices the young are prone of themselves: to avarice their fathers must train them (99–117). Accordingly they stint themselves and their household, and, the love of money growing with their wealth, they by fair means or foul possess themselves of their neighbours' estates (118–147). For now a single proprietor will own a larger tract than Rome did under the kings. It is this haste to be rich which causes crime (148–170). The Marsian father of old warned his sons against luxury; nowadays a father urges his sons to make money by any, even the meanest arts (171–199). What wonder, then, if the son goes a step farther, and seeks his fortune by perjury and murder? nay, if, to satisfy that love of gain which he has inherited from his parent, he attempts that parent's life? (200–247).—*Inviti quoque.* "Even against their will."—*Fallit enim vitium*, &c. "For vice sometimes deceives under the guise and covering of virtue." An instance of this is given immediately after in the case of avarice, which passes with many for frugality.— *Triste habitu.* "Grave in bearing."—*Frugi.* "A frugal character." —*Hesperidum serpens*, &c. "The serpent of the Hesperides or of Pontus." The former guarded the golden apples of the Hesperides, the latter the golden fleece among the Colchi. The Romans regarded Colchis as a part of Pontus, it having been made subject to this country by Mithradates Eupator.—*Hunc de quo loquor.* The avaricious man.—*Acquirendi.* "Of his own fortune." The common text has *atque verendum.*—*Sed crescunt quocunque modo*, &c. The idea is, But if one's fortune is thus to grow, every means must be employed, the forge must be always heated, the anvil always busy. —*Et pater ergo.* "The father, therefore, also," *i. e.*, the father, therefore, as well as the people (v. 107), admires the avaricious.

114–125. *Eidem sectæ.* The avaricious. — *Sunt quædam,* &c. "There are certain first elements of all vices," *i. e.,* certain rudiments or beginnings. The father does not all at once bid his sons to be covetous, but insinuates into their minds, by little and little, sordid principles. This he does first (*protinus*); but anon (*mox*), as the pupil advances, he inculcates an insatiable thirst for gain.— *Minimas ediscere sordes.* "To become adepts in the most petty means of stingy saving."—*Castigat.* "He pinches."—*Modio iniquo.* "With an unjust measure," *i. e.,* an unfair allowance of food. Slaves had a certain allowance of corn, olives, figs, vinegar, and wine, either by the month or the day.—*Neque enim,* &c. The idea is, For indeed he can never bring himself to eat up at once every crust of mouldy bread, but keeps some, along with a portion of yesterday's mince, for the succeeding day.—*Medio Septembri.* "Even in the middle of September." This was the hottest and most unhealthy month at Rome.—*Conchem æstivi,* &c. "The bean sealed up along with a portion of summer lacertus." The lacertus was a species of sea-fish. Some render it "stockfish," others "pilchard." Both it and the beans would be hard to keep in summer; hence the epithet *æstivi,* for which the common text has *æstivam.* These remains of food, however, are put away in some vessel, the cover or mouth of which is sealed, lest the half-starved slaves may steal it.— *Siluro.* Compare *Sat.* iv., 33. The *silurus* was a common and coarse Egyptian fish, sent over salted to Rome.—*Filaque sectivi,* &c. "And to lock up the very fibres of the chopped leek, after they have been counted." There are fibres resembling threads which hang downward from the bottom of the leek. These the miser is so stingy as to lock up after he has counted them. As regards the *porrum,* consult note on *Sat.* iii., 293.

126–143. *Invitatus ad hæc,* &c. "A beggar from a bridge, on having been invited to such a meal, would decline." Compare note on *Sat.* iv., 116.—*Sed quo.* Supply *habes* or *possides.*—*Hæc tormenta.* "This self-torture."—*Egentis vivere fato.* "To live with a beggar's fate," *i. e.,* to lead a beggar's life.—*Quum.* "Although."—*Et minus hanc optat,* &c. "And yet he who has it not wishes for it less." The poor man looks no farther than for a supply of his present wants; he never thinks of any thing more. Observe that *et* is here for *et tamen.*—*Et proferre fines libet,* &c. "And it takes your fancy to extend your boundaries, and your neighbour's corn-land seems to you more extensive and productive than your own."—*Arbusta.*

" Its groves."—*Canet.* The bloom of the olive is of a white or light-gray colour.—*Non vincitur.* " Is not prevailed upon."—*Boves macri*, &c. Lean through hard work and half starved, and therefore such as will make a thorough clearance. There was a law of the Twelve Tables *de pastu pecoris*, under which such injuries as are here described were punished.—*Hujus.* The owner who refuses to sell.—*Sævos.* " Ravenous."—*Novalia.* Put here for the crops on any good land. *Novale* properly means land recently cleared.—*Injuria.* " Wrongs like this."—*Venales fecerit.* " Have exposed to sale," *i. e.*, have brought to the hammer.

144–158. *Sed qui sermones*, &c. " But what remarks will be made about this ! How loudly will the trumpet of slanderous fame sound forth !" This is supposed to be the remark of the poet, and equivalent to, " But how the world will talk of this conduct of yours in ruining your neighbours' property !" To which the other replies, " Who cares for what the world says ? What harm does this do to me ?"—*Tunicam.* " The pod."—*Toto pago.* " Throughout the whole village."—*Secantem.* " While reaping merely."—*Scilicet et morbis*, &c. The ironical remark of the poet : " No doubt ! you will be free from," &c.—*Post hæc.* " Hereafter."—*Mox*, &c. The idea is, Afterward, even veterans who had served against Carthage or Pyrrhus received for their many wounds scarce two *jugera* a head.—*Molossos.* Compare *Sat.* xii., 108.—*Jugera.* The juger, though commonly translated " acre," was in reality about five eighths of an English acre, being a rectangle 240 × 120 feet, or 28,800 square feet.—*Curta.* " Scant." It did not appear a breach of faith on the part of their thankless country.

159–171. *Turbam.* " The troop," *i. e.*, the noisy brood.—*Infantes quatuor.* Children of different ranks used to be playmates in ancient times.—*Tres domini.* " Three young masters."—*A scrobe vel sulco redeuntibus.* Coming home from their day's work at digging and ploughing.—*Amplior.* " More plentiful." As for grown men after a hard day's work.—*Pultibus.* As this species of porridge was a national dish, we have the expression "*pultiphagus barbarus*" applied by Plautus in the sense of *Romanus* (*Most.*, iii., 2, 144).—*Inde.* He means from avarice.—*Properantis.* " Hastening to be rich."

172–179. *Marsus*, &c. Compare the language of Strabo (v., p. 241), as given by Mayor : " Above Picenum are the Vestini, Marsi, Peligni, &c., of the Samnite race. They occupy the high ground, and scarcely any where come down to the sea. These nations are but small, it is true, yet they are brave, and have proved to the Romans their valour."—*Hernicus.* The Hernici were a people in Latium, but not of the Latin stock. Their capital was Anagnia. In their war against Rome, however, B.C. 306, they did not justify their high reputation.— *Vestinusque.* The Vestini were the most northern tribe of Sabellian extraction, and occupied a tract lying between the Adriatic and Apennines, which was separated from Picenum by the Matrinus, and from the Marrucini by the Aternus.—*Quorum ope et auxilio*, &c. "By whose aid and intervention, since the boon of the kindly corn-blade, there happen to man loathings of the old oak," *i. e.*, it is man's fortune to loathe the oaks he fed upon before. — *Perone.* "Country boot." The *pero* was a boot reaching up to the calf of the leg, and made of raw-hide or untanned leather.—*Pellibus inversis.* "With skins having the hair inward." Literally, "with inverted skins."—*Quæcunque est.* "Whatever it is," *i. e.*, whatever it may be, I know not. Explanatory of *ignota*, which precedes.

180-187. *Præcepta.* Supply *dabant.*—*Media de nocte.* "At midnight." Compare Gesner (*Thes.*, *s. v.*): "*De* cum nominibus temporis significat, id tempus nondum plane effluxisse." — *Supinum.* "Asleep and lying on his back."— *Clamosus.* "Clamorous."—*Rubras.* In ordinary books, the titles and headings of the chapters were written in red letters. But in law-books the text was in *red* letter, and the commentaries and glosses in *black.*—*Aut vitem posce libello.* "Or ask by petition for the office of centurion." The badge of a centurion was a vine sapling cut into a stick or baton, and employed for punishing any of the men who had neglected their military duties. Hence *vitis* is often put for the office itself of centurion. — *Buxo.* "By the boxwood comb." This kind of wood was usually, on account of its hardness, employed for this purpose.—*Grandes alas.* "Your brawny shoulders." *Ala* is properly "the arm-pit."—*Lælius.* The general.

188-202. *Attegias.* The *attegia* was a Moorish hut or wigwam, made of reeds and thatch. They were commonly on wheels, like the huts of the Scythian nomadæ. Evans thinks that, when fixed, they were called *magalia.* Compare *Virg., Æn.,* i., 425.—*Brigantum.* The Brigantes occupied Lancashire, Durham, Westmoreland, Cumberland, with the south of Northumberland, and nearly all Yorkshire.—*Locupletem aquilam.* "The enriching eagle." The eagle was the main standard of the legion, and was carried by the oldest centurion. The post conferred the rank and *census* of an eques.— *Solvunt.* "Relax." The *cornua* were curved like a C; the *litui* were bent at one end like a tobacco-pipe.—*Pluris dimidio.* "For half as much again," *i. e.*, at a price greater by one half.—*Fastidia*

mercis, &c. " Disgust at any trade that must be banished," &c.
Tanning and similar offensive trades were restricted to the Trans-
tiberine region.—*Neu credas*, &c. The idea is, Think that hides,
if they bring in money, smell as sweetly as perfumes.—*Lucri bonus
est odor*, &c. The ancients tried the purity of their money by the
smell.—*Poetæ.* Ennius, who is said to have taken this sentiment
from the Bellerophon of Euripides.—*Unde habeas quærit nemo*, &c.
" No one asks how you get (wealth), but (wealth) you ought to get."
The idea is, Only take care to be rich ; no one will inquire how you
became so.—*Repentibus.* " While yet creeping along," *i. e.*, before
they can run alone.—*Ante alpha et beta.* " Before their A B C."

203–223. *Quis te festinare jubet.* " Who bids you make this
speed ?" There is no need of forcing avarice on your son. He
will soon be only too apt a scholar.—*Præsto.* " I warrant him."—
Securus abi. You may safely leave him to himself. —*Vinceris.*
" You will be surpassed." Your son will surpass you in this vice,
just as Ajax and Achilles surpassed their respective fathers in heroic achievements. — *Parcendum teneris.* Parodied from Virgil.
Georg., ii., 363.—*Nondum implevere medullas*, &c. " The evils of
matured vice have not yet filled the marrow of their bones," *i. e.*,
matured vice has not yet been bred in the bone.—*Et longi mucronem*, &c. " And to apply the edge of the long razor."—*Tangens.*
In swearing, the Romans laid their hands on the altars consecrated
to the gods, to whose deity they appealed.—*Elatam jam.* " To be
already carried forth for burial." Your son's wife, if she bring a
portion that makes it worth his while to take her life, is as good as
dead and buried from the instant she crosses the threshold.—*Limina subit.* The bride, when she came to the bridegroom's house,
was lifted across the threshold.—*Prematur.* Strangulation is meant.
—*Brevior via.* Murder. The *short cut* of crime.—*Olim.* " One
day."—*Mentis malæ.* " Of this depravity of heart."—*Est penes te.*
" Rests at your doors."—*Præcepit.* " Inculcated."—*Lævo monitu.*
" By sinister lessons."—*Producit.* " Trains up."—*Et qui per fraudes*,
&c. This line is wanting in several MSS., and is evidently spurious.
—*Dat libertatem*, &c. A father who has once entered his son in the
race of avarice, has given him the reins, and cannot bring him to a
stand when he will.—*Quem.* The same with the *illi* of line 223.

225–239. *Nemo satis credit*, &c. No one is content to sin just so
much as you allow, and no more.—*Adeo latius.* " So much the
more widely." So much the more unrestrained liberty do they allow themselves.—*Stultum.* Supply *illum hominem esse.* — *Circumscribere.* Compare *Sat.* x., 217.—*Amor.* " As great a love." Sup-

N

ply *tantus.—Deciorum.* Compare *Sat.* viii., 254.—*Menœceus.* Son of Creon, king of Thebes. He put an end to his life because Tiresias had declared that his death would bring victory to his country when the Seven marched against Thebes.—*Quorum.* Referring to *Thebanorum*, which is virtually contained in *Thebas.* The allusion is now to the story of Cadmus and the dragon's teeth, so that the "*si Grœcia vera*" applies mentally to this clause also.—*Capessunt.* "Eagerly engage in."—*Ergo.* Since your love of money is so ardent.—*Leo tollet alumnus.* "The lion-pupil will destroy." There is said to be here an allusion to a real incident which occurred under Domitian, where a tame lion tore in pieces his keeper who had brought him up. Consult *Mart., Ep. de Spect.*, x.

240-247. *Nota mathematicis*, &c. "Your nativity is known to the astrologers," *i. e.*, your horoscope, or the constellation in the ascendant at your birth. The idea is, Your son has learned from the astrologers your nativity, and the length of the thread of life spun out for you by the fates, but cannot wait until it has all run out.— *Grave.* "It is a tedious business."—*Jam nunc.* "Even now."— *Juvenem.* Your son.—*Cervina.* "Stag-like." It was a popular belief among the ancients that the stag was very long-lived. The old scholiast says that this animal lives for nine hundred years!—*Archigenen.* Compare *Sat.* xiii., 98.—*Mithridates.* Alluding to the famous antidote compounded by this monarch. The ingredients are given by the physician Serenus Sammonicus (xxx., 578).—*Et pater et rex.* The idea is, Both a father and a king, if they would live secure, must use antidotes against poison. Mithradates, as being both one and the other, needed them more than any one else. (*Mayor, ad loc.*)

248-256. *Monstro voluptatem*, &c. The train of ideas is as follows: It is a more diverting spectacle to watch the adventures of a man in pursuit of wealth than any theatre can offer. The hazardous balancings of the rope-dancer cannot compare with the risks of the merchant (248-266). Now more than half mankind live on shipboard, and all for the chance of bringing back full money-bags. If Orestes and Ajax were mad in one way, surely they are not less mad in another who will brave sea and storm rather than delay their ship a single day (267-294).—*Nulla prætoris*, &c. "No platform of the sumptuous prætor." The prætor now provided for the entertainment of the people by shows and games, a duty which, under the republic, had devolved on the curule ædile. The person who exhibited the games had a more elevated seat than the rest.— *Lautus.* This epithet is meant to apply not only to the sumptuous and splendid costume worn on these occasions by the prætor, but also to the expense which he necessarily incurred.—*Si spectes.* "If you can but witness."—*Incrementa domus constent.* "The additions to family property stand one in."—*Multus fiscus.* "The abundant store."—*Castora.* Money was deposited in the temple of Castor, as in a place of security, even in Cicero's time (*pro Quint.*, 17), and so, also, generally in temples. The temple of Castor was in the Forum. The epithet *vigilem* is here employed because a guard kept watch in the temple.—*Mars Ultor.* The temple of Mars Ultor was dedicated by Augustus, B.C. 2, in his forum. No other writer mentions the robbery here spoken of. It seems to have alarmed capitalists, so that they again committed their hoards to Castor's temple as more secure. (*Mayor, ad loc.*)

Floræ. The *Floralia* were first sanctioned by the government A.U.C. 514, the year that Livius Andronicus began to exhibit. They were celebrated with great license from April 28 to May 1.— *Cereris.* The *Cerealia* were celebrated by Circensian games, April 7. — *Cybeles.* The *Megalesia* were instituted B.C. 203, when the image of the Great Mother was brought from Pessinus to Rome. (Compare *Sat.* iii., 118.) These games were celebrated from April 4 to April 9.—*Aulæa.* "The scenic representations." *Aulæa* properly means the curtain of the theatre.—*Humana negotia.* "Is the actual business of life."

257–263. *Jactata petauro.* "Projected from the petaurum." The petaurum was a theatrical machine, the precise character of which has never been ascertained. Some make it to have been a kind of see-saw. Others, more correctly, describe it as a wheel hanging loose in the air, on which two jugglers took their seats, and the one endeavoured to keep it steady, the other to make it oscillate. If either were thrown off, he had to leap through flames and burning hoops. (*Mayor, ad loc.*)—*Rectum descendere funem.* Compare verse 264.—*Corycia.* Corycus was the name of a town, promontory, and cave in Cilicia. The town Corycus (now *Kurku*) lay between the mouths of the Lamus and Calycadnus, and became a place of great trade under the later Roman emperors. Twenty stadia to the north of the town was the Corycian cave, a deep valley inclosed by high rocks, where the best saffron grew.—*Coro.* Corus is properly the N.W. wind, and is called by the Italians *Maestro.*—*Tollendus.* "To be tossed up and down." — *Perditus ac vilis,* &c. "Reckless (of danger), and the trader in vile and strong-smelling sacks." *Sacci* is here the singular put for the plural. The bags of saffron are meant. It does not follow, however, from the language of Juvenal, that the cargo was either worthless or offensive to the smell. The poet merely wishes to express his contempt for such luxuries, which men risked their lives to procure, in order thereby to amass rapid fortunes.—*Pingue passum.* "The rich raisin-wine." Supply *vinum.* It was so called because made of grapes spread out (*pando, passus*) in the sun to dry.—*Municipes Jovis.* "The countrymen of Jove." In playful allusion to the legend of Crete's having been the birth-place of Jove.—*Lagenas.* Compare *Sat.* vii., 121.

264–275. *Hic tamen,* &c. The rope-dancer, however, if he haz-ards life, does so to avoid starvation ; you hazard yours, not to ob-tain necessaries, but superfluities, to add yet another to your 999 talents· or your 99 villas. (*Mayor, ad loc.*)—*Victum.* "His daily bread."—*Propter.* "For the sake of," *i. e.,* to make up the number of.—*Plus hominum,* &c. There are more men on the sea than on the land, such is their eagerness to be rich. — *Carpathium.* The part of the Ægean near Carpathus (now *Scarpanto*), an island be-tween Crete and Rhodes. Ships on their way to Asia Minor often met with rough weather here.—*Gætulaque.* The Gætuli, as remark-ed in a previous note (*Sat.* x., 158), occupied the country to the south of Morocco ; here, however, the *Gætula æquora* must lie to the east of Calpe (or *Gibraltar*). The Syrtes, so dangerous to the corn fleets from Libya, seem to be meant. — *Calpe.* Calpe (*Gibraltar*) and Abyla, on the opposite side, were known as the Pillars of Hercules, which are often spoken of as the extreme west ; yet even this "world's end" the adventurous trader leaves far behind him.—*Au-diet Herculeo,* &c. Posidonius and Epicurus pretended that when the sun sank in the Atlantic, it hissed like red-hot iron plunged into water. According to the popular belief, the Sacrum Promon-torium, on the Atlantic coast of Hispania, now Cape *St. Vincent,* was the place where the sun plunged with his chariot into the sea. —*Tenso folle.* "With well-distended purse." Compare *Sat.* xiii., 61. — *Tumida aluta.* "With swelled money-bag." *Aluta* is the leather purse softened by being steeped in alum-water. —*Juvenes marinos.* "Young mermen."

276–283. *Unus furor.* "One and the same kind of madness."— *Ille.* Orestes.—*Sororis in manibus.* "While in his sister's arms." Alluding to the scene in the Orestes of Euripides, where Orestes, in his madness, imagines that he sees the Furies come to punish him for slaying his mother Clytæmnestra, and where his sister Electra endeavours, by throwing her arms around him, to keep him from leaping in terror from his couch. (*Eurip., Orest.,* 260, *seqq.*)—*Igni.* "The torch."—*Hic.* Ajax, son of Telamon, who became insane

after the arms of Achilles were awarded to Ulysses, and in his madness committed great havoc among the herds and flocks of the
Greeks, mistaking them for his enemies.—*Ithacum.* "The Ithacensian." Ulysses.—*Parcat tunicis,* &c. "Though he spare tunics
and cloaks," *i. e.,* his tunic or his cloak. Prichard (*On Insanity,* p.
26) quotes from an Italian physician's description of raving madness, or mania : "A striking and characteristic circumstance is the
propensity to be quite naked. The patient tears his clothes to tat-
ters." (*Mayor, ad loc.*)—*Curatoris.* A curator or guardian was always appointed by the prætor in the cases of persons of unsound
mind, in accordance with the provisions of the Twelve Tables.—*Ad
summum latus.* "To the topmost edge," *i. e.,* to the very top of the
bulwarks.—*Tabula distinguitur unda.* "Is parted from the water by
a single plank."—*Titulos faciesque.* The legend and head of the
emperor on the coin.

284–294. *Solvite funem.* "Loose the cable."—*Piperis.* Indian
pepper was brought on camels to Alexandrea, and there shipped for
Rome.—*Fascia nigra.* A dark belt of clouds resting on the horizon.
—*Æstivum tonat.* "It is summer thunder," *i. e.,* it is only a summer thunder-shower.—*Zonam.* A broad belt is meant, worn by men
around their loins, and made double or hollow, like our shot-belts,
for the purpose of carrying money.—*Modo.* "But lately."—*Tagus.*
Compare *Sat.* iii., 55.—*Pactolus.* The Pactolus, now *Sarabat,* was
a small river of Lydia, rising in Mount Tmolus, flowing past Sar-
dis, and falling into the Hermus. Its golden sands were exhausted
in Strabo's time ; still, its riches were proverbial among the poets.
—*Frigida velantes inguina.* "Covering his nakedness."—*Et picta se
tempestate tuetur.* Those who had escaped from shipwreck or any
other imminent calamity used to carry about a painting of the occurrence, to excite compassion and obtain alms from the charitable.

295–299. *Tantis parta malis,* &c. The train of ideas is as follows :
The rich are troubled by fear of fire. Diogenes may break his tub,
but it will not trouble him. Nature is content with very little, and
he who desires no more is wise. He who is dissatisfied with a com-
petency would be dissatisfied even with the hoards of Crœsus.—
Dispositis hamis. "With leathern buckets all in rows." Observe
that *hami* are "hooks," but *hamæ* "leathern buckets." Originally
the *triumviri capitales* were intrusted with the protection of the city
from fires. From the time of Augustus, however, this became the
duty of the *Præfectus vigilum,* or prefect of the seven cohorts of
night police. Among the means employed for extinguishing fires
were *siphones* (syringes) and *hamæ* (buckets).—*Electro.* "His elec-

trum." Not amber, but a compound of four fifths of gold and one fifth of silver, and resembling amber in look.—*Phrygia*. Synnada, in Phrygia, was famed for its marble.—*Testudine*. Compare *Sat.* xi., 93.

300-323. *Dolia*. These were not made of wood, but of baked clay. —*Nudi*. The Cynics, besides wearing no tunics, used to leave one arm and shoulder bare, their cloak being thrown over the other.— *Commissa*. " Fastened."—*Magnum habitatorem*. Diogenes.—*Passurus gestis*, &c. Compare *Sat.* x., 97.—*Nullum numen habes*, &c. Compare *Sat.* x., 365.—*In quantum*. "Just as much as." Used by Ovid, Virgil, Livy, and later writers, where Cicero would say *quantum* alone. So, also, *in tantum* is found.—*Quantum Socratici*, &c. "As much as the home of Socrates contained before," *i. e.*, before the days of Epicurus. Socrates died B.C. 399 ; Epicurus, B.C. 270. —*Sapientia*. "Philosophy."—*Acribus*. "Too strict."—*Te claudere*. "To hem you in."—*Nostris*. "Of our own times."—*Effice summam*. "Make up the sum." Four hundred thousand sesterces. Compare *Sat.* iii., 140.—*Hæc quoque si rugam trahit*, &c. "If this also contracts your brow, and makes you put out your lip," *i. e.*, in token of dissatisfaction.— *Fac tertia quadringenta*. " Make the third four hundred (sestertia)," *i. e.*, make it, by the union of three equestrian fortunes, amount to 1200 *sestertia*, or 1,200,000 *sestertii*.—*Gremium*. " Your lap." The *sinus* or bosom of the toga is literally meant.— *Narcissi*. Narcissus, Pallas, and Callistus, three freedmen of Claudius, amassed enormous wealth.—*Uxorem occidere jussus*. Consult note on *Sat.* x., 304.

SATIRE XV.

ARGUMENT.

After enumerating with great humour the animal and vegetable gods of the Egyptians, the author directs his powerful ridicule at their sottish and ferocious bigotry, of which he gives an atrocious and loathsome example. The conclusion of the Satire, which is a just and beautiful description of the origin of civil society (infinitely superior to any thing that Lucretius or Horace has delivered on the subject), founded, not on natural instinct, but on principles of mutual benevolence implanted by Deity in the breast of man, and of man alone, does honour to the genius, good sense, and enlightened morality of the author. (*Evans.*)

1–7. *Volusi Bithynice.* "O Volusius Bithynicus." Who this Volusius was, and what was the origin of the word *Bithynicus*, is unknown. A Bithynicus was a friend of Martial (vi., 50, 5).—*Qualia demens*, &c. The train of ideas is as follows: The Egyptians worship all kind of monstrous things. They even regard it as a sin to eat an onion or a leek, but have no abhorrence of feeding on human flesh. Of all the marvellous stories told by Ulysses to the Phæacians, none are so strange and incredible as those of the cannibal Cyclopes and Læstrygones; but deeds of horror not less atrocious have been witnessed in Egypt, not in a fabulous antiquity, but in our own civilized days. (*Mayor, ad loc.*)—*Crocodilon.* Compare *Herodotus*, ii., 69.—*Ibin.* Compare *Cic., N. D.*, i., 36.—*Cercopitheci.* A long-tailed ape is meant.—*Dimidio magicæ*, &c. "Where the magic chords resound from the halved Memnon," *i. e.*, broken in half. Memnon, in the Æthiopis of Arctinus, one of the poems which formed the epic cycle, was described as son of Aurora and Tithonus, who was slain by Achilles before Troy, and afterward received the gift of immortality. By the Alexandrine writers this legend was connected with the statue of the Egyptian king Amenoph or Phamenoph, whose name can still be read on the statue. (*Mayor, ad loc.*) On the whole subject, consult Anthon's Classical Dictionary, *s. v. Memnon.*—*Atque vetus Thebe*, &c. By its so-called hundred gates Egyptian Thebes was distinguished from the Bœotian one, which had seven gates.

8–18. *Nemo Dianam.* They worship the hound, but forget to worship the goddess of the chase herself.—*Porrum et cæpe.* "A leek and an onion."—*Lanatis animalibus.* They never eat sheep or lambs.—*Fetum capellæ.* The goat was sacred to Pan, and worshipped in the Mendesian nome.—*Carnibus humanis*, &c. Cannibalism was not legalized in Egypt. Such an instance as is mentioned below (verse 33, *seqq.*) was exceptional. — *Quum narraret Ulixes.* "Were Ulysses to relate."—*Alcinoo.* Alcinous, the Phæacian king, to whom Ulysses related his adventures.—*Ut mendax aretalogus.* "As a lying babbler." The epithet *aretalogus* is properly applied to a Stoic or Cynic parasite, who would hold forth upon virtue for the entertainment of the company; hence it came to signify generally a babbler, a romancer.—*In mare nemo*, &c. The poet supposes one of the company, who had heard these strange stories told by Ulysses, to express his surprise that no one threw the narrator of such falsehoods into the sea.—*Abicit.* For *abjicit.* The other compounds of *jacio* are often subject to a similar change for the sake of the metre.—*Veraque Charybdi.* A real Charybdis, not a mere creature of the fancy, such as he had been romancing about.—*Fingentem.* "For inventing." More literally, inventing (as he does)." Referring to the story that they were cannibals.

19–25. *Concurrentia saxa Cyanca.* "The clashing Cyanean rocks." The Symplegades, rocky islands at the northern entrance of the Thracian Bosporus, now the Channel of Constantinople. They were fabled to have floated and crushed all vessels that passed the Straits, until the Argo passed through them, when they became fixed forever.—*Utres.* The bags of adverse winds.—*Percussum.* Supply *esse.*—*Elpenora.* Elpenor, when Ulysses left the palace of Circe, hearing the bustle, rose hastily to join his mates, and, falling backward, broke his neck. Homer does not mention by name the twenty-one of the crew who were transformed by Circe's wand, and consequently does not expressly include Elpenor among them. (*Mayor, ad loc.*)—*Populum Phæaca.* The Phæacians were identified by the ancients with the people of Corcyra, the modern *Corfu.*—*Et minimum qui,* &c. "And who had drawn a very small portion of potent wine from the Corcyrean bowl." The Phæacians were very luxurious in their habits, and much given to banqueting and carousing. (*Odyss.,* viii., 248.)

26–32. *Solus enim,* &c. Ulysses had lost all his crew before he reached Calypso's island; when the raft on which he sailed thence was wrecked, he landed alone in Phæacia. (*Odyss.,* v., 365, *seqq.*) —*Nullo sub teste.* "Supported by no testimony." The train of thought is, A sober Phæacian might well have rejected the unsupported assertions of Ulysses, but my story, though strange, may be proved true; for it relates what was done lately, at a specified time and place, and by a whole people. (*Mayor, ad loc.*)—*Junio.* To be read as a dissyllable, on account of the metre. The allusion is either to Q. Junius Rusticus, who was consul A.D. 119, or to Appius Junius Sabinus, consul A.D. 84. Some, in order to avoid the contraction, read *Junco,* but no consul of this name appears before A.D. 182, at which date Juvenal could not have been living.—*Super.* "Above," *i. e.,* to the south of, *up* the country. Coptus lay to the north of Ombi, and south of Tentyra. It was the capital of the Coptite nome, in Upper Thebais. Ships discharged their cargoes at the harbours of Berenice and Myoshormus, in the Arabian Gulf, from which caravans conveyed them to Coptos. There are ruins of the city at *Keft.*—*Vulgi.* "Of a whole people."—*Cothurnis.* The cothurnus, or thick-soled tragic buskin, is here put for tragedy itself. —*Quamquam omnia syrmata volvas.* "Though you turn over every tragic theme." The *syrma* was properly the long, sweeping train of tragedy.

33–36. *Inter finitimos.* "Between two neighbouring communities."—*Vetus atque antiqua.* The epithet *antiquus* is applied to what was long ago; hence *antiqui mores*, the good old times; *antiqui amici*, those who were friends in days of yore, as, for instance, Theseus and Pirithous: on the other hand, *vetus* indicates what has long been, hence "inveterate," "experienced," as *vetus miles.* Hence *novus* (what is seen for the first time, strange) is opposed to *antiquus*, and *recens* (fresh, what has lasted but for a short time) to *vetus.* (*Mayor, ad loc.*)—*Ombos.* Ombi, now *Kum Ombu*, north of Syene, on the right bank of the Nile, in Upper Egypt, or Thebais.—*Tentyra.* Now *Denderah*, in Upper Egypt, on the left bank of the Nile, and capital of the Tentyritic nome. As Ombi and Tentyra were separated by several important cities, they were not, strictly speaking, *finitimi;* it seems more probable that Juvenal uses this term somewhat laxly, than that he was mistaken as to the locality of either city. Relatively to the Romans, any two towns in the same district might be called neighbours.

37–46. *Odit uterque locus.* The Ombitæ worshipped crocodiles, the Tentyritæ were famous for their skill in taking them, hence they quarrel.—*Solos.* The exclusiveness of their worship, as of the Druidical and Jewish, was opposed to the Roman principle.—*Alterius populi.* The Ombites.—*Inimicorum.* The Tentyrites.—*Pervigilique toro.* "And the couch that knows not sleep." The couch on which they reclined while feasting."—*Septimus interdum sol invenit.* The number seven was held sacred by the Egyptians; hence their festivals were sometimes celebrated for seven days in succession. (*Schol., ad loc.*)—*Horrida sane Ægyptus.* The idea is, Egypt, it is true, is rude and savage, but in the article of luxury, the rabble, barbarous as they are, equal the people of Canopus themselves, at least in that part of the country where I have been. Compare, as regards Canopus, *Sat.* i., 24. — *Quantum ipse notavi.* Hence it appears that Juvenal had visited Egypt. Most lives of the poet, following the pseudo-Suetonius, relate that he was sent to Egypt, when eighty years of age, as prefect of a cohort stationed at Syene, and that this, under the appearance of an honorary appointment, was in reality meant as a species of exile. A story incredible in itself, and apparently derived from the present passage. (*Mayor, ad loc.*)

47–53. *Adde quod*, &c. One motive of the attack was the wish to spoil the sport of the revellers; a second was the hope that they, in their drunken helplessness, might fall an easy prey.—*De madidis.* "Over men soaked with wine."—*Mero.* "With the undiluted juice of the grape."—*Inde.* "On the one side." The Ombites.

—*Nigro tibicine.* "With a black to play the flute." Ablative absolute. The black was a Moor. The Ombites could not afford to employ a skilful Alexandrean; they had to be content with an inferior substitute. So, for the costly perfumes of Lower Egypt, they used such (*qualiacunque*) as they had. (*Mayor, ad loc.*)—*Hinc jejunum odium.* "On the other side was hungry hate." The Tentyrites, on the contrary, were fasting, and their hatred, like their hunger, was fierce and insatiable. Their hatred was like a hungry appetite, which longs after something to satiate it. (*Madan, ad loc.*)—*Tuba.* "The signal-blast."

54–71. *Nuda.* "Unarmed."—*Aspiceres.* "One might see." The second person of the subjunctive, used to denote an indefinite subject. (*Madvig,* § 370.) — *Vultus dimidios.* "Halved faces," *i. e.,* more or less mutilated.—*Alias facies.* "Features quite different from the usual ones," *i. e.,* so disfigured as not to be known for the same.—*Ruptis genis.* "From lacerated cheeks."—*Tamen.* Bloody as the fray is, "still."—*Et pueriles exercere acies.* "And to be engaged in boyish encounters."—*Et sane quo,* &c. And, indeed, says the poet, where is the use of so great a riot if no life is to be taken? — *Domestica.* "Familiar," *i. e.,* natural or handy.—*Hunc.* For *talem.*—*Et Turnus et Ajax.* Supply *torquebant.*—*Illis.* "To those of theirs." Equivalent to *illorum dextris.*—*Nam genus hoc vivo,* &c. Compare *Hom., Il.* v. 303, *seqq.*—*Malos homines,* &c. "Now rears poor and puny men."—*Ridet et odit.* Laughs at them, as *pusilli,* and hates them, as *mali.*

72–82. *A diverticulo repetatur fabula.* "Let our story be resumed after this digression." *Diverticulum* properly means "a cross-road," then "a place to which we turn aside from the high-road;" a halting or refreshing place.—*Pars altera.* The Tentyrites.—*Omnibus.* The Ombites are meant, who flee before the ré-enforced Tentyrites. Some editions read *præstant instantibus Ombis,* which will make the Ombites to be the re-enforced party, and the Tentyrites to be those who fled.—*Qui vicina colunt,* &c. "They who inhabit Tentyra, adjacent to the shady palm." The "shady palm" is put for "groves of palm."—*Hinc.* "Hereupon," *i. e.,* owing to the hasty flight.—*Quidam.* One of the Ombites.—*Frusta et particulas.* "Pieces and bits."—*Corrosis ossibus.* "The very bones being gnawed."—*Nec ardenti decoxit,* &c. "Neither did they boil him in a glowing cauldron, or roast him on spits." From *decoxit,* in the first clause, we must supply "roasted" with *verubus.* Similar instances of zeugma are far from uncommon.—*Longum usque adeo.* "So very long."

84–90. *Hic gaudere libet,* &c. The idea is, Here we may rejoice that fire, the gift of Prometheus, which was brought from heaven, and which is the symbol of civilization, was not profaned by these savages. — *Raptum.* " Stolen." — *Prometheus.* Compare *Sat.* iv., 132. — *Te.* Volusius. — *Mordere.* " To chew." — *An prima voluptatem*, &c. For, in the case of so great a crime, doubt not whether the first that ate was gratified; whether only in the first transport of rage they enjoyed their horrid feast. — *Ultimus autem*, &c. " The last one, too, who stood waiting for his turn," &c.

93-107. *Vascones.* Now the Basque nation, between the Ebro (Iberus) and Pyrenees, in the modern *Navarra* and *Guipuzcoa.*— *Produxere animas.* " Prolonged their lives." The chief cities of the Vascones were Calagurris (now *Calahorra*) and Pampelo (now *Pampeluna*). It is doubtful which of these two places held out in the manner alluded to in the text. They were besieged by Pompey and Metellus, and were so reduced by famine that, to maintain inviolate their engagements with Sertorius (who was then no more), they devoured their wives and children rather than surrender.— *Fortunæ invidia.* " The spite of Fortune." — *Ultima.* " The last extremity." Supply *discrimina.* — *Casus extremi.* " The very height of human suffering." Literally, " extreme sufferings." — *Egestas.* " Starvation." — *Hujus enim, quod nunc agitur*, &c. " For the example that is now under consideration, of such food as this ought to excite our compassion." — *Gens.* The Vascones. — *Furor.* " The gnawings." — *Fame.* " In their hunger." — *Viribus.* " To human energies." Abstract for concrete, energies for energetic men. Some read *urbibus*, others *ventribus*, but both are inferior. — *Zenonis.* The founder of the Stoic school. — *Quædam.* " That some things only." Not only did Zeno hold that a man should die rather than do wrong, but he even recommended suicide under certain circumstances.

108-114. *Cantaber.* The Cantabri occupied that part of Spain which now answers to Biscay, Santander, and the east of Asturias. The Vascones formed a part of them. — *Antiqui præsertim*, &c. Before arts, science, and philosophy flourished as they now do. Quintus Cæcilius Metellus Pius, consul with Sulla, B.C. 80, conducted the war against Sertorius (B.C. 79-72), and triumphed over Spain (B.C. 71). — *Graias nostrasque Athenas.* " The Grecian and our Athens." Equivalent to *Græcas et Romanas Literas.* — *Gallia causidicos*, &c. Among the seats of learning in Gaul were Massilia (*Marseille*), Angustodunum (*Autun*), Lugdunum (*Lyon*), Burdigala (*Bordeaux*), and Tolosa (*Toulouse*). — *De conducendo*, &c. " Thule now talks of hiring a teacher of oratory." The *rhetor*, or teacher of oratory, is different from the *orator*. Thule is generally supposed to have been one of the Shetland Isles. Some modern geographers, however, seek to identify it with Iceland or part of Norway. At all events, the ancients, especially the poets, use the name to denote generally the extreme north.—*Populus.* The Vascones.—*Major clade.* "Their more than equal in calamity."—*Saguntus.* Now *Mur Viedro*, in Valencia, south of the Iberus, on the River Palantias, about three miles from the coast. It was memorable for its obstinate resistance to Hannibal during a siege of eight months. The fidelity of the Saguntines to Rome was as famous as that of the Vascones to Sertorius; but their fate was more disastrous, as Hannibal took Saguntus and razed it to the ground after its people had endured the most horrible extremities, whereas the siege of Calagurris was raised. The more common form of the name is *Saguntum.*

115-128. *Mæotide ara.* The Tauri, who lived in the peninsula called from them Taurica Chersonesus (now *Crimea*), on the Palus Mæotis (*Sea of Azof*), used to sacrifice shipwrecked strangers on the altar of Diana.—*Illa inventrix.* The Tauric Diana.—*She* required the death only of her victims, and does not demand that their bodies be eaten.—*Jam.* Implying to go so far as to admit.—*Modo.* "If nothing more." (*Mayor, ad loc.*) Heinrich, however, makes it equivalent to *tamen.*—*Infesta vallo.* "Threatening their rampart."—*Tam detestabile monstrum.* "So detestable and monstrous a piece of wickedness."—*Anne aliam,* &c. "Would they, if the land of Memphis were parched with drought, bring (by some act of desperation) any other (and greater) infamy on the Nile unwilling to rise?" *i. e.,* would they, by any deed to which the last extremity of drought might drive them, bring any greater infamy on the Nile as the cause of their desperation, and so mediately of their crime? The words *nolenti surgere* further define the *invidia;* they would complain of the Nile's unwillingness to rise. (*Mayor, ad loc.*)—*Cimbri.* Compare *Sat.* viii., 249.—*Sauromatæ.* The Sauromatæ or Sarmatæ inhabited the country on the northeast of the Palus Mæotis, and east of the Tanais or *Don,* which separated them from the Scythians of Europe.—*Agathyrsi.* A people in European Sarmatia, on the River Maris, now *Marosch,* in *Transylvania.*—*Fictilibus phaselis.* "To their earthenware pinnaces." The deficiency of timber in Egypt forced the inhabitants to adopt any expedient as a substitute. Strabo mentions these vessels of pottery-ware, varnished over to make them water-tight. *Phaselus* is properly the Egyptian kidney-bean, from which the boats derived their name on account of their long and narrow form. (*Evans, ad loc.*)—*Pictæ testæ.* "Of their painted pottery-canoe."

131–136. *Ira atque fames.* From mere passion the Egyptians commit crimes great as any to which starvation could compel them. —*Quæ lacrymas dedit.* " In that she has given us tears." Sympathy between man and man is natural, and nature has given us outward symptoms of sorrow and compassion which are given to no other creature.—*Hæc nostri pars,* &c. Because, by flowing in pity and commiseration, they bespeak the most amiable qualities of the mind.—*Jubet.* " She bids us," *i. e.,* Nature.—*Rei.* "Of one accused." Those who were arraigned in any court of judicature used to appear in a squalid plight, in order to excite the commiseration of the judges.—*Circumscriptorem.* " His defrauder," *i. e.,* the guardian who had defrauded him. The fraudulent guardian might be deposed from his office by an *accusatio suspecti,* which was as old as the Twelve Tables, and might be brought before the prætor, but not by the ward himself. After the ward arrived at the age of puberty, the guardian was compelled to give him an account of the way in which he had fulfilled his office, and to make good any losses which the property had sustained. (*Mayor, ad loc.*)—*Cujus manantia fletu,* &c. " Whose girl-like locks make all uncertain to the view his visage flowing with tears," *i. e.,* render it almost uncertain to the beholders of which sex the youthful sufferer is.

138–149. *Adultæ.* " Just grown up."—*Et minor igne rogi.* " And one too young for the fire of the funeral pile." Infants under forty days old were not burned, but buried, and the place was called *suggrundarium.* — *Face dignus arcana.* Worthy to act as δᾳδοῦχος, or sacred torch-bearer in the Eleusinian mysteries. None were admitted to initiation in the mysteries of Ceres without a strict inquiry into their moral character, and the greatest purity of life was expected from them when initiated.—*Aliena sibi.* Compare Terence's *Heaut.,* i., 1, 25 : *"Homo sum, humani nihil a me alienum puto."* —*Separat.* " Distinguishes."—*Venerabile ingenium.* " The revered gift of intellect."—*Atque exercendis,* &c. " And possessing an aptitude for the practice as well as the reception of arts."—*Sensum.* " A moral sense."—*Conditor.* "Creator."—*Indulsit illis.* "Vouchsafed unto them."—*Animas.* " The vital principle." Compare the language of Accius : *"Animus est quo sapimus; anima qua vivimus."*

151–164. *In populum.* " Into one people." — *Laribus nostris.* " To our own homes."—*Tutos vicino limine,* &c. " That the confidence mutually inspired by a neighbouring threshold might bestow secure slumbers," *i. e.,* that by thus joining together dwellings (the original of cities and towns), each might receive and impart a notion of safety.—*Nutantem.* " Staggering."—*Sed jam serpentum,* &c.

But now we see the most savage creatures less fierce against their kind than man against man.—*Parcit cognatis maculis.* "Spares kindred spots," *i. e.*, the leopard recognizes the leopard, and avoids hurting him, whom he sees by his spots to be of the same species with himself.—*Fortior.* "Though stronger."—*Indica tigris.* Compare Pliny (*H. N.*, viii., 18): "*Tigris Indica fera velocitatis tremendæ est,*" &c.—*Convenit.* "There is agreement."

165-174. *Ast homini,* &c. Man's rage, however, can no longer be appeased with the sword, though the first smiths knew nothing even of that. Now we see people who are not content with the death of an enemy, but must convert his body into food.—*Produxisse.* "To have forged." Literally, "to have lengthened (or drawn) out."— *Sarcula.* Compare *Sat.* iii., 292.—*Marris.* Compare *Sat.* iii., 292. —*Extendere.* "To beat out." In the sense of *extundere,* which some editions actually read.—*Pythagoras.* Holding the doctrines of the metempsychosis, Pythagoras was averse to shedding the blood of any animal, and, according to the ordinary account, forbade the eating of flesh. According, however, to other authorities (*Diog. Laert.*, viii., 20), he enjoined abstinence only from the wether, and the ox used in ploughing. Aristotle, however, says only from certain parts of animals and some kinds of fish (*ap. Gell.*, iv., 11; *Diog. Laert.*, viii., 19).—*Hæc monstra.* "Such atrocities as these."—*Et ventri indulsit,* &c. "And did not even indulge his appetite with every kind of pulse." Pythagoras enjoined on his disciples abstinence from beans. The reason of this prohibition has never been clearly ascertained.

SATIRE XVI.

ARGUMENT.

Under the pretense of pointing out to his friend Gallus the advantages of a military life, Juvenal attacks with considerable spirit the exclusive privileges which the army had acquired or usurped, to the manifest injury of the civil part of the community.

1-15. *Felicis præmia militiæ.* "The advantages of military service when fortunate."— *Galle.* Martial often addresses a friend, named Gallus, perhaps the same with the one here mentioned.— *Nam si subeuntur,* &c. "For if a camp distinguished by success be only entered, then may its gate receive me, a timid recruit, under the influence of some auspicious star."—*Hora.* "One hour."—*Gen-itrix.* Juno, the mother of Mars. Samos was sacred to her, and here she had a famous temple.—7–15. The first privilege, which is common to all ranks in the army, is, they hold so fast together that no civilian dares to accuse them or give evidence against them.—*Ne te pulsare,* &c. "That no civilian must dare to strike you." *Ne* is used because "*subest notio impediendi vel prohibendi.*" (*Hand, Tursell.,* iv., 42. *Major, ad loc.*)—*Togata.* The *toga* was the robe of peace, as the *sagum* was of war.—*Dissimulet.* "That he must dissemble." Equivalent to *ut dissimulet,* the conjunction *ut* being supplied from *ne.*—*Et nigram in facie,* &c. "And the black bruise in his face with its livid swellings; and the eye left in its socket indeed, but the physician giving no hopes that it will be restored." Literally, "promising nothing."—*Bardaicus judex,* &c. "A Bardaic judge is assigned to him who wishes to get these things punished, namely, a soldier's shoe, and stout calves at the capacious benches." The epithet *Bardaicus* is derived from the name of an Illyrian tribe (*Bardaei* or *Bardiaei*), of rude and rapacious habits. Marius is said to have had a body-guard of slaves who flocked to him, chiefly Illyrian, whom he called his "Bardiaei." A Bardaic judge, therefore, in the present case, will be a rude, overbearing military man, from whom the civilian may expect no redress. The terms *calceus* and *surae* will then be in comic apposition with *Bardaicus judex,* and the general idea will be as follows: If the injured man of peace seek redress, a soldier's shoe and stout shanks sit in judgment on the bench. Some connect *Bardaicus* at once with *calceus,* in the sense of *militaris.* The idea, however, will be the same.—*Camilli.* Camillus first introduced a standing army; before which time the soldiers might, in winter, prosecute their suits at home.

17–24. *Justissima centurionum,* &c. "Most just (of course) is the decision of the centurions." Ironical, since the military judge will always favor his own comrades.—*Nec mihi deerit ultio,* &c. "Nor will due satisfaction be wanting unto me, if a ground for just complaint be alleged." Ironical again. He will get, in reality, no satisfaction.—*Curabilis ut sit vindicta,* &c. Their vengeance for your prosecution of their comrade will be matter of serious concern, and will fall heavier on you than the original injury.—*Declamatoris mulino corde Vagelli.* "The mulish heart of the declaimer Vagellius," *i. e.,* the mulish rhetorician Vagellius. He is here called "mulish" from his foolhardiness and obstinacy in undertaking causes which no man in his sober senses would have advocated. Vagellius was an advocate of Mutina (now *Modena*), and hence some read *Mutinensi* for *mulino.—Quum duo crura habeas,* &c. " When you have only two legs, to stumble against so many soldiers' shoes, so many thousands of hob-nails." As regards the *caliga,* compare note on *Sat.* iii., 229.

25-34. *Quis tam procul absit,* &c. The idea is, -Who will venture so far from the city to accuse a soldier ? Besides, what friend is ready, like Pylades, to devote his life for his friend?—*Molem aggeris ultra.* " Beyond the mole of the rampart," *i. e.,* within the rampart of the camp.—*Pylades.* Alluding to the legend of Orestes and Pylades, and the scene that took place at the altar of the Tauric Diana.—*Lacrimæ siccentur potius,* &c. Let us dry up our tears at once, and not importune our friends, who, on one pretext or another, will certainly put us off, to bear us company in our hazardous enterprises, and to give their evidence when the judge calls for witnesses. (*Mayor, ad loc.*)—*Audeat ille,* &c. " Will the man, whoever he may be, dare to say, ' I witnessed the transaction?' "—*Et credam dignum barba,* &c. The idea is, I will believe such a man deserving of being ranked with the noblest worthies of the good old times. The early Romans wore the hair of the head and of the beard uncut. Barbers were not introduced into Rome until A.U.C. 454, or B.C. 300. They came from Sicily.—*Paganum.* " A civilian." The term *paganus* properly means a rustic, or occupant of the country. It appears that, under the emperors, husbandmen were exempt from military service, in order that the land might not fall out of cultivation. The *paganus* then became opposed in meaning to *armatus,* and hence arose its signification of " civilian," which is very common with the silver age of Latinity.—*Pudorem.* " Honour."

35-42. *Præmia nunc alia,* &c. We come now to the second privilege of the soldiery. Civilians have to wait long for the decision of their suits, whereas soldiers meet with a speedy settlement.—*Sacramentorum.* " Of military life." The military oath (*sacramentum*) is here put for military life itself. — *Et sacrum effodit,* &c. " And has dug up the sacred stone from the intervening boundary-line." The stone that forms the common landmark between two neighbouring fields. He who removed his neighbour's landmark was held accursed among the Romans, as among the Jews.—*Patulo.* " Flat."—*Puls annua.* It was forbidden to offer bloody sacrifices to Terminus, or the god of landmarks.—*Vana supervacui,* &c. Repeated from *Sat.* xiii., 137.—*Expectandus erit,* &c. " The year of the whole people will have to be waited for to commence litigation," *i. e.,* the year in which the litigation of a whole people is to be settled will have to be waited for by us before we can bring on our suit for adjudication. The civilian cannot, like the soldier (verse 49), choose his own time; he must wait until, in the course of the people's year, his turn may come. Actions between civilians (before the *centumviri*) were heard in the order in which application had been made to the prætor.

44-50. *Subsellia tantum sternuntur.* "The benches alone are spread with cushions," *i. e.,* are got ready. The benches of the judges are got ready, but the judges are not ready, and there is no quorum to commence business. — *Tum.* While waiting for the judges to appear and open court.—*Facundo ponente lacernas,* &c. While the pleader Cædicius is laying aside his *lacerna,* and preparing to address the court (when it shall have opened) in his toga. The *lacerna* was worn over the toga.—*Micturiente.* "Obeying a call of nature." — *Parati digredimur,* &c. "Though prepared for the fray, we part combat, and fight in the dilatory lists of the law." The civilian at length leaves the court-room in despair, and the case stands again adjourned.—*Tempus agendi.* "A time for the hearing of their case." Literally, "for pleading." — *Longo sufflamine litis.* "By the tedious drag-chain of litigation."

51-60. *Solis præterea,* &c. A third privilege of soldiers. The right of acquiring property independently of the father, and also of making a will. A son who was *in manu patris* had no property of his own, strictly speaking. What he was allowed to enjoy as such (termed his *peculium*) was held on a precarious tenure, and might be taken from him by his father. But in imperial times this law was relaxed in favour of the soldiery. A soldier, when arming for battle, and even at ordinary times also, was allowed to name an heir in the presence of three or four witnesses.—*Non esse in corpore census.* "Should not be incorporated in the private fortune."— *Æra merentem.* "Earning the pay." — *Tremulus.* "Trembling with age."—*Captat.* "Pays court to." The father turns inheritance-hunter to his own son. — *Favor æquus,* &c. The idea is, Coranus is advanced by " well-merited favour," and his honourable exertions are crowned by the fitting reward. At least, it appears to concern the commander himself that his bravest soldiers be most quickly advanced, that all be gladdened by badges of distinction. (*Mayor, ad loc.*) The common text has *labor æquus,* but *labor* followed by *labori* in the next line makes an exceedingly harsh construction. We have therefore substituted *favor* with Ruperti, Jahn, and Mayor.

Torquibus omnes. Here the Satire terminates abruptly. The conclusion is too tame to be such as Juvenal would have left it, even were the whole subject thoroughly worked up. It is probably an

N *

unfinished draught. The commentators are nearly equally bal-
anced as to its being the work of Juvenal or not, but one or two of
the touches are too masterly to be by any other hand. (*Evans, ad
loc.*)

THE END.

Books for Schools and Colleges

PUBLISHED BY

HARPER & BROTHERS, FRANKLIN SQUARE, NEW YORK.

☞ HARPER & BROTHERS *will send either of the following Works by Mail, postage prepaid (for any distance in the United States under 3000 miles), on receipt of the Money.*

For a full Descriptive List of Books suitable for Schools and Colleges, see HARPER'S CATALOGUE, *which may be obtained gratuitously on application to the Publishers personally, or by letter inclosing Six Cents in Stamps.*

Alford's Greek Testament. The Greek Testament: with a Critically Revised Text; a Digest of various Readings; Marginal References to Verbal and Idiomatic Usage; Prolegomena; and a Critical and Exegetical Commentary. For the Use of Theological Students and Ministers. By HENRY ALFORD, B.D., Dean of Canterbury. Vol. I., containing the Four Gospels, 8vo, Muslin, $5 00; Sheep extra, $5 50; Half Calf extra, $6 00.

Andrews's Latin-English Lexicon, founded on the larger German-Latin Lexicon of Dr. WM. FREUND. With Additions and Corrections from the Lexicons of Gesner, Facciolati, Scheller, Georges, &c. Royal 8vo, Sheep extra, $5 00.

Abercrombie on the Intellectual Powers. Inquiries concerning the Intellectual Powers and the Investigation of Truth. With Questions. 18mo, Muslin, 45 cents; Half Bound, 50 cents.

Abercrombie on the Philosophy of the Moral Feelings. With Questions. 18mo, Muslin, 40 cents; Half Bound, 50 cents.

Abercrombie's Miscellaneous Essays. Consisting of the Harmony of Christian Faith and Christian Character; The Culture and Discipline of the Mind; Think on these Things; The Contest and the Armor; The Messiah as an Example. 18mo, Muslin, 37½ cents.

Alison on Taste. Essays on the Nature and Principles of Taste. Edited for Schools, by ABRAHAM MILLS. 12mo, Muslin, 75 cents.

Anthon's Latin Lessons. Latin Grammar, Part I. Containing the most important Parts of the Grammar of the Latin Language, together with appropriate Exercises in the translating and writing of Latin. 12mo, Sheep extra, 75 cents.

Anthon's Latin Prose Composition. Latin Grammar, Part II. An Introduction to Latin Prose Composition, with a complete Course of Exercises, illustrative of all the important Principles of Latin Syntax. 12mo, Sheep extra, 75 cents.

A Key to Latin Composition may be obtained by Teachers. 12mo, Half Sheep, 50 cents.

Anthon's Zumpt's Latin Grammar. From the Ninth Edition of the Original, by LEONARD SCHMITZ, Ph.D. 12mo, Sheep extra, 75 cents.

Anthon's Zumpt's Latin Grammar, Abridged. 12mo, Sheep extra, 50 cents.

Anthon's Latin Versification. In a Series of Progressive Exercises, including Specimens of Translation from the English and German Poetry into Latin Verse. 12mo, Sheep extra, 75 cents.

A Key to Latin Versification may be obtained by Teachers. 12mo, Half Sheep, 50 cents.

Anthon's Latin Prosody and Metre. 12mo, Sheep extra, 75 cents.

Anthon's Cæsar. Cæsar's Commentaries on the Gallic War, and the First Book of the Greek Paraphrase; with English Notes, Critical and Explanatory, Plans of Battles, Sieges, &c., and Historical, Geographical, and Archæological Indexes. Map, Plans, Portrait, &c. 12mo, Sheep extra, $1 00.

Anthon's Æneid of Virgil. With English Notes, Critical and Explanatory, a Metrical Clavis, and an Historical, Geographical, and Mythological Index. Portrait and many Illustrations. 12mo, Sheep extra, $1 25.

Anthon's Eclogues and Georgics of Virgil. With English Notes, Critical and Explanatory, and a Metrical Index. 12mo, Sheep extra, $1 25.

Anthon's Sallust. Sallust's Jugurthine War and Conspiracy of Catiline. With an English Commentary, and Geographical and Historical Indexes. Portrait. 12mo, Sheep extra, 75 cents.

Anthon's Horace. The Works of Horace. With English Notes, Critical and Explanatory. A new Edition, corrected and enlarged, with Excursions relative to the Vines and Vineyards of the Ancients; a Life of Horace, a Biographical Sketch of Mæcenas, a Metrical Clavis, &c. 12mo, Sheep extra, $1 25.

Anthon's Cicero. Cicero's Select Orations. With English Notes, Critical and Explanatory, and Historical, Geographical, and Legal Indexes. An improved Edition. Portrait. 12mo, Sheep extra, $1 00.

Anthon's Cicero's Tusculan Disputations. With English Notes, Critical and Explanatory. 12mo, Sheep extra, $1 00.

Anthon's Cicero de Senectute. The De Senectute, De Amicitia, Paradoxa, and Somnium Scipionis of Cicero, and the Life of Atticus, by Cornelius Nepos. With English Notes, Critical and Explanatory. 12mo, Sheep extra, 75 cents.

Anthon's Cicero de Officiis. M. T. Ciceronis de Officiis Libri Tres. With Marginal Analysis and an English Commentary. 12mo, Sheep extra, 75 cents.

Anthon's Tacitus. The Germania and Agricola, and also Selections from the Annals of Tacitus. With English Notes, Critical and Explanatory. Revised and enlarged Edition. 12mo, Sheep extra, $1 00.

Anthon's Cornelius Nepos. Cornelii Nepotis Vitæ Imperatorum. With English Notes, &c. 12mo, Sheep extra, $1 00.

Anthon's Juvenal. The Satires of Juvenal and Persius. With English Notes, Critical and Explanatory, from the best Commentators. Portrait. 12mo, Sheep extra, 90 cents.

Anthon's First Greek Lessons, containing the most important Parts of the Grammar of the Greek Language, together with appropriate Exercises in the translating and writing of Greek. For the use of Beginners. 12mo, Sheep extra, 75 cents.

Anthon's Greek Composition. Greek Lessons, Part II. An Introduction to Greek Prose Composition, with a Complete Course of Exercises illustrative of all the important Principles of Greek Syntax. 12mo, Sheep extra, 75 cents.

Anthon's Greek Grammar. For the use of Schools and Colleges. 12mo, Sheep extra, 75 cents.

Anthon's New Greek Grammar. From the German of Kühner, Matthiæ, Buttmann, Rost, and Thiersch; to which are appended Remarks on the Pronunciation of the Greek Language, and Chronological Tables explanatory of the same. 12mo, Sheep extra, 75 cents.

Anthon's Greek Prosody and Metre. For the use of Schools and Colleges: together with the Choral Scanning of the Prometheus Vinctus of Æschylus, and Œdipus Tyrannus of Sophocles; to which are appended Remarks on the Indo-Germanic Analogies. 12mo, Sheep extra, 75 cents.

Anthon's Jacobs's Greek Reader, principally from the German Work of Frederic Jacobs. With English Notes, Critical and Explanatory, a Metrical Index to Homer and Anacreon, and a copious Lexicon. 12mo, Sheep, $1 00.

Anthon's Xenophon's Anabasis. With English Notes, Critical and Explanatory, a Map arranged according to the latest and best Authorities, and a Plan of the Battle of Cunaxa. 12mo, Sheep extra, $1 25.

Anthon's Xenophon's Memorabilia of Socrates. With English Notes, Critical and Explanatory, the Prolegomena of Kühner, Wiggers's Life of Socrates, &c., &c. Corrected and enlarged. 12mo, Sheep extra, $1 00.

Anthon's Homer. The First Six Books of Homer's Iliad, English Notes, Critical and Explanatory, a Metrical Index, and Homeric Glossary. Portrait. 12mo, Sheep extra, $1 25.

Anthon's Manual of Greek Antiquities. From the best and most recent Sources. Numerous Illustrations. 12mo, Sheep extra, 88 cents.

Anthon's Manual of Roman Antiquities. From the most recent German Works. With a Description of the City of Rome, &c. Numerous Illustrations. 12mo, Sheep extra, 88 cents.

Anthon's Manual of Greek Literature. From the earliest authentic Periods to the close of the Byzantine Era. With a Critical History of the Greek Language. 12mo, Sheep extra, $1 00.

Anthon's Smith's Dictionary of Antiquities. A Dictionary of Greek and Roman Antiquities, from the best Authorities, and embodying all the the recent Discoveries of the most eminent German Philologists and Jurists. First American Edition, corrected and enlarged, and containing also numerous Articles relative to the Botany, Mineralogy, and Zoology of the Ancients. By CHARLES ANTHON, LL.D. Royal 8vo, Sheep extra, $4 00.

Smith's Antiquities, Abridged by the Author. 12mo, Half Sheep, 90 cents.

Anthon's Classical Dictionary. Containing an Account of the principal Proper Names mentioned in Ancient Authors, and intended to elucidate all the important Points connected with the Geography, History, Biography, Mythology, and Fine Arts of the Greeks and Romans; together with an Account of the Coins, Weights, and Measures of the Ancients, with Tabular Values of the same. Royal 8vo, Sheep extra, $4 00.

Anthon's Smith's New Classical Dictionary of Greek and Roman Biography, Mythology, and Geography. Numerous Corrections and Additions. Royal 8vo, Sheep extra, $2 50.

Anthon's Latin-English and English-Latin Dictionary. For the use of Schools. Chiefly from the Lexicons of Freund, Georges, and Kaltschmidt. Small 4to, Sheep extra, $2 00.

Anthon's Riddle and Arnold's English-Latin Lexicon, founded on the German-Latin Dictionary of Dr. C. E. Georges. With a copious Dictionary of Proper Names from the best Sources. Royal 8vo, Sheep extra, $3 00.

Anthon's Ancient and Mediæval Geography. For the use of Schools and Colleges. 8vo, Muslin, $1 50; Sheep extra, $1 75.

Barton's Grammar. With a brief Exposition of the Chief Idiomatic Peculiarities of the English Language. To which Questions have been added. 16mo, Muslin, 38 cents.

Beecher's (Miss) Physiology and Calisthenics. Over 100 Engravings. 16mo, Muslin, 50 cents.

Boyd's Rhetoric. Elements of Rhetoric and Literary Criticism, with copious Practical Exercises and Examples: including, also, a succinct History of the English Language, and of British and American Literature, from the earliest to the present Times. On the Basis of the recent Works of ALEXANDER REID and R. CONNELL; with large Additions from other Sources. Compiled and arranged by J. R. BOYD, A.M. 12mo, Half Roan, 50 cents.

Boyd's Eclectic Moral Philosophy: prepared for Literary Institutions and General Use. By J. R. BOYD, A.M. 12mo, Muslin, 75 cents.

Butler's Analogy. By Emory and Crooks. Bishop Butler's Analogy of Religion, Natural and Revealed, to the Constitution and Course of Nature. With an Analysis by the late ROBERT EMORY, D.D., President of Dickinson College. Edited, with a Life of Bishop Butler, Notes, and Index, by Rev. G. R. CROOKS, D.D. 12mo, Muslin, 75 cents.

Butler's Analogy. By Hobart. With Notes. Adapted to the use of Schools, by CHARLES E. WEST. 18mo, Muslin, 40 cents.

Buttmann's Greek Grammar. For the use of High Schools and Universities. Revised and enlarged. Translated by EDWARD ROBINSON, D.D., LL.D. 8vo, Sheep extra, $2 00.

Burke on the Sublime and Beautiful. 12mo, Muslin, 75 cents.

Calkins's Object Lessons. Primary Object Lessons for a Graduated Course of Development. A Manual for Teachers and Parents, with Lessons for the Proper Training of the Faculties of Children. By N. A. CALKINS. Engravings. 12mo, Muslin, $1 00.

Campbell's Philosophy of Rhetoric. 12mo, Muslin, $1 25.

Clark's Elements of Algebra. 8vo, Sheep extra, $1 00.

Collord's Latin Accidence. Latin Accidence and Primary Lesson Book; Containing a Full Exhibition of the Forms of Words, and First Lessons in Reading. By GEORGE W. COLLORD, A.M., Professor of Latin and Greek in the Brooklyn Collegiate and Polytechnic Institute. 12mo.

Comte's Philosophy of Mathematics. Translated from the Cours de Philosophie Positive, by W. M. GILLESPIE, A.M. 8vo, Muslin, $1 25.

Combe's Principles of Physiology. With Questions. Engravings. 18mo, Muslin, 45 cents; Half Sheep, 50 cents.

Crabb's English Synonyms. English Synonyms explained. With copious Illustrations and Explanations, drawn from the best Writers. By GEORGE CRABB, M.A. 8vo, Sheep extra, $2 00.

Daniell's Natural Philosophy. Edited by JAMES RENWICK. 18mo, Muslin, 45 cents.

Docharty's Arithmetic. A Practical and Commercial Arithmetic: containing Definitions of Terms, and Rules of Operations, with numerous Examples. The whole forming a complete Treatise for the use of Schools and Academies. By GERARDUS BEEKMAN DOCHARTY, LL.D., Professor of Mathematics in the New York Free Academy. 12mo, Sheep extra, 75 cents.

Docharty's Institutes of Algebra. The Institutes of Algebra. Designed for the use of Schools, Academies and Colleges. 12mo, Sheep, 75 cents.

Docharty's Geometry. Elements of Plane and Solid Geometry, together with the Elements of Plane and Spherical Trigonometry, and an Article on Inverse Trigonometrical Functions. 12mo, Sheep extra, 75 cents.

Draper's Physiology. Human Physiology, Statical and Dynamical; or, The Conditions and Course of the Life of Man: being the Text-Book of the Lectures delivered in the Medical Department of the University. By JOHN W. DRAPER, M.D., LL.D. Illustrated by nearly 300 fine Wood-cuts from Photographs. 8vo, 650 pages, Muslin, $4 00; Sheep, $4 25; Half Calf, $5 00.

Draper's Text-Book on Chemistry. A Text-Book on Chemistry, for the use of Schools and Colleges. With nearly 300 Illustrations. 12mo, Sheep extra, 75 cents.

Draper's Text-Book on Natural Philosophy. A Text-Book on Natural Philosophy, for the use of Schools and Colleges. Containing the most recent Discoveries and Facts, compiled from the best Authorities. With nearly 400 Illustrations. 12mo, Sheep extra, 75 cents.

Duff's Book-Keeping. The North American Accountant: embracing Single and Double Entry Book-Keeping, practically adapted to the Inland and Maritime Commerce of the United States. Exemplifying all Modern Improvements in the Science, with a New and Certain Method of detecting Errors and proving the Ledger. Embracing an Improved Plan of Instruction. Complete in Three Parts. By P. DUFF, Merchant. 8vo, School Edition, Half Sheep, 75 cents; Mercantile Edition, Muslin, $1 50.

Faraday on the Physical Forces. A Course of Six Lectures on the Various Forces of Matter, and their Relations to each other. By MICHAEL FARADAY, D.C.L., F.R.S., Fullerian Professor of Chemistry, Royal Institution. Edited by WILLIAM CROOKES, F.C.S. With numerous Illustrations. 12mo, Muslin, 50 cents.

Faraday's Lectures on the Chemical History of a Candle. A Course of Six Lectures on the Chemical History of a Candle, to which is added a Lecture on Platinum. Edited by WILLIAM CROOKES, F.C.S. With numerous Illustrations. 16mo, Muslin, 50 cents.

Findlay's Classical Atlas to illustrate Ancient Geography. Comprised in 25 Maps, showing the various Divisions of the World as known to the Ancients. Composed from the most Authentic Sources, with an Index of the Ancient and Modern Names. 8vo, Half Bound, $3 25.

Foster's First Principles of Chemistry. Illustrated by a Series of the most recently Discovered and brilliant Discoveries known to the Science. Adapted especially for Classes. 12mo, Sheep extra, 60 cents.
APPARATUS to perform the experiments laid down in this work, manufactured expressly for this purpose, carefully packed for transportation, for $23.

Foster's Chart of the Organic Elements. For the use of Schools and Academies. Beautifully colored, mounted on Rollers, with Cloth back, $4 00.

Fowler's English Language. The English Language in its Elements and Forms. With a History of its Origin and Development, and a full Grammar. For Colleges and Schools. By WILLIAM C. FOWLER, late Professor in Amherst College. 8vo, Muslin, $1 50; Sheep extra, $1 75.

Fowler's English Grammar for Schools. Designed for General Use in Schools and Families. 12mo, Sheep extra, $1 00.

Fowler's Elementary English Grammar for Common Schools. 16mo, Sheep extra, 50 cents.

Gieseler's Church History. Edited by Rev. H. B. SMITH, D.D., Professor in the Union Theological Seminary, N. Y. 4 vols. 8vo, Sheep extra, $2 25 per vol.

Gray's and Adams's Geology. 12mo, Sheep extra, 75 cents.

Gray's Natural Philosophy. Designed as a Text-Book for Academies, High Schools, and Colleges. 300 Wood-cuts. 12mo, Sheep extra, 75 cents.

Greek Concordance of the New Testament. The Englishman's Greek Concordance; being an Attempt at a Verbal Connection between the Greek and the English Texts: including a Concordance to the Proper Names, with Indexes, Greek-English and English-Greek. 8vo, Muslin, $3 50; Sheep, $4 00.

Greek-English and English-Greek Lexicon, for the use of Schools and Academies. By Prof. HENRY DRISLER, of Columbia College, Editor of " Liddell and Scott's Greek Lexicon." Small 4to. (*In Press.*)

Griscom's Animal Mechanism and Physiology. Illustrations. 18mo, Muslin, 45 cents.

Hackley's Algebra. School and College Edition. 8vo, Sheep extra, $1 50. A School Edition. 8vo, Muslin, $1 00.

Hackley's Geometry. 8vo, Sheep extra, 75 cents.

Hale's History of the United States. 2 vols. 18mo, Muslin, 90 cents.

Hamilton's (Sir William) Philosophy. With an Introductory Essay by ROBERT TURNBULL, D.D. 8vo, Muslin, $1 50.

Harper's Greek and Latin Texts. Cheap and Accurate Editions of the Classics for the use of Schools and Students. Superior in mechanical execution to other editions, and more convenient in form. 18mo, Flexible Cloth Binding, 40 cents a volume. CÆSAR.—VERGILIUS.—HORATIUS.—CICERO DE SENECTUTE and DE AMICITIA.—LUCRETIUS.—ÆSCHYLUS.—EURIPIDES, 3 vols.—HERODOTUS, 2 vols.—THUCYDIDES, 2 vols.

Harper's New Classical Library. Literal Translations of the Greek and Latin Authors. Portraits. 12mo, Muslin, 75 cents each. The following volumes are now ready: CÆSAR.—VIRGIL.— HORACE.— SALLUST.—CICERO'S ORATIONS.—CICERO'S OFFICES, &c.—CICERO ON ORATORY AND ORATORS.—TACITUS, 2 vols. — TERENCE. — JUVENAL. — XENOPHON. — HOMER'S ILIAD. — HOMER'S ODYSSEY. — THUCYDIDES. — HERODOTUS. — EURIPIDES, 2 vols.—SOPHOCLES.—ÆSCHYLUS.—DEMOSTHENES, 2 vols.

Harper's School History. Narrative of the General Course of History, from the Earliest Periods to the Establishment of the American Constitution, Prepared with Questions for the use of Schools, and illustrated with 150 Maps and Engravings. Square 12mo, Muslin, $1 25; Sheep, $1 38.

Harrison's Latin Grammar. An Exposition of some of the Laws of the Latin Grammar. By GESNER HARRISON, M.D., Professor of Ancient Languages in the University of Virginia. 12mo, Sheep extra, $1 00.

Haswell's Mensuration. For Tuition and Reference, containing Tables of Weights and Measures; Mensuration of Surfaces, Lines, and Solids, and Conic Sections, Centres of Gravity, &c. To which is added, Tables of the Areas of Circular Segments, Sines of a Circle, Circular and Semi-elliptical Arcs, &c., &c., &c. By C. H. HASWELL, Marine Engineer. 12mo, Sheep, 75 cents.

Henry's History of Philosophy. Epitome of the History of Philosophy. For Colleges and High Schools. 2 vols. 18mo, Muslin, 90 cents.

Herschell's Natural Philosophy. 12mo, Muslin, 60 cents.

Hooker's Child's Book of Nature. The Child's Book of Nature, for the use of Families and Schools; intended to aid Mothers and Teachers in training Children in the Observation of Nature. In Three Parts. PART I. Plants. —PART II. Animals.—PART III. Air, Water, Heat, Light, &c. By WORTHINGTON HOOKER, M.D., Yale College. Illustrated by Wood-cuts. The Three Parts complete in one vol. Small 4to, Muslin, $1 25; Separately, Muslin, 50 cents each.

Hooker's Natural History. For the use of Schools and Families. 12mo, Muslin, $1 00.

Hooker's Science for the People. An Elementary Work on Natural Philosophy, for Schools and Families.

Kane's Chemistry. With Additions and Corrections. By JOHN WILLIAM DRAPER, M.D. With about 250 Wood-cuts. 8vo, Muslin, $1 50; Sheep extra, $1 75.

Lee's Elements of Geology. Engravings. 18mo, Half Sheep, 50 cents; Muslin, 45 cents.

Lewis's Platonic Theology. Plato against the Atheists; or, The Tenth Book of the Dialogue on Laws, accompanied with Critical Notes, and followed by extended Dissertations on the main Points of Platonic Philosophy and Theology, especially as compared with the Holy Scriptures. By TAYLER LEWIS, LL.D. 12mo, Muslin, $1 50.

Liddell's School History of Rome. (*See Student's Historical Text-Books.*)

Liddell and Scott's Greek-English Lexicon. Based on the German Work of FRANCIS PASSOW. With Corrections and Additions, and the Insertion, in Alphabetical Order, of the Proper Names occurring in the Principal Greek Authors, by Professor HENRY DRISLER, M.A., Columbia College, N. Y. Royal 8vo, Sheep extra, $5 00.

Loomis's Treatise on Arithmetic. A Treatise on Arithmetic, Theoretical and Practical. By ELIAS LOOMIS, LL.D., Professor of Mathematics in Yale College. 12mo, 352 pages, Sheep extra, 75 cents.

Loomis's Elements of Algebra. Elements of Algebra. Designed for the use of Beginners. 12mo, 281 pages, Sheep extra, 62½ cents.

Loomis's Treatise on Algebra. A Treatise on Algebra. 8vo, 350 pages, Sheep extra, $1 00.

Loomis's Elements of Geometry. Elements of Geometry and Conic Sections. 8vo, 234 pages, Sheep extra, 75 cents.

Loomis's Trigonometry and Tables. Trigonometry and Tables. 8vo, 360 pages, Sheep extra, $1 50.
The *Trigonometry* and *Tables*, bound separately. The Trigonometry. $1 00; Tables, $1 00.

Loomis's Elements of Analytical Geometry. Elements of Analytical Geometry, and of the Differential and Integral Calculus. 8vo, 286 pages, Sheep extra, $1 50.

Loomis's Elements of Natural Philosophy. Elements of Natural Philosophy. Designed for Academies and High Schools. 12mo, 352 pages, Sheep extra, $1 00.

Loomis's Practical Astronomy. An Introduction to Practical Astronomy, with a Collection of Astronomical Tables. 8vo, 497 pages, Sheep extra, $1 50.

Loomis's Recent Progress of Astronomy, especially in the United States. A thoroughly Revised Edition. Illustrations. 12mo, 396 pages, Muslin, $1 00.

Loomis's Meteorology and Astronomy. Elements of Meteorology and Astronomy, for the use of Academies and High Schools. 12mo, Sheep extra. (*In Press.*)

Lowry's Universal Atlas. From the most Recent Authorities. 4to, Half Roan, $5 00.

M'Clintock's First Book in Latin. Comprising Grammar, Exercises, and Vocabularies, on the Method of Constant Imitation and Repetition. With Summaries of Etymology and Syntax. By Rev. J. M'Clintock, D.D., LL.D., President of Troy University, and Rev. Geo. R. Crooks, D.D., late Adjunct Professor of Languages in Dickinson College. 12mo, Sheep extra, 75 cents.

M'Clintock's Second Book in Latin. Containing Syntax and Reading Lessons in Prose; forming a sufficient Latin Reader. With Imitation Exercises and a Vocabulary. 12mo, Sheep extra, 75 cents.

M'Clintock's First Book in Greek. Containing a full View of the Forms of Words, with Vocabularies and copious Exercises, on the Method of Constant Imitation and Repetition. With brief Summaries of the Doctrine of the Verb, and of the Rules of Syntax. 12mo, Sheep extra, 75 cents.

M'Clintock's Second Book in Greek. Containing Syntax, with Reading Lessons in Prose; Prosody and the Dialects, with Reading Lessons in Verse. Forming a sufficient Greek Reader. With Notes and a copious Vocabulary. 12mo, Sheep extra, 75 cents.

Markham's (Mrs.) History of France. A History of France, from the Conquest of Gaul by Julius Cæsar to the Reign of Louis Philippe. With Conversations at the End of each Chapter. Map, Notes, and Questions, and a Supplement, bringing down the History to the Present Time. By Jacob Abbott. 12mo, Muslin, $1 00.

Maury's Principles of Eloquence. With an Introduction, by Bishop Potter. 18mo, Muslin, 45 cents.

Mill's Logic. A System of Logic, Ratiocinative and Inductive: being a connected View of the Principles of Evidence, and the Methods of Scientific Investigation. By J. S. Mill. 8vo, Muslin, $1 50.

Mills's Literature and Literary Men of Great Britain and Ireland. By Abraham Mills, A.M. 2 vols. 8vo, Muslin, $3 50; Half Calf, $5 50.

Morse's School Geography. A New System of Geography, for the use of Schools. Illustrated by more than 50 Cerographic Maps, and numerous Engravings on Wood. 4to, Half Bound, 50 cents.

Noel and Chapsal's French Grammar. 12mo, Muslin, 75 cents.

Olmsted's Astronomy. Engravings. 12mo, Muslin, 75 cents.

Parker's Outlines of General History. Outlines of General History, designed as the Foundation and Review of a Course of Historical Reading. By Richard Green Parker, A.M., Corresponding Member of the New York Historical Society; Author of "Aids to English Composition," &c. New Edition, with Additions. 12mo, Sheep extra, $1 00.

Parker's Aids to English Composition. Aids to English Composition, Prepared for Students of all Grades, embracing Specimens and Examples of School and College Exercises, and most of the higher Departments of English Composition, both in Prose and Verse. A New Edition, with Additions and Improvements. 12mo, Muslin, 80 cents; Sheep extra, 90 cents.

Parker's Geographical Questions. Adapted for the use of Morse's, Woodbridge's, Worcester's, Mitchell's, Field's, Malte-Brun's, Smith's, Olney's Goodrich's, or any other respectable Collection of Maps: embracing, by way of Question and Answer, such Portions of the Elements of Geography as are necessary as an Introduction to the Study of the Maps. To which is added a concise Description of the Terrestrial Globe. 12mo, Muslin, 20 cents.

Proudfit's Plautus's "Captives." With English Notes for the use of Students, by Professor JOHN PROUDFIT, D.D. 18mo, Paper, 38 cents.

Potter's Principles of Science. The Principles of Science applied to the Domestic and Mechanic Arts, and to Manufactures and Agriculture, with Reflections on the Progress of the Arts, and their Influence on National Welfare. By Rt. Rev. ALONZO POTTER, D.D. With Illustrations. 12mo, Muslin, 75 cents.

Potter's Political Economy. Political Economy: Its Objects, Uses, and Principles; considered with Reference to the Condition of the American People. With a Summary for the use of Students. 18mo, Half Sheep, 50 cents.

Potter's Hand-Book for Readers and Students, intended to assist Private Individuals, Associations, School Districts, &c., in the Selection of Useful and interesting Works for Reading and Investigation. By A. POTTER, D.D. 18mo, Muslin, 45 cents.

Renwick's Natural Philosophy. Engravings. 18mo, Half Sheep, 75 cents.

Renwick's Mechanics. Applications of the Engravings. 18mo, Half Sheep, 90 cents.

Renwick's Chemistry. Engravings. 18mo, Half Sheep, 75 cents.

Robinson's Greek Lexicon of the Testament. A Greek and English Lexicon of the New Testament. By EDWARD ROBINSON, D.D., LL.D., Professor of Biblical Literature in the Union Theological Seminary, N. Y. A New Edition, Revised, and in great part re-written. Royal 8vo, Muslin, $4 50; Sheep extra, $4 75.

Robinson's Buttmann's Greek Grammar. (*See Buttmann's Greek Grammar.*)

Russell's Juvenile Speaker. The Juvenile Speaker; comprising Elementary Rules and Exercises of Declamation, with a Selection of Pieces for Practice. By the Rev. FRANCIS T. RUSSELL, A.M. 12mo, Muslin, 60 cents; Half Bound, 70 cents.

Salkeld's Roman and Grecian Antiquities. With Maps, &c. 18mo, Muslin, 38 cents.

Salkeld's First Book in Spanish. A First Book in Spanish; or, A Practical Introduction to the Study of the Spanish Language. Adapted to every Class of Learners; containing full Instructions in Pronunciation; a Grammar; Reading Lessons, &c. 12mo, Sheep extra, $1 00.

Schmucker's Psychology. 12mo, Muslin, $1 00.

School (the) and the Schoolmaster. A Manual for the use of Teachers, Employers, Trustees, Inspectors, &c., &c. By Rt. Rev. ALONZO POTTER, D.D., and GEORGE B. EMERSON, A.M. Engravings. 12mo, Muslin, $1 00.

Smith's Mechanics. Illustrations. 8vo, Muslin, $1 50; Sheep extra, $1 75.

Smith's (Dr. Wm.) New Classical Dictionary. (*See Anthon's Smith's New Classical Dictionary.*)

Smith's (Dr. Wm.) Dictionary of Antiquities. (*See Anthon's Dictionary of Greek and Roman Antiquities.*)

Smith's Student's Gibbon. (*See Student's Historical Text-Books.*)

Smith's History of Greece. (*See Student's Historical Text-Books.*)

Smith's Smaller History of Greece. (*See Student's Historical Text-Books.*)

Strong's Harmony of the Gospels. A Harmony of the Gospels, in the Greek of the Received Text. With the most important various Readings, brief Grammatical Explanations, Select Biblical References, and Chronological Notes. For the use of Students and others. By Rev. JAMES STRONG, S.T.D. 12mo, Muslin, $1 25.

Student's (the) Historical Text-Books:

Liddell's School History of Rome. A School History of Rome, from the Earliest Times to the Establishment of the Empire. With Chapters on the History of Literature and Art. By HENRY G. LIDDELL, D.D., Dean of Christ Church, Oxford. Illustrated by numerous Wood-cuts. 12mo, Muslin, $1 00.

Dr. Smith's History of Greece. A History of Greece, from the Earliest Times to the Roman Conquest. With Supplementary Chapters on the History of Literature and Art. By WILLIAM SMITH, LL.D., Editor of the Dictionaries of "Greek and Roman Antiquities," "Biography and Mythology," and "Geography." Revised, with an Appendix, by GEORGE W. GREENE, A.M. For Schools and Students. Illustrated with 100 Wood-cuts. 12mo, Muslin, $1 00.

Dr. Smith's Smaller History of Greece. A Smaller History of Greece, from the Earliest Times to the Roman Conquest. By WILLIAM SMITH, LL.D. Illustrated by numerous Engravings on Wood. 16mo, Muslin, 60 cents.

The Student's Gibbon. The History of the Decline and Fall of the Roman Empire. Abridged. Incorporating the Researches of Recent Commentators. By WILLIAM SMITH, LL.D., Editor of the "Classical Dictionary," "A School Dictionary of Greece," &c. Illustrated by 100 Engravings on Wood. 12mo, Muslin, $1 00.

The Student's Hume. A History of England, from the Earliest Times to the Revolution in 1688. By DAVID HUME. Abridged. Incorporating the Corrections and Researches of Recent Historians; and continued down to the Year 1858. Illustrated by Engravings on Wood. 12mo, Muslin, $1 00.

Spencer's Greek New Testament. The Four Gospels and Acts of the Apostles, in Greek. With English Notes, Critical, Philological, and Exegetical, on the Gospels and Acts; Maps, Indexes, &c., together with the Epistles and the Apocalypse. The whole forming the Complete Text of the New Testament. For the use of Schools, Colleges, and Theological Seminaries. By Rev. J. A. SPENCER, D.D. 12mo, Muslin, $1 00; Sheep extra, $1 25.

Upham's Mental Philosophy. Elements of Mental Philosophy; embracing the two Departments of the Intellect and Sensibilities. By Rev. THOMAS C. UPHAM, D.D., Professor of Moral and Mental Philosophy in Bowdoin College. 2 vols. 12mo, Sheep extra, $2 50. 12mo, Sheep, $1 25. ABRIDGED EDITION.

Upham on the Will. Philosophical and Practical Treatise on the Will. Forming the Third Volume of a System of Mental Philosophy. By T. C. UPHAM, Professor in Bowdoin College. 12mo, Sheep extra, $1 25.

Whately's Logic. Elements of Logic: comprising the Substance of the Article in the Encyclopædia Metropolitana. With Additions, &c. By RICHARD WHATELY, D.D., Archbishop of Dublin. 18mo, Muslin, 38 cents.

Willson's Readers. A Series of School and Family Readers: Designed to teach the Art of Reading in the most Simple, Natural, and Practical Way: embracing in their Plan the whole range of Natural History and the Physical Sciences; aiming at the highest degree of Usefulness, and splendidly Illustrated. Consisting of a Primer and Seven Readers. By MARCIUS WILLSON. The Primer, and First, Second, Third, Fourth, and Fifth Readers now ready. Prices 15, 20, 30, 50, 66 cents, and $1 00.

Harper's Catalogue.

A New Descriptive Catalogue of Harper & Brothers' Publications, with an Index and Classified Table of Contents, is now ready for Distribution, and may be obtained gratuitously on application to the Publishers personally, or by letter inclosing Six Cents in Postage Stamps.

The attention of gentlemen, in town or country, designing to form Libraries or enrich their Literary Collections, is respectfully invited to this Catalogue, which will be found to comprise a large proportion of the standard and most esteemed works in English Literature —COMPREHENDING MORE THAN TWO THOUSAND VOLUMES — which are offered, in most instances, at less than one half the cost of similar productions in England.

To Librarians and others connected with Colleges, Schools, &c., who may not have access to a reliable guide in forming the true estimate of literary productions, it is believed this Catalogue will prove especially valuable as a manual of reference.

To prevent disappointment, it is suggested that, whenever books can not be obtained through any bookseller or local agent, applications with remittance should be addressed direct to the Publishers, which will be promptly attended to.

www.ingramcontent.com/pod-product-compliance
Lightning Source LLC
Chambersburg PA
CBHW021214270326
41929CB00010B/1122